Understanding the Sociology of the Accounting Profession

Jasvinder Sidhu · Soma Pillay · Mahesh Joshi

Understanding the Sociology of the Accounting Profession

The Case of Australia

palgrave
macmillan

Jasvinder Sidhu
Business Discipline, Institute
of Innovation, Science
and Sustainability
Federation University Australia
Mt Helen, VIC, Australia

Soma Pillay
Business Discipline, Institute
of Innovation, Science
and Sustainability
Federation University Australia
Berwick, VIC, Australia

Mahesh Joshi
Department of Financial Planning
and Tax
RMIT University
Melbourne, VIC, Australia

ISBN 978-981-99-1571-2 ISBN 978-981-99-1572-9 (eBook)
https://doi.org/10.1007/978-981-99-1572-9

This Palgrave Macmillan imprint is published by the registered company Springer Nature Singapore Pte Ltd.
The registered company address is: 152 Beach Road, #21-01/04 Gateway East, Singapore 189721, Singapore

Acknowledgments

I would like to thank my co-authors Dr. Soma Pillay and Dr. Mahesh Joshi for their contributions to this book.

I would like to express my sincere gratitude to my mentors, Professor Garry Carnegie, and Associate Supervisor, Professor Brian West, for their continuous support, patience and motivation and for sharing their immense knowledge.

Dr. Jasvinder Sidhu

Contents

List of Tables

CHAPTER 1

Introduction

This book examines the four unsuccessful attempts to merge the two major professional accounting bodies in Australia from the late 1960s to the late 1990s. This chapter provides an outline of the book in 12 sections. The first section provides a brief statement about the research project. The second section provides the context and background of this book, including the key features of the Australian accounting profession and the emergence of the two major rival professional accounting bodies. The third section provides an overview of the four merger attempts between these two bodies, while the fourth and fifth sections discuss the scenario for investigation and the time period covered by this project. The sixth section explains the motivation for conducting this research, while the seventh section specifies the research objectives and lists the five research questions. The eighth and ninth sections, respectively, provide an overview of the literature used in this project and discuss the two complimentary theoretical frameworks applied to analyse the findings. The tenth section provides an overview of the research methodology and data collection methods. The eleventh section discusses the limitations of this project, while the final section provides a conclusion to this chapter. An outline of the structure of this book is provided at the end of this chapter, listing the details of the 11 chapters and appendices.

J. Sidhu et al., *Understanding the Sociology of the Accounting Profession*, https://doi.org/10.1007/978-981-99-1572-9_1

1.1 Research Statement

For at least the last five decades, the landscape of the organised accounting profession in Australia has been dominated by two high-profile, large membership professional bodies:

- CPA Australia (formerly the Australian Society of Accountants [ASA], as the body was known during the period of this book, and later renamed the Australian Society of Certified Practising Accountants [ASCPA]; hereafter referred to as "the Society").
- Chartered Accountants Australia and New Zealand (CAANZ; known as the Institute of Chartered Accountants in Australia until 2014; hereafter identified as "the Institute").[1]

There have been four unsuccessful attempts to merge these two professional accounting bodies during the last five decades, which comprise the subject of this book. All four merger proposals presented to the members of each body, which were voted on in 1969, 1981, 1991 and 1998, failed, and, as a result, the Australian accounting profession is not fully unified. It is notable in professional accounting in Australia that, while there has been a long and successful history of unification, it seems that this "last hurdle" could not be overcome to the time of writing. In each case, the merger proposal was supported overwhelmingly by the membership of the Society, but the Institute failed to deliver the minimum voting threshold required to enable a merger to proceed. Consequently, the Australian accounting profession today remains characterised by a distinctive binary structure. While there may be a general understanding within the Australian accounting profession of the reasons for this ongoing dichotomy, "many who are outside the two associations

[1] A third professional accounting body in Australia is the Institute of Public Accountants (IPA), formerly the National Institute of Accountants. This organisation has about 25,000 members and was formed in Melbourne in 1923 as the Institute of Factory and Cost Accountants. The IPA is described on its own website as "one of three professional accounting bodies gazetted by the Department of Immigration and Citizenship of the Australian Government to complete qualifications assessments for the Australian and New Zealand Standard Classification of Occupations code encompassing occupations of Accountant (General), External Auditor, Management Accountant, Taxation Accountant, Finance Manager and Corporate Treasurer". See www.publicaccountants.org.au/about-us/what-makes-us-unique (last accessed 4 November 2014).

are puzzled by this failure to unify" (Carnegie, 2009, p. 292). This book examines the failure of these four merger attempts.

It has been more than 160 years since the earliest professional accountancy bodies were formed in the United Kingdom (UK). Since then, accountants around the world have made numerous attempts to create a structure, such as the formation of a body, for their profession or, in some instances, to restructure the occupation, such as the dissolution or merger of a body with other bodies. According to Carnegie and Edwards (2001, p. 301), "professionalisation is a dynamic process involving a diversity of ... 'signals of movement' by an occupational group towards occupational ascendency", which are evident in periods before and after the formation of professional associations. One such signal exists in the restructuring of a profession, including mergers, dissolutions and divisions of professional bodies. The Australian accounting profession has witnessed a series of successful merger attempts, where professional bodies have merged to form larger and stronger bodies.[2] The last successful merger of two professional accounting bodies in Australia was the merger of the Australian Institute of Cost Accountants with the Society in 1966. Moves to unify the accounting profession by means of the merger of professional bodies are recognised as a way to strengthen the profession, giving a stronger or even single voice to represent that profession (United States: 1986a, 1986b; Britain: Shackleton & Walker, 1998, 2001; Walker & Shackleton, 1995, 1998; Willmott, 1986; Canada: Richardson, 1989a; Richardson & Jones, 2007). The argument that merger would enable the profession to speak with one voice was also present in the case of the four unsuccessful merger attempts in Australia, which are discussed in detail in the specific chapters to follow that are dedicated to the merger attempts and in the analysis section of this book.

This book employs two complementary theoretical constructs to explain the operational implementation and, in particular, maintenance of professional boundaries in the Australian accounting profession. The first draws on the "boundary-work" concepts of Thomas Gieryn (Gieryn, 1983, 1995, 1999; Gieryn et al., 1985) and Marcia Annisette (2017), while the second construct is "one of the basic *casus belli* in the world of expert occupations—the dilemma of exclusiveness versus market control"

[2] Appendix A1: Accounting Bodies Formed Before 1901, Appendix A2: Parent Bodies of the Society and Appendix A3: Parent Bodies of Institute provide a comprehensive list of all bodies including formation, mergers and dissolution.

(Macdonald & Ritzer, 1988, p. 257). The first theoretical construct, boundary work, is used to help explain how accounting professionals have delineated different forms of professional services, leading to the dichotomy between the members in public practice (MIPP) and members not in public practice (MNIPP). This dichotomy was important to create, and ultimately maintain, boundaries between the memberships of the Institute and the Society. Annisette (2017) extended the application of boundary work in her study of Ontario's accounting profession. Her work adds further interpretations to the boundary-work framework, emphasising that boundaries are created and maintained through public discourse as a means of differentiating different groups of professionals from one another. This book extends her work and applies it in the analysis of findings and to understand their implications. Annisette (2017) is applied in understanding how members of the Institute and leaders of the Institute engaged in two competing public discourses, with many members opposing changes to boundaries while the Institute's leaders were projecting changes to the organisation's boundaries. The second theoretical construct, namely, an occupational group's need to choose between the strategies of elitism and market dominance, complements the first framework and permits more comprehensive explanations in the context of professions.

1.2 Book Context and Background

The context of this book is set in a period of 30 years, spanning the late 1960s to the late 1990s. During this period, many major changes affected the Australian accounting profession. For example, higher education for accountants became mandatory and structured.[3] As Australia proceeded through a series of economic cycles, both accounting bodies, the Society and the Institute, implemented many modifications to their structure and operations, with both bodies making major changes to their professional entry programs.[4] Additionally, the Australian corporate

[3] Future Education Policy of the Society, 1 October 1965, submitted to General Council by L. A. Braddock; Vatter (1964a, 1964b) report.

[4] ASA and ICAA (1969), Report of Joint Meeting of Education Committees on 30 November 1969. A joint meeting of the Education Committees of both the ASA and ICAA was held, and the ICAA's Education Committee proposal, in particular, was discussed.

sector experienced sporadic turbulence, such as the financial crisis of the early 1960s, which witnessed a spate of corporate collapses (Carnegie & O'Connell, 2012; Clarke et al., 2003; Sykes, 1998). The early to mid-1970s saw another series of corporate collapses, in which accountants and auditors faced criticism (Henderson, 1997). In the early 1980s, the accounting profession encountered some other major developments, such as the preparation of a draft *Accountants and Auditors Bill* and the formation of the Accounting Standards Review Board. The next section discusses the early features of the accounting profession and the events that led to the development of the two chief rival accounting bodies by the late 1960s.

1.2.1 Features of the Australian Accounting Profession: Regionalism, Duplication and Unification

The professionalisation of accounting in Australia was initiated in the late nineteenth century, with the key structural and other features of the profession formalised during the early decades of the twentieth century. Regionalism, duplication and successive unification around the notion of members involved in public practice and those not in public practice were key characteristics of the early Australian accounting profession.[5]

Several accounting bodies were formed on a state basis and were largely independent of direct government control while the six states of modern Australia were each still independent colonies of Britain (Parker, 1986). This resulted in the initial regionalism and duplication of associations (Parker, 1989), which was primarily evident between 1885 and the 1920s (Graham, 1972). During these initial years in Australia many accounting bodies were formed which had a regional or colony-wide focus (Carnegie & Edwards, 2001), such as the Adelaide Society of Accountants (ADSA), the Queensland Institute of Accountants (QIA) and the Incorporated Institute of Accountants of Victoria (IIAV) (Carnegie & Parker, 1999; Gavens, 1990; Gynther 1967; Walton, 1970). Similarly, in Britain accountancy bodies established in "Edinburgh,

[5] Australian accountants had a choice of possible structures through which the organisation of professional activity could proceed. This included aligning with established overseas accounting bodies or strategies around the nature of the membership and its geographical coverage (Carnegie, 2016; Carnegie et al., 2003).

Glasgow, Aberdeen, Liverpool, London and Manchester by the early 1870s proclaimed their localism" (Parker, 2014, p. 176).

During the initial years of development of the accounting profession, every state in Australia had at least one accounting body (Parker, 1989) and regional interests were even reflected in the names of the professional accounting bodies (Carnegie, 1993). Poullaos (1994) noted that regionalism was quite strong because the six British colonies in Australia had vast differences in climate, natural resources, laws, infrastructure, custom duties and so forth (Poullaos, 1994).

Gavens (1990) provided a comprehensive list of 32 professional accounting bodies that were formed between 1885 and 1952, most of which eventually merged with other bodies or disappeared from the professional association scene. In 1898, there were 12 associations across the six British colonies of pre-Federation Australia (Gavens, 1990). Between 1908 and 1945, three of those bodies were dissolved, five became part of the Society, and the remaining four merged to form the Institute (Appendix A4). Thus, over time, regionalism gradually became weaker and duplication decreased, and this reduction in the number of bodies was an overwhelming advance in promoting the wider national interests of the accounting profession (Graham, 1972). These mergers led to the formation of larger accounting bodies and, by 1952, there were two strong professional accounting bodies in Australia, that is, the Institute and the Society. This process of unification continued largely unabated, resulting in further successful mergers by the 1960s. The next subsection explains the background context that led to the formation of the two major professional accounting bodies. As noted, a total of 32 professional accounting bodies were originally formed in Australia, representing the accounting profession primarily between 1885 and 1928, with the formation of the Society in 1952 being the last of the 32 bodies formed.

1.2.2 Emergence of Two Professional Bodies: The Society and the Institute

The Society and the Institute emerged from the aforementioned unification processes and were largely a result of the surviving bodies developing respective memberships around the notion of MIPP and MNIPP. This polarisation in the Australian accounting profession was the result of two different strategies adopted by Australian accountants (Carnegie,

2016; Carnegie & O'Connell, 2012; Carnegie et al., 2003), which are summarised with the phrase: "the dilemma of exclusiveness versus marker control" (Macdonald & Ritzer, 1988, p. 257). Some accountants, including some leaders of the profession, held the belief that public practice constituted a superior occupational status to roles played in commerce, industry and government (Poullaos, 1993). This notion has been shown "to have exerted a profound and lasting influence on the institutional structure of the Australian accounting profession" (Carnegie et al., 2003, p. 792), as will be further elucidated in this book. Similar to the Australian case, tensions between public practitioners and accountants who worked in industry or government also led to divisions in the Canadian and British accounting professions (Richardson, 1987).

One of the earliest accounting bodies in Australia, and the first to be formed in Victoria, was the IIAV. Established in Melbourne on 12 April 1886, incorporated on 1 March 1887 (Carnegie & Edwards, 2001; Edwards et al., 1997) and the earliest antecedent body of CPA Australia, the IIAV adopted an inclusive strategy because "openness had more to offer than closure" (Chua & Poullaos, 1998, p. 170) and opted for a unified model of the profession (Carnegie et al., 2003). As a result, some key founding members who were seeking higher professional status defected and formed the Sydney-based Australasian Corporation of Public Accountants (ACPA) in June 1907, which was incorporated in February 1908 (Carnegie & Edwards, 2001) and "restricted membership to those engaged in public practice" (Carnegie et al., 2003, p. 793), thereby drawing a distinctive organisational boundary created around the work of MIPP.

The ACPA was formed through the merger of the Sydney Institute of Public Accountants (SIPA), the Tasmanian Institute of Accountants (TIA), and the Corporation of Accountants of Australia (CAA) (Gynther, 1967). Thus, the establishment of the ACPA made the distinction between MIPP and MNIPP clearly visible at the national, rather than state, level. According to Carnegie et al. (2003, p. 791), "this was a turbulent era in the development of an organised accounting profession in Australia". The ACPA became the Institute of Chartered Accountants in Australia on 19 June 1928, when a Royal Charter was granted to 28 accountants in public practice, which added further credit to this category of professional accountant (Institute of Chartered Accounts in Australia [ICAA], 1969, p. 6). The formation of the Institute crystallised the division of MIPP and MNIPP in the Australian accounting profession.

Professional accounting bodies that mainly represented MNIPP, but also had MIPP, merged over time, and the Society was incorporated on 13 October 1952 with the amalgamation of the Commonwealth Institute of Accountants (CIA), the Federal Institute of Accountants (FIA) and the Association of Accountants in Australia (AAA). In all, a total of 15 bodies contributed to the composition of the Society (Appendix A1). Around that time, members of the Society were mainly employed in commerce, industry and government, while the Institute members were largely involved in public practice (Carnegie & O'Connell, 2012; also see Carnegie et al., 2003). The Institute and the Society were in competition to attract members and advance their status, but were recognised as adopting different organisational strategies (Carnegie & O'Connell, 2012). The Institute positioned itself as the elite accounting association in Australia with its long-held public practice orientation and exclusive Royal Charter, while the Society was comfortable with a strategy that focused on market control by means of membership growth and the associated financial security that this provided in contrast to smaller associations.

The two bodies did not become involved in any significant joint activity until they confronted a crisis in the 1960s following a spate of corporate collapses, in which accounting and accountants were implicated and the legitimacy of the profession was challenged (see Carnegie & O'Connell, 2012). Around that time, both the Institute and Society faced challenges that precipitated pressure for change in their organisational boundaries, including the possibility of consolidating the profession through the merger of the two bodies. Members of both bodies were informed by their respective general councils in mid-1968 that preliminary merger discussions had commenced for the first time. On 1 August 1969, both bodies publicly released a unity plan to their respective members (ICAA & ASA, 1969). They proposed that the merged organisation would be elite in a different way, as the only major accounting association in Australia. This would assure it of market control, and subsequently ensure a prominent position among professional associations of any kind in Australia.

1.3 Four Unsuccessful Merger Attempts

This section provides a comparative overview of the outcomes of the member votes for each of the four merger attempts, using the data presented in Table 1.1, as well as presenting other details associated with each attempt. Table 1.1 provides a comparison of the voting patterns of all four merger attempts and provides the membership numbers for both bodies at the time of each merger attempt vote. The Institute membership showed the lowest level of support in the first and fourth merger attempts. The Society membership overwhelmingly supported all merger attempts, with the lowest level of "yes" vote at 88.5% of the voting membership in 1969. As shown in Table 1.1, the third merger attempt, mounted in 1991, came closest to unifying the Australian accounting profession. In this attempt, the Society's membership demonstrated the highest level of support of all four merger attempts. A detailed analysis of each merger attempt is presented in each of the chapters dedicated to discussing these mergers. Chapter 5 is dedicated to the first merger attempt, while Chapters 6, 7 and 8 examine the second, third and fourth merger attempts, respectively. These chapters provide detailed accounts of the four merger proposals, including the background, process adopted and outcomes, and then apply the theoretical framework to analyse each merger episode and provide evidence to answer the research questions.

Table 1.1 Comparison of voting outcomes for the four merger attempts

Attempt	*Year*	*Total members of institute*	*Total members of society*	*Members voting "yes" on merger proposal (% of total members who voted)*	
				Institute	*Society*
First	1969	5,488	31,793	41.8	88.5
Second	1981	11,941	46,562	56.5	90.1
Third	1991	21,219	62,465	64.0	94.0
Fourth	1998	30,868	86,881	41.0[6]	90.0

Sources ASA and ICAA annual reports (1969, 1981, 1991)

[6] A market research study conducted in the same quarter showed that 61% of Institute members were supporting the merger with a "yes" vote (Anon, Charter 1999, p. 12).

1.3.1 *Background to the Merger Attempts*

A series of developments occurred during the early 1960s that contributed to the advent of favourable conditions for mounting the first merger attempt. During this period, after several companies failed, the Australian corporate sector faced a challenging climate (Clarke et al., 2003; Sykes, 1998), with the years 1961 and 1962 being particularly bleak for many companies (Irish, 1963). In a joint response to this developing professional crisis, both accounting bodies, the Institute and the Society, established the Accountancy Research Foundation (ARF) in 1965 (Boehme & Braddock, 1965), which was a major move "in the quest for better research and higher standards" (Graham, 1972, p. 5). Before the first merger attempt, Reg Gynther conducted a "pathfinding survey on the Australian accounting profession" (Linn, 1996, pp. 175–176) and elucidated the general mood of accountants. The findings of his study showed that members of the Society overwhelmingly favoured the idea of a single national body, while the majority of the Institute's members were in opposition to the full unification of the profession.

1.3.2 *First Merger Attempt*

The first merger attempt was mounted in the late 1960s, following a series of corporate failures and other developments that posed a threat to the legitimacy of the Australian accounting profession (Carnegie & O'Connell, 2012). It was proposed that the new body would adopt the existing title of "the Institute", being the Institute of Chartered Accountants in Australia. As shown in Table 1.1, the outcome of the vote on 3 December 1969 resulted in a majority of 58.2% of the Institute's members rejecting the merger, while 88.5% of the Society's members supported the merger (ICAA, 1970, p. 8). In the aftermath of the vote, both bodies pledged to work jointly on various fronts, including in the development of corporate regulation (Gibson, 1979; Graham, 1972).

1.3.3 Second Merger Attempt

The 1970s faced another series of corporate collapses,[7] in which accountants and auditors once again faced criticism (Henderson, 1997). After the failure of the first attempt, both bodies re-initiated merger discussions, which continued for more than 10 years until the second proposal was put to vote in 1981. In supporting the second merger, both bodies argued that "we need, as professionals, to be able to negotiate and consult with governments as one strong unified body" (ASA & ICAA, 1981, p. 3). Joint activities by both bodies, such as the joint organisation of the Tenth International Congress of Accountants in 1972, kept the merger spirit alive. In order to consider a second merger proposal, the bodies formed a joint Integration Policy Committee (IPC) in 1979 under independent chairperson J. D. Norgard (Anon, 1981). The outcome of the 1981 merger attempt was that the Society members voted 90.1% in favour of the merger, as shown in Table 1.1, while the majority support from the Institute members at 56.5% did not reach the required level of 66.6%, namely two-thirds of voting members (Anon, 1982, p. 5; Linn, 1996, p. 194).

1.3.4 Third Merger Attempt

The third merger attempt mounted in 1991 fell slightly short of the two-thirds vote required by the Institute members (Leon, 1998). Neither the annual reports nor the journals of the Institute or the Society published the details of the vote, although a brief mention was made in each of the annual reports expressing disappointment with the outcome. The annual report of the Society reported that both bodies subsequently called for cooperation in the areas of accounting and auditing standards, international representation and the accreditation of tertiary institutions (ASA, 1991, p. 5). However, on 23 March 1991, The Age reported that 64% of the Institute members voted in favour, while 94% of the Society members voted in favour. This third attempt was the closest to success among all four merger attempts. It fell short by only 2.67 percentage points, about

[7] These included Mineral Securities Australia Ltd., "a loose collection of companies known as the Minsec group managed by Ken McMahon and Tom Nestel in the late 1960s and early 1970s"; Cambridge Credit Company, which went into receivership on 30 September 1974 and was one of the biggest corporate failures in Australian history at the time; and the Hutcheson Conglomerate (Clarke et al., 2003, p. 12).

250 votes in total, from the Institute. Many members of the Institute were concerned about a possible loss of status. The most concerning issue for them was that a large number of Society members would become full Institute members, and that the Institute members would be swamped by the Society members (Anon, 1991; Minter, 1991).

1.3.5 *Fourth Merger Attempt*

The fourth merger attempt was the shortest in terms of the time between starting merger discussions and the final vote. The final merger attempt met some early challenges, and an initial planned vote was delayed after leaders of both bodies felt that there was insufficient support for the merger to succeed (Anon, 1998). When the vote was finally undertaken, 59% of the Institute's members rejected the merger, in contrast to 90% of the Society's members who voted in favour (Anon 1999, p. 12; Leon 1998). After the fourth unsuccessful attempt, the president of the Institute urged its membership not to distance themselves "from fellow professionals with similar interests and aims" (Harrison, 1999, p. 6) and called for cooperation among the members of the Institute and the Society in areas of common interest.

In summary, all four attempts proved unsuccessful and raised major questions for the leadership of both bodies. It seems that the Institute's leadership has repeatedly failed to understand adequately the mood of a significant majority of its members. Additionally, in four decades, the Institute's leadership could not convince the Chartered Accountants (CAs) of the potential benefits of supporting a merger with the Society so as to create a dominant national body.

1.4 Scenario for Investigation

This historical book examines the four unsuccessful attempts to unite the two major professional accounting bodies in Australia, the Society and Institute. After the early years of regionalism and duplication, the Australian accounting profession witnessed various successful unifications, as has been noted earlier and will be addressed further in later chapters. Some attempts at unification were regional and some were based on the notion of public versus non-public practice. Appendix A1 presents a summary of these successful unifications. However, while there have been many successful unifications, the last successful merger of two professional accounting bodies in Australia occurred in 1966, which was 50 years ago, at the time of writing this book. After this last successful unification in 1966, all further attempts to unify and consolidate the Australian accounting profession have failed, and the episodes of merger attempts between the two dominant bodies have covered a period of nearly four decades, i.e. from the late 1960s until the late 1990s. This research examines the unique nature of these episodes and their effect on the structure and operations of the accounting profession.

1.5 Period Selection

This book focuses on the period from the late 1960s until the late 1990s, and the four merger attempts voted upon between 1969 and 1998. However, as the first merger attempt began to develop in the late 1960s, a particular commencing year is not selected to seek information related to the matter. Both bodies first made official announcements about merger intentions in the late 1960s. Additionally, this book also examines some years before these official announcements because of the identification of some "signals of movement" (Carnegie & Edwards, 2001, p. 301) associated with the notion of full unification of the Australian accounting profession, based on earlier statements and activities.

1.6 Motivation and Contributions

The accounting profession has great importance to a country's social and economic context due to its role in business, services, the community and governmental work. Key historical developments in Australia's society, economy and business world have shaped the present structure and operations of the accounting profession, and the three remaining professional bodies at the national level. Thus, studying history is crucial to understanding professional accounting in Australia, and solutions to current problems may emerge by understanding past contexts (Carnegie & Napier, 1996). The outcomes of events such as unsuccessful mergers have influenced and shaped the policies and strategies of the bodies involved in these processes (Previts et al., 1990).

Based on a reading of the relevant literature, it is apparent that there is no other example of any other professional group in general, or national accounting profession in particular, either globally or in Australia, in which two relatively strong and successful professional bodies have mounted four unsuccessful merger attempts. Thus, a research of this prominent case is valuable and promises a significant contribution by providing historical explanations that better inform understandings of the present, and enlighten thinking and decisions about the future. The findings of this book are also intended to inform professional accounting bodies, as well as their members and regulators, about how contemporary structures and processes have emerged from historical events. This book can also assist in assessing viable strategies and pathways for the future to enable change in the Australian accounting profession's structure and operations.

Studies of merger attempts by accounting associations in various other countries have been a fertile area of research and have been published in leading refereed journals (see, for example, Lee, 2010; Miranti, 1986a, 1986b; Richardson, 1989a, Richardson & Jones, 2007; Shackleton, 1995; Shackleton & Walker, 1998, 2001; Walker, 2004; Walker & Shackleton, 1995, 1998). These strong precedents of research in similar scenarios strengthen the case for this Australia-specific research, with the express aim of contributing to the literature on this subject. Individuals may learn from failures at least as much as from successes. This is the first non-European and non-North American research of this kind which is intended to augment knowledge by providing explanations for the failures of merger attempts, rather than the successes in other contexts that many other studies have examined. These factors all contribute to the originality and significance of this book. This book also responds to calls that have invited researchers to examine whether factors that contribute to the mounting merger attempts of accounting associations and their consequential failures are observable internationally (Lee, 2010), or whether certain factors or themes are only relevant to a specific country.

1.7 Objectives and Research Questions

1.7.1 Research Objective

The express objective of this Australian historical research is to critically examine the four unsuccessful merger attempts between the Society and the Institute, and identify the factors that contributed to the failures of these mergers. The book seeks to identify the factors that precipitated the merger proposals and the strategies adopted by both bodies in each attempt. This book will also analyse the implications of these failures for the structure and operation of the Australian accounting profession.

This book has five main research questions stemming from the key research objective. All these research questions will be answered in the chapters on each merger attempt, while a comprehensive comparative discussion will be provided in Chapter 9.

1.7.2 Research Questions

This book's research questions are as follows:

1. What were the reasons for mounting each of the four merger attempts between the Society and the Institute?
2. What strategies were adopted by the Society and the Institute in each of the four merger attempts?
3. What key factors contributed to the failure of each merger attempt?
4. What were the reactions of various stakeholders to the proposals for unification and their subsequent failures?
5. What were the long-term implications of the unsuccessful merger attempts for the Australian accounting profession?

There are five chapters dedicated to the merger attempts, one for each merger attempt, and a subsequent chapter comparing the facts, causes and consequences of each merger attempt.

1.8 Literature Review and Identification of Research Gap

This book is informed by two key branches of the accounting literature, being historical studies of the Australian accounting profession and of the mergers of professional accounting bodies internationally.

Previous Australian studies provide context-specific background information, that is, historical explanations of the structure and operations of the accounting profession, both before and during the period under investigation. These studies addressed issues related to the earliest efforts to professionalise the accounting occupation in Australia, including the import of the British model; regionalism, duplication and divisions of associations; attempts to gain a Royal Charter; and the changing closure strategies adopted by accounting bodies (Carnegie, 1993; Carnegie & Edwards, 2001; Carnegie & Parker, 1999; Carnegie et al., 2003; Chua & Poullaos, 1993, 1998; Gavens, 1990; Gavens & Gibson, 1992; Parker, 1989; Poullaos, 1993, 1994). These studies have drawn upon, and contributed to, the literature on the sociology of professions in general, and extended and enriched the accounting literature. Official and unofficial histories of major accounting bodies have also been written (see, for example, Creaney, 1984; Graham, 1978; Kenley, 1963; Marshall, 1978; Walton, 1970). Some studies have briefly discussed the merger attempts by both Australian professional accounting bodies (Carnegie, 2009; Carnegie & O'Connell, 2012; Carnegie et al., 2003; Velayutham, 1999) and provided detailed accounts of earlier developments in the structure and operations of the accounting profession. However, apart from brief mentions no previous studies have specifically covered the four attempts to unify the two bodies.

The second branch of the literature that informs this book relates to studies on mergers in the accounting profession in other countries. Mergers of accounting bodies have been one of the most common strategies used by associations, both in Australia and overseas, to secure their professional territory, as mergers can provide an opportunity to gain more lobbying power and tighten control over the operations and structures of an occupation (Richardson & Jones, 2007). Examples of merger attempts and their consequential successes or failures overseas are found in the United States (US) (Miranti, 1986a, 1986b), Britain (Shackleton & Walker, 1998, 2001; Willmott, 1986; Walker & Shackleton, 1995, 1998) and Canada (Guo, 2012; Richardson & Jones, 2007; Richardson, 1989a). The state has sometimes played a key role in encouraging mergers of accounting bodies to create a single professional body in order to establish ethical standards and enforce internal discipline (Richardson & Jones, 2007). Mergers have also been promoted independently of state intervention by accounting professionals as a strategy to achieve market dominance, reduce costs, defend legitimacy and strengthen their professional brand as a response to market dynamics (Richardson, 2002; Richardson & Jones, 2007). A review of this literature assists in identifying gaps which this research aims to fill.

1.9 Conceptual Framework

According to West (2003, p. 13), the "dissonant character of the sociology of professions literature means that it does not offer a generally accepted theory of professions that is 'ready-made' for application in explaining and evaluating the circumstances of particular occupational groups". Thus, this book blends two complementary theoretical constructs to assist in explaining the business model adopted by both accounting bodies for accepting their members and the operational implementation of professional boundaries within the Australian accounting profession. The first draws upon the boundary-work concepts of Thomas Gieryn (Gieryn, 1983, 1995, 1999; Gieryn et al., 1985), who focused on the delineation between "science" and "non-science" as a means of constructing a social boundary involving processes of inclusion and exclusion. Gieryn's boundary-work concept has been used "to study the construction of differences between 'us' and 'them'" (Grbic, 2010, p. 109). It embraces "boundary setting, maintenance, blurring, bridging, shifting, etc." (Grbic, 2010, p. 109). In her application of boundary-work concepts to the divide between local and foreign-trained accountants in Ontario, Annisette (2017, p. 1) emphasised the importance of "discursive resources" in "sorting people into groups" and creating "conceptual distinctions between them". That is, "Boundary-work refers to a specific type of linguistic practice" (Annisette, 2017, p. 3; also see Chua & Poullaos, 1998; Kirkham & Loft, 1993; McKinstry, 2014; Walker, 1991). Annisette (2017) provides the most recent and distinctive application of boundary-work concepts in accounting literature, building upon the original boundary-work concept of Gieryn (1983), who also identified the use of language to distinguish between "us" and "them" as individuals invoke discursive arguments to claim their superiority.

The boundary-work concept has been used by several researchers in a wide array of research settings (Allen, 1997, 2001; Anagnostopoulos, 2006; Bach et al., 2012; Best et al., 2021; Carmel, 2006; Glucina et al., 2020; Golyagina & Valuckas, 2020; Hunter, 2005; Jasanoff, 1995; Lamont, 1992, 2000; Mitchell & Boyle, 2021; Pacholok, 2009; Pachucki et al., 2007; Perry, 2002; Sherman, 2005, 2006; Wood et al., 2022; Wray, 2006). Boundary work has also been used in studies of the accounting profession (Annisette & Trivedi, 2013; Young, 2014) and to examine the regulation of the audit profession in France (Hazgui & Gendron, 2015). As aforementioned, the second theoretical construct is the "dilemma of exclusiveness versus market control" as a "*basic casus belli*" in connection with expert occupations (Macdonald & Ritzer, 1988, p. 257).

The boundary-work construct is used to help explain how accounting professionals delineated different forms of professional services, leading to the MIPP and MNIPP dichotomy. This categorisation was important in creating and ultimately maintaining boundaries between the memberships of the Institute and the Society. As Annisette (2017) explains, language is used as a tool to create different categories that place individuals into a hierarchy. The second theoretical construct complements the first framework and permits more comprehensive explanations to be provided, specific to the context of professional groups and their organisational strategies. This construct is applied in this book to show how professional boundaries were part of the distinctive strategic positioning of each of the two major professional accounting bodies in Australia and were then jointly reinterpreted in the form of the proposed strategy of the merged organisation. The "dilemma of exclusiveness versus market control" has been a key feature of the British, Canadian and Australian accounting professions (Annisette & O'Regan, 2007; Carnegie & Parker, 1999; Carnegie et al., 2003; Carr-Saunders & Wilson, 1964; Poullaos, 1993; Richardson, 1989b; Walker & Shackleton, 1995).

1.10 Methodology and Data Collection Methods

This book is "grounded firmly in the archive" (Carnegie & Napier, 1996, p. 31) and provides a critical and interpretive account of the four merger attempts. Primary sources and oral evidence are drawn upon, supplemented by secondary sources. The relevant archival records were largely drawn from the Jill Bright Archives of CPA Australia. Unfortunately, most minute books and many other official records of the Institute relating to the period under examination and the episodes under examination have not survived. However, the CPA Australia library has kept most of the original documents released by the Institute to the public and its members. The collection of merger-related archival records available from CPA Australia is augmented with oral history interviews conducted with four former presidents of the Society, two former presidents of the Institute and a seventh individual who was a member of the general council of the Society.

For the first merger attempt, two members of the Society who held positions on the organisation's general council in the late 1960s were interviewed, one of whom was the president of the Society at this time. Another four interviews covering the second and third merger attempts were conducted with the president of the Society and president of the Institute who were incumbent when these merger attempts took place. For the fourth merger attempt, only the then president of the Society was available for interview.

In this book, the process of data collection and analysis had three main steps: (i) collection of data from archives, including published official and non-official documents; (ii) collection of oral history information; and (iii) interpretation of findings.

1.10.1 Archives and Written Documents

The use of archives to conduct accounting studies has been advanced by several researchers (Carnegie & Napier, 1996; Miller et al., 1991; Napier, 1989; Previts et al., 1990). Carnegie and Napier (1996, p. 8) stated that "historical research in accounting gains its strength from its firm basis in the 'archive'". A form of inquiry "firmly rooted in the contents of the archive" responds to the calls of postrevisionist sociologists to examine historical variations in professionalisation projects (Walker & Shackleton, 1998, p. 34). This book also responds to the suggestions of Walker and Shackleton (1995) that critical accounting researchers need to rely more prominently on primary sources of information than on official versions of histories by professional bodies.

The archival source had two categories: official and non-official publications. The first source included officially published documents, such as unity proposals, reports of unity committees, press releases and letters from presidents to members. This source also included the minutes of various decision-making committees of both professional bodies, where access was permitted, particularly of their general councils and executive councils, and articles published in *The Australian Accountant*, *The Chartered Accountant in Australia* and the *Charter* which were the official journals of both bodies. The second archival source comprised unofficial publications, including academic journal articles, media and newspaper articles, letters to editors and other categories. The targeted newspapers included *The Sydney Morning Herald*, *The Age*, *The West Australian*, *The Telegraph*, *The Courier-Mail*, *The Australian* and *The Australian Financial Review*. The CPA Australia library has a set of scrapbooks that contain press clippings for the periods under investigation.

1.10.2 *Oral History*

According to Tosh (2010), documentary sources do not provide answers like an open book, and only provide raw data and a partial picture of events (also see Napier, 1989). Therefore, where possible, oral history evidence was obtained to supplement the formal records available in the archives and understand relevant themes to better explain the factors leading to the mounting of the four merger attempts and their subsequent failures. As aforementioned, six interviews were conducted with the presidents of the Society and the Institute who were available for these interviews and a seventh interview was conducted with a former member of general council of the Society.

1.10.3 *Analysis*

The data collected from the written documents and oral histories was subject to "critical examination in pursuit of enhanced understanding" (West, 2003, p. 10). In the analysis phase, the first step was to understand the context of Australian merger attempts from archival sources, and draw out relevant themes. Following this, through oral history interviews, contextual themes were further identified and analysed. Finally, the two theoretical frameworks were applied to analyse the findings and provide answers to the five research questions. As stated earlier, each of the four merger attempts is allocated a separate chapter, and these chapters collectively respond to the research questions.

The evidence and the researcher's analysis were combined to elucidate an interpretation of the findings. The process of interpretation involved attaching significance to what was found in the descriptive and narrative sources. This process involved "making sense of findings, offering explanations, drawing conclusions, extrapolating lessons, making inferences, considering meanings" (Patten 2002, p. 480). As outlined earlier, this book employs the boundary-work concept of Thomas Gieryn (Gieryn, 1983, 1995, 1999; Gieryn et al., 1985), as informed by the interpretation of Annisette (2017), as well as the "dilemma of exclusiveness versus market control" construct (Macdonald & Ritzer, 1988, p. 257). Historical studies can combine three forms of literary techniques: description, narrative and analysis. The first two *recreate* the past, while analysis adds *interpretation* to the findings (Tosh, 2010). This book attempted to justify all three forms of literary techniques by recreating detailed accounts of the four merger attempts and adding interpretation and analysis to historical information about them.

1.11 Book Limitations

The major limitations of this book include a lack of available surviving records for examination, as well as the inability to interview some of the key actors who were involved in each of the four periods due to their passing, migration from Australia, unwillingness to participate or inability of the researcher to trace the individuals. For example, the president of the Institute for the first merger attempt could not be traced, as the period covered by the first merger attempt was 50 years ago. For the fourth merger attempt, the then president of the Institute did not respond to a request for interview.

In addition, not all documented sources survived for this book, while publicly available written records have the drawback that they only capture what was considered relevant for public consumption. In all cases, there is a predefined purpose for prepared and distributed documents, which can limit, distort or falsify facts. In addition, professional bodies depend on a measure of confidentiality (Tosh, 2010); thus, some documents that are available in archives may not be accessible for research of the genre presented in this work (Bryman, 2008). This was the case for the Society's minutes of meetings of its general councils, as access to them was declined.

Further, oral history has many limitations. It is costly and time-consuming to conduct interviews, which can be exacerbated because potential interviewees may reside anywhere in the world or be dispersed throughout Australia (Tosh, 2010). This was overcome in one instance by conducting a telephone interview with one interviewee. For others, interstate and long distance travel was undertaken to conduct the interviews. Tosh (2010) added that interviewees may be reluctant to cooperate, unable to recall facts or happenings, or unwilling to give their perspective on specific events and conditions. Interviewees may also feel that certain facts are too private or that revealing them may attract controversy. However, for this book, all seven interviewees were found to be very open and frank in their discussion about the merger attempts.

Additionally, as time passes, people have memory lapses that can result in errors of omission. People also sometimes make assertions that may not be carefully thought out. There is a limit to the number of people who can be interviewed, and people's memories may be modified by the effect of subsequent experience and recollections of other people (Tosh, 2010). This was a particular limitation for a couple of interviews in which the interviewees stated that they could not recall certain details when responding to the interview questions. However, others seemed to have good recollections of the dated merger attempts.

1.12 Summary

This chapter has provided an overview of the book and its structure. This book is concerned with the background and factors leading to the mounting of four merger attempts between the Institute and the Society in order to outline and discuss the merger processes and to explain the reasons for their failure, using insights from the theoretical perspectives employed. These findings then provide the foundation for some broader inferences about the operational implementation and maintenance of professional boundaries in the Australian accounting profession, and the strategic positioning of different professional associations within "a pecking order" (Carnegie & Parker, 1999, p. 96). More specifically, the book addresses how accounting professionals created a hierarchy within different types of professional services, primarily to create a distinction between MIPP and MNIPP. This was an important boundary between the memberships of the Institute and the Society, and the failed merger attempts tended to perpetuate this distinction. The next chapter provides a review of relevant literature and identifies the gap in the extant research that this book aims to fill.

1.12.1 Book Structure

- Chapter 1: Introduction
- Chapter 2: Sociology of professions and accounting
- Chapter 3: Examining the Accounting Profession—Development, Structures and Operations
- Chapter 4: Understanding accounting history through critical and interpretative research
- Chapter 5: Understanding the failed merger attempts through theoretical frameworks
- Chapter 6: The first attempt to unite the dominant professional accounting associations

- Chapter 7: Second merger attempt
- Chapter 8: Third merger attempt
- Chapter 9: Fourth merger attempt
- Chapter 10: Similarites and differences across all merger attempts
- Chapter 11: Summary and implications
- References
- Appendices

References

Allen, D. (1997). The nursing-medical boundary: A negotiated order? *Sociology of Health and Illness, 19*(4), 498–520.

Allen, D. (2001). *The changing shape of nursing practice*. Routledge.

Anagnostopoulos, D. (2006). Real students and true demotes: Ending social promotion and the moral ordering of urban high schools. *American Educational Research Journal, 43*(1), 5–42.

Annisette, M. (2017). Discourse of the professions: The making, normalizing and taming of Ontario's foreign-trained accountant. *Accounting, Organizations and Society, 60*, 37–61.

Annisette, M., & O'Regan, P. (2007). Joined for the common purpose: The establishment of the Institute of Chartered Accountants in Ireland as an all-Ireland institution. *Qualitative Research in Accounting & Management, 4*(1), 4–25.

Annisette, M., & Trivedi, V. U. (2013). Globalization, paradox and the (un) making of identities: Immigrant chartered accountants of India in Canada. *Accounting, Organisations and Society, 38*(1), 1–29.

Anon. (1981, March). Integration forum. *The Australian Accountant*, 90–93.

Anon. (1982, January/February). No to integration. *The Australian Accountant*, 5.

Anon. (1991, February 21). The unification debate: The house divided. *New Accountant*, 18.

Anon. (1998, May). New national president: David Boymal. *Australian CPA*, 18–19.

Anon. (1999). Summit convened after merger plans abandoned. *Charter, 70*(1), 12.

Australian Society of Accountants and the Institute of Chartered Accountants in Australia. (1969). *Report of Joint Meeting of Education Committees*. ASA Melbourne and ICAA Sydney, 1–19.

Australian Society of Accountants and Institute of Chartered Accountants in Australia. (1981). Draft proposals for the integration of the accountancy profession in Australia, Australian Society of Accountants and the Institute of Chartered Accountants in Australia, issued March 1, 1981, 1–20.

Australian Society of Certified Professional Accountants. (1991, March). *The Society and Institute merger—A vote crucial to your future*. Pamphlet issued to members with vote papers.

Bach, S., Kessler, I., & Heron, P. (2012). Nursing a grievance? The role of healthcare assistants in a modernized National Health Service. *Gender, Work and Organisation, 19*(2), 205–224.

Best, S., Beech, C., Robbé, I. J., & Williams, S. (2021). Interprofessional teamwork: the role of professional identity and signature pedagogy–a mixed methods study. *Journal of Health Organization and Management*.

Boehme, T. C., & Braddock, L. A. (1965, November). The Accountancy Research Foundation. *The Australian Accountant*, 573–574.

Bryman, Alan. (2008). Of methods and methodology. *Qualitative Research in Organizations and Management: An International Journal, 3*(2), 159–168.

Carmel, S. (2006). Boundaries obscured and boundaries reinforced: Incorporation as a strategy of occupational enhancement for intensive care. *Sociology of Health & Illness, 28*(2), 154–177.

Carnegie, G. D. (1993). The Australian Institute of Incorporated Accountants (1892–1938). *Accounting, Business and Financial History, 3*(1), 61–80.

Carnegie, G. D. (2009). The development of accounting regulation, education and literature in Australia, 1788–2005. *Australian Economic History Review, 49*(3), 276–301.

Carnegie, G. D. (2016). The accounting professional project and bank failures. *Journal of Management History, 22*(4), 389–412.

Carnegie, G. D., & Edwards, J. R. (2001). The construction of the professional accountant: The case of the Incorporated Institute of Accountants, Victoria (1886). *Accounting, Organisations and Society, 26*(4/5), 301–325.

Carnegie, G. D., & Napier, C. J. (1996). Critical and interpretive histories: Insights into accounting's present and future through its past. *Accounting, Auditing & Accountability Journal, 9*(3), 7–39.

Carnegie, G. D., & O'Connell, B. T. (2012). Understanding the responses of professional accounting bodies to crises: The case of the Australian profession in the 1960s. *Accounting Auditing and Accountability Journal, 25*(5), 835–875.

Carnegie, G. D., & Parker, R. H. (1999). Accountants and empire: The case of co-membership of Australian and British accountancy bodies, 1885 to 1914. *Accounting, Business & Financial History, 9*(1), 77–102.

Carnegie, G. D., Edwards, J. R., & West, B. P. (2003). Understanding the dynamics of the Australian accounting profession: A prosopographical study of the founding members of the Incorporated Institute of Accountants,

Victoria, 1886 to 1908. *Accounting, Auditing & Accountability Journal, 16*(5), 790–820.
Carr-Saunders, A. M., & Wilson, P. A. (1964). *The professions*. Frank Cass.
Chua, W. F., & Poullaos, C. (1993). Rethinking the profession-state dynamic: The case of the Victorian Charter attempt, 1885–1906. *Accounting, Organisations and Society, 18*(7/8), 691–728.
Chua, W. F., & Poullaos, C. (1998). The dynamics of 'closure' amidst the construction of market, profession, empire and nationhood: An historical analysis of an Australian accounting association, 1886–1903. *Accounting, Organisations and Society, 23*(2), 155–187.
Clarke, F., Dean, G., & Oliver, K. (2003). *Corporate collapse: Accounting, regulatory and ethical failure* (2nd ed.). Cambridge University Press.
Creaney, E. (1984, July). The history of the I. A. A., An address by the National Secretary, Perth, WA.
Edwards, J. R., Carnegie, G. D., & Cauberg, J. (1997). The Incorporated Institute of Accountants, Victoria (1886): A study of founders' backgrounds. In T. E. Cooke & C. W. Nobes (Eds.), *The development of accounting in an international context: A festschrift in honour of R. H. Parker* (49–67). Routledge.
Gavens, J. J. (1990). A historical perspective of integration of the Australian accounting profession. In R. H. Parker (Ed.), *Accounting in Australia: Historical essays* (pp. 381–407). Garland.
Gavens, J. J., & Gibson, R. W. (1992). An Australian attempt to internationalize accounting professional organisations. *The Accounting Historians Journal, 19*(2), 79–102.
Gibson, R. W. (1979). Development of corporate accounting in Australia. *Accounting Historians Journal, 6*(2), 23–38.
Gieryn, T. F. (1983). Boundary-work and the demarcation of science from non-science: Strains and interests in the professional ideologies of scientists. *American Sociological Review, 48*(6), 781–795.
Gieryn, T. F. (1995). Boundaries of science. In S. Jasanoff, G. E Markle, J. C Petersen, & T. Pinch (Eds.), *Handbook of science and technology studies* (pp. 393–443). SAGE.
Gieryn, T. F. (1999). *Cultural boundaries of science: Credibility on the line*. University of Chicago Press.
Gieryn, T. F., Bevins, G. M., & Zehi, S. C. (1985). Professionalization of American scientists: Public science in the creation/evolution trials. *American Sociological Review, 50*(3), 392–409.
Glucina, T. T., Krägeloh, C. U., Farvid, P., & Holt, K. (2020). Moving towards a contemporary chiropractic professional identity. *Complementary Therapies in Clinical Practice, 39*, 101105.

Golyagina, A., & Valuckas, D. (2020). Boundary-work in management accounting: The case of hybrid professionalism. *The British Accounting Review, 52*(2), 100841.

Graham, A. A. (1972, May). The profession in Australia: Problems and developments. *The Chartered Accountant in Australia*, 4–14.

Graham, A. W. (1978). *Without fear or favour: A history of the Institute of Chartered Accountants in Australia, 1928–1978*. Butterworths for Institute of Chartered Accountants in Australia.

Grbic, N. (2010). 'Boundary work' as a concept for studying professionalization processes in the interpreting field. *Translation and Interpreting Studies, 5*(1), 109–123.

Guo, K. H. (2012). Understanding why and how some chartered accountants object to the proposed merger of the three accounting professions in Canada. *Accounting Perspectives, 11*(2), 111–130.

Gynther, R. S. (1967). *Practising accountants in Australia*. Queensland University Press.

Harrison, S. (1999, February). Are we still talking to the Society? *Charter, 70*, 6.

Hazgui, M., & Gendron, Y. (2015). Blurred roles and elusive boundaries: On contemporary forms of oversight surrounding professional work. *Accounting, Auditing & Accountability Journal, 28*(8), 1234–1262.

Henderson, S. (1997). The expectations gap and the Australian accounting profession. *Accounting Forum, 21*(2), 175–188.

Hunter, B. (2005). Emotion work and boundary maintenance in hospital-based midwifery. *Midwifery, 21*(3), 253–266.

Irish, R. (1963, August). Should we blame the accounting profession? *The Chartered Accountant in Australia*, 79–96.

Jasanoff, S. (1995). *Science at the bar: Law, science, and technology in America*. Harvard University Press.

Kenley, W. J. (1963). *History of the Australian Society of Accountants and its antecedent bodies, 1887 to 1962*. Australian Society of Accountants (evidence of authorship in *The Australian Accountant*, June 1977, 27).

Kirkham, L. M., & Loft, A. (1993), Gender and the construction of the professional accountant. *Accounting, Organizations and Society, 18*(6), 507–58.

Lamont, M. (1992). *Money, morals, and manners: The culture of the French and American upper-middle class*. University of Chicago Press.

Lamont, M. (2000). *The dignity of working men: Morality and the boundaries of race, class, and immigration*. Harvard University Press.

Lee, T. A. (2010). Consolidating the public accountancy profession: The case of the proposed Institute of Chartered Accountants of Great Britain, 1988–9. *Accounting History, 15*(1), 7–39.

Leon, G. (1998, December 15). Merger numbers fall well short. *The Age*, 3.

Linn, R. (1996). *Power, progress and profit: A history of the Australian accounting profession*. Australian Society of Certified Practising Accountants.
Macdonald, K. M., & Ritzer, G. (1988). The sociology of the professions: Dead or alive? *Work and Occupations, 15*(3), 251–272.
Marshall, N. J. (1978). A jubilee history 1928–1978 (Melbourne: The Institute of Chartered Accountants in Australia). Partly reprinted in R. H. Parker (Ed.). (1990a) *Accounting in Australia: Historical essays* (pp. 408–434). Garland Publishing.
McKinstry, S. (2014). From "colonial reciprocity" to international supremacy: Scottish chartered accountancy and its "discourse of superiority" in context, 1854 to the present. *Accounting History, 19*(1–2), 77–96.
Miller, P., Hopper, T., & Laughlin, R. (1991). The new accounting history: An introduction. *Accounting, Organisations and Society, 16*(5/6), 395–403.
Minter, E. (1991, March 23). Rebel group blocks accountancy merger. *The Age*, 7.
Miranti, P. J. (1986a). Associationalism, statism, and professional regulation: Public accountants and the reform of the financial markets, 1896–1940. *Business History Review, 60*(3), 438–468.
Miranti, P. J. (1986b). From conflict to consensus: The American Institute of Accountants and the professionalization of public accountancy, 1886–1940. *Business and Economic History, 15*(2nd series), 93–126.
Mitchell, R., & Boyle, B. (2021). Understanding the role of profession in multidisciplinary team innovation: Professional identity, minority dissent and team innovation. *British Journal of Management, 32*(2), 512–528.
Napier, C. J. (1989). Research directions in accounting history. *British Accounting Review, 21*(3), 237–254.
Pacholok, S. (2009). Gendered Strategies of self: Navigating hierarchy and contesting masculinities. *Gender, Work and Organisation, 16*(4), 471–500.
Pachucki, M. A., Pendergrass, S., & Lamont, M. (2007). Boundary processes: Recent theoretical developments and new contributions. *Poetics, 35*(6), 331–351.
Parker, R. H. (1986, November). Accounting in Australia. *The Australian Accountant*, 85–87.
Parker, R. H. (1989). Importing and exporting accounting: The British experience. In A. G. Hopwood (Ed.), *International pressures for accounting change* (pp. 7–29). Prentice-Hall.
Parker, R. H. (2014). The first 32 importers of an English professional accountancy qualification: Opportunities, incentives, impact. *Accounting History, 19*(1–2), 171–192.
Perry, P. (2002). *Shades of white: White kids and racial identities in high school*. Duke University Press.

Poullaos, C. (1993). Making profession and state, 1907 to 1914: The ACPA's first charter attempt. *Abacus, 29*(2), 196–229.

Poullaos, C. (1994). *Making the Australian chartered accountant*. Garland.

Previts, G. J., Parker, L. D., & Coffman, E. N. (1990). Accounting history: Definition and relevance. *Abacus, 26*(1), 1–16.

Richardson, A. J. (1987). Professionalization and intra-professional competition in the Canadian accounting profession. *Work and Occupations, 14*(4), 591–615.

Richardson, A. J. (1989a). Corporatism and intraprofessional hegemony: A study of regulation and internal social order. *Accounting, Organisations and Society, 14*(5), 415–431.

Richardson, A. J. (1989b). Canada's accounting elite: 1880–1930. *The Accounting Historians Journal, 16*(1), 1–21.

Richardson, A. J. (2002). Professional dominance: The relationship between financial accounting and managerial accounting, 1926–1986. *The Accounting Historians Journal*, 91–121.

Richardson, A. J., & Jones, D. B. (2007). Professional 'brand', personal identity and resistance to change in the Canadian accounting profession: A comparative history of two accounting association merger negotiations. *Accounting History, 12*(2), 135–164.

Shackleton, K., & Walker, S. P. (2001). *A future for the accountancy profession: The quest for closure and integration, 1957–1970*. Institute of Chartered Accountants of Scotland.

Shackleton, K. (1995). Scottish chartered accountants: Internal and external political relationships, 1853–1916. *Accounting, Auditing & Accountability Journal, 8*(2), 18–46.

Shackleton, K., & Walker. S. P. (1998). *Professional reconstruction: The coordination of the accountancy bodies, 1930–1957*. Institute of Chartered Accountants of Scotland.

Sherman, R. (2005). Producing the superior self: Strategic comparison and symbolic boundaries among luxury hotel workers. *Ethnography, 6*(2), 131–158.

Sherman, R. (2006). *Class acts*. University of California Press.

Sykes, T. (1998). *Two centuries of panic: A history of corporate collapses in Australia*. Allen & Unwin.

The Institute of Chartered Accountants in Australia. (1970). *Annual report*. Sydney, Australia

Tosh, J. (2010). *The pursuit of history: Aims, methods and new directions in the study of modern history* (5th ed.). Pearson Longman.

Velayutham, S. (1999). The professional accounting body in the 21st century: The global franchise. *Pacific Accounting Review, 11*(1/2), 163–171.

Walker, S. P. (1991). The defence of professional monopoly: Scottish chartered accountants and 'satellites in the accountancy firmament' 1854–1914. *Accounting, Organisations and Society, 16*(3), 257–283.

Walker, S. P. (2004). *Towards the 'great Desideratum': The unification of the accountancy bodies in England, 1870–1880.* Institute of Chartered Accountants of Scotland.

Walker, S. P., & Shackleton, K. (1995). Corporatism and structural change in the British accountancy profession, 1930–1957. *Accounting, Organisations and Society, 20*(6), 467–503.

Walker, S. P., & Shackleton, K. (1998). A ring fence for the profession: Advancing the closure of British accountancy 1957–1970. *Accounting, Auditing & Accountability Journal, 11*(1), 34–71.

Walton, S. J. T. (1970). *History of the Institute of Chartered Accountants in Australia and its antecedent bodies with reference to the personalities concerned.* The Institute of Chartered Accountants in Australia.

West, B. P. (2003). *Professionalism and accounting rules*. Routledge.

Willmott, H. (1986). Organising the profession: A theoretical and historical examination of the development of the major accountancy bodies in the UK. *Accounting, Organisations and Society, 11*(6), 555–580.

Wood, A., Copley, J., Hill, A., & Cottrell, N. (2022). Interprofessional identity in clinicians: A scoping review. *Journal of Interprofessional Care*, 1–12.

Wray, M. (2006). *Not quite white: White trash and the boundaries of whiteness.* Duke University Press.

Young, J. J. (2014). Separating the political and technical: Accounting standard-setting and purification. *Contemporary Accounting Research, 31*(3), 713–747.

CHAPTER 2

Sociology of the Professions and Accounting

2.1 Introduction

Professions represent social groups formed within a wider social context by skilled individuals around their common economic interests. In particular, the formation of these groups is directed by various factors which are subject to numerous enquiries of sociology. This chapter introduces the sociology of professions and various themes within this domain drawing from the available literature. This is done with an objective to set a clear path for the current study and to identify a potential gap in the contemporary literature especially around mergers of accounting associations. To understand the context of development of the Australian accounting profession, a good understanding of sociology of the professions (SOP) is important. The SOP helps us understand the dynamics of the origins of organising into groups by professionals and formation of associations. Such organising is usually done at social levels first and then around common economic interests. Hence, we need to rely on SOP to understand the dynamics of professionalisation of accounting. Attempts to achieve control over the service market are often linked with self-interest of individuals, whether economic or status related. SOP also enables us to extract themes in the development of any profession and how an occupation evolves into an organised profession, how a profession develops abilities to influence and how that is used for promoting self-interest.

J. Sidhu et al., *Understanding the Sociology of the Accounting Profession*,
https://doi.org/10.1007/978-981-99-1572-9_2

With this aim, we provide an overview of SOP literature and various themes in the development of professionalisation studies. We then move our focus to the accounting profession to identify popular themes in the professionalisation of accounting literature. This assists us to explore current gaps in our understanding of the development of Australian accounting profession's current structures and operations.

Prior research has revealed that social class, race and gender often played important roles in the professionalisation of the accounting occupation (Carnegie & Edwards, 2001; Sidhu & West, 2014). This highlights that early accountants relied upon other, more problematic, characteristics to elevate the status of their occupation rather than the traditionally ascribed traits of specialist knowledge and commitment to ethical public service. In other words, mechanisms of exclusion were used to further the special interests of accounting professionals.

This chapter is divided into six sections. The second section begins the discussion with reference to the sociology of professions literature and attempts to explain the term "professions" and "professionalisation". The third section briefly explains the three main approaches to the study of professions, along with their key features. After some initial contention, accounting was successful in gaining recognition from sociologists as a profession. The historical origins and initial developments of the accounting profession are discussed in the fourth section.

This section finds that in recent years, an increasing body of research from non-Anglo-Saxon countries indicates that there is a clear demarcation between Anglo and non-Anglo-Saxon countries in the themes and issues surrounding the professionalisation of accounting. The fifth section provides a summary of the main themes in the professionalisation of accounting, that is, the influence of the state, imperialism and closure based on racism, gender and social class. The last section offers concluding remarks to this chapter.

2.2 Professions and Professionalisation

Individuals in every society have been engaged in both skilled and unskilled occupations since the beginning of civilised social systems. In order to gain collective mobility and influence, the formation of groupings and guilds was part of ancient and medieval economic systems. While in recent times, professions were organised into institutional forms as a response to the social and economic changes which resulted from a range of changes in society and its operations. These include increased migration of population from rural areas to urban settings, centralisation of economic activity in certain regions and increased demand for the provision of organised and structured forms of professional services. Increase in commerce and trade activity in regions and across national boundaries further added to this need. Over the last 100 years or so, in developed countries the role of religion has diminished, and elected government representatives play far more direct and active role in sanctioning the status of profession to any trait. The result of such fast pace changes was the emergence of a new middle class of professionals in the last decades of nineteenth century (Lee, 1995). Modern professions are structured around an occupation and their authority is vested in special knowledge and skill-based training with their ultimate role being service provision to the society. In other words, at the core of foundation of any profession is public interest and their utility to the functioning of a given society.

Researchers have struggled to provide a concise explanation about some key questions, what professions are, what is their role in a society, and how one can provide a definition of a profession? Some claim that a profession is an occupation based on tactical and technical knowledge (Evetts, 2003), which means an occupation without those features may not be termed as a profession. Such claims are open for scrutiny and criticism. Lee (1995) formed a view that the formation of formal institutions is termed the birth of any profession while Carnegie and Edwards (2001) held contrasting views about professionalisation.[1] They argued against the notion that professions are born with the formation of formal institutions and rather called it a simplification of the whole process. They viewed the formation of a profession as a dynamic process involving various "signals of movement" by an occupational group to achieve occupational ascendency. Such signals are evident both before and after the formation of professional (occupational) associations. Therefore, the formation of associations does not mean the birth of a profession, but it is a milestone in achieving the status of a profession.

Larson (1977) is one of the pioneers who provided a mechanism to sociologists for understanding the complexities of professionalisation.

[1] In this book, professionalisation is understood as a process for the formation of a profession; that is, how an occupation gains professional status. In some instances, the term "professional project" is used which is understood as a name given to the process of professionalisation.

Since publishing her Ph.D. thesis as a book which she completed at the University of California, she has influenced a domain of research which also guides this work. Larson (1977) argued that the process of professionalisation is an attempt to translate one order of scarce resources such as special knowledge and skills into another such as social status and economic rewards. Professional groups achieve these by creating a scarcity of such knowledge and skills with a tendency to create a monopoly of expertise in the market. Monopoly is also achieved over status in system of stratification. If we simplify her statement, then it means professionalisation is a process based on exclusion of large number of potential members from entering the profession. This is done by setting entry level requirements, minimum qualifications, tests and experience requirements. This process of exclusion creates scarcity of those services thus delivers economic rewards and social status to member which is often linked with high income too.

Willmott (1986) provided a critical socio-economic perspective of professions. He argued that professions are self-governing bodies safeguarding private interests within the context of the market, the state and the community. The sociology of professions literature does not provide any concise definition of the term "professions" and due to the absence of common understanding, different claims and counterclaims have been made (e.g. development of different approaches). Irrespective of prevalent approaches and an extensive body of research, West was sceptical of the usefulness of the literature related to the study of professions. In response to the ambiguity in the sociology of professions literature surrounding the term "professions", West (2003) addressed such confusion by arguing that the major substance of any profession is the presence of "occupational authority" which is enjoyed and exercised by a profession. Based on analysis of different arguments put forward by researchers we conclude that a profession is an occupation organised via formal associations, requires special training, skills and entry level education, and as West stated these features provide a form of authority which a profession uses in providing service to society. In order to exert control and save its position of strength, professions do need to engage in political lobbying and advocacy work. Often there are challenges from other professions to capture service market, such as provision of advisory service by accountants and lawyers and overlap of certain aspects. Next, we look at sociology of profession literature as it evolved across three key approaches and finally settled in the development of critical approach.

2.3 Approaches to the Study of Professions

Primarily, there are three approaches within the sociology of professions literature: the functionalist; the interactionist; and the critical approach. These approaches have progressively emerged one after the other in the last century and it is difficult to separate them out in periodic frames. The first two approaches dominated the sociology debate in the pre-1970 period and the later period registered a strong presence of the critical approach which draws heavily upon the work of Weber and Marx (Willmott, 1986).

2.3.1 Functionalist

The first approach is the functionalist approach, and it is based on the traditional or functional view of professions. The proponents of this approach viewed professions as a commodity for the service of society (Carr-Saunders & Wilson, 1964). This approach was also labelled the "trait", "attribute" or "taxonomic" model of professions (West, 2003).

Sociologists suggested that an occupation claiming to be a profession required the possession of certain attributes such as "esoteric knowledge, independence, altruism and self-discipline" (Willmott, 1986) and with some researchers providing a list of these attributes. Despite many attempts to prepare a list of traits that occupation must hold to make claims of a profession, it is impossible to provide a comprehensive enough to cover all types of professions, which defies the usefulness of such lists. According to this approach, professional bodies are responsible for ensuring competence, discipline and service standards (Willmott, 1986) and members of professions are expected to act in the public interest to justify need for their social utility and a legitimate position (Lee, 1995). This is the simplification of seeing professions as mere groups of skilled individuals who fulfill their role in the functioning of society. Here a professional is seen as someone who is offering his or her service to others. Professional bodies are expected to act in the best interest of society ensuring members act in the best interest of their clients. However, this seemed like a simplification of complex process of professionalisation which sees members not act in public interest.

2.3.2 *Interactionist*

Due to much weakness in the first approach, the study of professions evolved into the interactionist approach. This approach[2] viewed professions as special interest groups that strive to convince others that their claims of professional recognition are valid and legitimise (Willmott, 1986). The contributors to this approach include Becker (1962), Bucher and Strauss (1961), Dingwall (1976), Haug and Sussman (1969), Hughes (1975) and Roth (1974). According to this approach, there are two stages of interaction: first, the profession's interaction with society at individual or group level; second, the interaction of members within the profession. The interaction with society is aimed at securing respectability and claiming a distinguished social niche for the occupation. The interaction within a profession can be between individuals, and between individuals and groups.

In the next stage of interaction and their pursuit of recognition from society as valued social elements, interest groups are also exposed to intra-group rivalries within the profession. The professional organisation provides a platform for interactions and for the institutional politics which results from such interactions. Willmott (1986) found the capacity of the first two approaches insufficient for the study of professions and called for a more critical approach to understand the institutional politics, i.e. a critical study of intra-profession interactions. Although the first two approaches are criticised in later studies due to their limited capacity to provide clear directions and understandings about professions, the third approach evolved from the weaknesses of the earlier two approaches. We may not have had an advanced understanding of professions without first knowing why previous approaches failed to answer certain questions from sociologists. For example, why professionals engage in exclusion or lobbying with the state, what is the role of auditors in corporate scandals and so on. The next approach views such questions from a critical lens and makes an attempt to provide an analytical response.

[2] Many researchers identified this approach (e.g. Chua & Poullaos 1993, 1998; Willmott 1986) as an independent approach in the sociology of professions, but some did not separately identify this approach and discussed only the traditional and the critical approaches (e.g. Lee, 1995; Walker, 1995).

2.3.3 *Critical*

A major change in the sociology of professions research was observed during 1960s which led to major paradigm shift in the sociology of professions. After more than three decades during the late 1990s, the functionalist and the interactionist approaches within the sociology of professions literature were firmly rejected (Carnegie et al., 2003) as they did not serve the purpose of studying professions as special interest groups. The earlier two approaches were replaced by the critical approach, which considers professions as a medium for capitalists' exploitation (West, 2003) and is motivated by neo-Weberian and Marxist ideology (Willmott, 1986).

Looking at the accounting profession, Lee (1995) argued that the professional project gets more motivation from the economic self-interest of accountants than their duty to protect the public interest. Professions seek economic and other tangible rewards, such as those related to status, prestige and market dominance, which is achieved through the creation of monopoly and the practice of explicit and implicit exclusion (Larson, 1977; Macdonald, 1995; Willmott, 1986). Therefore, professions are groups striving for control over the service market and they operationalise their strategy of exclusivity by setting strict entry requirements into the profession such as academic education, work-related training and experience (Lee, 1995). The implication is clear that individuals must satisfy these requirements and without meeting them professional membership is impossible and certain service opportunities linked with economic rewards and status are denied.

The case of the four Australian merger attempts aligns with the arguments presented by Lee and other researchers, where the two major bodies in the Australian accounting profession were faced with challenges (discussed and explained in later chapters) and saw opportunities to change the structure of the Australian accounting profession to exert more control and influence. Both accounting associations were aiming to achieve market control and exclusivity. As Larson stated making strict entry level requirements creates scarcity and thus makes a profession exclusive. While allowing a large number of members to join a professional body risks the exclusivity but at the same time creates market dominance and control.

This approach rejects the notion that status is merely achieved by acquiring certain attributes or as a result of an interaction with society;

rather it is achieved through more complex social and political processes (West, 2003). This means that professions achieve economic rewards and safeguard their economic and status by entering into political processes of exclusion and lobbying. This is what led to the mounting and failure of four merger attempts.

It appears that various approaches have been developed while trying to distinguish one from the other, supplanting the old and proving the new approach as superior to the existing. Despite that, West (2003) argued that specialist expertise is a universally agreed feature of professions among all approaches. So, accounting profession with its specialist technical knowledge does satisfy the definition of a profession. Next, we expand on this argument bit further and provide contextual background of professionalisation of accounting.

2.4 Accounting Profession

Researchers have argued that accounting profession is not only the concern of accountants but governments, and in pluralistic societies, the public as well. This is because of the role played by accounting profession in the orderly functioning of any society, economic activity and assistance offered in running government apparatus which undoubtedly makes it of significant social and political importance (Willmott, 1986). After some initial hesitation, the majority of sociologists accepted accounting as an emerging profession in their social inquiry (West, 2003).

The accounting profession was formally institutionalised in Britain during and immediately after the industrial revolution (Lee, 1995). However, the main reason for its development was the rising demand for the services of public accountants after the failure of many joint stock companies (Bailey, 1992) and the enactment of new legislation such as the Bankruptcy Act (Macdonald, 1985). Therefore, it can be argued that the accountancy profession did not evolve as an absolute science as many other professions but its development was a response to economic and social factors (Briston, 1978). However, this does not subdue the importance of the rise of accountants as an important social as well as a sociological category.

The first accounting body in the English-speaking world was formed by the Scottish accountants in 1853 (Brown, 1905; Walker, 1995) as a response to the mounting pressures of industrialisation and likely competition from the legal profession (Walker, 1995). In the US accountants made their first attempt to organise in 1882 by forming the Institute of Accounts (Lee, 1995). The first global attempt to organise the accounting profession was, however, made by accountants in Venice in 1581 by forming an accounting association (Annisette, 1999), but it might not have been successful in gaining recognition and status. Similarly, the Scottish accountants also made several attempts to organise before finally succeeding in 1853 (Lee, 1995).

The Institute of Chartered Accountants in England and Wales (ICAEW) was set up in 1880 (Lee, 1995). One common theme in the professionalisation attempts was the pursuit of economic self-interest by accountants in the name of public interest (Lee, 1995). The professionalisation of accounting was also taking place in Austria, France, Germany and Italy (Bailey, 1992).

In addition to the demand for accounting services, another compelling reason that led accountants to organise into groups was the legal requirement imposed on companies to have their financial statements audited (West, 2003). The history of the British and US accountancy professions is marked by intra-professional rivalry (Lee, 1995) and members expedited pursuits to exercise control and monopoly over the profession (West, 2003). In contemporary times, there has been a fundamental bi-polarisation of professional accounting bodies around the world: one inspired by the British concept, Chartered Accountant (CA), and the other inspired by the American concept, Certified Public or Practising Accountant (CPA).

British colonialism has strongly influenced the development of corporate legislation, auditing and the accounting profession in its former colonies (Briston, 1978; also see Carnegie & Parker, 1999). In fact, the British imported double entry bookkeeping (a technique) and have exported professional accountancy (an institution) to colonies and other parts of the world (Parker, 1989). The export of British qualifications became a large-scale industry in the twentieth century and the British took the modern accounting profession to other parts of the world, primarily to colonies to run their colonial affairs.[3]

[3] Parker (2005) found a dominating British influence in naming accounting bodies in Commonwealth countries. In 2003, out of the total membership of the International Federation of Accountants (IFAC), 36% member countries were a part of the British Empire. By 2003, 19 Commonwealth countries had a Chartered Accountant body and 11 had a CPA body.

The British bodies also used an examinations regime as means of closing-off and controlling the accountancy service market (Willmott, 1986). The new entrants into the profession were seen as potential threats because existing members feared the dilution of their special privileges. The social class, gender and political acuity of early accountants contributed to the elevation of accounting within the occupational continuum, assisted by changes in the legislative and economic environments (West, 2003). Broadly seen, in the course of over a century accounting has become entrenched as a profession and in this process, it has developed all the pre-requisites to achieve the identity of a profession. This makes the accounting profession a complex and multi-dimensional entity, thus inviting multiple enquiry points from different angles and employing various themes. The next section briefly discusses this issue.

2.5 Themes in the Professionalisation of Accounting

What are the basic constituents of this profession and what strategies are used to continue the social controls within it? These are the two fundamental areas of enquiry that reveal certain themes. A clear understanding of any profession, and moreover its real role in local and global contexts, needs an analysis of various factors. These factors are active at international, cultural, political, economic, social and legal levels, influencing and constraining its development. The development of an accounting system is also the function of a range of factors ranging from historical, political, economic and social (Briston, 1978). Such perspectives are understood as different themes in the study of professions.

Evidenced by the availability of vast literature, this book claims attempts at closure and the role of the state are the most prominent themes in the sociology of the accounting profession. Groups have tried to establish control and create monopoly and closure is a means to this end. Closure has been achieved through gender, race coupled with imperial influence, social class and the sanctions of the local state as discussed in the next sections.

2.5.1 State Influence

The study of the role of the state in the professionalisation of accounting has been the subject of many studies (Bailey, 1992; Caramanis, 1999;

Chua & Poullaos, 1993, 1998; Poullaos, 1993; Walker, 1995; Walker & Shackleton, 1995).

The state/profession relationship has been a central theme in the sociology of the professions with a particular emphasis on the state's role and its ability to exert influence. According to Uche (2002), the state/profession nexus is dynamic and quite complex, and it is subject to structure and type of state mechanism. For example, whether there is a democratic, military or communist state, it will effect the professionalisation of accounting differently.

Professions strive to secure favorable legislation, engage in effective lobbying and successfully eliminate any external challenges. This is all possible if there is a strong nexus between the State and professional bodies. Uche (2002) also claimed that the development of the accounting profession cannot be understood in the absence of the political and social environment, which makes the relationship of a profession with the state of critical importance.

The influence of the state is recognised as a key theme in the professionalisation of accounting by many studies (Australia: Chua & Poullaos, 1993; England: Chua & Poullaos, 1998). In the UK, although the initial steps in the professionalisation of accounting were driven by collective self-interest motives, the state later played a major role, including the introduction of legislation (Walker & Shackleton, 1995). According to Puxty et al. (1987), "the state does not simply license the existence of organised interest groups but incorporates them into its own centralised, hierarchical system of regulation. In doing so, the state simultaneously recognises its dependence upon these associations and seeks to use them as an instrument in the pursuit and legitimation of its policies" (p. 284). Therefore, it is up to professional bodies to engage in effective negotiations with the State for desired policy and legislative changes. The State does not proactively introduce regulation of any profession unless the profession is such where unorganised profession may have significant public interest implications. A profession such as accounting does not fall into that category such as medicine, law and even trade occupations such as electrician and plumbing. A bad accounting service is not as of public interest as a bad treatment by a doctor or a faulty electric connection which can have massive implications for public safety.

The importance of the state is emphasised by Larson (1977) who claimed that professions ultimately depend upon the power of the state because the emergence of profession requires assistance form powerful protectors, i.e. state. The professional monopoly is established when the state grants exclusive rights to provide service only to certain individuals and registration is one such means. Therefore, the professions create and maintain their monopoly and control on the basis of autonomy granted by the state, which is specific to social context and time frame.

The state can either grant an unrestricted autonomy, a restricted autonomy or create interference for the management of a harmonious social order as we just explained in previous paragraphs. As a result, the role of the state in professionalisation cannot be understood through a universal model but it is the context and time-specific forces which drive this relationship. The state may also set the specific roles for the profession in a particular time and context. For example, in the early twentieth century, the duty of the accounting profession to the state was given the utmost importance in Russia and Germany (Bailey, 1992).

Ballas (1998) concluded that during the civil war, the Greek state perceived the auditing profession as a tool to establish and maintain economic and political control; which in Dingwall's words is harmonious social order. Therefore, the beneficiary and dominant actor, in this case, appears to be the state rather than the profession. Bopta et al. (2007) claimed that the form of state significantly affects the professionalisation process. The social expectations and government actions are linked to its form, whether it is a military or democratic government. They also claimed that mere active involvement of the state is not sufficient for a profession's development; rather the active participation of additional actors is required as well. For example, the implications of actions of professional practitioners on the general public. As we discussed earlier with examples of a doctor or an electrician.

Hao (1999) and Yee (2009) analysed the state structure in the Chinese context, which is a communist state. Yee (2009) concluded that the accounting profession in China re-emerged in 1980s under the direct state supervision. Hao (1999) observed that the change in the state structure significantly affected the accounting profession. According to Yee (2009), the Chinese state had a dominating and authoritative role when compared to Anglo-Saxon countries in the professionalisation of accounting. However, she associated it with the cultural features of Chinese society. The Chinese accountants did not make proactive attempts to organise themselves and it was the state that mobilised accountants to achieve its economic agenda. This can be attributed to the political structure in China where government plays an active role in the regulation of society, business and professions.

Sakagami et al. (1999) found that in Japan, the accounting profession accepted the state dominance and failed to make any attempts to obtain or claim control over the profession. An ineffective and insufficient role of the state is also evident in some non-Anglo-Saxon studies (Trinidad and Tobago: Annisette, 1999). A number of studies in sociology of accounting profession has looked at Asian countries such as Cambodia, China, Indonesia, South Korea, Sri Lanka and India (Sidhu & West, 2014). Of these, some of these studies looked at the role of State in the development of professional accounting in respective countries.

According to Yapa (1999) a structured accounting profession does not exist in Brunei. In a Sri Lankan study, Yapa (2006) found that the role of the local accounting institute and the state to be ineffective and attributed this directly to the failure of the professionalisation process. This theme from new and emerging economies (which are predominantly non-Anglo-Saxon) shows that the accounting profession was not organised enough to effectively get regulation and deliver rewards for its members. Such rewards are economic and also linked with social status. For example, the term doctor commands high respect in most societies, but the term accountant may not command same level of respect in all contexts. If profession is not able to restrict untrained people from engaging in providing services then it is obvious that society, business world and state would not give it due respect or attention.

Bopta et al. (2007) studied the re-emergence of the accounting profession in Cambodia in the aftermath of the Khmer Rouge massacre which killed more than one million people. The radical changes in the Cambodian accounting profession were driven by changes in the state structure. During Khmer Rouge, accountants faced clear rejection while accounting was used as a tool for state control (Yapa et al., 2016). Dyball and Valcarcel (1999) provided evidence of weak state control in Philippines and claimed that society and social networks are more powerful than the state and have the capacity to influence the accounting profession.

Bakre (2005) concluded that through the local accounting board in Jamaica, the government has passed control to the British bodies, which has left the state in a very weak role. Similarly, in Trinidad and Tobago (T&T) the state is not in a position to influence the accounting profession and the British bodies have a significant control (Annisette, 1999). Since gaining independence from Britain in 1960, Nigeria has witnessed many political structures and upheavals including parliamentary democracy, presidential democracy, military dictatorships (coups) and civil wars. Although the social developments and influence of special interest groups have also affected the accounting profession, the political state of affairs seems to have particularly and critically affected the accounting profession. Sidhu and West (2014) found that the state played an indirect role in the professionalisation of accounting in India which is not much different from the case of Australia.

2.5.2 *Closure Through Imperialism and Colonial Bodies*

According to Ali, Lee and West (2008), the imperial influence has also been a dominating theme as identified in both Anglo-Saxon and non-Anglo-Saxon studies (Briston, 1978; Parker, 1989). These two factors are not separated in this study because the British bodies gained their dominating position due to their imperial origins.

The pioneering work of Johnson (1973, 1982) and Johnson and Caygil (1971) evidenced this aspect in settler and non-settler colonies. Briston (1978) claimed that the British imperial influence was so powerful that it was virtually impossible for any colony to avoid it. The British bodies were used as a medium to influence the professionalisation process (Annisette, 1999) outside the British territory. Their role was in no way less influential than a direct form of colonialism.

In fact, it was the superior position of the British accounting bodies which played a strong role to determine the context of the development of the accounting profession in its former colonies. For example, Willmott (1986) explained that the ICAEW used its influence through examinations and certifications to close off and control the accounting profession. Johnson (1982) indicated that the policies of ICAEW had the presence of an implicit racial element, e.g. the residency condition to sit for its exams literally excluded non-whites from becoming accountants and the institute was able to create a scarcity of services and achieved monopoly and status.

Chua and Pollaos (1998, 2002), Carnegie and Edwards (2001) and Carnegie and Parker (1999) provided the Australian story from a settler colony's perspective. Carnegie and Parker (1999) did not find an overt influence of the British bodies because the profession was imported from Britain, rather than accountants. Australian accountants were able to form local bodies and copied the model of profession from the UK. They did not need an active influence of parent country's professional association.

Yapa (2006) identified a dominating colonial influence in Sri Lanka through the imperial bodies. Accountants are in under supply and in the last four decades the Institute of Chartered Accountants of Sri Lanka (ICASL) followed the agenda of "occupational closure" and left the Sri Lankan accounting profession at the mercy of an interplay between the Association of Chartered Certified Accountants (ACCA) and the Chartered Institute of Management Accountants (CIMA). This also indicates inter-professional rivalry between the British bodies beyond the national boundaries of Britain.

In a study of the Malaysian accounting profession, Ali et al. (2008) found that the British system did not fit a developing country which had a different social culture and corporate environment. But with the spread of modern developments, the imported system has been suitable and thus added another nation subject to colonial influence. Briston (1978) found that the Indonesian accounting profession had been influenced by the Dutch imperialism. Tanzania, a former colony, not only depended on Britain for education and exam contents, but also required the British bodies to monitor the local examination system.

Annisette (1999) observed a significant presence and influence by British bodies in T&T and found that T&T failed to indigenise professional training and examinations. Similarly, other studies conducted in the African continent also identified a strong presence of imperialism and colonial bodies (Sian, 2006). Some Asian studies also felt the strong influence of the former coloniser after independence, e.g. Yapa (1999) found an overt colonial influence in Brunei. Similarly, Bopta et al. (2007) found the persistence of French colonialism in Cambodia, and in the Filipino context, Dyball et al. (2006) found the influence of its former ruler on the initial development of the accounting profession.

In some studies of the Sri Lankan accounting profession, it was found that the British influence is still quite strong. Sidhu and West (2014) concluded that the Indian accountants adopted the British model of accounting profession. The development of accounting profession in India had started while it was still a British colony. The departure of British imperial government did not change much for the development of accounting profession. India adopted the Chartered Accountant title although it is meant to be associated with granting of Charter by the British monarch.

2.5.3 *Closure Based on Racism, Gender and Social Class*

As discussed earlier, social closure achieved through exclusion is identified as a major theme in the sociology of professions. Social closure is understood as a process through which a profession maintains a privileged identity, a kind of exclusivity with certain restrictive postures. Weber is one of the early sociologists to theorise concepts of social closure and exclusion and researchers have used his concepts as an initial point of their social enquiry (e.g. Chua & Poullaos, 1998).

According to Parkin (1979) "social closure broadly defines a situation where an interest group seeks to regulate market conditions in their favour by restricting access to specific opportunities to other group members. This is usually done in the face of actual or potential competition from outsiders" (p. 44). Studies in professionalisation have identified social closure based on gender, race and social class. Gender as a means of closure has been identified and analysed by many researchers.

In some studies, race has been a dominating theme in the study of professionalisation of accounting, particularly in African and Asian countries (Annisette, 1999; Sian, 2006). The racial discrimination towards Afro-Americans has also attracted some serious attention. Social class as a central theme in the professionalisation of accounting is the subject of many studies which examined the British and the American accounting profession.

Cooper and Robson (2006) found that the excluded groups were primarily women, black people and those doing clerical/manual work. The labels of being "ineligible" or not possessing sufficient qualities were used in the pursuit of closure. However, as explained by Carnegie and Parker (1999), in specific contextual settings the professional body may not always follow the closure strategy because if the aim is to achieve market dominance and control as it contradicts the need to achieve exclusivity (e.g. Kenya: Sian, 2006). Social closure was achieved even at the formation of early accounting bodies in the UK in 1880s through the registration of accountants (Macdonald, 1985).

Gender bias has also been a dictating theme in the sociology of professions as a means used to exclude women. Shackleton (1999) analysed the political and social struggle of women to penetrate the implicit and explicit[4] restrictions to entry into the Scottish Chartered Accountancy profession in the first quarter of the twentieth century. Scottish accountants adopted various strategies which included initial denial of women and then their acceptance at low status jobs as a response to mounting awareness and pressure. In a study ranging over sixty years, Kirkham and Loft (1993) have clearly shown that women were confined to jobs which were considered to be of low status in England. During this period, women accountants only rose to 1.4% of total accountants in 1931 from a near absence in 1871. However, the low status job of clerk appears to have been granted to women, and women clerks rose from 1.1% in 1871 to 42% of total clerks in 1931. Their analysis indicates that in order to meet market demand for clerical jobs, but at the same time to save its exclusive status and control, the male-dominated profession of accountancy disassociated itself from clerical work and achieved occupational ascendancy to gain elite status. The low status work was then passed onto women.

In another comprehensive study covering eighty years, Lehman (1992) analysed the exclusion of women from the accounting profession in the UK and the US and found that economic, political and ideological factors were employed to operationalise the strategy of exclusion. The exclusion of women was also prevalent in Australia where there were no women among the founders of the Incorporated Institute of Accountants, Victoria (Carnegie & Edwards, 2001). The case in India was also same; the initial membership of the first three Indian Accountancy Boards which were formed by nominating members by the state between 1932 and 1939 had no female members.[5]

Evans and Rumens (2020) examined historical data related to Price Waterhouse Coopers (PwC), which showed that professionalisation of accounting was centred around masculinity of that occupation. The ideal accountant was coded as male with an image of professional skills and

[4] E.g. the legal advice that Chartered Accountancy bodies received, explicitly stated that the three Royal Charters did not have provision to allow admission of women to accountancy. However, it was proposed to permit the entry of women if they accepted lower salary than men for the same role after undergoing similar training requirements.

[5] See membership lists of first Accountancy Board formed in 1932 (Kapadia, 1972, pp. 88–89), the Second Accountancy Board formed on 30 March 1935 (p. 95) and the third Accountancy Board formed on 1 July 1939 (pp. 122–123). The membership list of 1953 of the Institute of Chartered Accountants in India is used in this study. There were only two women members, one being Parsis by religion and the other Hindu.

knowledge making construction of the accountant's identity as a masculine process. During wartime women were employed in accounting roles but this did not make PwC inclusive organisation for women. In a similar prior study looking at gendered processes of professionalisation of accounting, Whiting (2013) found that exclusionary mechanisms hinder women's progress in accounting firms and assist their exit. Internal socialising in accounting firms is a complex process which leads women to leave accounting work looking for more flexibility, work under less pressure and achieve work/life balance. Social expectations from women outside their work put additional pressures on them to perform in high pressure roles such as those in accounting firms. Rather than juggling between professional and personal gendered roles they prefer to exit accounting firms. Indonesian women find that social norms do play a key role in their exclusion from accounting profession. They are expected to behave in a proper way while fulfilling their domestic roles as well as meet pressures of accounting professional roles. In China, there is a negative perception about women's performance after they have a child. The traditional Chinese social culture continues to impact how women's role is perceived in professional accounting work. Women are expected to perform home duties in addition to professional roles. This theme is common across many traditional societies as reflected by some studies of professionalisation of accounting in Asia.

Racism as a means of exclusion and closure is also analysed by a number of studies, particularly the fate of black people. Probably a significant contribution is made by Teresa Hammond. She looked at the extremeness of exclusion of African Americans from the accounting profession in the US over several decades in the last century, based on highly reliable first-hand information sources such as interviews with the earliest black Certified Public Accountants. The literature surveyed also provides clear evidence of racism in former colonies. The conditions related to gaining accounting qualification and registration almost excluded the Jamaicans from entering the profession. Like other African countries, Kenya also suffered racism and exclusion. As a result, three layers of accountants' social class emerged. The top layer was British, the middle was Asian and the lowest was local Kenyan accountants (Sian, 2006). According to Annisette (2003), even in the post-independence era, the recruitment procedures of companies ensured the exclusion of blacks in T&T and its effects are still evident four decades after independence.[6]

Over the years Indian accounting profession and its interplay with caste has been examined (Sidhu & West, 2014). The distinctive Indian caste system divides Hindu society into a hierarchy of four varnas, each of which also has a traditional association with particular categories of occupations. They revealed a significant over-representation of the Brahman upper caste relative to this caste's presence in the general population. This Brahman presence is posited as having endowed a status to the accounting occupation that aided the replication in India of the British model of professional organisation. However, it also meant that the formation of the Chartered Institute would predominantly benefit an already privileged social stratum and contribute to perpetuating traditional caste hierarchies within the modern occupation of professional accounting. Sidhu and West (2014) found that Brahmans with just 5% of population share represented over 50% of membership in the Chartered Institute.

In order to achieve the group objective of monopoly and control, the role played by individuals has been studied by Carnegie and Edwards (2001, pre-1886) and Carnegie et al. (2003, between 1886 and 1908). They looked at the role of individuals in the professionalisation of accountancy in Australia as set in time and social context. Some other studies also looked at the role played by members in the professional project (Australia: Edwards et al., 1997).

There are also some examples of dedicated studies looking at the role played by influential individuals in the professionalisation of accounting. Bailey (1992) identified the significant role of F. V. Ezerskii in Russian accounting. Caramanis (2005) supported the idea of the study of individuals' influences on the accounting profession and claimed with reference to Weber that social, political and economic actors can be brought together by a charismatic personality.

[6] In 2003 blacks (Afro and Indo Trinidadians) constituted 80% of the population but only 33% of accountants were from this group. Asians and white accountants comprised 67% of the total number of accountants; however, their share in the population was 1.2%.

2.6 Conclusion

Professionalisation is an attempt to create monopoly of a domain and achieve status and tangible rewards because of this process. The accounting profession is no exception. In this process, it has built up multiple layers and points of social closure. Though in most cases the state had a substantive influence, it was more confined to constitutional recognition and legal structure of the profession. There were other substantive sociological factors like race, gender, caste and others too.

The discussion also indicated that the professionalisation of accounting has been partially successful in many Asian countries but has literally failed in majority of the African countries. The Asian countries have similar trends in terms of the state dominance and strict control which, however, cannot be generalised because each country has specific political and socio-economic conditions. In numerous studies of Anglo and non-Anglo-Saxon countries, many themes have been studied but there is no study which has looked at Australian accounting profession in recent five decades in its attempts to unite divided professional bodies.

References

Annisette, M. (1999). Importing accounting: The case of Trinidad and Tobago. *Accounting, Business & Financial History, 9*(1), 103–133.

Bailey, D. (1992). The attempt to establish the Russian accounting profession 1875–1931. *Accounting, Business & Financial History, 2*(1), 1–23.

Barber, J. H. (1981, September). Form of prejudice, Integration Forum. *The Chartered Accountant in Australia*, 14.

Briston, R. J. (1978). The evolution of accounting in developing countries. *International Journal of Accounting Education and Research, 14*(1), 105–120.

Brown, R. (1905). *A history of accounting and accountants*. T. C. & E. C. Jack.

Caramanis, C. (1999). International accounting firms versus indigenous auditors: Intra-professional conflict in the Greek auditing profession, 1990–1993. *Critical Perspectives on Accounting, 10*(2), 153–196.

Carnegie, G. D., & Edwards, J. R. (2001). The construction of the professional accountant: The case of the Incorporated Institute of Accountants, Victoria (1886). *Accounting, Organisations and Society, 26*(4/5), 301–325.

Carnegie, G. D., & Parker, R. H. (1999). Accountants and empire: the case of co-membership of Australian and British accountancy bodies, 1885 to 1914. *Accounting, Business & Financial History, 9*(1), 77–102.

Carnegie, G. D., Edwards, J. R., & West, B. P. (2003). Understanding the dynamics of the Australian accounting profession: A prosopographical study of the founding members of the Incorporated Institute of Accountants, Victoria, 1886 to 1908. *Accounting, Auditing & Accountability Journal, 16*(5), 790–820.

Carr-Saunders, A. M., & Wilson, P. A. (1964). *The professions*. Frank Cass.

Chua, W. F., & Poullaos, C. (1993). Rethinking the profession-state dynamic: The case of the Victorian Charter attempt, 1885–1906. *Accounting, Organisations and Society, 18*(7/8), 691–728.

Chua, W. F., & Poullaos, C. (1998). The dynamics of 'closure' amidst the construction of market, profession, empire and nationhood: An historical analysis of an Australian accounting association, 1886–1903. *Accounting, Organisations and Society, 23*(2), 155–187.

Edwards, J. R., Carnegie, G. D., & Cauberg, J. (1997). The Incorporated Institute of Accountants, Victoria (1886): A study of founders' backgrounds. In T. E. Cooke & C. W. Nobes (Eds.), *The development of accounting in an international context: A festschrift in honour of R. H. Parker* (49–67). Routledge.

Evetts, J. (2003). The sociological analysis of professionalism: Occupational change in the modern world. *International Sociology, 18*(2), 395–415.

Johnson, T. J., & Caygill, M. (1971). The development of accountancy links in Commonwealth. *Accounting and Business Research, 1*(2m), 155–173.

Larson, M. S. (1977). *The rise of professionalism: A sociological analysis*. University of California Press.

Lee, T. A. (1995). The professionalization of accountancy: A history of protecting the public interest in a self-interested way. *Accounting, Auditing & Accountability Journal, 8*(4), 48–69.

Macdonald, K. M. (1985). Social closure and occupational registration. *Sociology, 19*(4), 541–556.

Macdonald, K. M. (1995). *The sociology of the professions*. SAGE.

Parker, R. H. (1989). Importing and exporting accounting: The British experience. In A. G. Hopwood (Ed.), *International pressures for accounting change* (pp. 7–29). Prentice-Hall.

Poullaos, C. (1993). Making profession and state, 1907 to 1914: The ACPA's first charter attempt. *Abacus, 29*(2), 196–229.

Sidhu, J., & West, B. (2014). The emergent Institute of Chartered Accountants of India: An upper-caste profession. *Accounting History, 19*(1–2), 115–132.

Sidhu, J., Carnegie, G. D., & West, B. (2021). Australia's divided accounting profession: The 1969 merger attempt and its legacy. *The British Accounting Review, 53*(3), 100975.

Sian, S. (2006). Inclusion, exclusion and control: The case of the Kenyan accounting professionalisation project. *Accounting, Organisations and Society, 31*(3), 295–322.

Walker, S. P. (1995). The genesis of professional organisation in Scotland: A contextual analysis. *Accounting, Organisations and Society, 20*(4), 285–310.
Walker, S. P., & Shackleton, K. (1995). Corporatism and structural change in the British accountancy profession, 1930–1957. *Accounting, Organisations and Society, 20*(6), 467–503.
West, B. P. (2003). *Professionalism and accounting rules*. Routledge.
Willmott, H. (1986). Organising the profession: A theoretical and historical examination of the development of the major accountancy bodies in the UK. *Accounting, Organisations and Society, 11*(6), 555–580.

CHAPTER 3

Examining the Accounting Profession—Development, Structures and Operations

3.1 Introduction

This chapter provides a review of relevant literature from two perspectives, (i) previous historical studies that examined the development, structures and operations of the Australian accounting profession and (ii) studies examining the mergers of professional accounting bodies, primarily in Australia and Canada. The reason to limit mergers studies to these two countries is that they both adopted the British model of accounting profession. Conditions that led to the formation and mergers of accounting associations had many commonalities and are also unique in the British model. Moreover, the process of professionalisation has common themes as well; developed nation, regionalism and duplication of associations, English-speaking society, settled colonies, divide between public and non-public accountants, legal framework, economic and business conditions. Also, the social structure and the state play inactive roles in the regulation of non-essential professions such as accounting.

Any comparison of Australian case with mergers of associations in other countries would not provide a comparative analysis. We also limit literature to accounting profession because of unique factors that led to the professionalisation in accounting industry. For example, medicine profession in Australia would have completely different factors than that of accounting. One always goes to general practitioner who are regulated at national level through qualifications and accreditations. Whereas there

J. Sidhu et al., *Understanding the Sociology of the Accounting Profession*, https://doi.org/10.1007/978-981-99-1572-9_3

are many options available when one needs an accountant. Accounting profession is nationally organised but it is not fully regulated like many other professions. Considering the main objective of this book, we focused only on the sociology of the accounting profession.

This chapter is structured in three sections. The second section provides a review of studies on the accounting profession, with a particular focus on Australian studies. The third section examines studies on the merger of accounting associations in the UK and Canada, because the Australian accounting profession has a similar structure to the professional associations of those two countries. The subject matter of this study, the four merger attempts between the Institute and the Society in Australia, is a relatively unexplored area in the context of historical accounting research. However, it should be noted that some accounting researchers have briefly outlined or discussed these merger attempts as part of a broader context while investigating other topics (Carnegie, 2009; Carnegie & O'Connell, 2012; Carnegie et al., 2003; Linn, 1996; Poullaos, 1994; Velayutham, 1999). Hence, the comparative literature on the mergers of accounting associations is mainly available in the international context, which presents a strong case for this book.

3.2 Australian Studies

The professionalisation of accounting in Australia began with the formation of Australia's first accounting body in 1885. Following this, numerous other bodies were formed as the Australian accounting profession progressed through the process of professionalisation. Various previous studies have addressed issues related to the earliest efforts to professionalise the accounting occupation in Australia, encompassing the import of the British model of profession, coupled with issues of regionalism, duplication and divisions of associations; attempts to gain a Royal Charter; and the changing closure strategies adopted by accounting bodies (Carnegie, 1993; Carnegie & Edwards, 2001; Carnegie & Parker, 1999; Carnegie et al., 2003; Chua & Poullaos, 1993, 1998; Gavens, 1990; Gavens & Gibson, 1992; Parker, 1989; Poullaos, 1993, 1994). These studies have contributed to the accounting history literature, while simultaneously making key additions to the literature on the SOP. As the model of the Australian accounting profession was inherited from Britain (Parker, 1989), the inherent features of duplication and regionalism were also imported. These features also spread to New Zealand, South Africa and Canada, where the British accounting model was also imported by local accountants (Parker, 1989). Initiatives for the inclusion of staff who identify as lesbian, gay, bisexual, transgender and intersex (LGBTI) have also attracted the attention of recent studies. Professional accounting bodies in Australia have developed a bureaucratic control over the education process that oversees membership and accreditation of accounting degrees. They have used this control as a means of closure and exclusion.

Official histories of each of the two major accounting bodies, the Institute and the Society, have been written (see, for example, Graham, 1978; Kenley, 1963; Linn, 1996; Marshall, 1978; Walton, 1970). There are also some examples of unofficial histories compiled by senior members of the profession (see, for example, Creaney, 1984). These studies provide an account of earlier developments in the structure and operations of the accounting profession. They also provide a descriptive historical account of various phases and periods in the development of the Australian accounting profession. Although the majority of these studies were conducted in the period covered by this research project, it is important to note that these studies do not address the issue of the merger of both bodies. Some studies presented an overall historical account of the accounting profession, but did not examine in detail the four unsuccessful merger attempts (Linn, 1996).[1] Generally, official histories do not provide critical analysis of historical events and processes which lead to the development of professional bodies (Carnegie & Napier, 1996, 2012). Hence, this strengthens the case for the current study, which specifically examines the failure of the four merger attempts and provides a critical analysis of the reasons for mounting the attempts, as well as an analysis of their consequential failures.

Towards the end of the nineteenth century, the accounting profession in Australia was seen to lack an overarching formal structure and the process of professionalisation was still in its infancy. Thus, several bodies were emerging on a regional basis within the six British colonies in Australia, known as Australian states from 1901 (Carnegie & Edwards,

[1] Linn (1996) provided brief details of three unsuccessful mergers, which are part of current study, with slightly more information provided on the first merger. In addition, Linn (1996) provided details of various other successful mergers, including the 1966 merger of the Society with the Australasian Institute of Cost Accountants, and commented that this successful merger marked a major change in the structure of the Australian accounting profession.

2001). Therefore, duplication of associations was a key characteristic of the Australian accounting profession. Initially, accounting bodies in Australia were organised on a colony or state basis (Carnegie, 1993), with their names reflecting their regional interests in specific states, such as the Incorporated Institute of Accountants, Victoria (IIAV) formed in Victoria in 1886, the Adelaide Society of Accountants (ADSA) formed in 1885 in South Australia, the Queensland Institute of Accountants (QIA) formed in 1891 in Queensland, the Sydney Institute of Public Accountants (SIPA) formed in 1894 in New South Wales, and the Tasmanian Institute of Accountants (TIA) formed in 1897 in Tasmania (Carnegie, et al., 2003). These organisations were formed while the six states of modern Australia were independent colonies. Parker (1989) noted that, in the initial years of development of the accounting profession in Australia, every state had at least one body, while larger states had multiple bodies. Victoria had the greatest duplication of associations, with four competing bodies formed by the 1900s, including the IIAV as the earliest antecedent body of the CPA Australia (Carnegie, 1993).

The characteristic of regionalism in the organisation of the accounting profession was natural due to all states in modern Australia historically being independent former colonies of Britain. It was not until the Federation on 1 January 1901 that the Commonwealth of Australia was formed, thereby uniting the colonies (Carnegie & Edwards, 2001; Chua & Poullaos, 1993, 1998).[2]Thus, the formation of the Commonwealth of Australia and the ongoing professionalisation of accounting occurred simultaneously (Chua & Poullaos, 1993). Among the various bodies that existed at the inception of the Commonwealth of Australia in 1901, the Victorian regional body of the IIAV was the largest and strongest in terms of both members and financial strength during the first few decades of Federation (Chua & Poullaos, 1993). A body that narrowly took the edge from IIAV as the earliest body of accountants formed in Australia was the ADSA, formed in 1885 (Carnegie, et al., 2003; Chua & Poullaos, 1993, 1998; Gavens, 1990; Parker, 1961), merely five months earlier than the IIAV (Edwards et al., 1997). The Adelaide body was formed with an interest in acquiring a Royal Charter; however, it later did not pursue its stated objectives and the IIAV made the first (unsuccessful) charter attempt between the periods of 1904 to 1906 (Chua & Poullaos, 1993).

[2] Six British colonies, New South Wales, Queensland, South Australia, Tasmania, Victoria and Western Australia, became states in the Commonwealth of Australia.

Thus, the first attempt to create exclusive boundaries, by means of a Royal Charter, around the membership of a professional accounting body failed. A second attempt to create boundaries around the public profession and the membership of an accounting association failed between 1907 and 1914, when the ACPA also attempted to gain a Royal Charter.

The initial years in the development of Australian accounting profession from 1886 to 1908 were quite turbulent in terms of organising and development of associations (Carnegie, et al., 2003). During this period especially around 1903 a view had been developed outside accounting circles that, perhaps, there was a danger in salaried and "public" accountants being represented by the same association because accountants were staking claims to the audit field and the accountancy industry was in its formative stages (Chua & Poullaos, 1993). These are the early signs of boundary construction, while the boundaries were later settled around the membership of both bodies. Chapter 5 discusses the construction of boundaries, which echoes the views expressed by Chua and Poullaos (1993). In addition to the formation of bodies concentrated on public practice membership, other bodies were formed around specialisations. This included associations such as the Institute of Factory and Cost Accountants, formed in 1926, and the Corporation of Consulting Accountants, formed in 1922. Other bodies were either formed to internationalise their efforts as far as the adopted name had indicated, such as the International Institute of Accountants formed in 1933 (see Gavens, 1990), or through some form of national status (such as the Association of Accountants of Australia formed in 1910; see Gavens, 1990) or beyond Australian boundaries in the South-Pacific region, such as the Australasian Institute of Cost Accountants formed in 1921 (see Gavens, 1990).

As the introductory chapter mentioned, between 1885 and 1952, 32 professional accounting bodies were formed in Australia (Appendix A1). The majority of these bodies were formed during the first four decades after the formation of Australia's first accounting body (Carnegie, 1993; Carnegie & Parker, 1999; Gynther, 1967; Linn, 1996; Parker, 1989) and demonstrated both rivalry and cooperation among themselves (Carnegie et al., 2003). The IIAV, one of the earliest organisations, has been the main subject of many studies. For study by Garry Carnegie looked at the formation of the IIAV. One of such study prosopographical method of data collection was used to study the occupational and commercial backgrounds of the 45 founders of the IIAV (Carnegie & Edwards, 2001; Carnegie et al., 2003). The failure of the charter attempt by the IIAV in

1904 has also been extensively studied. The expansion strategies of IIAV, as evident in its large membership base, including influential accountants of the time was a key focus. When the IIAV made its application for a Royal Charter in 1904, it was firmly opposed by groups of accountants who would have been excluded. Their opposition was also strong because for them it was a matter of fighting to retain their market position (Chua & Poullaos, 1993).

Hence, objections to the charter application by other accounting bodies and an inability to demonstrate support from other stakeholders, such as the state, precipitated its failure. By employing Max Weber's class–status–party model, Chua and Poullaos (1998) examined the earliest years of the formation of IIAV and the shift in its strategies. They studied the period from 1886 to 1903 and asserted that the IIAV had strong reasons to promote openness in its organisational structure, rather than a closed formation. Thus, the failure of first charter attempt was also the first failure to construct boundaries around membership of an organisation, using exclusivity as organisational strategy. The motivation behind constructing boundaries around the possession of a Royal Charter was the status associated with the title CA. Regionalism was quite strong and differences within states varied in contentiousness, but included issues such as the climate, natural resources, laws, infrastructure and customs duties. Even with Federation and the formation of the Commonwealth, tensions among states around their regional pride and autonomy did not disappear and politicians such as Alfred Deakin were well aware of the depth of opposition to Federation before its inception (Poullaos, 1994).

The timing of the IIAV's formation was directly related to a proposal of the (English) Society of Accountants and Auditors (SAA), formed in London in 1885, to establish its first branch in Melbourne in December 1885 under a "British Empire" policy (Garrett, 1961), with the strategy of market control at its core. The SAA was formed in response to the closure practices of the ICAEW: in other words, it was an attempt to challenge the exclusiveness strategy adopted by the ICAEW, with boundaries set around the membership of that body, and to follow the strategy of market control. Among other objectives of the SAA, one aim was to expand its base in overseas countries by increasing its membership within the British Empire (Carnegie et al., 2003; Garrett, 1961; Johnson & Caygill, 1971; Parker, 1999). By market control SAA intended to include a large number of members in the UK and in overseas countries and capture a major part of market of accounting services. While the elite accounting associations formed around Royal Charters would continue to have exclusive and small membership base creating status and potentially high income for their members.

The local accountants rejected the branch formation proposal presented by Charles A Cooper of the SAA as Commissioner for Australia, and proceeded to establish their own local organisation in the form of the IIAV. While the 45 foundation members of IIAV, all of whom were men and well-established in public practice, decided that new members of the IIAV, to be known as "associates", would be of similar reputation of the founders, but sourced from an array of organisations beyond the realm of public practice and from among the principal clerks in accountants' offices (Carnegie & Edwards, 2001). This key development was probably due to the influence of Cooper, who proceeded to form a local branch of the Empire-focused SAA in Melbourne as a competitor to the new local accounting association.

The SAA itself was effectively unable to build exclusivity in Britain due to the earlier establishment of the three chartered accounting associations in Scotland from 1853, and due to the formation of the ICAEW in 1880 (Chua & Poullaos, 1998). Thus, the SAA was essentially operating outside the domain of public practice in Britain, which resulted from the earlier construction of MIPP membership boundaries by the three associations of CAs. This situation was similar to the nineteemth-century Scottish controversy regarding the authority of phrenology when anatomists engaged in boundary work in order to push phrenologists outside the boundaries of astronomy (Gieryn, 1983). The IIAV adopted an inclusive strategy because, in the local time-specific context, opening up the association had more benefits than than closure (Chua & Poullaos, 1998). In short, the organisational strategy of the SAA premised on market control effectively became the organisational strategy of the IIAV, thus creating flexible boundaries around its membership based in a wide array of organisations and firms, which guided the IIAV from the time of formation, with an initial focus on Victoria, to the time of writing, as the ongoing CPA Australia with a strong international orientation.

Subsequently, key founding members of the IIAV who were seeking higher professional status controversially defected from that body and helped form the ACPA in 1907, which was incorporated in 1908, in Sydney (Carnegie et al., 2003). This body decided to restrict membership to those engaged in public practice (Carnegie et al., 2003) and drew members from other state-based accounting associations, thereby creating a distinctive organisational boundary based on exclusivity. The ACPA was formed exclusively for accountants as MIPP, with the aim of elevating their collective professional status based on occupational closure and exclusion (Carnegie & Edwards, 2001; Carnegie et al., 2003). In other words, this was the first national attempt to create boundaries around the membership of a professional body based on public practice. The Australian accountants behind the move to form the ACPA had examined the British bodies as models of professional associations. Most of the charter-based British bodies had adopted strict closure strategies and emphasised exclusivity by restricting boundaries around their membership. The public practice was clearly viewed as a means to elevate professional status in society, particularly in the class- and status-conscious British society. It was due to the fact that offering public practice had been established as one of the most elevated mediums for professional status and that applied to the accounting profession as well (Carnegie et al., 2003). The higher status for MIPP is derived from the greater authority and freedom they have in offering their services. Further, it is associated with the type of work done and opportunity to gain experience across different sectors and with different organisations. Public practitioners enjoy autonomy and hold the right to select or reject clients and such opportunities offer them an avenue to escape from being working class. In other words, public practice is linked with high economic rewards and higher social and professional status.

The establishment of the ACPA[3] made the distinction between MIPP and MNIPP clearly visible at the national level, as opposed to the colony or state level. The ICAEW had a strong effect on the development of the Australian accounting profession because, in the initial years, Australian bodies such as the IIAV and others aimed to model themselves on the ICAEW (Chua & Poullaos, 1993). However, it is also noteworthy that the IIAV did not follow the organisational strategy adopted by the ICAEW; rather, it later adopted the market control strategy which was due to the influence of SAA making attempt to form a local body (Carnegie, 2016). Thus, the ACPA was created by applying the notion of boundary work by excluding MNIPP from the membership of this new national body. According to Gieryn (1983, pp. 787–788), this is a "useful ideological style when monopolizing professional authority and resources

[3] The ACPA was formed through the merger of the SIPA, the TIA and the CAA of Australia (Gynther, 1967).

in the hands of some". Thus, the ACPA attempted to exert control over entry to the market of public practice via members who were specialists in the delivery of public practice services, monopolising access to this service delivery only to its members.

Later, the IIAV and ACPA became the first antecedent bodies of the contemporary CPA Australia and CAANZ, respectively. Members of both bodies developed key intra-professional status differences which were based on the main occupation of their members, i.e. public practitioners vis-à-vis those employed in industry, government and other areas (Carnegie et al., 2003). The adopted membership strategy was a key distinguishing feature between prominent bodies, such as the IIAV, with an inclusionary strategy and the ACPA which adopted an exclusive strategy. This book's Chapter 5 on theoretical frameworks explains one of the interpretive frameworks applied in this study: "the dilemma of exclusiveness versus market control" (Macdonald & Ritzer, 1988, p. 257). This framework is applied to further understand the "business model" adopted by professional accounting associations in Australia. For example, the IIAV decided to have fewer restrictions to its membership because, as aforementioned, the IIAV had strong incentives to adopt a less exclusive strategy to target a broader membership base (Chua & Poullaos, 1998). Hence, it adopted a membership strategy that was based on not distinguishing between different types of accounting work. In contrast, the ACPA adopted a more exclusive model and only accepted members who were engaged in public practice (Carnegie et al., 2003). In other words, the boundaries of membership were relaxed in the case of IIAV, while the ACPA created significant boundaries around its membership. That is, the "business model" of creating an exclusive body was implemented at the micro level by restricting entry by creating boundaries.

In fact, during the early years after formation, most bodies adopted the exclusive model. This was the case for the ADSA, which restricted its membership between 1885 and 1890 to accountants who were engaged in public practice only. Most organisations were formed with a view of replicating the exclusive model of the ICAEW, but did not pursue this objective in their long-term strategies. The IIAV's founder initially sought to form and develop an association of "public practitioners" (Carnegie et al., 2003). However, it quickly switched to what became a long-term strategy of market control. Thus, the initial plan of the IIAV founders did not eventuate, as explained in later sections of this book (Carnegie, 2016). The adoption of two different strategies led to intra-professional conflict in the Australian accounting profession, and the formation of the Society and the Institute.

The formation of the ACPA was the result of developments within the IIAV and was also related to the ambitions of accountants to form an accounting body exclusively for MIPP. The founder members of IIAV held senior positions in the first 23 years and shaped ACPA policies (Carnegie et al., 2003). The IIAV was formed with the aim of modelling an ICAEW-type body, which was formed with a Royal Charter. However, the IIAV founders realised that their territory was small compared with Britain, and decided to include members who were in industry, mercantile and government positions. As Carnegie (2016) stated that there was a danger of competition from SAA as well which was planning to establish a local body in Victoria equipped with a market control strategy. This meant that the IIAV adopted a market control strategy, rather than a strategy based on exclusiveness. Accordingly, the early objectives of the IIAV demonstrated the adoption of a strategy of market control and did not confine membership only to public practitioners. Therefore, a specialist public practice association, as an established profession, did not exist in those times in Australia, and someone not in public practice could be reputable and influential. As Chua and Poullaos (1993) demonstrated, the IIAV sought to include influential salaried accountants who had influence within state bodies. In this situation, influential professionals, such as the Comptroller of Accounts from Railways, could not be excluded from membership to the IIAV. Hence, the market control strategy, or having relaxed boundaries around the membership of a professional body, was an automatic choice for the IIAV.

Researcher noted, the IIAV founders decided not to confine the body to members only in public practice, and, in order to expand the membership base, they opted to include a viable number of memberships (Carnegie et al., 2003; Chua & Poullaos, 1993). This strategy was also adopted in light of anticipated competition from the London-based SAA which proceeded to establish a local branch in Australia. Consequently, the IIAV relaxed entry conditions and thus attracted a higher number of members, although this led to a dilution in the quality of membership (Carnegie et al., 2003). In 1904, the IIAV made a failed attempt to gain a Royal Charter. This outcome upset members who aspired to model the IIAV in a similar manner to the ICAEW. Therefore, these members attempted to distance themselves from the IIAV (Carnegie et al., 2003; Chua & Poullaos, 1993) in two ways. First, by 1910, of the 19 surviving founders of the IIAV, seven founder members had resigned and joined the ACPA, 10 remained with the IIAV and two had become members of both bodies (Carnegie et al., 2003). More importantly, these members who left the IIAV were founding members of the ACPA. When the ACPA was formed, even the then president of the IIAV, Fred Wilson, took a seat on the Victoria State Council of the ACPA. This was not considered a conflict of interest; rather, his presence was seen as safeguarding the interests of the IIAV. Second, the sons of the IIAV's founders entering the accounting profession preferred to join the ACPA than the IIAV. The ACPA had 13 sons of IIAV founders, of whom five had defected from the IIAV and eight had shifted from the SAA (Carnegie et al., 2003).

The ACPA subsequently became the Institute of Chartered Accountants in Australia on 19 June 1928, when a Royal Charter was granted to 28 accountants in public practice, adding further kudos to this category of a professional accountant (ICAA, 1969). The formation of the Institute as an elite body equipped with a Royal Charter crystallised the professional boundaries between MIPP and MNIPP in the Australian accounting profession. The founding members of the ACPA and the Institute pushed MNIPP outside their boundaries because construction of boundaries was useful in their "pursuit of professional goals: acquisition of intellectual authority and career opportunities, denial of these resources" to MNIPP (Gieryn, 1983, p. 781). The Melbourne-based Society was incorporated on 13 October 1952 from the amalgamation of three professional accounting bodies that mainly represented MNIPP: The CIA, previously known as the IIAV, the FIA and the AAA (Kenley, 1963). Subsequently, the Australasian Institute of Cost Accountants merged with the Society in 1966, as explained in Appendix A, which presents a summary of the antecedent bodies of both the Institute and the Society.

Members of the Society were mainly employed in commerce, industry and government, while the Institute's members were largely involved in public practice (Carnegie & O'Connell, 2012; also see Carnegie et al., 2003). At the time, public practitioners in accounting typically accrued experience operating in several different industries and different organisations in the same industry, thus securing a diverse knowledge and broad understanding of the discipline. In contrast, the Society members of the era were more likely to be confined to the general accounting and administrative affairs of a single organisation across given periods, thus generating an understanding of accounting that tended to be limited to specific organisational contexts, which may have provided narrow professional experience, especially for those who did not commonly change their employers.

The Institute positioned itself as the elite accounting association in Australia, with its long-held public practice orientation and exclusive Royal Charter, while the Society was comfortable with a strategy that focused on market control and associated financial security in comparison with smaller professional associations. The Institute and the Society were in competition with each other to attract members and advance their status, but were recognised as adopting different organisational strategies (Carnegie & O'Connell, 2012). The professional accounting practice roles played by members of both organisations assisted in making their boundaries firmer until, finally, the boundaries were commonly settled around the membership affiliations of qualified accountants of these two associations, which resulted from two different organisational strategies. The original professional boundaries were created around MIPP as a generally perceived superior vocation. However, as the share of the Institute members engaged in public practice gradually decreased over several decades, its boundaries shifted towards emphasising its status as an elite organisation with a Royal Charter, rather than an association comprising only public practitioners. The Chartered Accountant title became a premier professional brand in Australia and a boundary was created around its exclusiveness, and subsequently around membership to the Institute.

Carnegie and et al., (2003, p. 811) provided a summary of the intra-professional rivalry and creation of boundaries in the Australian accounting profession that led to the formation of the two rival accounting bodies:

> The ACPA, armed with its Royal Charter and renamed the ICAA, continued with its essentially elitist stance and maintained a restrictive membership policy. In contrast, the future of IIAV lay in the procession of mergers of associations with generally more permissive entry requirements that led to the creation of the Australian Society of Accountants (ASA) in 1952. The professionalisation strategy evident in these circumstances was that of exerting influence through the amassing of members and resources.

The four unsuccessful attempts to unite the Society and Institute as key professional accounting bodies in Australia were not the first merger failures experienced by the Australian accounting profession and there have been other unsuccessful merger attempts to create a united profession in Australia. Such efforts were first made in 1901, along with the formation of the Commonwealth of Australia, when the earliest attempts by professional accounting bodies were made to work out grounds for creating a common association for all accountants (Chua & Poullaos, 1993). A merger of all bodies was viewed as an organisational strategy and the IIAV, the ADSA, the TIA, the Incorporated Institute of Accountants in New Zealand, the SIPA and the QIA were involved in such discussions during three conferences held from 1901 to 1903. Dating back to 1897, accountants attempted to achieve some form of cooperation so that the regional associations formed in different states could expand their domains. They discussed mutual recognition of members, holding joint examinations for accountants and forming a national accounting body, namely, the Australasian Institute of Public Accountants (Chua & Poullaos, 1993). The most contentious issue was including members from perceived lower-status organisations that were heavily represented by MNIPP. Professional bodies were divided over the issue of exclusivity versus market control. Some bodies proposed the idea of a unified profession that included practitioners from all sorts of roles that were directly or indirectly related to accounting, with some reasonable claims to competence. This led to the first failed attempt to unify the accounting profession in 1901: at the Sydney conference of accounting bodies from Australia and New Zealand on the issue of including members from non-public domains and perceived lower-status work. This motion failed at the Sydney conference by show of hands, based on disagreement around the status of MNIPP. During these discussions, the dispute was also on the domicile of any new body. Both the SIPA and IIA wanted to have the head office of new body in Sydney and Melbourne, respectively, which was associated with colonial pride and identity (Chua & Poullaos, 1993).

This provides an important historical background to the formation of the two accounting bodies and the construction of boundaries in the Australian accounting profession. Even during the initial years of the professionalisation of accounting, the issue of contention was that of MIPP and MNIPP. Attempts to form a national organisation to represent all accountants failed for similar reasons, which ultimately led to the failure of four merger attempts. The factors creating a regional divide between accountants included regional pride and identity among accountants in New South Wales and Victoria. Even after the formation of Federation, accountants and people in general were still thinking themselves as belonging to the independent British colonies of New South Wales and Victoria, which had long competed with each other for primacy both economically and culturally (Chua & Poullaos, 1993). The last successful merger of two professional bodies in Australia was in 1966 when the Australasian Institute of Cost Accountants merged with the Australia Society of Accountants. Since then, the accounting profession has struggled to successfully work together on the issue of moving to the full unification of the profession and, to date, all further attempts to unify the accounting profession in Australia have failed. The next section provides a review of studies in the UK and Canada where professional accounting bodies have attempted to merge.

3.3 Mergers Between Professional Associations—Case of the UK and Canada

Previous studies on mergers between professional associations help position the current study and indicate the relevance of the theoretical framework of boundary management and the "dilemma of exclusiveness versus market control" applied in this study. Reviewing the literature on mergers of accounting associations in the UK and Canada helps identify gaps in the research related to the case of Australia's four unsuccessful merger attempts.

In other national settings, mergers of accounting associations have been the subject of numerous studies (see, for example, Lee, 2010; Miranti, 1986a, 1986b; Richardson, 1989a; Richardson & Jones, 2007; Shackleton, 1995; Walker, 1991, 1995, 2004; Walker & Shackleton, 1995, 1998). In these studies, many different issues were evident, although challenges to existing professional boundaries represented a common theme. In some cases, members supported changes in boundaries, while, in other cases, the boundaries were successfully defended leading to the failure of merger attempts (see, for example, US: Miranti, 1986a, 1986b; Britain: Shackleton & Walker, 1998, 2001; Walker & Shackleton, 1995, 1998; Willmott, 1986; and Canada: Richardson, 1989a; Richardson & Jones, 2007).

Mergers between accounting bodies have been one of the most common strategies used by associations to secure their professional domain (Richardson & Jones, 2007). Sometimes mergers are mounted as an attempt to gain market control, or provide economic rewards to its members by allowing them access to greater markets and to offer economies of scale. Mergers are also mounted to gain legitimacy and to achieve and maintain professional brand as a response to changing regulatory and market conditions. Mergers of associations may also be used to define and redefine the roles of members in market of accounting services. The state has sometimes played a key role in encouraging mergers to create a single professional body in order to establish ethical standards and enforce internal discipline (Richardson & Jones, 2007). In other cases, mergers have been motivated by desires to achieve market dominance, reduce costs, defend legitimacy and strengthen the professional brand as a response to market dynamics (Richardson, 2002).

Regionalism, duplication and divisions between MIPP and MNIPP have been key features of the British, Canadian and Australian accounting professions (Annisette & O'Regan, 2007; Carnegie & Parker, 1999; Carr-Saunders & Wilson, 1964; Poullaos, 1993; Richardson, 1989b; Walker & Shackleton, 1995). In the US, the accounting profession was divided until a unified national body, the American Institute of Certified Public Accountants, emerged from several successful mergers proving additional political leverage to American accountants (Miranti, 1986a, 1986b). In Britain, a common official rationale apparent in the majority of merger attempts has been the perceived benefits of being able to negotiate with the state with one strong and clear voice (Walker & Shackleton, 1995).

3.3.1 Britain's Merger Attempts

In Britain, many accounting bodies were formed during the initial years of professionalisation, such as the ESA, ICAEW, the Institute of Chartered Accountants in Ireland (ICAI), the Society of Accountants in Aberdeen and the Institute of Accountants in Glasgow. These bodies were formed with a view to achieving higher professional status and monopoly over accounting services. Accountants of the time aimed to achieve a status similar to that of the legal and medical professions. These professional accounting bodies were partially successful in meeting these objectives. They achieved professional status and occupational closure by securing

Royal Charters,[4] thereby creating professional boundaries around the membership of these associations. However, it is important to note that these bodies did not create a complete professional monopoly, which was the first motivation to lobby for charters. The literature on the merger attempts of British accounting associations provides various perspectives on the motivations for mounting such merger attempts, and the causes of their failures (Shackleton & Walker, 1998, 2001; Walker, 1991, 1995; Walker & Shackleton, 1995).

British accountants have regularly attempted to restructure the profession in order to gain elevated status, ensure economic rewards and achieve further occupational closure through boundary management. Several studies have covered various eras of the British accounting profession's quest to achieve these objectives (Walker, 1991, 1995; Walker & Shackleton, 1995, 1998, 2001). After 75 years of struggle, accounting associations in the UK gave up their attempts to create a legal monopoly for the accounting profession (Macdonald, 1985). By the 1930s, an evident division between MIPP and MNIPP emerged in the UK. This was an issue of contention and cause of failure in the merger attempts of 1957 (Shackleton & Walker, 1998, 2001). In other words, opposition to changes in the boundaries of membership of higher-status associations, such as chartered bodies, was a major factor that contributed to the failure of numerous merger attempts in the UK. The main body opposing the changes in professional boundaries was the ICAEW.

During the initial decades of the professionalisation of accounting in the UK, duplication and regionalism were key features (Parker, 1989). In order to have strong control over the profession and create a monopoly of services after gaining a Royal Charter, accounting bodies[5] aimed to secure state registration between 1890 and 1930 (Macdonald, 1985). However, they repeatedly failed because the charter bodies could not convince the government as to the manner in which MNIPP were damaging the reputation of the overall profession, which was the argument presented by the

[4] For example, on 13 September 1854, the ESA was formed with a Royal Charter, and later became the ICAS. The ICAEW was formed on 24 March 1880 and the ICAI was formed by Royal Charter in 1888.

[5] This included the Institute of Chartered Accountants in England and Wales, the Society of Accountants and Auditors, the Edinburgh Society of Accountants, the Glasgow Institute of Accountants and Actuaries and the Aberdeen Society of Accountants. By 1896, four bills were drawn up by various bodies and all were unsuccessful. Between 1901 and 1912 four more attempts were made before the matter was finally dropped.

charter bodies (Shackleton & Walker, 1998). At various times, attempts to coordinate the British profession failed because bodies that held a higher status were not willing to compromise and accept a dilution of their status in order to achieve greater benefits for accounting profession as a whole (Shackleton & Walker, 1998). In other words, similar to the case of Australia's four unsuccessful merger attempts, the British bodies that held a charter and higher professional status defeated attempts to change the boundaries of the profession, which were drawn around MIPP and membership to charter bodies.

Scottish accounting bodies enjoyed a near professional monopoly over the provision of public practice, and their members achieved a status associated with the title CA. The accounting profession and the term "chartered accounting" were promoted as synonyms by the media of the time (Walker, 1991). The accounting profession was clearly established as a public accounting profession in Scotland. For example, in 1895, 85.4% of Scotland's public audit work was completed by Scottish CAs (Walker, 1991). From 1884 to 1905, there were nine attempts to challenge the Chartered Accountant monopoly by altering the boundaries of Scotland's accounting profession (Walker, 1991). These attempts were all successfully quashed by the chartered bodies in Scotland. In 1886, the Scottish Institute of Accountants, which was perceived to be a lower-status professional body, sought to implement a joint effort by all bodies to unify the Scottish accounting profession. This was an attempt to alter the boundaries of the Scottish accounting profession and was similar to the case of the four Australian merger attempts. However, the Chartered Accountant bodies refused to cooperate at the leadership level. Any attempt to dilute Chartered Accountant status was successfully challenged by the claim that it was against the public interest and that the non-Chartered Accountant body members were not professional. The Chartered Accountant bodies made attempts to provide arguments which were derogatory for members of non-Chartered Accountant associations. These claims included that members of non-Chartered Accountant bodies were not professional primarily because they were engaged in commercial occupations than public practice. Roles held in commercial occupations accorded a lower status in the Victorian society. Another argument was that the examinations used for CAs had higher quality than those at the Scottish Institute (Walker, 1991). Thus, chartered bodies in the UK used boundary management to protect the boundaries of their professional associations and memberships in order to project their exclusive status.

Accounting was defined as a public profession by the bodies that were formed during the early years of professionalisation of accounting in the UK, comprising MIPP (Shackleton & Walker, 2001). These bodies largely closed entry to the profession to accountants working in government positions and industry. As a result, the excluded members formed various other bodies and, by 1929, there were 17 accounting bodies (Shackleton & Walker, 1998). This situation was similar to the Australian accounting profession, where multiple bodies were formed due to early stages of boundary construction around the notion of public practice. During 1930 and 1935, the ICAEW entered discussions with Scottish bodies for a merger, but the top management of the ICAEW rejected the idea (Shackleton & Walker, 1998). The idea of a merger meant changes to the traditional strategies of adopting exclusive status and changes in their respective boundaries. This example indicates how higher-status organisations are likely to be circumspect about proposals to merge with associations that they perceive to be of lower status. In other words, higher-status organisations and their members continue to justify and protect the boundaries of their membership and any modifications to their organisational strategies by rejecting mergers with lower-status organisations. These examples highlight the similarities between these prior situations and the way in which all four merger attempts in Australia failed for comparable reasons.

Key British studies indicate that the ICAS and its members generally perceived the ICAS to be of higher status than other organisations, which also resulted in the failure of the most recent attempt to combine the ICAEW and ICAS (Lee, 2010; Walker, 1991, 1995). Other chartered accounting bodies also have a perceived higher professional status. Contention between various accounting bodies has always been a key feature of the British accounting profession. For example, during a movement to coordinate the accounting profession in the UK during World War II and later years, some bodies were not included in the discussions, such as the Institute of Cost and Works Accountants, the Institute of Municipal Treasurers and Accountants and the Association of International Accountants (Shackleton & Walker, 1998). A key reason behind the failure of various merger attempts in the UK profession has been occupational closure based on boundary construction. As the model of the Australian accounting profession was imported from the UK (Parker, 1989), the inherent features of duplication, regionalism and occupational closure based on boundary construction were also imported.

Professional accounting bodies in the UK sought complete market control and to elevate their professional status further. They continued to propagate that MNIPP were damaging the status of the profession. In 1966, the Board of Trade sought evidence from the ICAEW to support its view that unqualified members were not fit to undertake accounting work; however, the ICAEW refused to supply any objective evidence. The major attempts to create professional boundaries using state registration were made in the 1890s and 1930s. All 17 accounting bodies in the UK at that time made submissions to the Groschen Enquiry, which was an official state body set up to consider the issue. The profession was divided into three ways (Shackleton & Walker, 1998). First, the chartered institutes feared the dilution of their status and opposed the register that included members of all bodies, although chartered bodies were in favour of registration that only included members of chartered bodies. Second, junior societies strongly favoured the register, as they saw registration as an opportunity to be placed alongside CAs (Shackleton & Walker, 1998). The third submission was from those outside the profession, who were against the register. In August 1930, the Groschen Report rejected the need for state registration of accountants because it perceived that this was not in the public interest. In other words, the government did not want to become a party to assist in creating professional boundaries in the accounting profession. Therefore, the UK's first attempt to unify the accounting profession failed, and the chartered institutes managed to save their status and avoid the dilution of the profession that they feared. Thus, this was the first successful defence of boundaries in the British accounting profession. On two occasions in 1930 and 1935, the SIAA entered discussions with the ICAEW for the merger of both bodies, but the ICAEW rejected the idea of a merger on both occasions at the top management level (Shackleton & Walker, 1998), again due to a fear of diluting current members' status with the influx of more members. In the context of the British accounting profession, many accounting merger discussions have failed due to perceived higher-status organisations withdrawing from merger discussions (Shackleton & Walker, 1998). The case of the four Australian merger attempts has unique facts to the British merger attempts. In contrast to the British charter institutes, the Australian Institute took the first initiative in all four cases. This unusual and unique case demands a critical analysis of the factors leading to the Australian merger attempts and failure.

In later years in Britain, during World War II, less attention was paid to the structure of the accounting profession because it served the state in times of national crisis, with many prominent accountants assisting the state during the war. However, during the reconstruction period after the war, the UK government became more centralised and the accounting profession attempted to coordinate its efforts. However, the decentralised structure of the accounting profession proved a hindrance to coordinating the profession's activities, even during times of crisis, when the public interest would have been the foremost objective. This caused the minister responsible for reconstruction, William Jowitt, to comment that the accounting profession needed to put its house in order (Shackleton & Walker, 1998) which was a strong comment coming from the top level of the British government.

Later in 1942, the ICAEW and SIAA formed a joint subcommittee to consider issues affecting the profession, and primarily to consider the issue of the profession's structure. Discussions were again focused on the old agenda of excluding perceived ineligible accountants who were not working in public practice through the means of a Public Accountants Bill. However, government agencies, such as the Board of Trade and Federation of British Industries, and excluded accounting bodies, such as the ICAI, objected and viewed the new Bill as an attempt by the accounting bodies to establish a professional monopoly or create boundaries to exclude others. It became difficult to coordinate the process with the Scottish bodies, and the ICAEW president subsequently ignored their presence. Hence, the Scots objected to the Bill and viewed it as a means of gaining registration only. After the ICAEW President Charles Palmour visited Scotland, the Scottish bodies agreed to cooperate after he clarified that the minister had requested that they organise their affairs, and highlighted that the Association of Chartered Certified Accountants (ACCA) membership was growing at a rate that posed a possible danger to chartered bodies. Following this, there was agreement from the Scottish bodies when it was accepted that there would be a separate Public Accountants' council for Scotland (Shackleton & Walker, 1998). For the first time, the ACCA was included in discussions by the chartered bodies; previously, it was considered an outsider. The ACCA objected to the issue of a separate council for Scotland, while the Scottish bodies claimed that it was necessary to uphold the standards of the profession and education in Scotland, which was self-perceived to be the most superior of all bodies. The ACCA also sought government support in its objections; however, a compromise was not reached. The ICAI was also initially not included; however, after some deliberations and interference from the Board of Trade, it was included as a recognised body (Shackleton & Walker, 1998).

Looking at some of the key reasons for the failure to achieve coordination among the ICAEW, ACCA and SIAA in 1957, we conclude that this failure could be partially attributed to the different decision-making processes of the various bodies. The higher-status institutes were not ready to accept dilution in their status with claims of years of hard work and that keeping public practice separate from non-public practice-based associations was in the public interest (Shackleton & Walker, 1998). Although such claims were made to continue to pursue economic self-interest of their members. These claims were counterproductive for merger attempts because when seeking support from government bodies, the proposals of mergers must be able to show that they were in the wider public interest and not designed to preserve the self-interests of some of all of the professional bodies (Shackleton & Walker, 1998). Government representation concluded that all bodies were pursuing their own narrow private interests. Ultimately, government support was not extended for state-sponsored intervention regarding the structure of the profession (Shackleton & Walker, 1998).

The central reasons for the various unsuccessful merger attempts in Britain included a lack of attention being given to previous failures, a lack of consideration of merger alternatives, continuous disregard of the disagreement about the worth of merger proposals, poor levels of lobbying with the government and the detachment of office bearers from membership (Shackleton & Walker, 2001). Such detachment could be disastrous, given that the ultimate authority to approve any merger scheme rests with the membership (Shackleton & Walker, 2001). The 1988 failure to merge the ICAEW and the Institute of Chartered Accountants of Scotland (ICAS) to create the Institute of Chartered Accountants of Great Britain, had the detachment of leaders from their members as a principal cause of the merger failing. Leaders of both associations were pursuing agenda of control while trying to keep reputation of accounting profession intact as a response to state pressure. The state had the view that the accounting profession should have a joint voice when responding to regulatory matters (Lee, 2010). The boundary management literature concluded that individuals in lower-status groups support social mobility strategies to gain access to higher-status groups in order to achieve an enhanced social identity (Keohane & Milner, 1996). This discussion of

Britain's accounting history highlights that the factors that caused the British merger attempt to fail may also have been present in Australia's four unsuccessful merger attempts.

3.3.2 *Canada's Merger Attempts*

Following the above comprehensive discussion of the British mergers, this subsection provides a review of the literature on Canada's merger attempts. In fact, after the UK, Canada was the second country in the world to formally organise its accounting profession by forming associations of accountants. The origin of accounting profession in Canada can be traced to Montreal and Toronto which were the financial market centres at that time. Initially the demand for accountants arose mainly for dealing with bankruptcies of businesses. Similar to that of Australia and in the UK, the professionalisation process had many challenges, conflicts and multiple failed and successful merger attempts. Between 1880 and 2014, there have been many waves of formation of new accounting associations and successful merger attempts that changed the structure and operations of accounting profession. At the same time there were multiple failed merger attempts as well. The history of Canadian accounting profession covers over 130 years which is marked by constant struggles for achieving market control, intra-professional conflicts, regulatory changes leading to major changes in the market for accounting services and division of labour within the accounting profession. There have been six waves of successful merger attempts by the Canadian accounting profession. Unlike the Australian accounting profession, the accounting associations in Canada made at least 18 unsuccessful attempts at merger which are publicly known. This number does not include formal and informal discussions which did not proceed to the next stages. A key theme among these failed merger attempts is that they followed a successful attempt in one province which probably acted as a motivating factor for accounting associations in another provinces (Richardson & Kilfoyle, 2012).

The first accounting associations in Canada were formed in 1879 in Quebec and Ontario. These earlier associations adopted the Chartered Accountant title because it had gained status and prestige in Britain. Accountants in Canada also imported the British model of accounting profession just was the case in Australia. A key theme in the professionalisation of accounting in the UK and Australia, regionalism, spread in Canada as well, where associations were formed in Manitoba and Nova

Scotia in 1901, who also adopted the Chartered Accountant designation (Richardson, 1987). These associations were functioning independent of each other and often competed for accounting services market (Richardson & Kilfoyle, 2012).

In 1902, an independent federal association, the Dominion Association of Chartered Accountants (DACA), was formed under a federal charter. One of the objectives for forming a federal body was to create a designation which could be used across all Canadian provinces. Soon after its formation, DACA faced conflicts with the Institute of Chartered Accountants of Ontario and various regional CA Institutes. After negotiations between all associations, DACA became the federal body representing all provincial Institutes. DACA encouraged the formation of CA Institutes in those provinces where none existed to secure a market of accounting services (Richardson, 2002). By 1910, all Chartered Accountant associations in Canada had merged with the DACA, which acted as a federal coordinating body. This was achieved after a series of conflicts and negotiations (Richardson, 1987).

The CA Institutes in Canada were focused on public practice which was similar to that of the UK and Australia. Entry requirements included an examination to test knowledge of potential members in auditing and financial reporting. However, there were increasing number of accountants who worked in commerce, industry and government. Although the boundaries of professional accounting were constructed around the title of Chartered Accountant, and then expanded to include all Chartered Accountant associations. However, this did not stop the formation of other associations, that offered a professional designation outside the boundaries of the Chartered Accountant title. In 1908, the Certified General Accountants Association of Canada (CGA) was formed. CGA offered membership to those accountants who did not work in public practice firms and gradually their number was increasing as compared to accountants working in public practice. Initially, it was formed by accountants working within Canadian Pacific Railways in Montreal as an attempt to organise themselves. The Chartered Institutes saw the formation of CGA as a challenge to their domain and responded to the threat by creating the Canadian Society of Cost Accountants (CSCA). This led to a competition between CSCA and CGAs to offer professional designation for their members.

After World War I, business and personal income taxes were introduced which created an additional branch of accountants offering that service. In

1920 tax accountants and tax auditors working in government tax offices formed the Certified Public Accountants Association (CPA Canada). In later years CPA Canada started developing public accounting firms in addition to traditional services offered by their members for preparing and auditing personal and business taxes. This created further professional conflict in the Canadian accounting profession. After World War II there were many attempts to consolidate the accounting profession. There were some successful initiatives to create larger organisations by merging smaller groups with arguments of increased lobbying powers to negotiate self-regulatory mechanisms and ability to offer better services to public (Richardson, 1989a; MacDonald & Richardson, 2004). Further mergers took place when entry of public accounting practice was raised to match the entry level of CA profession (Richardson & Jones, 2007). This shows that earlier mergers were achieved to reduce duplication of organisations or as a response to changes in government legislation regulating services of accountants. Some initiatives were motivated by a desire to create a federal brand for accountants in Canada and were driven by a uniform title for accountants in the US.

The successful merger in the 1960s between the Institute of Chartered Accountants of Ontario and Certified Public Accountants of Ontario was the result of the charter institute's attempt to attain market control due to direct state intervention. Hence, external factors drove changes in the traditional strategies of the chartered institute, which were the same in the case of the Australian merger attempts (Richardson & Jones, 2007). In 2004, the merger discussions between the Canadian Institute of Chartered Accountants and CMA failed at the initial level only. In fact, the merger failed largely because of the reaction of members of each association to either the potential loss of their designation (in order to join the merged body) or the dilution of their "brand" equity (by granting the continuing designation to new members through the merger rather than through traditional entry processes) (Richardson & Jones, 2007). External factors such as state intervention did play a role in the successful attempt of 1960s while in 2004 merger attempts the state did not play an active role.

Another wave of formation and mergers of accounting associations was linked to creating organisations for specialised accounting functions such as "vocational accountants". Such organisations do have arrangements with vocational training institutes to offer certificates and training to their members (Richardson & Kilfoyle, 2012). The final and successful attempt to unite Canada's accounting profession was the merger of Certified General Accountants of Ontario (CGA) with the Chartered Professional Accountants of Ontario (CPA Ontario) and the Certified Management Accountants (CMAs). About 97 per cent CGA members voted in favour of merger, while 74 per cent CPA Ontario members supported this merger attempt. This was a complex process which needed approvals from over 40 accounting bodies, national associations for Chartered Accountants (CAs), CMAs and CGAs and the regional bodies for each of these three groups across 10 provinces and two territories. This agreement brings together 185,000 CAs, CMAs and CGAs under the new title Chartered Professional Accountants (CPA). The new professional title CPA will be common in each province and territory.

The three national accounting associations in Canada had originated from various successful mergers and had created their own position within the accounting profession. They differentiated themselves partly on the basis of functions their members performed and partly on the basis of status of their members. The ongoing struggle in the accounting profession across the UK, Canada and Australia has been around roles and associations created for members in public practice and those not in public practice. So the boundaries of profession are drawn around public practice and they exclude those who are not in public practice. The protection of professional legitimacy is a factor that generally influences the decision to mount mergers of professional accounting associations (Richardson & Jones, 2007). In other merger contexts, changes in the organisational strategies of exclusivity versus market control have been a starting point for merger discussion (Walker & Shackleton, 1995) and eventually led to changes in associations' boundaries. These themes are common in most of the merger discussions whether failed or successful in the UK, Canada and Australia.

3.4 Conclusion

This chapter demonstrates that the early stages of the professionalisation of accounting in the UK, Canada and Australia had many similarities. The main point of contention was constructing boundaries around the membership of perceived higher-status organisations and excluding others who did not meet the entry standards. The excluded members formed rival organisations, many of which developed large membership numbers and the financial strength associated with this large group of members. However, the changing economic, social and political contexts created conditions favourable for various mergers. Thus, various merger attempts posed challenges to professional boundaries based on exclusivity strategies. This triggered boundary protection either at the leadership or membership level by perceived higher-status organisations.

Despite their similarities, the Australian case has many unique factors. First, in each of the four merger attempts in Australia, the perceived higher-status organisation always approached the perceived lower-status organisation to discuss matters of mutual interest or instigate merger talks. Second, the outcomes of all four merger attempts were the same, yet both bodies made four attempts with a gap of nearly one decade between each. Third, in each of these merger attempts, the reasons that led to the failures of the attempts were essentially the same. This unique and unusual case demands special attention and critical scrutiny of the factors that resulted in this outcome, even though it has many similarities to the British and Canadian mergers.

The boundary management tensions in the Australian accounting profession were a particular consequence of perceived status differentials between MIPP and MNIPP initially, and then later as a differentiation between members of the Institute and the Society. However, a changing social and economic context, including corporate failures, the need to lift education standards and the legitimacy crisis, presented the profession with new challenges, which resulted in both bodies mounting the merger attempts. Resistance to the mergers was a result of the Institute's members' fear of losing their higher status.

Gieryn (1983) argued that professional boundaries are not permanent structures, and the ongoing conflict for control and authority leads to changes in these boundaries. In Australia's various unsuccessful merger attempts between accounting associations, the motion to combine forces failed because, in many cases, the members of the perceived higher-status association voted against the merger attempt. Thus, the central reason for failure has been contention between MIPP and MNIPP, and the associated perceived superior status of MIPP. The factors that led to the mounting of merger attempts in Canada and the UK were replicated in similar scenarios in Australia during the four merger attempts examined in this study. The consequential failures in the UK and Canada also had overlapping factors that were collectively shared by the episodes of failure of the four merger attempts in Australia. The next chapter discusses research methodology adopted in this project and provides a detailed account of data collection methods.

References

Annisette, M., & O'Regan, P. (2007). Joined for the common purpose: The establishment of the Institute of Chartered Accountants in Ireland as an all-Ireland institution. *Qualitative Research in Accounting & Management, 4*(1), 4–25.

Carnegie, G. D. (1993). The Australian Institute of Incorporated Accountants (1892–1938). *ABFH, 3*(1), 61–80.

Carnegie, G. D. (2009). The development of accounting regulation, education and literature in Australia, 1788–2005. *Australian Economic History Review, 49*(3), 276–301.

Carnegie, G. D. (2016). The accounting professional project and bank failures. *Journal of Management History, 22*(4), 389–412.

Carnegie, G. D., & Edwards, J. R. (2001). The construction of the professional accountant: The case of the Incorporated Institute of Accountants, Victoria (1886). *Accounting, Organisations and Society, 26*(4/5), 301–325.

Carnegie, G. D., & Napier, C. (2012). Accounting's past, present and future: The unifying power of history. *Accounting, Auditing & Accountability Journal, 25*(2), 328–369.

Carnegie, G. D., & Napier, C. J. (1996). Critical and interpretive histories: Insights into accounting's present and future through its past. *Accounting, Auditing & Accountability Journal, 9*(3), 7–39.

Carnegie, G. D., & O'Connell, B. T. (2012). Understanding the responses of professional accounting bodies to crises: The case of the Australian profession in the 1960s. *Accounting Auditing and Accountability Journal, 25*(5), 835–875.

Carnegie, G. D., & Parker, R. H. (1999). Accountants and empire: The case of co-membership of Australian and British accountancy bodies, 1885 to 1914. *Accounting, Business & Financial History, 9*(1), 77–102.

Carnegie, G. D., Edwards, J. R., & West, B. P. (2003). Understanding the dynamics of the Australian accounting profession: A prosopographical study of the founding members of the Incorporated Institute of Accountants, Victoria, 1886 to 1908. *Accounting, Auditing & Accountability Journal, 16*(5), 790–820.

Carr-Saunders, A. M., & Wilson, P. A. (1964). *The professions*. Frank Cass.

Chua, W. F., & Poullaos, C. (1993). Rethinking the profession-state dynamic: The case of the Victorian Charter attempt, 1885–1906. *Accounting, Organisations and Society, 18*(7/8), 691–728.

Chua, W. F., & Poullaos, C. (1998). The dynamics of 'closure' amidst the construction of market, profession, empire and nationhood: An historical analysis of an Australian accounting association, 1886–1903. *Accounting, Organisations and Society, 23*(2), 155–187.
Creaney, E. (1984). The history of the I. A. A., An address by the National Secretary, Perth, WA, July.
Edwards, J. R., Carnegie, G. D., & Cauberg, J. (1997). The Incorporated Institute of Accountants, Victoria (1886): A study of founders' backgrounds. In T. E. Cooke, & C. W. Nobes (Eds.), *The development of accounting in an international context: A festschrift in honour of R. H. Parker* (pp. 49–67). Routledge.
Garrett, A. A. (1961). *History of the society of incorporated accountants 1885–1957*. Oxford University Press.
Gavens, J. J. (1990). A historical perspective of integration of the Australian accounting profession. In R. H. Parker (Ed.), *Accounting in Australia: Historical essays* (pp. 381–407). Garland.
Gavens, J. J., & Gibson, R. W. (1992). An Australian attempt to internationalize accounting professional organisations. *The Accounting Historians Journal, 19*(2), 79–102.
Gieryn, T. F. (1983). Boundary-work and the demarcation of science from non-science: Strains and interests in the professional ideologies of scientists. *American Sociological Review, 48*(6), 781–795.
Graham, A. W. (1978). *Without fear or favour: A history of the Institute of Chartered Accountants in Australia, 1928–1978*. Butterworths for Institute of Chartered Accountants. in Australia.
Gynther, R. S. (1967). *Practising accountants in Australia*. Queensland University Press.
Johnson, T. J., & Caygill, M. (1971). The development of accountancy links in Commonwealth. *Accounting and Business Research, 1*(2m), 155–173.
Kenley, W. J. (1963). *History of the Australian Society of Accountants and its antecedent bodies, 1887 to 1962*. Australian Society of Accountants (evidence of authorship in *The Australian Accountant*, June 1977, 27).
Keohane, R. O., & Milner, H. V. (Eds.). (1996). *Internationalization and domestic politics*. Cambridge University Press.
Lee, T. A. (2010). Consolidating the public accountancy profession: The case of the proposed Institute of Chartered Accountants of Great Britain, 1988–1989. *Accounting History, 15*(1), 7–39.
Linn, R. (1996). *Power, progress and profit: A history of the Australian accounting profession*. Australian Society of Certified Practising Accountants.
MacDonald, L. D., & Richardson, A. J. (2004). Identity, appropriateness and the construction of regulatory space: The formation of the public accountant's council of Ontario. *Accounting, Organizations and Society, 29*(5–6), 489–524.

Macdonald, K. M. (1985). Social closure and occupational registration. *Sociology, 19*(4), 541–556.
Macdonald, K. M., & Ritzer, G. (1988). The sociology of the professions: Dead or alive? *Work and Occupations, 15*(3), 251–272.
Marshall, N. J. (1978). A jubilee history 1928–1978 (Melbourne: The Institute of Chartered Accountants in Australia). Partly reprinted in R. H. Parker (Ed.). (1990a) *Accounting in Australia: Historical essays* (pp. 408–434). Garland Publishing.
Miranti, P. J. (1986a). Associationalism, statism, and professional regulation: Public accountants and the reform of the financial markets, 1896–1940. *Business History Review, 60*(03), 438–468.
Miranti, P. J. (1986b). From conflict to consensus: The American Institute of Accountants and the professionalization of public accountancy, 1886–1940. *Business and Economic History, 15*(2nd series), 93–126.
Parker, L. D. (1999). Historiography for the new millennium: Adventures in accounting and management. *Accounting History, 4*(2), 11–42.
Parker, R. H. (1961, December). Australia's first accountancy body—The Adelaide Society of Accountants. *The Chartered Accountant in Australia*, 337–340.
Parker, R. H. (1989). Importing and exporting accounting: The British experience. In A. G. Hopwood (Ed.), *International pressures for accounting change* (pp. 7–29). Prentice-Hall.
Poullaos, C. (1993). Making profession and state, 1907 to 1914: The ACPA's first charter attempt. *Abacus, 29*(2), 196–229.
Poullaos, C. (1994). *Making the Australian chartered accountant*. Garland.
Richardson, A. J. (1987). Professionalization and intra-professional competition in the Canadian accounting profession. *Work and Occupations, 14*(4), 591–615.
Richardson, A. J. (1989a). Corporatism and intraprofessional hegemony: A study of regulation and internal social order. *Accounting, Organisations and Society, 14*(5), 415–431.
Richardson, A. J. (1989b). Canada's accounting elite: 1880–1930. *The Accounting Historians Journal, 16*(1), 1–21.
Richardson, A. J. (2002). Professional dominance: The relationship between financial accounting and managerial accounting, 1926–1986. *The Accounting Historians Journal*, 91–121.
Richardson, A. J., & Kilfoyle, E. (2012). Merging the profession: A historical perspective on accounting association mergers in Canada. *Accounting Perspectives, 11*(2), 77–109.

Richardson, A. J., & Jones, D. B. (2007). Professional 'brand', personal identity and resistance to change in the Canadian accounting profession: A comparative history of two accounting association merger negotiations. *Accounting History, 12*(2), 135–164.

Shackleton, K., & Walker, S. P. (2001). *A future for the accountancy profession: The quest for closure and integration, 1957–1970*. Institute of Chartered Accountants of Scotland.

Shackleton, K. (1995). Scottish chartered accountants: Internal and external political relationships, 1853–1916. *Accounting, Auditing & Accountability Journal, 8*(2), 18–46.

Shackleton, K., & Walker. S. P. (1998). *Professional reconstruction: The coordination of the accountancy bodies, 1930–1957*. Institute of Chartered Accountants of Scotland.

The Institute of Chartered Accountants in Australia. (1969). *Annual report*. Australia.

Velayutham, S. (1999). The professional accounting body in the 21st century: The global franchise. *Pacific Accounting Review, 11*(1/2), 163–171.

Walker, S. P. (1991). The defence of professional monopoly: Scottish chartered accountants and 'satellites in the accountancy firmament' 1854–1914. *Accounting, Organisations and Society, 16*(3), 257–283.

Walker, S. P. (1995). The genesis of professional organisation in Scotland: A contextual analysis. *Accounting, Organisations and Society, 20*(4), 285–310.

Walker, S. P. (2004). *Towards the 'great Desideratum': The unification of the accountancy bodies in England, 1870–1880*. Institute of Chartered Accountants of Scotland.

Walker, S. P., & Shackleton, K. (1995). Corporatism and structural change in the British accountancy profession, 1930–1957. *Accounting, Organisations and Society, 20*(6), 467–503.

Walker, S. P., & Shackleton, K. (1998). A ring fence for the profession: Advancing the closure of British accountancy 1957–1970. *Accounting, Auditing & Accountability Journal, 11*(1), 34–71.

Walton, S. J. T. (1970). *History of the Institute of Chartered Accountants in Australia and its antecedent bodies with reference to the personalities concerned*. The Institute of Chartered Accountants. in Australia.

Willmott, H. (1986). Organising the profession: A theoretical and historical examination of the development of the major accountancy bodies in the UK. *Accounting, Organisations and Society, 11*(6), 555–580.

CHAPTER 4

Research Methodology: Understanding Accounting History Through Critical and Interpretative Research

This book adopts a critical and interpretative research approach to the study of four merger attempts and comprises part of the "new accounting history" paradigm (Fleischman et al., 1996; Miller et al., 1991; Parker, 1999). The study of accounting history and accounting institutions makes an important contribution to the accounting literature in particular and other literature in general because the importance of historical understanding applies to accounting as much as to other fields of human endeavour. We can learn from history and appreciate the contemporary accounting thought and practice as it evolves through past and present and future (Carnegie & Napier, 2012).

Chapter 3 provided a historical account of the development of accounting profession in Australia. As analysed in the previous chapter duplication of associations, regionalism and mergers around the notion of members in public practice and members not in public practice were key themes in the development of accounting profession. The study of history of development of accounting profession using a non-descriptive lens requires application of a critical and inter-preparative framework. Critical history research in accounting provides an analysis of contemporary practices and explains how institutional structures were formed as a result of social and political changes over many decades.

The domain of critical and interpretive research paradigm has dominated the accounting history research for the last three decades. The scope

J. Sidhu et al., *Understanding the Sociology of the Accounting Profession*, https://doi.org/10.1007/978-981-99-1572-9_4

of accounting history research is broader now than it was 20 to 30 years ago, as it currently includes the study of institutions and the professionalisation of accounting (Parker, 2015). Researchers such as Garry Carnegie and Lee Parker have provided insight into the methods used to conduct accounting history research during the three decades from 1983 to 2012, and argue that, during this period, a key development has been the rise of "new accounting history" research, which is explained in later parts of this chapter. This chapter provides the context for conducting historical research and provides details of the historical insights. This is important as accounting history research provides analysis of events that had a significant influence on the development of the accounting profession in any society.

This chapter is structured into six sections. The first section provides introduction and second section provides the context for conducting historical research and provides details of the research technique adopted in this book. The third section explains how data were collected from public archives, such as CPA Australia, other libraries and other sources. The fourth section provides details of the methodology for data collection. The fifth section summarises the limitations of the adopted research methods and techniques, while the last section provides a conclusion to this chapter.

4.1 Introduction

This study adopts a qualitative approach using a historical research methodology to source surviving business records from public archives and other data gathered from oral history interviews to investigate the historical developments related to the four attempts to merge the two major accounting bodies in Australia. The project is constituted by multiple historical case studies (Carnegie & Napier, 1996; Eisenhardt, 1989; Eisenhardt & Graebner, 2007; Yin, 2009). A historical study can identify factors that led to important historical events (such as the case of the four merger attempts) and add interpretations when writing a historical account to provide answers to research questions in a given study (Previts et al., 1990a).

Qualitative research involves the collection, analysis and interpretation of the data. Data collection is far more important task in qualitative research than the quantitative approach. It is because these data related to the social world and the concepts and behaviours of people within it.

Such data is not available in ready to use forms and often researchers need to conduct data search and then test it against research objectives and questions (Anderson, 2010). Then further data collection is done to meet research needs. The nature of the current project warranted the use of a qualitative research methodology because it was not possible to accurately predict the intensity of the work involved in searching for potential sources of information, the extent to which information was available from different sources and the depth of data collection from the available sources. In fact, for this project, data collection for the first merger attempt was the most challenging. Based on the experiences gained in collecting data for the first merger attempt, the authors developed a systematic process that streamlined further data collection and provided clear directions to source data for the next three merger attempts. This also reduced the amount of time spent collecting data from archives after investing a significant amount of time in data collection for the first merger attempt and subsequently developing a systematic approach.

An interdisciplinary approach to accounting history research and aspiring to write in an informative and engaging manner makes this research more appealing to a wider audience, which is the main aim of the adopted research methodology in this project (Gomes et al., 2011). This chapter is structured into six sections. The next section provides the context for conducting historical research and provides details of the research technique adopted in this project. The third section explains how data were collected from public archives, such as CPA Australia, other libraries and other sources. The fourth section provides details of the oral history interviews that were conducted for data collection. The fifth section summarises the limitations of the adopted research methods and techniques, while the last section provides a conclusion to this chapter.

4.2 Research Methodology in Accounting History Research

Accounting history research provides analysis of events that had a significant influence on the development of the accounting profession in society (Napier, 1989). Historical research centres on documenting and explaining the context of past events, their causes and consequences, decisions that led to those events and complex dynamics that played a role in background (Bedeian, 1998). These arguments match the process adopted to conduct the research underpinning this study, which examined different events, major decisions and actions, such as the mounting of merger attempts, and their consequences for the operation and structure of the Australian accounting profession. Before the first merger attempt was mounted, a series of corporate failures occurred in the early 1960s, and the accounting profession faced a legitimacy crisis (Carnegie & O'Connell, 2012). These incidents forced the two major professional bodies to engage in joint activities and, this spirit of cooperation assisted in creating the favourable conditions that ultimately led to the mounting of the first merger attempt (Carnegie, 2009; Carnegie & O'Connell, 2012). Calls by scholars to conduct historical studies firmly rooted in the contents of archives (Walker & Shackleton, 1998) motivate our work and also respond to the calls of post-revisionist sociologists to examine historical variations in professionalisation projects. In fact, this book examines historical variations in the professionalisation of accounting in Australia, whereby two major institutions attempted to restructure themselves to form a single unified body.

Accounting history research cannot be rigidly based solely on facts; rather, it must also be based on the interpretations of findings of historical inquiry, which are underpinned by surviving evidence that elucidates the facts to the extent known (Miller et al., 1991). In the current research project, factual information, as it appears in primary documents, is combined with interpretations to provide appropriate responses to the research questions. Therefore, interpretations of historical information become crucial, and such interpretations are tested with documentary evidence and crosschecked with data collected from oral history interviews. The current research project falls in the category of critical and interpretative history. It examines surviving evidence of historical events and adds a critical perspective by interpreting various decisions taken by the councils of both accounting bodies and the responses of members to the decisions made regarding merger proposals. This approach places the current project in the branch of new accounting history, which:

> involves attention to a variety of agents and agencies, the conditions of possibility of transformations in accounting knowledge and practice, the institutional forces that shape actions and outcomes and the rationales that set out the objects and objectives of accounting. (Miller et al., 1991, p. 395)

There is a key difference between the conventional accounting history and critical and interpretative accounting history, where many conventional historians are more comfortable with a descriptive portrayal of accounting's past, but "new accounting history" uses interdisciplinary theories and provides interpretative perspectives to the study of history (Fleischman et al., 1996; Miller et al., 1991). The application of theories underpins this study, meaning that it does not merely seek to portray a highly descriptive account of past actors and events but to provide a critical and interpretive orientation of the study of the four merger attempts using interdisciplinary theoretical frameworks.

The new accounting historians tend to expose hidden agendas, and reveal the politicisation of related institutions and practices (Parker, 1999) which makes the approach quite complex and at the same time critically important to present a balanced account of history. These arguments align well with the aims and objectives of the current research project. The strength of critical and interpretative history is that its criticisms can only stand when it is established that interpretations are inconsistent with the assumptions made or the facts available (Previts et al., 1990a). However, researchers must establish that source materials are authentic, credible and adequate for drawing inferences. Any inferences can be crosschecked if multiple sources of information are available (Previts et al., 1990b).

History research uses "communicative evidence", which can be in written forms, such as found in surviving documents, or can be collected through oral history techniques (Fleischman et al., 1996). As stated previously, this study falls within the realm of "critical and interpretive histories" (Carnegie & Napier, 1996). It draws on the available surviving archival records and other secondary sources and uses the oral evidence of key individuals who officially represented the Society and the Institute in the merger negotiations. Thus, it provides a critical perspective to identify the reasons for mounting the four merger attempts and identifies the potential causes for the failures of these mergers.

Developments in accounting history research since the mid-1990s were described by Parker (1999, p. 29) as an "eclectic reading of history encompassing social, political, cultural and ideological contexts in which institutions have operated". In any historical study, it is important to understand the context in which historical events occurred and decisions were made because central to this effort is a grasp of society in which events of interest occurred (Fleischman et al., 1996). In the current project, for each of the four merger attempts, this study seeks to explore the context, including some of the major changes in society and the economy at that time. The events affecting the accounting profession such as corporate collapses and a legitimacy crisis, are also considered.

After an early start and strong reception, critical accounting history received criticism which encouraged for calls that accounting historians needed to improve the significance of their research to make accounting history matter. In order to persuade others of the importance of accounting history, researchers need to draw out the contemporary relevance and implications of their research findings (Gomes et al., 2011). The importance of history depends on how the contemporary audience perceives its relevance and contribution to knowledge. This project provides a critical and interpretative account of the four merger attempts and makes an effort to add contemporary significance by assessing the implications of these merger failures for the Australian accounting profession.

The set key research objectives of the current research project examine the reasons for mounting the four unsuccessful merger attempts between the Society and the Institute and identify the factors that contributed to the failures of these mergers. This study also seeks to identify the factors that precipitated the merger proposals. Hence, this project also studies the relationships between historical events and their causation or effect on the mounting of the four merger attempts. The relationship between the Society and the Institute before the first merger attempt, and since the formation of the two bodies, is also studied based on the available literature and evidence. This thesis also considers the effect of certain historical events connected to the developments studied, such as corporate collapses and their influence on the standing of the accounting profession.

The importance of accounting history research has been contemplated by many researchers. The present and past are strongly linked, and the study of history presents a more meaningful account of past events to a contemporary audience (Fleischman & Tyson, 1997). Our key objective of this book also includes the analysis of the implications of the failure of the four merger attempts for the structure and operation of the Australian accounting profession. Therefore, it connects the effect of past events and endeavours to make the research relevant for a contemporary audience. The study of accounting history is also important because it supports contemporary research in policymaking and practice and in standard setting (Previts et al., 1990a). Writing about the contrast between the traditional descriptive form of accounting history and interpretive and critical accounting history, Funnell (1996) stressed the importance of studying accounting history because it informs the present by illuminating the path that was taken to get there. This is what the current project aims to achieve by unfolding the factors that led to the mounting of the four merger attempts and their consequential failures.

The process of data collection, writing the narrative using archival materials and analysis has three main steps: collection of data from archives, including published official and non-official documents; collection of oral history and interpretation of findings. This chapter discusses the data collection from written archival sources and oral history interviews, while subsequent chapters discuss the writing, analysis and interpretation of data. The next section provides details of the sources that were accessed for archival data collection and the methods adopted during that process.

4.3 Data Collection from Archives and Written Documents

This study is grounded firmly in the archive, with the main emphasis on the available primary sources and supplemented by oral history evidence that, in the words of Fleischman et al., (1996, p. 61), constitutes "communicative evidence". However, where necessary, the evidence and arguments are supplemented by relevant secondary sources because an archive is simply a record, or a set of records (Robson, 2002). We also need to consider the fact that the documents in an archive were prepared for purposes other than those of historical research. Such sources may include media releases, the minutes of meetings, annual reports and letters that were written either for official purposes or to inform stakeholders, such as the members of both bodies, about decisions that would affect their membership in their respective bodies.

Primary archives provide an important and key data source for historical research because they provide the original account of accounting history. The examination of primary accounting documents is crucial in offering empirical content to our theories and generalisations (Napier, 1989). This means that using original records is crucial for accounting history research, and most studies in the accounting history domain have relied on archives for their data sources (Carnegie & Napier, 1996; Miller et al., 1991; Napier, 1989; Previts et al., 1990b). Historical research in accounting gains its strength from its firm basis in the 'archive. This study also responds to the suggestions of Walker and Shackleton (1995) that critical and interpretative histories, such as the current research project, need to rely more prominently on primary sources of information than on the official versions of the histories of professional bodies.

Fleischman and Tyson (1997) argued that much critical history work is based on archival resources. They stated that accounting history research has many forms, such as "well-researched archival investigation, well-reasoned interpretation and evaluation, and combinations thereof" (Fleischman & Tyson, 1997, p. 105), while Robson (2002, p. 355) noted that "archival research is not limited to the re-analysis" of historical evidence. Accounting history research relies on archival data, which has two main source categories: primary and secondary. However, in this book, primary records were mostly sought as evidence of events occurring around the time of mounting each of the four merger attempts. Two categories of written archival sources were used: official and non-official publications. The first of these sources included officially published documents of the Institute and the Society, including unity proposals, press releases, letters from presidents to members, minutes of meetings of general councils[1]and executive councils and articles published in the official journals of both bodies, the Australian Accountant and Chartered Accountant in Australia. Some of these documents were jointly issued by both bodies, while others were issued separately by the Institute and the Society. Such official sources are at risk of being biased either through selection or editing (Richardson & Jones, 2007). Hence, efforts were made to supplement official publications with unofficial sources, that is, those not under the imprimatur of the professional bodies, which included unofficial items, such as media and newspaper articles, academic journals, commentaries, letters to editors and opinion pieces. The relevant newspapers include The Sydney Morning Herald, The Age, The Australian Financial Review and The West Australian. The CPA Australia library has a set of scrapbooks that contain press clippings for the period under study, dating from the early 1960s to the late 1990s.

[1] In an email, CPA Australia wrote: "Sorry to have to confirm that access to minutes pertaining to the mergers, therefore including those of the unity committee and personal papers of staff/committee members, are not permitted" (CPA Australia, 2013, pers. comm., 16 April). This email was written in relation to the first merger attempt only, but access to similar resources for the other mergers proposals was also refused. Access to meeting minutes of the general council of the Society was allowed for the first merger attempt only.

Previts et al., (1990b, p. 150) presented arguments about the importance of explaining the selected research methods:

> In historical research, as in all similar efforts, the findings must be facilitated by a clear explanation of the research method employed and the justification of its appropriateness to the questions being investigated and/or the hypothesis being tested. The researcher should provide a rationale for each element of the process, including source selection; analysis and verification of sources; a justification for time periods selected.

Similar to their argument this chapter not only provides details of which sources of data were selected and which data collection methods were adopted, but also justifies the selection of sources and their time period. It was unfortunate that almost all of the records of the Institute relating to each of these four periods and the episode under examination have not survived. However, this did not become a major limitation because the CPA Australia library in Melbourne has kept official documents that were issued by the Institute with respect to these mergers. Moreover, most of the key documents related to the merger, such as unity proposals, were jointly issued and were accessible for this project. For the first merger attempt, the archival records available from CPA Australia were augmented with oral history interviews with two members of the Society who held positions on the organisation's general council in the late 1960s. For the second and third merger attempts, the presidents of the Institute and the Society at the time of the merger attempt were available and willing to assist in this research project. For the fourth merger attempt, only the then-president of the Society was available for interview.

The primary documentary data were mainly sourced from the Jill Bright Archives of CPA Australia, with the valuable assistance of Kerrie Ludekins, Senior Knowledge Management Coordinator. A significant volume of data was made available for examination and was collected. Other sources of information were the State Library of Victoria and Document Delivery Service of RMIT University library, as well as numerous other libraries that were accessed through the Document Delivery Service. These sources included annual reports, the professional journals of both bodies and press clippings, which were otherwise not available, even at the CPA Australia library, for different reasons. For example, some of the annual reports of the Institute were not available or not kept at the CPA library. Due to the high volume of original documents and difficulty in photocopying all relevant materials, a high-resolution digital camera was used and a total of 4,555 photographs were taken, which added up to more than 7,000 pages of original records. Some photographs were taken with two pages of document covered in one picture.

Two methods were adopted for this step of data collection involving taking photographs. The first method was used at the CPA Library and State Library of Victoria. To better facilitate data collection of records containing information relevant to the four merger attempts, photographs of all relevant information were taken. Between 2011 and 2015, during a 44-month period, data were progressively collected. The highest number of visits was to the CPA library, where an estimated 40 visits were made on a regular basis, with each visit being, on average, almost three hours. Kerrie Ludekins helpfully ensured that relevant source documents were ready and sorted according to months and years, which made data collection more manageable. During all visits, the emphasis was on taking photographs of the available records, which included meeting minutes of the general council of the Society (for the first merger attempt only; as mentioned earlier in this chapter, access to meeting minutes for later mergers was denied, while the Institute completely denied access to its archives or advised that they did not keep any archives dating for all four mergers[2]), newspaper clippings from scrapbooks, press releases, letters to members by presidents (CPA Australia also kept letters written by the Institute presidents to members), joint letters and statements issued by both presidents at respective mergers, various volumes of merger proposals and so forth.

Numerous visits were made to the State Library of Victoria, Melbourne, where some documents, mainly annual reports, were accessed that were unavailable through the RMIT Documentary Delivery Service or the CPA Australia Library. These documents mainly included annual reports of the Institute; however, in some cases, the annual reports of the

[2] On 7 May 2013, the Institute sent the following email: "Thank you for your email. Unfortunately, the Knowledge Centre is only for chartered accountants who have completed the CA programme or those who have enrolled to become chartered accountants. We're not able to assist you with minutes to meetings as we do not hold any here in the Knowledge Centre, I'm sorry that we cannot provide you with what you're looking for. I'd recommend contacting CPA as they may have an archive which contains the minutes to meetings of the unity committee".

Society were procured by means of this library as well. The CPA library did not hold all the annual reports of the Society.

The second method of data collection was adopted with regard to resources accessed through the RMIT University libraries. This was a major source of documentary evidence related to the official journals of both bodies, academic journals and, in some cases, newspaper articles. During 2011, documents were accessed from the RMIT University's library which allowed for the borrowing of more than 70 large volumes of bound academic journals and books. These references were taken away from the library for data collection and analysis. In this step, all the historical volumes of books, journals and annual reports were thoroughly analysed and images of relevant pages were taken only when they had information related to the merger attempts. This included pages containing material that had only indirect links with the proposed mergers. This method made data collection a slightly lengthier activity than the time spent at the CPA library for the same process; however, it reduced the time spent reading and analysing such sources, as only the most relevant materials were included.

The images were stored in more than 130 folders and systematically read and analysed during the period May 2011 to February 2016. Four main categories of archival data were identified: (i) annual reports of both bodies (1,285 photographs), (ii) press and newspaper clippings (1,145 photographs), (iii) journals of both bodies (1,246) and (iv) other documents (879) (Table 4.1).

Data were progressively collected because data collection for the first merger attempt and its analysis assisted in developing a systematic process for further data collection. After collecting all the relevant data for the first merger attempt, a detailed analysis was conducted, which then led to writing a research paper. From reading the materials and writing an account of the first merger attempt, a process was developed that assisted in the systematic collection of data for the remaining mergers. This included steps to identify the most relevant sources and ways to access these sources. For example, merger-related discussions appeared in particular sections of the journals of both bodies and in certain sections of newspapers. Hence, data analysis assisted in refining the data collection method and reduced the time spent. Some newspaper clips were collected from online searches using the websites of RMIT University and the State Library of Victoria. Various online databases were accessed through these libraries.

Table 4.1 Photographs taken using digital cameras

	Annual reports	*Press and newspapers clippings*	*Journals of both bodies*	*Other documents*	*Total*
First merger	203 (1961 to 1970)	209	171 (1961 to 1970)	429[3]	1,012
Second merger	355 (1970 to 1981)	319	353 (1970 to 1981)	178	1,205
Third merger	370 (1981 to 1991)	300	310 (1981 to 1991)	121	1,101
Fourth merger	357 (1991 to 1999)	317	412 (1991 to 1999)	151	1,237
Total	1,285	1,145	1,246	879	4,555

Data were primarily collected using a digital camera because, after an initial few weeks of using photocopying, that approach was abandoned because digital photographs were easier to take, save, sort and read. The images were saved using representative names. For example, all images related to the annual report of the Society for 1989 were saved as "ASA1989(1).jpg" and so forth, in a folder named "ASA Annual Report 1989". Similar naming conventions were specifically developed by the researcher for crosschecking and validating cited sources in case of doubt at a later stage. This was supplanted with the "search" command available in the Windows operating system, where the first few letters of any file can be used to search for an item. For example, if the cited source is an annual report of the Society from 1989, then entering "ASA1989" would return the details of folders containing all files relevant to that search. The use of digital photographs and coded naming conventions made data validation and verification very efficient and fast. Using the search command "Control + F" on the keyboard to search for original source photographs was very easy, especially because of the unique naming conventions adopted.

[3] For the first merger attempt, access to the minutes of meetings of the Society's general council was allowed. This proved a valuable source of information because the oral history information and details of the merger proposal in other sources were very limited.

Napier (1989) wrote that a key objective of accounting history work has been linked with understanding the past, knowing more about it and how it may have shaped the present. This has been the main motivating force behind much of historical accounting research. In fact Napier (1989) provided a good summary of key objectives for studying accounting history:

> The intellectual justification covers an interest in the past for its own sake, but more importantly it illuminates the process by which accounting thought, practices and institutions develop, identifying the factors in the environment that induce change and revealing how this change actually occurs. The utilitarian justification is the light that history is considered to throw 'on the origins of concepts, practices and institutions in use today, yielding insight for the solution of modern accounting practices'. (Napier, 1989, p. 239)

To understand accounting's past, it must be discovered through studying original accounting records and secondary sources. The primary motivation behind this study was the desire to understand the events that occurred, the roles of historical actors, and subsequently the context of each of the four merger attempt failures, which is largely an unexplored topic in the past of the Australian accounting profession. The data collection process was lengthy; however, Napier (1989) cautioned accounting historians of this circumstance pointing out that historical data collection processes are time- and labour-intensive. We do experienced this difficulty in data collection and the process was quite lengthy. However, the use of technology and a systematic approach made things easier than they would have been in the past for accounting historians.

The reading of primary documents led to the preparation of draft notes for each merger attempt. These notes were given appropriate headings for respective subsections. For the first merger attempt, the original notes were the lengthiest, largely because a lot of unnecessary details were collected and recorded, as later ascertained. However, for the next three merger attempts, the experience acquired from the data collection for the first merger attempt proved to be valuable, including when classifying and arranging draft notes under appropriate and relevant sections and subsections. These notes became the foundation for writing each of the four chapters to address the four merger attempts. The next subsection explains the process of data collection using oral history techniques.

4.4 Data Collection: Oral History Interviews

Due to the limitations of documentary sources in addressing issues raised in research projects, and the inability to provide direct responses to the questions (Tosh, 2010), this study's data source was supplemented with oral history. As a tool for data collection, oral history has been endorsed by several researchers (Carnegie & Napier, 1996; Collins & Bloom, 1991; Hammond & Sikka, 1996; Previts et al., 1990b). Any examination of primary records only provides us with raw data of history which can be supported with evidence from oral history.

Hammond and Sikka (1996, p. 79) recommended that oral history be used "more frequently in assessing accounting's past, present and future". They further stated that the use of oral history is important for two reasons, as follows:

> Oral histories are important because, first they focus on individual experiences, interpretations, reactions and aspirations. Focusing on these qualitative aspects of history problematizes the notion that accounting, and accounting history, can be neutral, objective and verifiable. Second, most accounting history ignores the role of human agency and struggles (except in the case of a few accounting 'heroes').

Suki Sian (2006) used oral history extensively to conduct research on the professionalisation project in Kenya. Her study found that documentary evidence mainly provided the documented official view of events which was insufficient to provide the context of development of accounting profession in Kenya. Though she used oral history interviews and explored the personal experiences and views of key actors to provide an accurate historical accounting of professionalisation project (Sian, 2006). Oral history provides a unique approach to gathering historical data because it allows the researcher to question the makers of history face to face (Perks, 1995). In this study, interviewees were invited to participate in semi-structured interviews and respond to specific preset questions. Their responses were recorded, transcribed and subjected to analysis. The oral history data were combined with and triangulated against the archival and documentary data gathered in order to assemble a credible story that speaks to our audience (Parker, 1999).

The study of available archival records provided some context, which was further supplemented with the help of oral history to better understand the reasons that led to the mounting of the four merger attempts and their consequential failures. It can be argued that oral history added credibility and validation to the data found in the archives. Researchers have argued that the use of oral history techniques has a key role in making accounting history a mature research discipline. Oral history can be a very effective research tool if the researcher is thoroughly prepared and able to conceal personal feelings (Collins & Bloom, 1991). Arguing the case for the use of oral history, Collins and Bloom (1991) claimed that oral history constitutes verbal recollections of events and circumstances that have occurred in the past from individuals knowledgeable by virtue of their position at the time of their expertise. The process of gathering oral history involves a number of steps, which include "identification of source available", "selection of knowledgeable person as an interviewee", "preliminary research" and "conducting the interview" (Collins & Bloom, 1991). With this description in mind, in this study, individuals who had influence[4] in the accounting profession were listed for interviews, alongside other senior members of the profession, and academic and media commentators.

Many interviews were conducted with relevant historical actors because "no history of developments in the accountancy profession can be related without a consideration of the personalities of leading players" (Walker & Shackleton, 1998, p. 2). Thus, this project sought to capture the experiences of leaders of the accounting profession using oral history techniques because the scope of gathering such evidence becomes limited as time passes. It was already difficult to trace actors from the late 1960s who were active during the period of the first merger attempt.

As a methodology to conduct historical research, oral history has several advantages when used in conjunction with archival research methodology. First, oral history interviews have the potential to unearth documents that are otherwise unknown to the researcher (Parker, 1999; Douglas et al., 1988). Second, oral history can provide new perspectives on research, resulting in new evidence. Third, oral history helps us understand the actions and motivations of those who were involved in taking action (Parker, 1997). Fourth, oral history has the ability to shed light

[4] In all four merger attempts, the final decisions on the proposals were taken by the general and national councils of both bodies. Hence, presidents, vice-presidents and other senior members were included in the scope of interviewees. Other members of the unity committees or integration committees, as these were called across different merger proposals, were also added to the scope for interviews.

on neglected or unknown dimensions of accounting history. Finally, oral history allows us to connect the present with the past (Tyson, 1996). However, the use of information provided by oral history interviews is limited by the fact that people generally more accurately remember those details that were more important to them (Prins, 1991). Despite this limitation, oral history interviews with individuals who made decisions in policy-making, standard setting and developing accounting institutions can make significant contributions to accounting history research (Tyson, 1996). This argument aligns with the objectives of conducting oral history interviews for the current project, where interviews were conducted primarily with those who were involved in the unity discussions via participating in general council meetings, commenting or voting on unity-related decisions taken by the councils, releasing media statements or as members of the committees that were formed to finalise the merger proposals and prepare a schedule of merger votes. Oral history gives us the opportunity to open windows into the past and reconstruct a brief part of previous incidents and events (Tyson, 1996).

The process of contacting all the interviewees involved Kerrie Ludekins first contacting the former presidents, vice-presidents and other council members in the case of the Society. While contacting potential interviewees, Kerrie requested whether she could pass on their contact details to the researcher. All members who responded agreed to be contacted and gave interviews. As already stated, the Institute was unable to provide any assistance of this nature. Thus, a Google search was conducted using various keywords to locate the whereabouts of former presidents of the Institute's general council. By doing so, the former presidents of the Institute for each of the three later merger attempts were able to be contacted, of whom two responded and were interviewed. An attempt was made to contact all the members of respective unity committees and other senior members of the general and national councils of both bodies. However, apart from seven interviewees others could not be traced or contacted. Moreover, major decisions related to the merger were taken by the most senior members of both bodies, that is, presidents or vice-presidents, which further limited the pool of individuals who could be interviewed to justify the stated objectives of this research.

For the first merger attempt, two oral history interviews were conducted: one with Geoffrey Orr, the president of the Society in 1968, and, in that capacity, a member of the unity committee, and one with James Dunkley, a member of the general council in 1969. Geoffrey Orr was interviewed in his home at Harvey Bay, Queensland, while James Dunkley was interviewed at his residence in Adelaide, South Australia. These interviews were based on a series of structured and semi-structured questions and were conducted on 17 May 2014 and 26 April 2014, respectively. Both interviewees responded to questions to the extent they could recall.

For the second merger attempt, two further oral history interviews were conducted. Fortunately, the presidents of the Institute and the Society at the time of the second merger attempt were available for interviews. The president of the Institute at the time of the second merger attempt was Geoff Neilson AM, who was interviewed on 20 February 2015 at his office in Geelong, Victoria. The president of the Society at the time of the second merger attempt, and immediately afterwards, was John Miller. An interview was conducted with John Miller on 26 April 2015 at his residence in Toorak, Victoria. Both interviewees responded to questions to the extent they could recall. Their permission was gained to cite them using the same process as for other interviewees.

For the third merger attempt, the president of the Society, Graeme McGregor, was interviewed on 14 December 2015 at his residence in Portarlington, Victoria. The president of the Institute, Nick Burton Taylor, gave a telephone interview on 21 March 2016. For the fourth merger attempt, the president of the Society during that period, David Boymal, was interviewed at his home on 8 February 2016 in Armadale, Victoria. The then-president of the Institute, Robert Atkinson, did not respond to requests for an interview.

All interviewees were requested to give permission which was duly gained to cite them from interview transcripts in research publications, including citation of their names and the names of any other individuals referenced in their responses. Drafts of the transcripts were provided to both interviewees, who were afforded the opportunity to correct or edit the transcripts as appropriate.

4.5 Conclusion

The limitations of the archival research method are that the quality of the research depends on the archival information available and the skills of researcher (Anderson, 2010). In this study, the time consumed during data collection made the collection process challenging; however, this was overcome because data were collected for a period of nearly four years while work on other chapters was also conducted. Coincidently, oral history interviews including associated travel commitments, also have limitations because recollections of interviewees may be contaminated by past grievances and nostalgia (Tyson, 1996). Oral history interviews and creating transcripts for use in historical research is also a time-consuming process. This process includes the time spent in data collection and in analysing the volume of data gathered (Collins & Bloom, 1991). Oral history interviews also have problems with differing recollections, reluctance to reveal any sensitive or controversial information, self-motivated interpretations and the desire to correct or censor information (Collins & Bloom, 1991).

According to Sevilla et al. (1992, p. 87):

> historical research can only give a fractional view of the past; its knowledge is never complete and is derived from surviving records of a limited number of past events. It is, therefore, a matter of conjecture how history can represent past events adequately.

Further use of oral history allowed this project to overcome the issue of conjecture outlined by these authors. A key limitation of historical research is that since past events and personalities cannot be re-created, the researcher needs to rely on observations and materials which will make the facts certain to them (Sevilla et al., 1992). We considered this statement by referencing all available resources and interviewing the individuals who were involved in making key decisions regarding the mounting of the four merger attempts.

This chapter has explained the methodology that was adopted to collect data from public archives and oral history interviews. The experience gained from the data collected for the first merger attempt assisted in collecting data for the next versions. This chapter has also contrasted the strengths of critical and interpretative historical research and explained how the current research project fits within this category. The next chapter provides an overview of theoretical frameworks used in this book and how they are applied to understand the findings of this project.

References

Anderson, C. (2010). Presenting and evaluating qualitative research. *American Journal of Pharmaceutical Education, 74*(8), 141.

Bedeian, A. G. (1998). Exploring the past. *Journal of Management History, 4*(1), 4–15.

Carnegie, G. D. (2009). The development of accounting regulation, education and literature in Australia, 1788– 2005. *Australian Economic History Review, 49*(3), 276–301.

Carnegie, G. D., & Napier, C. (2012). Accounting's past, present and future: The unifying power of history. *Accounting, Auditing & Accountability Journal, 25*(2), 328–369.

Carnegie, G. D., & Napier, C. J. (1996). Critical and interpretive histories: Insights into accounting's present and future through its past. *Accounting, Auditing & Accountability Journal, 9*(3), 7–39.

Carnegie, G. D., & O'Connell, B. T. (2012). Understanding the responses of professional accounting bodies to crises: The case of the Australian profession in the 1960s. *Accounting Auditing and Accountability Journal, 25*(5), 835–875.

Collins, M., & Bloom, R. (1991). The role of oral history in accounting. *Accounting, Auditing and Accountability Journal, 4*(4), 23–31.

Douglas, L., Roberts, A., & Thompson, R. (1988). Oral history: A handbook. (No Title).

Eisenhardt, K., & Graebner, M. E. (2007). Theory-building from cases: Opportunities and challenges. *Academy of Management Review, 50*(1), 25–32.

Eisenhardt, K. M. (1989). Building theories from case study research. *Academy of Management Review, 14*(4), 532–550.

Fleischman, R. K., & Tyson, T. N. (1997). Archival researchers: An endangered species? *Accounting Historians Journal, 24*(2), 91–109.

Fleischman, R. K., Mills, P. A., & Tyson, T. N. (1996). A theoretical primer for evaluating and conducting historical research in accounting. *Accounting History, 1*(1), 55–75.

Funnell, W. (1996). Preserving history in accounting: Seeking common ground between 'new' and 'old' accounting history. *Accounting, Auditing & Accountability Journal, 9*(4), 38–64.

Gomes, D., Carnegie, G. D., Napier, C. J., Parker, L. D., & West, B. (2011). Does accounting history matter? *Accounting History, 16*(4), 389–402.

Hammond, T., & Sikka, P. (1996). Radicalizing accounting history, the potential of oral history. *Accounting, Auditing & Accountability Journal, 9*(3), 79–97.

Miller, P., Hopper, T., & Laughlin, R. (1991). The new accounting history: An introduction. *Accounting, Organisations and Society, 16*(5/6), 395–403.

Napier, C. J. (1989). Research directions in accounting history. *British Accounting Review, 21*(3), 237–254.

Parker, L. D. (1997). Informing historical research in accounting and management: Traditions, philosophies, and opportunities. *The Accounting Historians Journal, 24*(2), 111–149.

Parker, L. D. (1999). Historiography for the new millennium: Adventures in accounting and management. *Accounting History, 4*(2), 11–42.

Parker, L. D. (2015). Accounting historiography: Looking back to the future. *Meditari Accountancy Research, 23*(2), 142–157.

Perks, R. (1995). *Oral history: Talking about the past* (vol. 94.). Twayne Publishers.

Previts, G. J., Parker, L. D., & Coffman, E. N. (1990a). Accounting history: Definition and relevance. *Abacus, 26*(1), 1–16.

Previts, G. J., Parker, L. D., & Coffman, E. N. (1990b). An accounting historiography: Subject matter and methodology. *Abacus, 26*(2), 136–158.

Richardson, A. J., & Jones, D. B. (2007). Professional 'brand', personal identity and resistance to change in the Canadian accounting profession: A comparative history of two accounting association merger negotiations. *Accounting History, 12*(2), 135–164.

Robson, C. (2002). *Real world research: A resource for social scientists and practitioner researchers*. Blackwell.

Sevilla, C. G., Ochave, J. A., Punsalan, T. G., Regala, B. P., & Uriarte, G. G. (1992). *Research Methods*. Rex Book Store.

Sian, S. (2006). Inclusion, exclusion and control: The case of the Kenyan accounting professionalisation project. *Accounting, Organisations and Society, 31*(3), 295–322.

Tosh, J. (2010). *The pursuit of history: Aims, methods and new directions in the study of modern history* (5th ed.). Pearson Longman.

Tyson, T. (1996). Rendering the unfamiliar intelligible: Discovering the human side of accounting's past through oral history interviews. *The Accounting Historians Journal, 23*(2), 87–109.

Walker, S. P., & Shackleton, K. (1995). Corporatism and structural change in the British accountancy profession, 1930–1957. *Accounting, Organisations and Society, 20*(6), 467–503.

Walker, S. P., & Shackleton, K. (1998). A ring fence for the profession: Advancing the closure of British accountancy 1957–1970. *Accounting, Auditing & Accountability Journal, 11*(1), 34–71.

Yin, R. K. (2009). *Case study research: Design and methods* (4th ed.). Sage.

CHAPTER 5

Understanding the Failed Merger Attempts Through Theoretical Frameworks

5.1 Introduction

The mergers of accounting associations is a complex process that is impacted by many factors. To understand such complexities and provide a critical analysis of developments that led to the mounting and failure of mergers, we apply two complementary theoretical frameworks. The first framework is the boundary-work construct used in the sociology of science (Gieryn, 1983, 1995, 1999; Gieryn et al., 1985), and augmented by Annisette (2017) in the study of accounting profession, and the second framework is "the dilemma of exclusiveness versus market control" (Macdonald & Ritzer, 1988) which has been widely used in understanding the development of professional accounting associations. These two frameworks are complimentary as both explain the interplay of factors at both the organisational level and membership level. One set of factors operate at macro level and are impacted by decisions taken by leadership teams of both professional bodies. Such decisions are taken by leaders of profession organisations keeping the best interest of the organisation and profession in mind. On the other hand, the final decision to approve merger of professional accounting associations lied with members of both organisations who voted to accept or reject any merger proposal. The way membership of perceived elite accounting association, i.e. the Institute responded, we argue that their voting choices to reject proposed mergers were impacted by individual self-interest. In other words, these

J. Sidhu et al., *Understanding the Sociology of the Accounting Profession*,
https://doi.org/10.1007/978-981-99-1572-9_5

factors played a role at micro level. Two theoretical frameworks analyse the interplay of factors at micro and macro levels and provide analysis of findings.

Boundary work is used as the main theoretical framework and is complemented by the second framework, the dilemma of exclusiveness versus market control. The first theoretical framework is applied to the strategies of both bodies in creating entry-level requirements for new members. These are understood as boundaries around the membership of each professional body. The boundaries of the Institute's membership feature stricter requirements for admittance as a member than do those of the Society; thus, this model's application is at a micro level. The reasons for the Institute's stricter requirements for becoming a member are that higher standards of professional practice are expected from members due to the entry of most new members into public practice. The four merger attempts that are the focus of this book were supported by the leaders of both professional bodies amidst discursive claims of the benefits of "oneness". However, a second and distinctive discourse was also mobilised at the membership level as some CAs asserted their superiority over the members of the Society. Members of the Institute applied linguistic claims of their superiority to reinforce boundaries around their membership and to exclude any new entrants. Discursive claims are used to label members outside the organisation, with low levels of competency and abilities (Annisette, 2017) and boundary work is applied to understand and analyse these two competing linguistic claims that ultimately led to three further failed merger attempts. The second theoretical framework is adopted to gain understanding of the business models of each professional accounting association at a macro level.

This chapter examines the theoretical models via three sections. The first two sections build the case for applying each of these theoretical models, while the third section provides a summary of the theoretical models. This chapter concludes with comparisons made of both frameworks and explanations of their applicability to this study.

5.2 Boundary Work

The proposed concept of Gieryn (1983) of boundary work and boundaries (such as boundary setting, maintenance, management, shifting, blurring and bridging) has been used in a broad spectrum of disciplines in many studies (Allen, 1997, 2001; Anagnostopoulos, 2006; Annisette,

2017; Bach et al., 2012; Carmel, 2006; Hunter, 2005; Jasanoff, 1995; Lamont, 1992, 2000; Pacholok, 2009; Pachucki et al., 2007; Perry, 2002; Sherman, 2005, 2006; Wray, 2006; Young, 2014) covering research in medicine, accounting, ethnicity, racism, gender bias, professionalisation, religion and risk management (Annisette, 2017; Pachucki et al., 2007). In his framework, Gieryn (1983, p. 782) stated that:

> the focus is on ***boundary-work*** of scientists: their attribution of selected characteristics to the institution of science (i.e. to its practitioners, methods, stock of knowledge, values and work organisation) for purposes of constructing a social boundary that distinguishes some intellectual activities as 'non-science' [emphasis in original].

Boundary work involves boundary shaping, construction, maintenance, management and blurring (Gieryn, 1983, 1999). Before Gieryn (1983), Kohler (1982) gave a general definition of disciplinary boundaries. According to Kohler (1982, p. 1), disciplines are "political institutions that demarcate areas of academic territory, allocate privileges and responsibilities of expertise, and structure claims on resources". This definition applies to the Australian accounting profession where both professional bodies created membership levels with minimum academic entry level requirements, and acquired privileged roles to provide specialised services, such as auditing and taxation, that were ultimately associated with economic rewards. These occupational roles were protected by the membership of professional bodies, particularly for the Institute, whose entry level requirements for membership were stricter due to the use of a macro-level business model of exclusivity, which is explained in the latter part of this chapter. Disciplinary boundaries are not rational but again the result of past battles and in a state of permanent tension (Cash, 1997). The four merger attempts that are the subject of this investigation led to an ongoing tension around efforts to change the boundaries of the Institute's membership. This issue is discussed in detail in the four chapters that follow.

Although boundary work has been extensively used in other disciplines, a recent study by Annisette (2017) has specifically applied boundary-work concepts in research on the Canadian accounting profession. According to Gieryn (1983, p. 792) "boundary-work excludes rivals from within by defining them as outsiders with labels such as 'pseudo', 'deviant', or 'amateur'". Therefore, the dynamics of inclusion and exclusion are central to the processes of boundary construction and in creating hierarchies within the professions (Lamont & Molnár, 2002). In the context of Canadian accounting profession exclusionary processes were used in boundary construction to exclude "foreign-trained" immigrant accountants. This was achieved through linguistic claims by the "labelling of immigrant accountants" as "foreign-trained" or "internationally trained", which in itself is part of the everyday practice of separating "us" from "them". In this way, public discourse was used to create boundaries to exclude "immigrant accountant as one whose training and experience being labelled as 'foreign'; is 'not known and suspicious' and is of low worth in the domestic order" (Annisette & Trivedi, 2013, p. 14).

In her more recent study, Annisette (2017) has applied boundary-work concepts to the professional accounting setting in Canada, supplemented by insights drawn from Mary Douglas' anthropology of pollution (Douglas, 1966; Douglas & Wildavsky, 1982). In that study boundary-work concepts were extended through a distinctive emphasis on the discursive aspects of boundary construction and this study is also important in differentiating boundary work from the more traditional emphasis on "closure" within professionalisation studies. The sharp analytical distinction between boundary work and closure is due to the operationalisation strategy of both, the objective of closure is control of the market, the objective of boundary work is control over meanings (Annisette, 2017). Annisette's study is set within the context of an intra-professional demarcation: between local-trained and foreign-trained accountants in Ontario. As such, its broad setting is analogous to that of the current study which focuses on the four failed attempts to unify the two main professional accounting bodies in Australia and the two "classes" of accountants that they embodied. That is, the focus is not on the closure of the Australian accounting profession, which had been attained, but rather on the internal boundaries that have persisted in the post-closure era. Of particular importance are the discursive tactics employed by some members of the Institute, in defiance of their leadership, in seeking to continue to remain separate from non-Chartered Accountants. In this way, the boundary work is depicted as a "useful ideological style" (Gieryn, 1983, p. 787) and when viewed from this perspective can augment understanding of the failure of the four merger attempts between the Institute and the Society.

The case of the four merger attempts relates to these arguments, with membership of the Institute implying an associated higher status. This also meant that accounting professionals who were not members of the Institute were labelled as not possessing the same educational and professional rigour as members of the Institute using linguistic claims. Gieryn (1983) studied how scientists distinguish themselves from non-scientists, and it is possible to apply similar boundary construction regarding MIPP and the Chartered Accountant title, where involvement in public practice was linked with discursive claims of higher intellectual activity, in a comparable manner to the claims of the scientists in Gieryn's (1983) work. Such discursive claims of higher status and better standards were not only made by members of the Institute, but were even accepted by the Society's general council. Evidence of the Society's acceptance is apparent in the following statement of the president of the Society, H. R. Irving (1966):

> The title, 'Chartered Accountant', flows—there is no similar generic title for the public accountant member of the Society. Attempts to gain such a title were defeated some years ago and indicate a lack of appreciation of the problem by members not in public practice, amongst other things. It seems unlikely that any other attempt to create special conditions for public practitioners within the Society would meet with greater success.

The higher status associated with members of the Institute and the branding of the title "Chartered Accountant" or "CA" was achieved using similar discursive arguments to those that Gieryn (1983, p. 781) presented in his studies, where the term "boundary work" was used to describe "an ideological style found in scientists' attempts to create a public image for science by contrasting it favourably to non-scientific intellectual or technical activities". In the case of the Australian accounting profession, boundaries were defined and constructed around permanent constructs: the membership of two professional bodies and the roles played by professional accountants (MIPP and MNIPP). These were then defended and maintained by members of the Institute using linguistic claims of superiority in the terms of Annisette (2017).

According to Gieryn (1983, pp. 787–788), "boundary-work is also a useful ideological style when monopolising professional authority and resources in the hands of some scientists by excluding others as "pseudo-scientists". Gieryn (1983, p. 784) argued that the boundaries of science are not permanent and that "professional conflict for authority and prestige" continues to occur. Such issues also arose in the case of the merger attempts. Norris (2001) studied boundary maintenance by different sub-occupations in the medical profession via a case study of musculoskeletal problems, and concluded that boundary management is an important aspect of occupational control.

In his study, Gieryn (1983) hinted at the potential to apply boundary-work concepts in other occupations, such as accounting. Jasanoff (1995, cited in Annisette, 2017) acted on this suggestion to distinguish between "'good' and 'bad' work within a single discipline, between different disciplines, and between 'science' and other forms of authoritative knowledge". Swedlow (2007) reaffirmed the broad application of boundary-work concepts, stating that they not only have application to distinguish scientists from non-scientists, but can also be used to distinguish among scientists. In a similar manner, boundary-work constructs may also be applied to distinguish members of the Institute and the Society based on claims of higher expertise. Annisette (2017) provides the most recent and refined application of boundary work and thereby aids the interpretation and application of its concepts. Hence, in this thesis Annisette (2017) informs the analysis of the research findings.

In addition, as aforementioned, boundary construction and management is not only limited to membership with professional bodies or categories of professional work, but can also be applied to gender bias. Past studies found that boundaries were drawn around the genders of medical practitioners, arguing that epistemic authority of nursing knowledge is determined by factors such as the gender structure of nursing (Cash, 1997). Due to the existence of gender bias, knowledge products of the nursing profession are given low epistemic status by both nurses and non-nurses. Hence, the masculinised profession of doctors is accorded a higher status than nursing. This is a classic example of boundaries being created and maintained on the basis of a prevalent gender bias in a given society.

In the case of the Swedish Armed Forces study by Persson (2010) found that occupational boundaries were drawn around male gender but as entry of women increased in armed forces these boundaries were redrawn. Due to a changing environment, the Swedish Armed Forces are now engaged in peacekeeping operations, which requires employment to be opened up to civilians, including women. When women enter settings traditionally occupied by and associated with men, established gender patterns tend to rupture. Hence the traditional boundaries around armed forces work are gradually modified due to blurring of roles associated with male gender. Similar to the case of the Swedish Armed Forces, the merger of two accounting associations is likely to challenge the existing dominant roles played by public practitioners in the Institute.

With a change of context, a profession deploys defensive strategies to protect boundaries (Fournier, 2000). A key strategy is to reconstitute boundaries along which the professions build new strategies of legitimisation (Fournier, 2000). By making four attempts to merge and create a single professional accounting body, the Institute and the Society sought to redraw the traditional boundaries around membership of both bodies. Just as Persson (2010) argued that including women in roles associated with men can "rupture" the traditional boundaries of a masculinised profession, similarly, in the merger attempts, the boundaries created around public practice, and, by implication, primarily around membership of the Institute, faced a potential threat: the inclusion of large numbers of members who were perceived to hold lower status.

Authors argue that boundaries are not permanent structures and are subject to change as a consequence of developments in the social, political and economic spheres (Annisette & Trivedi, 2013). Similarly, in the case of four merger attempts both professional bodies were proposing changes to the boundaries of their membership. The racial boundaries in the US constructed around "white" identities expanded over time to incorporate Irish immigrants (Ignatiev, 1995) and Jews (Brodkin, 1998). These groups were earlier cast as racial "non-whites" (Annisette & Trivedi, 2013). This shows a dynamic nature of social boundaries and successful changes with change of context.

Boundary-work concepts were applied in the case of masculinised hospital administration in the US, which is otherwise a female-dominated occupation. The hospital administration was masculinised because the American Hospital Association defined the personal characteristics of hospital administrators in a manner that created a male image of practitioners, and advocated formal training in the field that further linked the occupation to management in the private sector. Management in the private sector was male dominated. By doing this, the association created boundaries to deter women entering senior levels of hospital administration (Arndt & Bigelow, 2005). Hence, boundary work was aimed at reducing the number of women in this occupation in senior leadership roles. The boundaries of hospital administration favoured male leadership and, despite being a female-dominated profession, it was masculinised.

Using a case study of a catastrophic fire in western Canada in 2003, Pacholok (2009) applied boundary-work concepts to understand the creation of hierarchies within the firefighting effort, which positioned some occupational groups as superior and others as subordinate. Particular status differences existed between wildland and structural firefighters: some structural fire departments were reluctant to receive forest fire training from wildland firefighters because they were seasonal workers and were subsequently viewed as less professional. Additionally, the wildland firefighters did not carry the same cultural capital as structural firefighters, who had been granted heroic status by the media and the public in the wake of the attacks in the US on 11 September 2001 (Pacholok, 2009). Studies also found that the firefighters used self-identity to create boundaries between themselves and those to whom they felt superior (Lamont, 2000).

Lamont (1992) also studied status hierarchies between working-class and upper-middle-class men in the US and France. She extended the boundary work to include the "identity process", which is used by people to differentiate themselves from others (Lamont, 1992). This is achieved by individuals placing themselves as superior to other groups (Lamont, 2000). Sherman (2005, 2006) made further contributions to boundary work by extending its original concepts. In the case of service workers in luxury hotels and a study explored how they maintained their dignity and status while performing service work that automatically positioned them as inferior to privileged hotel guests (Sherman, 2005, 2006).

Another development in boundary work included the expansion of its application to the strategic management of collective identities, cultural classification, construction of authenticity, moral boundary maintenance and genre crossing. This work has also been extended to ethno-racial boundaries that intersect with class, immigration and nationhood. In other words, boundary work also includes dynamic and symbolic boundaries (Pachucki et al., 2007).

An example of boundary work used in ethno-racial contexts can be seen in its application to a case study of multiracial schooling (Perry, 2002). Students from white backgrounds drew boundaries around their racial identities by depicting what it meant to be white when distinguishing themselves from students of other races. Further, studies showed ethnic boundary construction among white working-class people by examining the everyday interactions between black and white people (McDermott, 2006). This framework has also been applied in historical contexts, including when Wray (2006) applied this work to distinguish between high- and low-income white people. Wray found that the use of labels such as "white trash" were common to identify people with low incomes. These works relate to the current project because they encompass micro-level boundary construction. In both these studies, boundaries were constructed and maintained by the assumed "higher" group, which was achieved by disassociating black people through the use of labels of superiority. In other words, these were discursive claims to distinguish and separate black people (Annisette, 2017). In the case of the Australian accounting profession, such boundaries were constructed by members of the Institute, initially around public practice and then around membership of their professional body and the Chartered Accountant title. Similar to the cited studies, this work was undertaken at a micro level.

Young (2014, p. 713) also applied this concept, using it to explain how the US-based Financial Accounting Standards Board "appears to have successfully established and maintained a boundary between a technical accounting process and politics". As indicated in this chapter, the boundary-work concept embraces boundary maintenance or boundary management (see, for example, Allen, 1997, 2001; Bach et al., 2012; Carmel, 2006; Hunter, 2005). Allen (1997, 2001) focused attention on the maintenance of boundaries in examining instances of conflicts between nurses, doctors and healthcare workers. Hunter (2005, p. 253) studied the case of midwives in the UK and found that, after creating social boundaries between senior and junior levels of the occupation, midwives used different strategies to "maintain intra-occupational boundaries". Discursive claims of higher expertise and experience were used to create and defend those boundaries.

In a similar regulatory context, Hazgui and Gendron (2015) applied the concept of boundary work to the study of the French audit profession, where a regulatory system of "co-regulation" was developed that was a mix of independent regulation and self-regulation. Challenges to the professional boundaries of public accounting practice have also been scrutinised. Wood, Hill and Cottrell (2022) found that interprofessional collaborative practice does not always occur in practice. They found that a key reason can be the clinician's identity and its interplay with interprofessional identity. This is an example of interprofessional boundary work. Glucina et al. (2020) looked at the professional identity perceptions of chiropractors. They found that chiropractors consider themselves as primary care practitioners with a broad scope and not just limited to musculoskeletal management. Mitchell and Boyle (2021) looked at the potential for professional identity salience to enhance healthcare team innovation. Best et al. (2021) found that the mobilisation of professional identity is a determinant of interprofessional teamwork which made it harder for practitioners to think like others while in an interprofessional team.

Further studies examined boundary maintenance between sub-occupational groups of doctors, nurses and other submedical professions. For example, Allen (1997) examined relationships between nurses and doctors in the light of "blurring boundaries". In a later study, Allen (2001) found that nurses were "negotiating" and redrawing boundaries not just with doctors, but also with other classes of healthcare workers. Carmel (2006) concluded that, following the blurring of boundaries in an intensive care unit, new boundaries at the organisational level, particularly between senior nurses and junior doctors over shared roles and responsibilities, were enforced between the intensive care unit and other parts of the hospital. Bach et al. (2012) examined the case of health workers and the maintenance of boundaries between doctors and nurses and between various nursing roles based on different specialisations. For example, nurses were found to have distinguished themselves from lower status occupations, such as healthcare assistants, within the nursing hierarchy.

A paper by Golyagina and Valuckas (2020) provides discussion and investigation of employing expansion boundary work in globalisation and hybrid professionalism contexts. Key areas of exploration were the boundary work of IMA officials and IMA members in Russia with a focus on linking boundary work to globalisation. The study suggests that the properties of professional boundaries influence the professionalisation process. Professional boundaries constructed around auditor's identity is positively associated with commercialisation. Construction of professional identities is linked with self-privilege (Guo, 2012). In South Korean context Ahn and Jacobs (2019) found that Korean accountants perceived that working in non-public practice was demeaning. They held beliefs that their professional identify and image were at risk if they worked in non-public accounting roles. Over time symbolic value of their accounting degrees became weaker which was the result of increase in qualified accountants. This led to South Korean accountants constructing boundaries of their professional identity account public service.

This Australian study extends the application of the concept to the context of mergers between professional accounting associations. This study involves accounting professionals working in a self-created hierarchy of different types of professional accounting services. It examines the ideological efforts of CAs, namely, members of the Institute, who have a tradition of providing a range of specialised professional accounting services to the public as MIPP, to continue to remain separate from non-CAs, who are generally employed in a wide variety of accounting roles in specific organisations as MNIPP. The boundary-work concept is seen as a "useful ideological style" (Gieryn, 1983, p. 787) to augment an understanding of the failure of the four merger attempts between the Institute and the Society. Thus, the current study is not concerned primarily with the construction of boundaries, but with how particular members of an occupation, specifically, accounting, negotiated and defended boundaries. Of particular importance is the boundary constructed around the membership of the Institute, which distinguished itself with its Royal Charter and its primary representation of members engaged in public practice.

Within the accounting profession, discursive claims of higher accounting expertise by public practitioners, based on prolonged training and rigorous entrance and education standards, meant that boundaries were drawn around public practice. Voting against the proposed mergers meant successful maintenance of these boundaries, which were defended using linguistic claims of superiority by members of the Institute (Annisette, 2017). In this book, we focus on the boundary maintenance aspect of boundary work by applying the theoretical perspective to the unsuccessful merger attempts in the Australian accounting profession, where tensions similar to those existing in a medical setting arose, and where the behaviour of a sufficient number of members of the higher-status group precluded a major change to the existing boundaries.

This section concludes by drawing on many past studies on boundary work. As discussed earlier, this framework is applied at the micro level of professional control because it relates to the creation and maintenance of occupational boundaries. The next section examines the second framework, which is adopted as a complementary model I, applied at the macro level of professional control and relates to the structure of the Australian accounting profession. Although linked to closure, boundary work is distinct from it, in "providing the professional project with a unique set of resources and challenges" (Annisette, 2017, p. 3). Closure of the accounting profession in Australia had commenced with the formation of professional bodies in the late nineteenth century and this "project"

(Larson 1977) was essentially completed by the mid-twentieth century (see, for example, Carnegie & Edwards, 2001; Carnegie et al., 2003; Chua & Poullaos, 1998). However, while the profession had collectively won the battle for jurisdiction over accounting work (Abbott, 1988), an internecine battle persisted between different classes of accountants within that jurisdiction. This battle would be characterised by claims and counterclaims: in short, a "war of words" about issues such as the superiority or inferiority of certain classes of accountants and the possible benefits or costs of unifying the profession.

5.3 Exclusivity Versus Market Control

The second interpretive framework applied in the study, "the dilemma of exclusiveness versus market control" (Macdonald & Ritzer, 1988, p. 257), is intended to assist in further understanding the outcome of the merger proposals under investigation. In particular, this second framework focuses attention on the new "business model" proposed by the two professional accounting bodies, whose four merger attempts are under examination. Professional associations have a choice to either adopt an exclusiveness-based membership strategy or adopt market control strategy with a large number of members. In the first instance, membership of professional associations is strongly guarded with strict entry-level requirements. Bu controlling inflow of membership, an exclusive or elite association of paractioners is created. In the second case, membership requirements are relaxed and a large number of members enable an association to achieve market control with the sheer volume of work, membership strength and ability of association to run market campaigns due to revenue generated from a large membership base.

According to Macdonald and Ritzer (1988, pp. 257–258), "In order to control the market, the occupational body must include anyone with a reasonable claim to expertise, but such inclusion brings in marginal practitioners who lower the standing of higher-status members". Thus, a professional body must decide whether to include marginal practitioners, who may lower professional standing and reputation. In contrast, those who Macdonald and Ritzer (1988, pp. 257–258) called "higher-status members" provide a foundation to build exclusive status. The accountants have been involved in the process of exclusion, struggle to ensure market control and especially their ability to "self-regulate" (MacDonald, 1985).

The strict enforcement of boundaries constructed around the memberships of professional associations meant that those who were excluded were left to create their own associations. The status differentials between members engaged in public practice and individuals employed in industry, government and other sectors led to a proliferation of accounting associations in many countries (Caramanis, 1999, 2002, 2005; Carnegie et al., 2003; Carnegie & O'Connell, 2012; Carnegie & Parker, 1999; Chua & Poullaos, 1993, 1998; Linn, 1996; Macdonald & Ritzer, 1988; Noguchi & Edwards, 2008; Poullaos, 1994; West, 2003, Chap. 3).

Edwards et al. (2013) studied the development of the Accounting Researchers International Association (ARIA) in 1974. The ARIA leadership was faced with the "dilemma of exclusiveness versus market control" (Macdonald & Ritzer, 1988, p. 257). The authors argued:

> ARIA, although an elite organisation, recognised the need to move beyond its initially narrow membership base if it were to wield influence within the accounting domain. However, the strict admission criteria proved a significant stumbling block. (Edwards et al., 2013, p. 371)

Therefore, ARIA's strategy was finally settled as that of exclusivity, establishing it as an elite association of academic researchers. According to Parker (2014, p. 176), selection of either of the two strategies is a difficult choice because:

> If they become too exclusionary, elite bodies risk loss of control of the market for their professional services by failing to admit to membership a sufficient proportion of the total number of the suppliers of those services. On the other hand, a more inclusive strategy risks the admission of marginal practitioners.

In a study of naming and branding practices, accountants and accounting bodies in the British Empire and Commonwealth between 1853 and 2003, Parker (2005) applied Macdonald and Ritzer (1988) and found that "Exclusionary names and designations are those that indicate the occupation and, sometimes, the territory over which an occupational body is claiming jurisdiction" (Parker, 2005, p. 10). Other applications of the Framework include Annisette (1999) who examined post-independence change in Trinidad and Tobago from importing British professional accountants to the importing of British professional qualifications. Annisette (1999) examined how changes in the political and social context led to the development of a local accounting profession. Edwards et al. (2005) explored the formation of the ICAEW and its organisational strategy, including the inclusion of members of its antecedent bodies. They argued:

> The choice is either to confine membership to high status practitioners, thus ensuring the almost certain emergence of competitor institutions, or to include all members of an occupational group and thereby accept the risk, at least in the short term, of a diminished public perception of a group's professional ranking within society. (Edwards et al., 2005, p. 229)

Anderson and Chandler (2005) found the application of the Framework in the British accounting profession where multiple attempts to create an exclusive accounting profession failed. These included attempts to get Bills passed for state registration of accounting and an attempt to make it unlawful for any person not on the register of accountants to engage in public practice (Anderson & Chandler, 2005).

The formation of professional accounting associations based on "exclusiveness versus market control" has been a key feature of the British, Canadian and Australian accounting professions (Annisette & O'Regan, 2007; Carnegie & Parker, 1999; Carr-Saunders & Wilson, 1964; Poullaos, 1993; Richardson, 1989b; Walker & Shackleton, 1995). It is also noteworthy that the IIAV, one of the predecessor bodies of the Society, was initially formed with the notion of an association of "public practitioners", having a standard for service to the public in order to gain confidence and support. According to one of the 45 founders of the IIAV, Thomas Brentnall, the founding members looked at the ICAEW, SAA and the Scottish chartered bodies and decided to emulate the British bodies by following their lead (Carnegie et al., 2003). However, leaders of the IIAV gradually "felt that openness had more to offer than closure" (Chua & Poullaos, 1998, p. 170).

The final strategy of IIAV was that of market control. However, originally it had planned to adopt exclusiveness strategy. The SSA planned to create a local branch in Melbourne in December 1885. As a result, the organisational strategy of the IIAV settled to that of market control. Carnegie (2016, p. 392) pointed out "It was probably the influence of Cooper and the constitution of the SAA as readily available to local accountants which resulted in the adoption of the IIAV's market control strategy". The IIAV's organisational strategy relied more on a broad membership and "did not distinguish between different types of accounting work" (Carnegie et al., 2003, p. 793). In other words, the boundaries of membership were relaxed in the case of the IIAV. The membership strategies of the IIAV were very different from those of the ICAEW. As Chua and Poullaos (1993, p. 702) noted:

> Its closure strategies were based not on the nature of work (i.e. public vs non-public) but on its capacity to make visible the intellectual ability and morality of one group of accountants. This group was largely drawn from the 'middle class'.

Thus, they adopted an inclusive model for the membership of the professional body. In contrast, the ACPA "restricted membership to those engaged in public practice" (Carnegie et al., 2003, p. 793). This means that the boundaries of the profession were created around the membership of a professional body, that is, the "business model" of creating an exclusive body was implemented at the micro level by restricting entry to the profession through creating boundaries.

A key theme leading to the failure of the four merger attempts was the contention between MIPP and MNIPP, that is, plans to change the traditional "business model" adopted by both professional accounting bodies. This contention was not only seen in the failure of the merger attempts but also in earlier instances of MIPP–MNIPP tensions. For example, Carnegie et al. (2003) noted that, in 1908, at a conference involving both sides in the IIAV, MNIPP objected to the presence of some members of the IIAV who were in public practice on ACPA councils.

It was not only the IIAV that originally adopted the "exclusiveness" model, and it appears that the initial choice of most professional accounting bodies was that of "exclusiveness". During the first five years after its formation (1885 to 1890), the ADSA restricted membership to accountants engaged in public practice only. It is clear that, although the majority of initial accounting bodies were formed with a view to create a profession consisting of MIPP, they could not practically pursue this objective. Later this issue became a serious contention, leading to a dichotomy in the Australian accounting profession that is still present, given the four failed merger attempts to unify the accounting profession in Australia.

Australian bodies were not the only ones that faced the dilemma of "exclusiveness versus market control". More evidence of these dilemmas can be seen in Scotland, where, between 1884 and 1900, nine attempts to challenge the monopoly of the Chartered Accountant title were successfully rejected by chartered bodies (Walker, 1991). In 1886, the lower-status Scottish Institute of Accountants attempted to foster joint efforts to unify the Scottish accounting profession; however, the leadership of the chartered bodies refused to cooperate because it challenged their "exclusiveness" model. As such, attempts to dilute the status of CAs through changes in boundaries were successfully challenged and defeated on the basis that it was against the public interest and that non-Chartered Accountant body members were "not professional" (Walker, 1991, pp. 268–269). In 1930, the British government rejected demands for the state registration of accountants. The chartered institutes, which feared dilution of their status, were opposed to the registration proposal. However, lower-status organisations strongly favoured state registration, viewing registration as an opportunity to be placed alongside CAs. In 1930 and 1935, the ICAEW entered discussions with the SIAA for the merger of both bodies, but the top management of the ICAEW rejected the idea (Shackleton & Walker, 1998). These examples reveal how members of higher-status organisations are likely to be circumspect about proposals to merge with associations that they perceive to be of lower status. Thus, higher-status organisations continue to protect the boundaries of their membership by rejecting mergers with lower-status organisations, thereby protecting their "business model" of "exclusiveness".

In Australia, CAs have traditionally been broadly recognised as holding higher professional status than non-CAs. The Institute prioritised the "exclusivity" dimension, while the Society focused on the pursuit of "market control", as distinct organisational strategies. Given this segmentation, the proposed mergers between the Institute and the Society effectively sought to combine the strategies of exclusivity and market control for adoption by a single accounting association in a unified accounting profession. As proposed, the merged accounting body was to become "exclusive" in the form of a single ongoing professional association, while also becoming a representative body that would seek market control.

When the complementary concepts of boundary work (Gieryn, 1983, 1995, 1999; Jasanoff, 1995; Swedlow 2003, 2007) are applied to exclusivity and market control in the case of the Australian accounting profession, the preferred choice of bodies, wherever possible, appears to be exclusivity. This is evidenced from the mutual struggle to gain a Royal Charter by the predecessor bodies of both the Society and the Institute, with the predecessor bodies of the Institute finally being successful in gaining a charter in 1928. It can be argued that exclusivity and market control are not automatic choices faced by professional bodies. However, exclusivity was the first choice of all bodies. The boundaries were also created around the membership and exclusive status of ACPA. However, the granting of a Royal Charter provided more status to the members of this professional group and the social construction of a status differentiation between MIPP and MNIPP. Unable to gain exclusivity, the excluded bodies adopted for the second strategy of market control.

5.4 Conclusion

The concepts of boundary work and the dilemma of exclusiveness versus market control are seen as complementary perspectives in this study. According to Gieryn (1983, p. 792), boundary work relates to creating and maintaining a monopoly by an occupational group because "expansion, monopolization and protection are generic features of 'professionalization'". As Annisette (2017) demonstrates, these protections are created and shaped by public discourse and linguistic claims. In contrast, Macdonald and Ritzer (1988) addressed the tension between the need for exclusivity and the drive for market control as a key determinant of the historical development of professional groups. Thus, proposed mergers of professional associations typically involve an attempt to dismantle designations and boundaries that have been cast by history, and to redraw underpinning organisational strategies in the event of mergers that are consummated. A paper examining the failure of the first merger attempt was published in The British Accounting Review that applied boundary work lens (Sidhu et al., 2021).

Both theoretical frameworks are applied across four chapters in this book in an attempt to examine changes in the traditional organisational strategies of both bodies; successful protection of the Institute's boundaries by its members; and consequently, the preservation of the different organisational strategies of each body. Chapters 9 and 10 present a comparative analysis and the implications of the study findings, with the application of both theoretical frameworks. The next chapter covers the first merger attempt in detail and applies both theoretical frameworks to the findings.

References

Abbott, A. (1988). *The system of professions: An essay on the division of expert labor*. The University of Chicago Press.

Allen, D. (1997). The nursing-medical boundary: A negotiated order? *Sociology of Health and Illness, 19*(4), 498–520.

Allen, D. (2001). *The changing shape of nursing practice*. Routledge.

Anagnostopoulos, D. (2006). Real students and true demotes: Ending social promotion and the moral ordering of urban high schools. *American Educational Research Journal, 43*(1), 5–42.

Anderson, M., Edwards, J. R., & Chandler, R. A. (2005). Constructing the 'well qualified' chartered accountant in England and Wales. *The Accounting Historians Journal, 32*(2), 5–54.

Annisette, M. (1999). Importing accounting: The case of Trinidad and Tobago. *Accounting, Business & Financial History, 9*(1), 103–133.

Annisette, M. (2017). Discourse of the professions: The making, normalizing and taming of Ontario's foreign-trained accountant. *Accounting, Organizations and Society, 60*, 37–61.

Annisette, M., & O'Regan, P. (2007). Joined for the common purpose: The establishment of the Institute of Chartered Accountants in Ireland as an all-Ireland institution. *Qualitative Research in Accounting & Management, 4*(1), 4–25.

Annisette, M., & Trivedi, V. U. (2013). Globalization, paradox and the (un) making of identities: Immigrant chartered accountants of India in Canada. *Accounting, Organisations and Society, 38*(1), 1–29.

Arndt, M., & Bigelow, B. (2005). Professionalizing and masculinizing a female occupation: The reconceptualization of hospital administration. *Administrative Science Quarterly, 50*, 233–261.

Bach, S., Kessler, I., & Heron, P. (2012). Nursing a grievance? The role of healthcare assistants in a modernized National Health Service. *Gender, Work and Organisation, 19*(2), 205–224.

Best, S., Beech, C., Robbé, I. J., & Williams, S. (2021). Interprofessional teamwork: the role of professional identity and signature pedagogy–a mixed methods study. *Journal of Health Organization and Management*.

Brodkin, K. (1998). *How the Jews became white folk and what that says about race in America*. Rutgers University Press.

Caramanis, C. (1999). International accounting firms versus indigenous auditors: Intra-professional conflict in the Greek auditing profession, 1990–1993. *Critical Perspectives on Accounting, 10*(2), 153–196.
Caramanis, C. (2002). The interplay between professional groups, the state and supranational agents: Pax Americana in the age of globalisation. *Accounting, Organisations and Society, 27*(4/5), 379–408.
Caramanis, C. (2005). Rationalisation, charisma and accounting professionalisation: Perspectives on the intra-professional conflict in Greece, 1993–2001. *Accounting, Organisations and Society, 30*(3), 195–221.
Carmel, S. (2006). Boundaries obscured and boundaries reinforced: Incorporation as a strategy of occupational enhancement for intensive care. *Sociology of Health & Illness, 28*(2), 154–177.
Carnegie, G. D. (2016). The accounting professional project and bank failures. *Journal of Management History, 22*(4), 389–412.
Carnegie, G. D., & Edwards, J. R. (2001). The construction of the professional accountant: The case of the Incorporated Institute of Accountants, Victoria (1886). *Accounting, Organisations and Society, 26*(4/5), 301–325.
Carnegie, G. D., Edwards, J. R., & West, B. P. (2003). Understanding the dynamics of the Australian accounting profession: A prosopographical study of the founding members of the Incorporated Institute of Accountants, Victoria, 1886 to 1908. *Accounting, Auditing & Accountability Journal, 16*(5), 790–820.
Carnegie, G. D., & O'Connell, B. T. (2012). Understanding the responses of professional accounting bodies to crises: The case of the Australian profession in the 1960s. *Accounting Auditing and Accountability Journal, 25*(5), 835–875.
Carnegie, G. D., & Parker, R. H. (1999). Accountants and empire: The case of co-membership of Australian and British accountancy bodies, 1885 to 1914. *Accounting, Business & Financial History, 9*(1), 77–102.
Carr-Saunders, A. M., & Wilson, P. A. (1964). *The professions*. Frank Cass.
Cash, K. (1997). Social epistemology, gender and nursing theory. *International Journal of Nursing Studies, 34*(2), 137–143.
Chua, W. F., & Poullaos, C. (1993). Rethinking the professional-state dynamic: The case of the Victorian charter attempt, 1885–1906. *Accounting, Organizations and Society, 18*(7/8), 691–728.
Chua, W. F., & Poullaos, C. (1998). The dynamics of 'closure' amidst the construction of market, profession, empire and nationhood: An historical analysis of an Australian accounting association, 1886–1903. *Accounting, Organisations and Society, 23*(2), 155–187.
Douglas, M., & Wildavsky, A. B. (1982). *Risk and culture: An essay on the selection of technical and environmental dangers*. University of California Press.

Douglas, M. (1966). *Purity and danger: An analysis of concepts of pollution and taboo*. Praeger.
Edwards, J. R., Anderson, M., & Chandler, R. (2005). How not to mount a professional project: The formation of the ICAEW in 1880. *Accounting and Business Research, 35*(3), 229–248.
Edwards, J. R., Dean, G., Clarke, F., & Wolnizer, P. (2013). Accounting academic elites: The tale of ARIA. *Accounting, Organisations and Society, 38*(5), 365–381.
Fournier, V. (2000). Boundary work and the (un) making of the professions. Professionalism, boundaries and the workplace, 67.
Gieryn, T. F. (1995). Boundaries of science. In S. Jasanoff, G. E Markle, J. C Petersen, & T. Pinch (Eds.), *Handbook of science and technology studies* (393–443). Thousand Oaks.
Gieryn, T. F. (1983). Boundary-work and the demarcation of science from non-science: Strains and interests in the professional ideologies of scientists. *American Sociological Review, 48*(6), 781–795.
Gieryn, T. F. (1999). *Cultural boundaries of science: Credibility on the line*. University of Chicago Press.
Gieryn, T. F., Bevins, G. M., & Zehi, S. C. (1985). Professionalization of American scientists: Public science in the creation/evolution trials. *American Sociological Review, 50*(3), 392–409.
Glucina, T. T., Krägeloh, C. U., Farvid, P., & Holt, K. (2020). Moving towards a contemporary chiropractic professional identity. *Complementary Therapies in Clinical Practice, 39*, 101105.
Golyagina, A., & Valuckas, D. (2020). Boundary-work in management accounting: The case of hybrid professionalism. *The British Accounting Review, 52*(2), 100841.
Guo, K. H. (2012). Understanding why and how some chartered accountants object to the proposed merger of the three accounting professions in Canada. *Accounting Perspectives, 11*(2), 111–130.
Hazgui, M., & Gendron, Y. (2015). Blurred roles and elusive boundaries: On contemporary forms of oversight surrounding professional work. *Accounting, Auditing & Accountability Journal, 28*(8), 1234–1262.
Hunter, B. (2005). Emotion work and boundary maintenance in hospital-based midwifery. *Midwifery, 21*(3), 253–266.
Ignatiev, N. (1995). *How the Irish became white*. Routledge.
Irving, H. R. (1966). Report on professional awards for accountants (designation of CPA) submitted on behalf of the Executive Committee by President, *The Australian Society of Accountants*. 7 October 1966, 1–27.
Jasanoff, S. (1995). *Science at the bar: Law, science, and technology in America*. Harvard University Press.

Kohler, R. E. (1982). *From medical chemistry to biochemistry: The making of a biomedical discipline* (Vol. 5). Cambridge University Press.

Lamont, M. (1992). *Money, morals, and manners: The culture of the French and American upper-middle class*. University of Chicago Press.

Lamont, M. (2000). *The dignity of working men: Morality and the boundaries of race, class, and immigration*. Harvard University Press.

Lamont, M., & Molnár, V. (2002). The study of boundaries in the social sciences. *Annual Review of Sociology, 28*(1), 167–195.

Larson, M. S. (1977). *The rise of professionalism: A sociological analysis*. University of California Press.

Linn, R. (1996). *Power, progress and profit: A history of the Australian accounting profession*. Australian Society of Certified Practising Accountants.

Macdonald, K. M. (1985). Social closure and occupational registration. *Sociology, 19*(4), 541–556.

Macdonald, K. M., & Ritzer, G. (1988). The sociology of the professions: Dead or alive? *Work and Occupations, 15*(3), 251–272.

McDermott, M. (2006). *Working-class white: The making and unmaking of race relations*. University of California Press.

Mitchell, R., & Boyle, B. (2021). Understanding the role of profession in multidisciplinary team innovation: Professional identity, minority dissent and team innovation. *British Journal of Management, 32*(2), 512–528.

Noguchi, M., & Edwards, J. R. (2008). Harmonising intergroup relations within a professional body: The case of the ICAEW. *British Accounting Review, 40*(2), 123–147.

Norris, P. (2001). How 'we' are different from 'them': Occupational boundary maintenance in the treatment of musculo-skeletal problems. *Sociology of Health & Illness, 23*(1), 24–43.

Pacholok, S. (2009). Gendered Strategies of self: Navigating hierarchy and contesting masculinities. *Gender, Work and Organisation, 16*(4), 471–500.

Pachucki, M. A., Pendergrass, S., & Lamont, M. (2007). Boundary processes: Recent theoretical developments and new contributions. *Poetics, 35*(6), 331–351.

Parker, R. H. (2005). Naming and branding: Accountants and accountancy bodies in the British Empire and Commonwealth, 1853–2003. *Accounting History, 10*(1), 7–46.

Parker, R. H. (2014). The first 32 importers of an English professional accountancy qualification: Opportunities, incentives, impact. *Accounting History, 19*(1–2), 171–192.

Perry, P. (2002). *Shades of white: White kids and racial identities in high school*. Duke University Press.

Persson, A. (2010). Soldiers and secretaries: Gendered boundary work in the Swedish Armed Forces. *Scandinavian Journal of Management, 26*, 166–175.

Poullaos, C. (1993). Making profession and state, 1907 to 1914: The ACPA's first charter attempt. *Abacus, 29*(2), 196–229.

Poullaos, C. (1994). *Making the Australian chartered accountant. New York.* Garland.

Richardson, A. J. (1989b). Canada's accounting elite: 1880–1930. *The Accounting Historians Journal, 16*(1), 1–21.

Shackleton, K., & Walker. S. P. (1998). *Professional reconstruction: The coordination of the accountancy bodies, 1930–1957*. Edinburgh, Institute of Chartered Accountants of Scotland.

Sherman, R. (2005). Producing the superior self: Strategic comparison and symbolic boundaries among luxury hotel workers. *Ethnography, 6*(2), 131–158.

Sherman, R. (2006). *Class acts.* Berkeley. University of California Press.

Sidhu, J., Carnegie, G. D., & West, B. (2021). Australia's divided accounting profession: The 1969 merger attempt and its legacy. *The British Accounting Review, 53*(3), 100975.

Swedlow, B. (2003). Scientists, judges, and spotted owls: Policymakers in the Pacific Northwest. *Duke Environmental Law and Policy Forum, 8*(2, Spring), 187–278.

Swedlow, B. (2007). Using the boundaries of science to do boundary-work among scientists: Pollution and purity claims. *Science and Public Policy, 34*(9), 633–643.

Walker, S. P. (1991). The defence of professional monopoly: Scottish chartered accountants and 'satellites in the accountancy firmament' 1854–1914. *Accounting, Organisations and Society, 16*(3), 257–283.

Walker, S. P., & Shackleton, K. (1995). Corporatism and structural change in the British accountancy profession, 1930–1957. *Accounting, Organisations and Society, 20*(6), 467–503.

West, B. P. (2003). *Professionalism and accounting rules.* Routledge.

Wood, A., Copley, J., Hill, A., & Cottrell, N. (2022). Interprofessional identity in clinicians: A scoping review. *Journal of Interprofessional Care*, 1–12.

Wray, M. (2006). *Not quite white: White trash and the boundaries of whiteness.* Duke University Press.

Young, J. J. (2014). Separating the political and technical: Accounting standard-setting and purification. *Contemporary Accounting Research, 31*(3), 713–747.

CHAPTER 6

The First Attempt to Unite the Dominant Professional Accounting Associations

6.1 Introduction

This chapter considers the first merger attempt by the Society and the Institute, which was voted upon by members of both bodies on 3 December 1969. The initial unity proposal was overwhelmingly supported by the Society members but was rejected by Institute members. Since the formation of the Institute in 1928 and of the Society in 1952, there has been very little, if any, cooperation between the two bodies. As such, the first merger attempt was a somewhat unexpected step, coming after years of professional rivalry and especially given that the Institute was created as an elite association to represent MIPP on a national basis. The formation of the Institute reflected a boundary construction whereby accountants not involved in public practice were to be kept outside the domain of this professional body. On the other hand, the earliest antecedent body of the Society, the IIAV, was formed in Melbourne in April 1886 and incorporated on 1 March 1887 (Carnegie & Edwards, 2001; Edwards et al., 1997). This association adopted market control as its organisational strategy, based on the inclusion of individuals drawn from both within and outside the domain of public practice. Hence, both the Society and the Institute were formed based on different organisational strategies in relation to their membership recruitments. After years of rivalry, the decision to try to merge the two bodies marked a modification of their traditional organisational strategies. The three further

J. Sidhu et al., *Understanding the Sociology of the Accounting Profession*, https://doi.org/10.1007/978-981-99-1572-9_6

unsuccessful merger attempts that followed resulted from the continuous dialogue, joint activities and cooperation that stemmed from the first merger attempt.

This chapter is arranged in five sections. Following this introductory section, the second section of this chapter provides various aspects of background context. The first subsection provides a background to the Australian accounting profession and historical developments. The next subsection provides the context before the first merger attempt. This includes the relationship between the Society and the Institute in the pre-1960s period and an overview of the major developments during the 1960s, such as experiences of corporate collapses and their effect on the standing of the accounting profession. The education of accountants, which also received attention because of criticism of the accounting profession, is described in this section. Further, a summary of attempts and concerns of the Society to gain a title associated with status, and a comparison between the Society and the Institute across various levels are provided in this subsection. The last part of the second section provides an overview of the joint activities between the two bodies that eventually led to the mounting of the first merger attempt. The third section of this chapter provides a detailed account of the merger proposal and its outcomes. The fourth section provides responses to the research questions. The last section concludes this chapter.

6.2 Background Context

This section outlines the background context that led to the mounting of the first merger attempt.

6.2.1 Background to the Australian Accounting Profession

The advent of professional accounting associations in Australia occurred in the late nineteenth century from 1885, with the key structural and other operational features of the profession formalised during the early decades of the twentieth century. As noted in earlier chapters of this book, regionalism and duplication were the major features of the early organised Australian accounting profession (Carnegie, 1993; Carnegie & Parker, 1999; Parker, 1986, 1989). Most accounting bodies that were formed between 1885 and 1952 merged with other bodies or disappeared from the professional association scene (Carnegie, 1993; Gavens,

1990; Gynther, 1967). The Institute and the Society emerged out of successful unification processes that largely involved coalescence around notions of MIPP and MNIPP. This was the result of organisational strategies of "exclusiveness versus market control" (Macdonald & Ritzer, 1988, p. 257) adopted by the Institute and the Society respectively. The strategy of exclusiveness adopted by the Institute was implemented with boundary work (Gieryn, 1983, 1995, 1999) which excluded a large number of potential members from joining. The concept of boundary work includes not just boundary setting, but also the maintenance and management of those demarcations, which may be subject to movement, blurring and bridging. Boundary work plays a key role in constructing identities such as elite status associated with membership of the Institute. This mechanism also includes means of excluding others, that is, members of the Society in this instance and others not involved in public practice (Grbic, 2010). The formation of the Institute was essentially premised on a social boundary constructed by highlighting differences between MIPP and MNIPP (Grbic, 2010). The boundaries were then fortified by linguistic claims asserting the superiority of MIPP (Annisette, 2017). Therefore, the polarisation of the Australian accounting profession can be viewed as a manifestation of different strategies adopted by the Australian accountants (Carnegie et al., 2003). The literature review has provided a comprehensive account of studies that examined the formation of various professional associations and other structural changes in the Australian accounting profession.

6.2.2 Pre-1960s

The Society was formed and incorporated in 1952, but its earliest antecedent body, the IIAV, was established in Melbourne, Victoria in 1886. While the Institute was formally constituted in 1928, it had much earlier antecedents. However, in spite of these long histories, the Institute, the Society and their antecedent bodies participated in very few joint activities of any consequence before the 1960s. The issuance of accounting pronouncements and compliance checks by companies was ad hoc. For example, evidence can be cited from a 1948 statement by T. A. Hiley, president of the Institute, in which he stated that there were too many companies that fail to follow many of the more important recommendations (Zeff, 1973). This shows that the Institute was unable to provide guidance to accounting profession in an effective and efficient manner.

In 1950, an attempt by the Commonwealth Institute, a predecessor of the Society, to form a joint committee of accounting bodies in Australia for issuing accounting pronouncements failed because of a lack of support from the Institute, which did not want to lose its right to issue its own statements on accounting practice (Zeff, 1973).[1] However, at the same time, and due to insufficient financial resources, the Institute could not afford any regular research staff (Zeff, 1973). Even if certain committees of state councils of the Institute did some work, there was no follow-up. J. K. Little, a member of the general council of the Institute, expressed concerns over the Institute's growth in different areas. It was also due to financial limitations. Due to a small membership base financial resources and growth of the Institute in financial standards setting areas was inadequate, resulting in a failure to keep pace with the competition.

On the other hand, the Commonwealth Institute gained enough financial strength to be in a position to afford a research officer once it merged with the numerically larger Federal Institute in 1952, leading to the formation of the Society (Zeff, 1973). Despite having greater financial viability to support such research, the Society did not want to take up an active research program to issue accounting pronouncements because this would put it in competition with the Institute (Zeff, 1973). This also shows that the Society was concerned about legitimacy of its authority because the Institute was seen as an association with higher technical abilities among its members. This situation posed a unique challenge, organisation with financial viability did not have required professional authority to issue standards. On the other hand, organisation with professional authority did not have sufficient financial resources.

The impact of uncoordinated research programs by both bodies to assist in guiding accountants is evident in the perceptions of practitioners. The ARF conducted a survey in the mid-1960s sponsored by both the

[1] The reality was that the Institute did not develop its own accounting guidelines, but closely followed and copied practices of the English Institute (Zeff, 1973) at this time. Later, during the mid to late 1960s, the influence of American and Canadian pronouncements could also be observed on the Institute's accounting guidelines. The pressures of reports issued by government inspectors on company failures and criticism by the financial press were compelling reasons for this change (Zeff, 1973).

Society and the Institute. This survey showed that accountants believed that financial statements did not provide enough information to users. Accountants demanded that more information should be provided and that standards of reporting should be improved (Anon, 1968d). It appears that neither body regarded itself to be working with the other on the development and growth of the accounting profession in Australia.

6.2.3 Developments During the 1960s

Developments in the 1960s brought the Society and the Institute bodies together for discussions on matters affecting them both. During the early stages of the decade, after a spate of corporate failures, the Australian accounting profession faced a legitimacy crisis (Carnegie & O'Connell, 2012). The Australian accounting profession was criticised by parties outside the profession as well as commentators within the profession. For example, the inspector appointed to investigate the collapsed Reid Murray Group of companies strongly criticised the accounting profession and its guiding principles (ASA, 1966a, p. 28). The inspector commented that there was a need for more precisely defined guiding principles for accountants and auditors (ASA, 1966a, p. 28). Criticisms of accountants and their profession, led by the press and government inspectors, meant both bodies felt the public backlash emanating from the corporate failures.

Initially, the Society tried to justify its position and attempted to reject the criticism. An example comes from the Queensland division of the Society, which requested the general council to take steps on behalf of the profession to refute promptly any damaging and unjust comments (ASA, 1967b). Another illustrative attempt to escape responsibility comes from an article that claimed the major causes of company failures were where "differences in expert opinions existed". There were only a few instances of criminal negligence. This meant that the best brains in accountancy needed to seek ways to settle criticisms emerging from corporate failures and criticisms by Govt. Inspectors (Anon, 1965c).

Eventually, mounting pressures forced both bodies to act jointly to respond to such criticisms. Both bodies reviewed their limited progress in developing and guiding the technical practices used by the accounting profession. A particularly important joint activity was the establishment and sponsorship by the Institute and the Society of the ARF, which was announced in the November 1965 issues of *The Australian Accountant* and *The Chartered Accountant in Australia* (Carnegie & O'Connell,

2012). The ARF was incorporated as a company limited by guarantee on 23 November 1966 (Burrows, 1996; Zeff, 1973). In later years, the ARF played a major role in the Australian accounting profession, though initially, it struggled to gain momentum and start its operations. Both bodies had planned to make an annual contribution of $AU20,000. However, the position of Research Director remained vacant for four years after it was first advertised, until P. W. Danby was appointed on 1 July 1969. Danby resigned within four months and the position was filled by W. J, Kenley from 1 January 1971 (Zeff, 1973). By the end of 1967, the ARF had $AU35,700 in unexpended funds in hand (Zeff, 1973). It was obvious that the initial planned joint contribution was not functioning effectively because money was not being spent on research activities. Therefore, despite their intentions and efforts, the bodies could not initiate the research activity that was planned through the ARF.

6.2.4 *Status of the Society Members*

The crisis of the 1960s and the subsequent sharp criticism of accountants and the accounting profession once again exposed status differentiation between the members of the Institute and the Society. The Institute was proud of its high standards and the Society was concerned that its members did not have a competitive professional title, such as the "Chartered Accountant" designation that was held by the members of the Institute. Irving (1966, p. 10), a member of the general council of the Society, stated:

> It is generally recognized that members of the Society are at an extreme disadvantage because of a lack of a generic name by which they can identify themselves in the community. The many letters of designation, indicating grades of membership of various professional bodies, are confusing and have little significance in the absence of a generic name … Unfortunately, the simple description 'accountant' has been so loosely used for so many years that, by itself, it has never had any real professional significance in the community. It is therefore necessary to add some other word or words in order to clearly identify an accountant qualified and trained at the professional level. Two combinations of words have gained general acceptance in other parts of the world, 'Chartered Accountant' and 'Certified Public Accountant'.

The arguments of Irving (1966) were linked with a public discourse of superiority that was used to elevate the status of the Institute members, casting them as superior to the Society members (Annisette, 2017). To overcome this significant barrier, in March 1966, the general council of the Society instructed its Central Public Accountants Committee (CPAC) to submit proposals to improve the status of its MIPP and overcome the serious disadvantages under which they practised (ASA, 1966b). The CPAC submitted its report and suggested an examination of the desirability of prohibiting those members of [the] Society, who were salaried officers of an accounting firm or other organisations from carrying on the practice of public accountant on their own. As the Society's members did not have any title to distinguish or identify themselves from accountants who were not qualified for Society membership, the CPAC proposed consideration of using the prefix "Royal" with the name of "Society" (Worley, 1967). Another attempt by the Society to adopt professional titles for its members failed due to the distinction drawn between MIPP and MNIPP (Irving, 1966).[2]

An additional confronting issue was that the Society's many MIPP did not associate themselves with the Society. As the general council expressed its worry:

> That General Council note that a great number of the Society Members in public practice find it necessary to refrain from describing themselves as members of the Society so that they can use their designation of membership of another professional body and request the Central Public Accountants Committee to report to the Executive as soon as possible on the steps that may be taken to raise the degree of acceptance of the Society

[2] The adoption of the generic titles of "Certified Public Accountant" and "Certified Accountant" failed because of the distinction drawn between the MIPP and MNIPP. The MNIPP objected and raised concerns that the privilege of public accountants to describe themselves as "Certified Public Accountants" or "CPAs" placed MIPP in an advantageous position because a greater status was attached to the description of "Certified Public Accountant" or the letters "CPA" when compared with the description of "Certified Accountant". Changing the name of the Society from the "Australian Society of Accountants" to the "Australian Society of Certified Accountants" was also discussed (Irving, 1966). Irving (1966) also mentioned that the use of the title "Certified Practising Accountants" for all members of the Society would have a prestige value. Further, it would conform to the practice of the Institute of Chartered Accountants in Australia whose members, whether in public practice or private employment, were now permitted to describe themselves as "Chartered Accountants" (Irving, 1966).

> Membership in the field of public accounting to the extent necessary for practitioners to be able to describe themselves as the Society Members without prejudicing their prospect of receiving certain appointments. (ASA, 1967a, p.10)

While comparing the status of the members of the Institute, Irving (1966) contrasted it with the Society's MIPP, adding, similar to the title "Chartered Accountant" there is no similar generic title for the public accountant member of the Society. The Society also had no objection to its MIPP using the Chartered Accountant title and disassociating themselves from the Society. It was due to the fact that recognition was given to the Chartered Accountant title as being in a specialist area—it is logical that members with dual membership practise under the title of "Chartered Accountant'. The Society's MIPP with dual membership did not disclose their membership of the Society when dealing with the public and mainly used the Institute's title of CA. Therefore, members with dual membership created a sub-boundary between themselves and other members of the Society who were not in public practice (Arndt & Bigelow, 2005; Cash, 1997; Gieryn, 1983; Lamont & Molnár, 2002). In the proposed merged association one of the incentives for the Society leadership was removing the intraorganisational boundary that was being constructed as a consequence of some the Society MIPP also being members of the Institute.

The Society also expressed concerns that outside Australia it did not have the same recognition as the Institute, something that became evident at the time of the Society and the Institute coming together to jointly organise the Tenth International Congress of Accountants in Australia. HR Irving, president of the Society, argued that, it was apparent that the distinction between the Society and the Institute was not clearly recognised in at least some other countries and, as a result, it became necessary for:

> [T]he acting President of the Society JG Orr to write to the General Secretary of the Ninth International Congress of Accountants, emphasising that the invitation in respect of the 1972 Congress had been extended on behalf of the accountancy profession in Australia, by the Presidents of both this Society and the Institute, and not just by one of the organisations in this country. (Irving, 1966, p. 8)

6.2.5 *Accountants' Education Policy Reforms*

The developments of the 1960s created the circumstances that led to the reassessment of the education of accountants. Three bodies, the Institute, the Society, and the Australasian Institute of Cost Accountants, sponsored a survey of the accounting profession by Professor W. J. Vatter, Professor of Accounting at the University of California, who submitted his report in 1964 (Anon, 1965b). Vatter's report suggested major changes in accounting education, including introducing graduate entry into the profession (Vatter, 1964a), and going so far as to say the profession of accountancy in Australia needed a general upgrading in all respects (Vatter, 1964b).

Vatter (1964b) exposed various inherent issues and problems in the accounting profession and in the education of accountants, commenting that the standards for admission to the profession were low, and that the accounting syllabi would be better abandoned than revised. The occupational roles played by accountants were also a matter for criticism by Professor Vatter who found that more than 25 per cent of the time spent by the Society members not engaged in public accounting was spent on non-accounting work. Not only were educational standards low but also accounting bodies, especially the Society, were not able to guide accountants to gain their professional territory.

In 1961, the Prime Minister of Australia Robert Menzies established a committee to inquire into the future of higher education in Australia. Leslie Harold Martin was appointed its chairperson, giving his name to the committee. The Martin Committee report was released on 24 March 1965. The Martin Committee report and the Vatter report acted as key motivations for the Society to make major changes in its education policy for potential members. Both reports had made quite similar recommendations and contributions in the general upgrading of the Australian accounting profession.

The report of the Society's committee on "Future Education Policy of the Society" was submitted by chairperson L. A. Braddock. This report mentioned that the new education policy of the Society was timely and important because the general situation in the educational field was one of turmoil (Braddock, 1965). It further mentioned that the objective of the Society's education policy should be the basic education and examination of candidates through universities and technological institutions with a qualifying examination taken by the Society for membership purposes

(Braddock, 1965). The Society approved the adoption of the new education policy at its general council meeting on 11 October 1965 (ASA, 1965).

As the previous subsection has discussed, the Institute's standards for the education of accountants and the general status of its members were perceived to be higher than the Society; hence, many changes and upgrades in the education policies of accountants were made by the Society.[3]

6.2.6 *Registration of Accountants*

The legitimacy crisis also revived the notion of creating legal boundaries through a process of registration for accountants, a proposal that gained strength in the context of the era's corporate failures. The Victorian division of the Society initiated the debate on state-based registration. In a presidential address delivered on 27 March 1963, the president of the Victorian branch of the Society H. F. Craig stated that accountants should not ignore criticism that surfaced after various recent corporate failures (Craig, 1963). He also mentioned that the Society and the Institute were not able to control the activities of non-member accountants, former member accountants and unqualified accountants. In concluding his argument, Craig presented a strong case for the state registration of accountants. In his words, just as with many other professions, statutory control of the accounting profession by means of registration or licences to protect the public was necessary. Later, in 1964, H. F. Craig reaffirmed the Society's stand and said that criticism of the accounting profession by government inspectors, the financial press and members of the public was "irresponsible and unjustified" and that it had directed attention to the desirability of statutory control over all accountants (Anon, 1964a).

On 19 March 1964, *The Age* reported that negotiations to bring about legislation for registration of accountants were continuing between accounting bodies and the Victorian Government. In a survey of the Society members, an overwhelming 97.5 per cent of members, from a

[3] For example, from 1 January 1967, students were required to obtain their basic accountancy education by taking an approved course at a university or technical institution for entry to which a matriculation standard of general education was required. On completion of this, graduates were required to pass a qualifying examination of the Society for admission to membership (ASA, 1967e).

response rate of 76.2 per cent, favoured the proposed Bill. The Attorney General of Victoria Arthur Rylah was also advised about the outcomes of the survey; Rylah considered it important that the Institute gave its full support to the proposal if the proposed state registration Bill went ahead in the parliament. The president of the Victorian division of the Society also told members that negotiations were being undertaken with the Victorian branch of the Institute (Anon, 1964c).

Speaking along the lines of projecting a case for state registration, on 20 April 1964, the national president of the Society, JMS Groom, declared that the public should be protected from unqualified and unethical accountants, and further said that the Society leadership wanted to see the term "accountant" applied only to those who were qualified accountants (Anon., 1964b). This marked an attempt to achieve occupational closure by means of state registration (Macdonald, 1985, 1995).

The 1965 annual report of the Society mentioned a joint discussion with the Victorian state government along with the Institute's Victorian division:

> General Council has continued its endeavour to achieve a form of statutory control of all sections of the profession on a basis which will enable it to govern its own affairs. General Council is convinced of the need for this statutory recognition throughout Australia and members can be assured that every effort is being made to bring this about. (ASA, 1965, p. 2)

The 1965 annual report of the Society further mentioned an agreement being reached with the Institute on the provisions of [a] draft Bill for statutory recognition of profession and control by the profession. Council claimed that it believed that the proposed legislation was in the best interests of the profession and was urgently needed to protect those we serve. Therefore, every effort was being made to have the Bill accepted by the Government (ASA, 1965).

It also appears that state registration was a more important issue for the Society than the Institute. The Society was prompt in discussing various options of statutory control. It clearly wanted to keep the autonomy of the profession, as it resolved that the General Council was opposed to any external control of professional standards (ASA, 1966a). Further, the Society claimed, statutory control by an outside authority may have restricted new thought and progress (ASA, 1966a). The issue was discussed in detail and it was even mentioned that the control of the profession should be entrusted by statute to the profession itself and not some statutory authority appointed by for the purpose (ASA, 1966a).

After some initial success, the attempts to gain statutory control in Victoria suffered a setback. Statutory control of the profession was promoted by the Society in Victoria. The Institute initially supported the idea. However, the National Institute of Accountants[4] bitterly opposed it directly and many other bodies opposed it indirectly. In an article published in *The Australian*, journalist John Lloyd mentioned that there was a veil of secrecy and that both the Society and the Institute were not discussing the contents of the proposed Bill (Lloyd, 1966). If the proposed Bill had become law then only members of the Society and the Institute could practise as accountants. In a big jolt to such efforts, the Premier of Victoria Henry Bolte made it clear that the issue of the registration of accountants was an internal issue within the accounting profession and that the Victorian Government was only acting in the interest of the profession. According to Lloyd (1966), because of rising public pressure, Henry Bolte did not want any involvement that could potentially cause embarrassment for his government.

In 1966, the general council of the Society gave authority to the divisional councils in all states to discuss the matter on an official basis with representatives of the Institute in their respective states (ASA, 1966b). In a May 1967 meeting of the general council of the Society, it was noted that "Government did not, at this stage, intend to proceed with the legislation" (ASA, 1967b). Therefore, the executive decided to raise this issue with representatives of the Institute at the sixth joint conference, with a view to create state registration as a means of constructing professional boundaries under the law. British accountants had made several attempts to create a mechanism of state-based registration to construct professional boundaries, as explained in earlier chapters (Shackleton & Walker, 1998). The first such British attempt to use state registration for creating professional boundaries failed between 1890 and 1930 (Macdonald, 1985). The failure in Britain was for similar reasons those arising in the Australian case, with the chartered bodies not being able to convince the government that accountants, who were not members of a professional body and had limited qualifications or experience, were damaging the reputation of the profession, an argument that was used to promote the case

[4] Name changed to the Institute of Commercial Studies in 1967.

for state registration (Shackleton & Walker, 1998). In 1967, the general registrar of the Institute informed the Society that "no action be taken" to implement the earlier decision of the general council. That earlier decision was to give authority to the state councils to initiate discussions with state representatives of the Institute (ASA, 1967d). As a result, the Society's executive committee decided to put the issue of statutory control on hold (ASA, 1967d).

6.2.7 Comparison of Both Bodies

The following data, drawn from the years 1968 and 1969, highlight some of the key similarities and differences between the Institute and the Society at this time. The total membership of the state councils of the Society was 103, while this number was 47 for the Institute. Overall administration, including admission of members and disciplinary action against members, was more departmentalised and decentralised in the case of the Society than the Institute. The Society had offices and full-time staff members in all states except Tasmania and owned its premises in Melbourne and Sydney. In contrast, the Institute had offices only in New South Wales and Victoria. The Society had 72 full-time staff members of whom 26 were in the Melbourne head office, while the Institute had only 26 full-time staff members with 20 based at the head office in Sydney (ASA & ICAA, 1968a). Fifty-five per cent of the Institute's members, numbering 2,954, were based in New South Wales, although the proportion of the Australian population living in that state was just 36 per cent (Australian Bureau of Statistics, 1968; ICAA, 1969). In contrast, while the Society had 10,175 members in New South Wales, this constituted just 33 per cent of its total membership. The Society drew 31 per cent (9,512) of its members from Victoria, which was home to just 22 per cent of the national population (Australian Bureau of Statistics, 1968). In short, the Institute's "home" was in Sydney, New South Wales, while Melbourne, Victoria, was the "home" of the Society, a factor that would compound the tensions surrounding the merger proposal.

The share of MIPP was 72 per cent in the Institute and just 15 per cent in the case of the Society (McEwen, 1967). Similarities between the bodies included the structure of general and state councils, the vesting of decision-making power with general councils, the frequency of meetings of councils and the functioning of bodies through executive committees

Table 6.1 Financial results of the society (1965–1970)

Year	*Revenue/Income ($AU)*	*Deficit/ surplus ($AU)*	*Deficit/ surplus (%)*
1965	529,158	79,096	14.9
1966	545,297	47,458	8.7
1967	549,594	(33,823)	(6.2)
1968	635,245	22,873	3.6
1969	641,672	4,548	0.7
1970	777,686	89,966	11.6
	Revenue deficit/surplus (%)		5.7

Source ASA 1965–1970

(ASA & ICAA, 1968b). The general councils of each body were also similar in size (18 at the Institute and 19 at the Society).

Table 6.1 provides details of revenue and the respective deficit or surplus for the Society between 1965 and 1970. The trend shows that the Society's financial performance was generally strong, with the exception of 1967 when it suffered a deficit of 6.2 per cent and 1969 when the surplus figure was merely 0.7 per cent. However, it regained its strong surplus position in the following year (1970), with an 11.6 per cent surplus in 1970. The overall average surplus for the years 1965 to 1970 was 5.71 per cent (Table 6.2).

The Institute recorded surpluses in 1966, 1967, 1969 and 1970, but in each instance, the surplus was less than 3 per cent of the total revenue. For

Table 6.2 Financial results of the institute (1965–1970)

Year	*Revenue/Income ($AU)*	*Deficit/ Surplus ($AU)*	*Deficit/ Surplus (%)*
1965	(7,000) pounds	41,392 pounds	(16.9)
1966	3,606	160,507	2.25
1967	1,108	167,837	0.66
1968	(20,327)	170,901	(11.9)
1969	6,034	237,949	2.2
1970	8,791	285,618	3.0
	Average surplus (%)		−3.5

Source Annual reports ICAA

1965 and 1968, significant deficits were reported by the Institute, respectively 16.9 per cent and 11.9 per cent of total revenue (ICAA, 1965, 1966, 1967, 1968, 1969, 1970). In 1969 and 1970, it recorded surpluses of 2.2 per cent and 3 per cent respectively. Overall, when compared with the Society, the Institute's financial performance was poorer. The Institute had an average 3.5 per cent deficit across the six-year period. This suggests that the Institute may have been under some financial stress while merger discussions were taking place. As mentioned above, because of a lack of financial capacity resulting from its smaller membership base, the Institute was unable to engage in an active research program, while the Society was cautious about engaging in such activity because this would place it in direct competition with the Institute (Zeff, 1973).

6.2.8 *Joint Activities*

Both bodies began to initiate joint activities in response to the challenges created by the corporate failures of the early 1960s, focusing on education standards for accountants and overcoming the difficulties in organising research activities for raising the standards of the profession. For example, when the Institute made its submissions on Commonwealth income tax legislation, the Society supported its recommendations (ASA, 1965, p. 3). Both bodies formed a joint committee to work together on issues of common interest, including upgrading the standards of recruitment to the profession and attracting students with the necessary standards of secondary education (Anon, 1965a).

Evidence of joint works and cooperation also comes from official documents. The 1965 annual report of the Institute mentions:

> This year has been notable for the liaison established in areas of common interest between the Institute and the Australian Society of Accountants. Conferences at Presidential level have been held between the two bodies and a number of projects have been accepted as being worthy of exploration on a joint basis. Members already have been informed of the proposed joint venture into research and subjects such as educational standards, legislation affecting the profession, Asian and Pacific conferences and recruitment into the profession have been discussed. (ICAA, 1965, p. 9)

The 1965 annual report of the Society printed a subcategory with the title "Joint Action within the Profession" and it reported:

> Members have been informed from time to time of discussions which have taken place between representatives of the Institute of Chartered Accountants in Australia and this Society on matters of mutual interest. One of the important areas of agreement was the need for the Institute and the Society to work closely together in the field of accounting research, so that the benefit of any work undertaken could be more widely disseminated and individual assignments undertaken in greater depth. Discussions have taken place over a considerable period of time with a view to establishing a basis for closer relationship between the Australian Society of Accountants and the Australasian Institute of Cost Accountants. (ASA, 1965, p. 1)

The Society's 1965 annual report also mentioned that history was made at the University of Western Australia in February when, for the first time, accountancy bodies combined with the Adult Education Board to present a seminar on Selected Problems in Accountancy.

The Institute and the Society agreed to make copies of their official journals available on a sale basis to the members of the other body (Anon, 1965a). They also agreed to make joint representations to governments and official bodies on matters affecting the accounting profession (Anon., 1965a). The Institute formally consulted with the Society before making submissions, revealing in its annual report that where appropriate, the [Parliamentary and Laws Committee] held discussions with the ASA to ensure that submissions from the profession were on parallel lines (ICAA, 1968).

The Institute and the Society organised joint seminars on accountants' education. One such seminar, held on 3 October 1968, dealt with bankruptcy in companies (Anon, 1968c). For the first time, both bodies made a joint representation on behalf of the Australian accounting profession at the Ninth World Congress of Accountants (Anderson, 1967). Another joint effort made in the interest of advancing the profession in Australia included a joint expression of interest to host the Tenth International Congress of Accountants, scheduled for 1972 (ICAA, 1967).

The Institute president contended that the Institute and the Society should direct their attention towards systematically improving the educational and training areas of the profession rather than just considering ad hoc matters from time to time (ASA, 1967b). In summary, after a long period of segregation, the two bodies were cooperating and engaging in joint works. The 1966 annual report of the Institute referred to maintaining an open door policy towards liaison with the Society on matters of common interest.

Before the first merger attempt, Gynther (1967) conducted a survey on the Australian accounting profession (Linn, 1996) and elucidated the general mood of accountants. The findings of his study showed that 84.2 per cent of the members of the Society overwhelmingly favoured the idea of a single national body, while a majority of the Institute's membership was in opposition and only 39.1 per cent were in favour of such a proposition. Gynther (1967, p. 289) wrote that:

> A combined professional body is essential if the accountancy profession is to play its role in the expanding Australian society in an efficient manner. There must be oneness in thought and action in such vital areas as formal education, continuing education and research especially.

Further, he argued that a single voice speaking for the whole profession would be much stronger and would be heard and listened to by many people than were the two smaller voices of the Society and the Institute (Gynther, 1967).

At a time when discussions for the first merger were still in their infancy in Australia, the six British professional accounting bodies were considering the unification of the British accounting profession. In 1968, a proposal was released and the primary rationale for unity was to reduce the confusion that had arisen due to the diversity and multiplicity of professional bodies. A second rationale, identified formally in the proposal, was the ability to speak with one voice to the government (Anon, 1968b). Unification of the accounting profession in India was under consideration at the same time, with the aim of merging the Institute of Chartered Accountants in India and the Institute of Cost and Works Accountants of India (Anon, 1968e). Interestingly, none of the three unity attempts would succeed and the respective bodies participating in the unity attempts in the UK, India and Australia are still separate bodies at the time of writing.

6.3 The Merger Proposal and Outcome

The previous section identified a series of developments that took place during the early 1960s that may have put pressure on both bodies to consider the merger option or, in other words, to modify their traditional strategies of exclusiveness or market control as adopted by the Institute and the Society respectively (Macdonald & Ritzer, 1988). The implications of this change would mean that members of the Society would gain status by becoming CAs accountants. For the Institute members, the implications of the proposed merger were linked with a potential dilution of status and they also feared dilution of the quality of professional services (Orr, 2014). The developments that mounted pressures to modify the traditional organisational strategies of both bodies included the threat to the legitimacy of the profession as a result of a series of corporate failures (Clarke et al., 2003; Sykes, 1998). This led to an increase in cooperation between the two bodies and ultimately resulted in the mounting of the first merger attempt (Carnegie, 2009; Carnegie & O'Connell, 2012). In response to the developing professional crisis centred on the inadequacy of accounting principles and practices, both bodies initiated many joint actions resulting in the formation of the ARF. This section examines the details of the merger proposal and its eventual failure and argues that this failure was the result of boundary protection by members of the Institute (Arndt & Bigelow, 2005; Fournier, 2000; Gieryn, 1983; Swedlow, 2007).

The initial attempt to start talks and commence joint operations was initiated by the Institute, as explained by Zeff (1973, p. 43):

> In March, 1964, Colin R. Kelynack, President of the Chartered Institute, telephoned the Society President Lyall A. Braddock to propose that the senior officials of both bodies attend an informal meeting at which 'matters of common interest' could be discussed. In prior years, the Institute and the Society had confined their co-operation largely to the joint sponsorship of accounting congresses. But by the 1960s, the leaders of both bodies felt the need for a closer link. The Institute President's suggestion for an informal meeting was readily accepted. (Zeff, 1973, p. 43)

The presidents and office bearers of the Institute and the Society met in Canberra on 23 June 1964 to discuss matters of mutual interest to both parties (Anon, 1964b), and several joint actions were initiated (Anon., 1965a). Following this initial coming together of the two bodies, the

ARF was jointly formed in June 1965. The ARF was incorporated in the Australian Capital Territory as a company limited by guarantee jointly sponsored by the Society and the Institute (ASA, 1965; ICAA, 1966). This was viewed by the Society as a significant development affecting the profession (ASA, 1965, p. 1). It was also one of the first major joint actions in the profession that contributed to the advent of the merger proposal. In the official history of the Institute, the formation of the ARF was mentioned as a major move within the accounting profession in the quest for better research and higher standards (Graham, 1972).

Both bodies also agreed to jointly host the Tenth International Congress of Accountants in 1972 (ICAA, 1967, 1968). The landmark joint activity between the bodies was the holding of a series of meetings between senior officials of each body, which were entitled "joint conferences", commencing with the April 1964 conference previously mentioned. From the beginning, these conferences comprised five representatives from each body: presidents, vice-presidents, registrars and two other members of the council (ASA, 1967a).

Formal discussions for unification emerged from these conferences, commencing from the second and third conferences held in Canberra on 8 October 1964 and 8 December 1964. The first four joint conferences occurred within a period of about 10 months from 23 June 1964 to 8 April 1965, respectively (Carnegie & O'Connell, 2012). No single clear trigger or event can be identified, through either documentary evidence or oral history, as precipitating the merger discussions. Rather, various factors exerted influence in a long and incremental process. The closeness in proximity of these conferences demonstrates the urgency of the matters addressed. The fifth joint conference was held on 14 March 1967 in Sydney (ASA, 1967d). Between March 1967 and October 1968, eight more conferences were held. After the tenth joint conference, held on 4–5 June 1968 in Sydney, the group was renamed the "unity committee". The unity committee would make all major decisions related to the proposed merger (ASA & ICAA, 1968a, p. 7). In summary, the joint conference aimed at discussing matters of mutual interest had become the forum for considering the proposition of merging the bodies. Tables 6.3 and 6.4 show the representation of both bodies on the unity committee.

Background work for the merger had started with a private meeting of senior council members of the Society and the Institute in Canberra in 1967 (Orr, 2014). Geoff Orr was the vice-president of the Society and he stated in an oral history interview held on 17 May 2014:

Table 6.3 Unity committee representation of the institute of chartered accountants in Australia

SN	*Name*	*Institute Designation*	*City*
1	A. B. Cleland	President	Sydney
2	E. W. Savage	Vice-President	Brisbane
3	J. R. Harrowell	Vice-President	Sydney
4	F. E. Trigg	General Councillor	Sydney
5	J. K. Little	General Councillor	Melbourne
6	S. J. Walton	Formerly General Registrar	Sydney
7	H. M. L. Hordern	General Registrar	Sydney

Source ASA & ICAA (1968b)

Table 6.4 Unity committee representation of the Australian society of accountants

SN	*Name*	*The Society Designation*	*City*
1	J. G. Orr	President	Brisbane
2	H. R. Irving	Immediate Past President	Sydney
3	G. W. Bottrill	Vice-President	Sydney
4	L. A. Braddock	General Councillor	Adelaide
5	R. F. Pascoe	General Councillor	Adelaide
6	C. W. Anderson	General Councillor	Adelaide

Source ASA & ICAA (1968b)

> We had a discussion in Canberra before the actual discussion on [a] merger. That was held in private. The Institute approached [the] Society and said that they would like to discuss a number of matters and the question of [a] merger did not come up at that stage. It was suggested that we might meet again confidentially. [The] second meeting as planned did not take place, but the following year the new president of [the] Institute contacted the new president of [the] Society and said that we have talked about all sorts of other things but I [would] really like to get to the real subject and that is the unity of [the] profession in Australia.

The earliest evidence of formal unity discussions comes from a meeting of the Society executive committee held in Melbourne on 13–14 June 1967, although some informal discussions may have taken place earlier, and probably did. The minutes of the meeting state:

> President of the Society H. R. Irving outlined, for the information of the Executive, the discussions he had with A. B. Cleland, the President of the Institute, arising from a decision taken by the General Council of the Institute that the desirability and practicability of achieving unity in the profession be discussed on a President to President basis. (ASA, 1967c)

This reveals that the idea of a merger was initially suggested by the Institute's general council. The report of the November 1967 meeting of the Society's executive committee confirmed that members of the general council were informed about the unity discussions underway. It mentioned:

> All members of General Council were informed on 28 June [1967] of the approach of the Institute to the Society for discussions on the desirability and predictability of achieving unity in the profession. They were informed also that at a recent meeting of the Executive, considerable time had been devoted to the preparation of an outline of fundamental questions as they affected members of the Society for the guidance of its representatives who would meet representatives of the Institute to pursue the discussions and the negotiations. (ASA, 1967d)

After informing members of the general councils, a decision was made unanimously during the sixth joint conference held on 12 July 1967 that all members of both bodies were to be advised that unity discussions were taking place. On 26 July 1967, the two presidents issued a joint official statement that stated:

> Acting under the authority of General Councils of the Institute of Chartered Accountants in Australia and of the Australian Society of Accountants, preliminary discussions are taking place between representatives of both bodies for the purpose of exploring ways and means of achieving unity between them in the interest of the profession in Australia and in the public interest. It may be expected that further announcements will be made as these discussions progress. (Anon, 1967a, p. 418; ICAA, 1967, p. 6; also see Anon, 1967b)

With this initial announcement the shape of public discourse changed and unity was projected as a necessary step in the public interest. A formal declaration that preliminary merger discussions were being held on unifying the profession was also made in the respective annual reports of the bodies (ASA, 1967e; ICAA, 1967, p. 6).

The Society's annual report mentioned:

> As announced by the respective Presidents in August 1967 representatives of the General Councils of the Institute of Chartered Accountants in Australia and of the Society have commenced discussions on ways and means of achieving unity between them in the interests of the profession and of the community generally. The discussions will be continued early in the new-year and further announcements will be made as they progress. (ASA, 1967f, p. 1)

Moreover, the Society's annual report of 1967 also defended merger discussions arguing that a complete consolidation of the accountancy profession in Australia was a must for the development of its services to the community and the advancement of its stature and standing (ASA, 1967f).

Further progress was made during the eighth joint conference in December 1967 where the representatives of the Institute and the Society discussed the proposed approach to achieve unity between the Institute and the Society using the Royal Charter of the Institute as a basis for the merged body. They also proposed to protect the rights and status of members of both bodies. The Institute representatives stated that preservation of the Royal Charter, possibly with an amendment, was fundamental. At this conference, the general registrar of the Institute S. J. T. Walton provided details of his discussions that took place in London and elsewhere while overseas in September 1967. He stated that the general attitude of personalities and kindred organisations towards the Australian unity was favourably received and that he had unofficially discussed the proposal in general terms with the Clerk of the Privy Council, the body which oversees the administration and activities of chartered bodies. Walton also shared the news that the Institute's London solicitors had been consulted and were alerted to the probable large expansion in membership under conditions not envisaged in the original charter, as amended. Further, Walton mentioned that the Clerk of the Privy Council had stated that the law lords were unlikely to raise any formal objections to amendments recommended by the Australian

Government in Canberra. After the eighth conference, the two registrars tentatively agreed to meet on 26–27 February1968 to deal with the matters referred to them (ASA & ICAA, 1967).

After hosting the tenth joint conference on 4–5June 1968 in Sydney (ASA & ICAA, 1968b), both the Society and the Institute made official announcements regarding unity talks on 2 July 1968. This was covered in the press across the country. Newspapers reported that in early 1968, the general councils of both the Society and the Institute had announced that both bodies had agreed upon certain broad proposals as a basis for the continuation of discussions aimed at producing an outline plan for unity of the profession (Anon, 1968a). In July 1968, the general councils of the Institute and the Society announced that they had agreed upon broad proposals aimed at achieving a merger (Anon, 1968a, 1968b). The joint conferences were held four times between March 1968 and October 1968. The draft version of 15 unity proposals was presented to the general councils of both the Society and the Institute (ASA, 1968b).

The process of preparing merger proposals, receiving feedback from state councils and moving forward to the merger was prompt and it appears that members were not given detailed disclosures. The annual reports only briefly mentioned unity-related discussions and this led to demands from members for better disclosures. One member, Sands, wrote a letter to the Secretary of the Western Australian division of the ASA (undated) showing curiosity related to merger discussions. Sands (n.d.) wrote:

> Am I right in assuming that negotiations are continuing with a view to a merger of this Society with the Chartered Institute ... If this is correct, who are the personnel appointed by our Society? ... What arrangements are being made for frequent reports to our members of the progress of negotiations and the bases upon which a proposed merger is being negotiated?

Sands (n.d.) seems to have represented the sentiments of those members who were taken by surprise at the release of the merger proposals.

Further, the Tasmanian branch of the Society expressed its disappointment at the terms of reference announced in the July 1968 issue of *The Australian Accountant*. The Tasmanian branch recommended that in the interest of ultimate acceptance by members of the proposals, a statement be published in the journal which provides members with as much information as possible. They also suggested that, as proposals would develop further, more information could be provided in the journal. The Tasmanian council also asked that they be kept fully informed of the developments so that if members had any inquiries the councillors were in a position to provide the required responses. At the same time, the Victorian council commended the announcement and the proposed plan to manage the proposals (ASA, 1968b).

In response to the criticism of the Tasmanian branch of the Society, the executive compared and contrasted public announcements of unity discussions in the UK and discussed that it was not desirable to make public announcements of the progress of unity discussions until the overall plan was logically developed. Any release of information before that had many associated risks (ASA, 1968b). Originally, the unity committee had decided to make regular public announcements regarding its progress. However, the experience in the UK indicated that such an approach led to submissions to the general council seeking the discontinuation of unity discussions. Such moves were planned and executed by a group of members. Therefore, the Tasmanian council was informed of this position and was assured that when the overall plan was logically developed they would be informed along with the other councils and members. In response, the Tasmanian council accepted this decision but suggested that unity discussions should be given more publicity in every future publication of the Society. The executive, however, decided that mere publicity, without giving the detailed background of the general principles of the unity scheme, was unwise. It did accept the view that it was desirable that the members should be informed in a general way, of the satisfactory progress being made with the negotiations (ASA, 1968b). Hence, the unity committee was requested to make appropriate public announcements as soon as practicable after both general councils had met in November 1968 (ASA, 1968b).

An outline plan consisting of 15 proposals was further considered at the November 1968 meetings of the general councils of both bodies. After the November 1968 meetings, both general councils approved and authorised the release of unity proposals to respective state and divisional councils throughout Australia for their confidential consideration and comments. Comments and suggestions received for expanding the unity plan, with explanatory notes, were considered by the unity committee and were submitted to the May 1969 meetings of the general councils of both bodies along with a recommendation that the unity proposals be sent to members as soon as practicable (ASA, 1969a; Orr, 1969, p. 214).

The president of the Society reported that in a meeting of May 1969, the general council of the Institute unanimously agreed that the unity of the accounting profession in Australia, as proposed, was desirable and that it had accepted the plan submitted by the unity committee (ASA, 1969a). The May 1969 issues of the journals of both bodies published an official statement by the two presidents, which stated that 1969 offered the exciting opportunity of further major steps towards unity within the profession in Australia (ASA, 1968a).

Finally, both bodies publicly released the unity plan on 1 August 1969 (ICAA & ASA, 1969). This document formally set out the rationale for the proposed merger (p. 2):

> The integration of these two organisations to form one body, comprising some 35,000 members drawn from all sectors of the profession, is a natural and logical culmination of the development of accountancy in Australia. It will strengthen the ability of our profession to meet the many challenges facing its members and facilitate effective action to develop and enforce the standards of accounting appropriate to the rapid economic expansion of Australia.

Therefore, three different yet complementary grounds for the merger were expressed: (1) to continue the development of the accounting profession by means of unification; (2) to increase the capacity of the profession to meet the challenges facing members and (3) to assist in the development and enforcement of standards of accounting as a means of contributing to further economic development. The overall rationale focused broadly on the advancement of accounting as a profession that had yet to reach its full potential in Australia. As such, the rationale was associated with profession-wide gains, which meant changes in the boundaries of the Australian accountancy profession as a whole and effects on individual members in each body. The formation of a single body would shift professional boundaries that were constructed originally around membership of the Institute (Gieryn, 1983; Lamont & Molnár, 2002). The strategy was that of a fusion between exclusivity and market control and is termed a modified strategy.

The official rationale for a merger indicated a change from the earlier public discourse that emphasised the superiority of the Institute members, with the linguistic claims modified in an attempt to persuade the Institute members to accept changes in the organisation's boundaries (Annisette, 2017). The statement by Institute president, EW Savage, claimed that accountancy was one profession, and ... every accountant, irrespective of mode of practice or employment, would gain from a united organisation which could facilitate the harnessing of the talents and abilities of all members for the advancement of the profession as a whole (Anon, 1969h). These arguments point to the adoption of a modified organisational strategy with inclusiveness at its core and a concomitant shift in the boundaries of both associations and especially the Institute. In a study of hospital administration, Arndt and Bigelow (2005) argued that professional boundaries are modified as context changes and as a response to external challenges. They found that these challenges were threats to male dominance in the hospital administration roles. In the Australian context, as earlier explained, threats to the legitimacy of profession posed a challenge (Carnegie and O'Connell, 2012), which led to proposed changes to traditional strategies and professional boundaries of both associations. Therefore, the professional boundaries are not permanent structures and there is an ongoing struggle for control and authority over the profession (Gieryn, 1983; Nancarrow & Borthwick, 2005; Niezen & Mathijssen, 2014).

In the case of the first merger attempt, it was proposed that the unification process would be undertaken between November 1968 and December 1969 (ASA & ICAA, 1968a) in three stages:

Stage I

Stage I would comprise a series of meetings in various centres to enable members to discuss the plan. Representatives of councils would be present to give further information and to answer questions and they would be available for discussion both before and after the meetings.

Stage II

In the case of the Institute, a proposed resolution would be submitted to members by means of postal ballot, when they would be asked to vote in principle on the plan.

Stage III

> After formal drafting had been completed:
>
> In the case of the Society, a meeting would be convened at which members would be asked to accept formally the basis on which they would become members of the Institute to be reconstituted in the manner necessary to give effect to the proposals outlined in the plan.
>
> In the case of the Institute, after the meeting of the Society had been held, a meeting at which a poll would be taken would be convened, when proposed resolutions to authorise the necessary amendments to the Royal Charter and Bylaws would give effect to the plan for unity. (ICAA & ASA, 1969)

For Stage I, meetings of members were planned to take place throughout Australia between 8 September 1969 and 6 October 1969 for the Society and between 11 September 1969 and 13 October 1969 for the Institute (ASA & ICAA 1968a). Voting papers for the postal ballot of the Institute and the referendum of the Society in Stage II were issued on 5 November 1969, returnable by 5 December 1969 (ASA, 1969a).

The underlying rationale of the professional bodies for mounting the unity attempt was to:

> Demonstrate clearly to the community that accountancy is a profession, whether it be practised for the benefit of the public generally or for the benefit of single enterprises in commerce, industry and government. (ASA, 1969b)

The basic objective of the unity of both bodies was to:

> Strengthen the ability of the profession to meet the many challenges facings its members and facilitate effective action to develop and enforce the standards of accounting appropriate to the rapid economic expansion of Australia. (ASA & ICAA, 1969)

The 1969 annual report of the Institute also attempted to advocate or promote the unity plan to its members:

> We have now reached a significant landmark in the history of the accounting profession in Australia and the coming year will determine the way ahead. It is vitally important that every member fully understands the proposals and, therefore, meetings have been arranged during September

> and October in all States with the objective of providing members with the opportunity of thoroughly discussing the proposals. This is known as Stage I. The three stages set out in the Plan and a message from the President to all members outlining these stages appeared on the inside front cover of August issue of the Journal. (ICAA, 1969, p. 7)

These statements show a major shift in public discourse and appear to be targeted at modifying the boundaries within the profession. The meeting of the executive committee of the Society was held in October 1969 where the committee reviewed the details of members' meetings held by divisional councils. The committee was informed that some members were disappointed and that there were some objections about certain aspects of the unity plan. However, it was also inferred from reports received that, in general, the Society's members were in favour of the plan. The Victorian division had more objections and divisional council made some suggestions, including for the use of the term "affiliate accountants" in the classification. However, when the executive committee met, it did not agree with the suggestions of the Victorian division and decided that no changes be suggested at that time. They also agreed that inclusion of members of the Institute of Commercial Studies[5] was a matter to be decided by the general council of the integrated body. The executive also decided to advise the unity committee that the Society was confident about the support of its members in favour of the proposal. The executive also decided that if the Institute wanted to distinguish MIPP this would be accepted, and it proposed the title of "Chartered Accountants in public practice".

It was reported that only small numbers had attended metropolitan meetings of members, but the general indication was that the Society members were in favour of the proposals. Some suggestions from the Victorian council were received but it was decided that no alterations be made at that stage, which was less than two months before the unity vote took place. The date by which the voting papers were returnable was changed to 3 December, by 5.00 pm. It was also proposed that the statement "it is important that you record your vote" be added after the text of voting instructions. Further, it was decided to provide business reply postal envelopes to the Society members following a decision at the previous meeting to do so in the case that the Institute did. The

[5] Name change from the National Institute of Accountants in 1967.

Society also decided to report to the unity committee for its October 15 meeting that it was confident that its members would vote in favour. It also reported some criticisms that had been received. It was decided to record votes for and against on a state basis with an analysis to be published in *The Australian Accountant*. The November issue featured a formal statement from the president including the principal objections raised by members with the replies given at the meetings. This was done as a reminder to those who attended and for the benefit of those who were unable to be present. The statement also asked all members to record their votes. An advance copy was sent to the Institute (ASA, 1969e).

Both bodies agreed that the voting results were to be discussed in divisional and state councils on a confidential basis. However, it was agreed that the overall vote of each association would be published. Any matter related to the issuance of statements to the press was left in the hands of the president of the Society (ASA, 1969f). The merger proposal, dated 1 August 1969 and titled "A Plan for the Unity of the Accountancy Profession in Australia", comprised 15 specific proposals for the unity of the Australian accounting profession and was sent to members for voting. The proposals covered matters such as name, constitution, designation of members, voting rights, education, conditions on public practice, professional conduct, journal, subscription and fees, governing bodies and administration.

The proposal, voted on 3 December 1969, failed because only 41.8 per cent of the members of the Institute endorsed the move and acceptance of the merger by the Institute required a two-thirds majority of voting members; however, a large majority of 88.5 per cent of the voting members of the Society supported the proposal (ICAA, 1970, p. 8). In the case of the Institute, voting papers were received from 77.2 per cent of the membership and in the case of the Society, from 69.7 per cent of the membership (ICAA, 1970, p. 8). The first attempt at unifying the accounting profession in Australia had failed at Stage II of the three-stage process outlined earlier in this chapter.

The outcome of the vote (see Table 6.5) was officially announced on 8 December 1969 by the president of the Society L. P. Crockett and the president of the Institute E. W. Savage (ICAA 1970, p. 8).

Contrary to the expectations and claims of both bodies, the members of the Institute rejected the idea of a merger, with only a minority of voting members being in favour, that is, far short of the two-thirds

Table 6.5 Outcome of vote

	Society (%)	*Society Ballots Returned (%)*	*Institute (%)*	*Institute Ballot Returned (%)*
		69.7		77.2
Yes	88.5	61.7	41.8	32.3
No	11.5	8.0	58.2	44.9

Source ICAA (1970, p. 8)

majority required. The leaders of the Institute had effectively failed to sell to its members the idea of a single accounting body.

It appears that despite showing public confidence, both bodies were mindful of the possibility of the merger failing. Just three days before the members of the Institute rejected the merger, the bodies held a joint meeting of their Education Committees on 30 November 1969. It was decided that uniform education policies would be sought irrespective of the unity proposal outcome (ASA & ICAA, 1969). Further coordinated efforts were mentioned in the annual report of the Institute, which provided details of cooperation with the Society for organising the Tenth International Congress of Accountants (ICAA, 1970, p. 10). After the failure of the first merger attempt, within six months the executive committees of two bodies began to meet regularly at quarterly intervals to exchange views and explore avenues of close cooperation and collaboration (Zeff, 1973).

Several newspapers reported briefly on the failure of the merger proposal. Most of these articles provided a descriptive account of what happened, including the voting outcomes and the official statements of both bodies. Some articles also mentioned that within the Institute opposition to the merger plan had been growing for some time, which resulted in its defeat (Anon, 1969d; Anon, 1969e; Anon, 1969f; Anon, 1969g).

6.4 Discussion and Analysis

Two significant findings emerge from this chapter: (1) the traditional organisational strategies of both bodies were modified and (2) there was a successful protection of the Institute's boundaries by its members and, consequently, the preservation of the different organisational strategies of each body. These respective findings are discussed in conjunction with four of the five research questions asked in this book.

6.4.1 *Reasons for Mounting the Merger Attempt*

This book's first research question is "What were the reasons for mounting the first merger attempt between the Society and the Institute?" Earlier sections of this chapter have covered the background context that led to the first merger attempt, which will be briefly discussed again in this section. When this question was posed to Geoff Orr, who was the first vice-president and then president of the Society during the years of discussions and votes on the first merger attempt, Orr (2014) replied by stating that when both bodies started discussions on joint activities, the Institute had already decided to initiate merger discussions. Orr (2014) said of the Institute that:

> They were dodging the issue in the first instance. I think the whole reason for it was because they saw the development of the Society, which was not tremendous in those days but it was a growing body. I think the Institute felt little bit under siege.

The reasons for mounting the merger attempt fell into three categories. First, were reasons that jointly affected both the Institute and the Society; second and third, were reasons specific to each body.

Common reasons included the corporate failures and the legitimacy crisis, which forced both bodies to become involved in joint activities (Carnegie & O'Connell, 2012) and created an environment that was favourable to the mounting of the first merger attempt. The development of accounting standards and guidelines was an uncoordinated activity, and this issue was repeatedly raised by many members. As discussed earlier in Sect. 6.2.2, JK Little, who was a member of the general council of the Institute, expressed concerns over the Institute's slow growth in different areas (Little, 1968). As such, these factors played a background role in creating favourable circumstances for a merger attempt.

The Institute had its own reasons for putting forward the idea of merger. Despite its exclusivity, the Institute seemed to struggle with the challenges of the 1960s. This included a legitimacy crisis arising from the failure of companies to follow its accounting pronouncements and widespread concerns about the state of accounting and auditing in

Australia. The financial results of the Institute were patchy at best and not as favourable as those of the Society were. Geoff Orr confirmed the Institute's difficult situation, which he may have inferred from his confidential discussions with the Institute president. Orr (2014) stated in his interview that "they [the Institute] felt if they didn't do something then the Society would swamp the profession". Dunkley (2014) added that the Institute had financial motivations for going ahead with the merger: "I think they wanted an element of financial stability—perhaps resulting from a larger number of members together with a larger element of members in industry and commerce". The Institute made initial attempts to initiate discussions with the Society on joint works, leading to the joint establishment and sponsorship of the ARF, and then it proceeded to merger discussions.

For the Society, the public status of its members when compared with the Institute members was an issue and the proposed merger provided an opportunity for a status upgrade. The higher status of CAs, as the Institute's longstanding professional title, was also recognised by the Society in various public discourses (see Parker, 2005 for a discussion of accounting "brand names" in Commonwealth countries). Evidence for this is available in a report submitted on "Professional Awards for Accountants" authored by the president of the Society, H. R. Irving. The report stated:

> There is no coincidence in the fact that the title 'Chartered Accountant' is well-known and generally well-accepted in the community. It is generally recognized that members of the Society are at an extreme disadvantage because of a lack of a generic name by which they can identify themselves in the community. (Irving, 1966, p. 9)

Access to the term "Chartered Accountant" by members of the Society had the potential to raise their status, irrespective of changes in professional competence and current work roles. The merger would lead to a change in public discourse, which was traditionally based on the differences between the membership profiles of each body (Annisette, 2017). While the Society's general council was keen to raise the status of its members, Irving (1966, p.9) raised a concern that:

> The Society could not expect in a short period—in say less than 10 years—to hope to match any title it adopted for its public accountants with that

> of any 'Chartered Accountant', even with the expenditure of considerable resources.

At the November 1967 meeting of the Society's executive, it was proposed to take "positive action for improving the image of the profession" (ASA, 1967g). It is apparent that the Society's leaders were ready to make an attempt to acquire enhanced status through a merger with the Institute. The invitations of the Institute, first, to engage in joint discussions to address matters of mutual interest, and second, to commence the merger discussions, were readily accepted. This was also confirmed in the oral history interview with James Dunkley, who stated that the then president of the Society, Geoff Orr, was promoting the merger attempt quite strongly. Dunkley (2014) stated that Geoff Orr had "thought the Chartered title would give the members of the Society of Accountants a better status". Hence, the Society was conscious of gaining exclusivity through obtaining access to the Chartered Accountant title for its members.

As discussed previously, the boundaries of the Australian accounting profession were created around a distinction between the Institute and the Society membership and the adoption of two different organisational strategies, as characterised by the response to the "exclusiveness versus market control" dilemma (Anderson et al., 2005; Carnegie et al., 2003; Carnegie & Parker, 1999; Edwards et al., 2013; Macdonald & Ritzer, 1988, p. 257; Parker, 2005). Section 2, above, discussion in this section and earlier chapters identified various factors that led both bodies to modify their traditional strategies. Each body had previously adopted a particular strategy. Whether to adopt an exclusiveness strategy or market control strategy is linked to conditions related to the membership, a decision taken at the leadership level at the time of formation of any professional body. In the case of the first merger attempt, the leadership of the Institute was prepared to modify the exclusive status earned by its membership over many years. Prior research reveals that compromises to a traditional strategy of exclusivity can deliver a form of market control in particular occupational contexts. In the case of the British medical profession, the three licensing bodies representing physicians, surgeons and apothecaries went through 20 years of political and legislative lobbying and infighting. However, the outcome was that:

> the Medical Act of 1958 set the seal on a series of compromises whereby the higher-status groups partially relaxed their exclusiveness and gained

> not only state regulation of the whole occupation, but control over the regulatory machinery. (Macdonald & Ritzer, 1988, p. 258)

However, in the case of the Institute, the modification of its traditional strategy was linked to the professional crisis that occurred in the early to mid-1960s as discussed above. Unlike the British medical profession, the Australian accounting bodies were not going to gain complete control over the profession; rather, they sought the market control created through a single large membership-based body that would remain relatively exclusive because of its size and its possession of a Royal Charter as a symbol of status. Hence, the new strategy may be described as exclusiveness by belonging to a single major professional body. In other words, the new strategy was an integrated strategy between exclusiveness and market control.

6.4.2 *Strategies Adopted by Both Bodies in Merger Attempt*

The second research question is linked with the strategies adopted by both bodies related to the first merger attempt. Considerable cooperation and mutual understanding existed between the two bodies. Merger discussions did not suffer any major setbacks and both bodies smoothly executed discussions through joint conferences initially and then via the unity committee. A degree of confidentiality was maintained, where any proposals were discussed and approved at the general councils of both bodies before being finalised by the unity committee. Major discussions were undertaken at national and general council levels and between councils and the unity committee.

Members sought more disclosures on the merger process, for instance regarding the mechanisms for creating a formal proposal, providing and receiving feedback to and from councils, and making decisions. The Tasmanian branch of the Society publicly asked for more disclosures. However, this request was rejected based on the example of merger discussions in the UK (ASA 1968b). Thus, the strategy was to maintain a degree of secrecy to avoid backlash on the merger attempt, especially from members of the Institute. This merger attempt was also unique in that it had three stages. In Stage I, throughout Australia, meetings of members were organised to allow members to seek questions and provide responses.

It is argued that the strategies adopted in this merger were based around modification of the traditional organisational strategies of "exclusiveness versus market control" (Macdonald & Ritzer, 1988, p. 257). This framework has been used in many accounting studies (Anderson et al., 2005; Carnegie & Parker, 1999; Carnegie et al., 2003; Edwards et al., 2013; Parker, 2005). In a study of the formation of ARIA, Edwards et al. (2013) found that founders followed a strict exclusive strategy that proved a stumbling block for gaining influence because the membership base was not enough. As discussed previously, the Institute was struggling financially and its membership size was 17 per cent the size of the Society (ASA, 1969d; ICAA, 1969). So when exclusivity was not enough to sustain it, the leaders decided to modify the organisational strategy, leading to proposed changes in boundaries, as Gieryn (1983) stated that boundaries are not fixed structures and, according to Fournier (2000, p. 83), they are "malleable and expandable".

Of the 5,377 members of the Institute in 1969, 1,900 or 35 per cent of its members were also members of the Society, and in the case of Institute's fellows, 1,182 or 42 per cent were also members of the Society (ICAA, 1969). In order to persuade its members, the general council of the Institute proposed that it was desirable to extend the accounting profession beyond a concentration on public accounting (Anon, 1969c). In his final letter, dated 5 November 1969, before members voted on the merger attempt, the president of the Institute, EW Savage, argued that more than 25 per cent of the Institute members were not in public practice. The discourse was based on the argument that the general trend in other countries was that more and more members were engaged in the profession outside public practice and that the future development of the Institute should also follow that pattern (Savage, 1969):

> General Council accepted the basic concept that accountancy is one undivided profession of which public practice is but one segment. The Council believes that to confine the profession to those in public practice is to run against world accounting opinion. The accounting skills and knowledge of those in public practice, commerce, industry and government are inextricably interwoven. (Savage, 1969, p. 1)

These sentiments show a modification of the traditional strategies adopted by the Institute based on the notion of exclusiveness, which had been ingrained into its organisational culture since its foundation. Instead of an emphasis on difference, the discursive claims brought the benefits of solidarity to the fore: "Unity is strength. The status of each individual accountant is related to the status and strength of the profession" (Anon, 1966, p. 241). Gieryn (1983) stated that demarcation is always based on certain discursive arguments that depend on what justifies the claim to authority. Demarcation in this instance arises from differences between members of the Institute and the Society. As Annisette (2017) showed, public claims are used to create meanings for categories; in this instance counterclaims were also used to defend the deconstruction of differences between members of the Society and the Institute. Although the business model of the new body was that of "inclusivity", it would retain a form of exclusivity by keeping the Royal Charter and Chartered Accountant professional status for all members, including those who were formerly members of the Society. By including a large number of members of the Society and by forming a large dominant professional body, it would attain more effective market control. The notion of exclusivity changed to one centred on a large professional body, representing most or virtually all professional accountants, with a Royal Charter as a symbol of earned status. This was a "step up" for the Society as the voting patterns showed. In other words, while "market control" was retained, the proposed merged body would be generally seen as more exclusive than the Society itself was before merger. The next parts of this section present further evidence and argue that members of the Institute, contrary to the recommendations of the Institute's leadership, rejected this proposed change and engaged in boundary work to protect the boundaries of their professional association.

6.4.3 *Reasons for Merger Attempt Failure*

The third research question identifies the major factors that resulted in the failure of the first merger attempt.

There are two angles in the analysis when responding to third research question. First, there was a detachment of leaders and members of the Institute (Lee, 2010; Shackleton & Walker, 2001). The second angle is that members of the Institute engaged in boundary protection work and preserved the existing boundaries. Within this response, the overwhelming support for changes in professional boundaries from the Society members is also discussed.

Successful mergers are the result of boundary work where members of the continuing association adjust their self-image based on the organisational strategies of professional associations to accommodate change (Richardson & Jones, 2007). This did not happen in the case of the first merger attempt as the Institute leaders failed to understand that its members were not prepared to accommodate sharing their professional titles with a large number of the Society members. This failure of leadership has also been termed as the detachment of leaders from members of professional bodies (Lee, 2010; Shackleton & Walker, 2001). This detachment was also visible in Britain, where one of the central reasons for various unsuccessful merger attempts was the detachment of office bearers of professional associations from members. Such detachment could be fatal, given that the ultimate authority to approve any merger scheme would vest with members (Lee, 2010; Shackleton & Walker, 2001).

There is discursive evidence that some members of the Institute did not agree with the organisation's leaders, writing that "we are the persons to make the decision not General Council" (Anon, 1969b). This indicated some detachment of the leaders from the members of the Institute (Lee, 2010; Shackleton & Walker, 2001). In a letter written to the editor of *The Chartered Accountant in Australia* dated 8 May 1969, RW Parry stated that there was a lack of open discussion in the Institute on the issue of unity and that "no opportunity is to be given for discussion through the columns of the Institute journal". In his discursive claims Parry also criticised the 1 July 1968 statement by both presidents "that steps will be taken to ensure that members have ample opportunity of considering the whole of the proposed plan for unity before any decisions were taken or implemented" (Parry, 1969, p. 1076). Members also asked to take a ballot first on whether the plan was acceptable or not before going ahead with the unity vote. This would mean extensive discussion and voting on the actual plan and, if this was approved, then going ahead with unity discussions (Anon, 1969a; O'Neill, 1969). The discursive argument continued as Parry (1969) further stated that since the unity announcements were made in 1968, he had "discussed the topic with quite a number of members and [was] yet to find one who regards the concept ... in the best interest of the profession" (Parry, 1969, p. 1076).

The leaders of the Institute faced strong opposition from members. As a member, Harriman (1968, p. 27) wrote to the editor of *The Chartered Accountant in Australia* that "my conclusion is that I do not have any faith in the present council of the Institute. They obviously do not know their members". These linguistic claims indicate that some members of the Institute were firm on preserving the distinction between the members of the two bodies (Annisette, 2017). This proved to be prophetic, given that a majority of members rejected the proposal and, thereby, the pleas of the Institute's general council. Richardson and Jones (2007) compared two merger attempts in Canada, where the unsuccessful attempt of 2004 was for similar reasons as the merger examined in this book when the merger discussions were scrapped at leadership level after it became evident that it would not be ratified by members of the Institute. In the Australian context, leadership of the Institute did not read the mood of its members. Gibson's (1970) letter presented a brief analysis of the failure of the merger from the perspective of members of the Institute. In his view, the Institute's council made a mistake by not taking members into its confidence: "Where perhaps the Institute's General Council erred was in not firstly asking its members to vote on the principle of unity, and enclosing a questionnaire to ascertain the acceptability of guidelines for a fusion".

The literature on boundary management contends that individuals in a lower status group support mobility strategies and readily accept changes in boundaries (Keohane & Milner, 1996; Milner, 1996), which helps explain the overwhelming support, at 88.5 per cent, given to the merger attempt by the Society members. As Gibson (1970) wrote, "As to the general councils, that of the Society was no task at all—practically all of its members obviously would accept the proposed automatic elevation in title from 'accountant' to 'Chartered Accountant'". In 1930, the British government rejected demands for the state registration of accountants when a similar situation of changes in boundaries of professional associations had arisen. The chartered institutes, which feared dilution of their status, were opposed to the registration proposal. However, similarly to this book, the lower status organisations, which saw registration as an opportunity to be placed alongside CAs, strongly favoured state registration. This was the case of boundary management by British accountants (Gieryn, 1983).

Next, the boundary protection by members of the Institute is analysed. As the context changes, defensive strategies are adopted to protect boundaries (Fournier, 2000). Members of higher-status groups, predictably, seek to defend against changes in boundaries of their groups (Keohane & Milner, 1996; Milner, 1996). Accordingly, in various unsuccessful merger attempts in the UK the attempts failed because the members of the perceived higher-status associations voted against the merger attempts. In examining the failure to achieve coordination among British accounting bodies in 1957, Shackleton and Walker (1998, p. vii) found part of the cause related to the higher-status institutes that were "unwilling to sacrifice a dilution in their status in order to achieve the greater object of rationalisation". More evidence of these tensions can be seen in Scotland, where between 1884 and 1900 nine attempts to dilute the status of CAs through changes in boundaries were successfully defeated on the basis that it was against the public interest and that the non-Chartered Accountant body members were "not professional" (Walker, 1991, pp. 268–269).

Boundary protection work was undertaken at individual and organised levels by the Institute members, with the many strong linguistic claims against the proposed merger revealing that members of the Institute were prepared to protect the organisation's traditional boundaries. A common theme in the public discourse of these members was that they had worked very hard to reach their present position and believed that the present form of the Institute should be kept intact (Anon, 1969c). An example of these discursive claims includes O'Neill (1969), a member of the Institute, who stated that unity was providing members of the Society with a "free ride on the sacrifice of the hard work of others and that the Institute was sacrificing its reputation, efficiency, standing and members by seeking to unite with the Society". In this discursive claim O'Neill (1969) further added that "it is hoped that no Chartered Accountant will vote for this unity proposal". Another example of linguistic claims of superiority is a letter by L. G. Boscoe to the editor of *The Australian Accountant* which stated that "devaluation of status is now to be wished upon the members of the Chartered Institute" (Boscoe, 1969, p. 522).

In his interview, Orr (2014) expressed a similar sentiment:

> The real question from the Institute's point of view [was] that they did not want to be swamped by people who didn't have the technical ability to deal with the public. They didn't want people to go out into public practice without any boundary.

Orr (2014) elaborated on why the Institute members voted against the merger proposal and pointed out:

> I reckon [their thinking was]... 'we are Chartered Accountants. We don't want to extend that title to a group of people we don't believe have the same professional qualifications.' That would be the main reason. I think there was a feeling in the Chartered Institute among younger members that personal financial considerations would outweigh the professional considerations. A group from Western Australia ran a campaign against [the] merger.

This portrayal is what Gieryn (1983) calls a demarcation based on special attributes that are used as the basis for the exclusion of certain practitioners, based on labels of lower technical abilities or not being "professional". This is congruent with Annisette's (2017) contention regarding the exclusion of "foreign" trained accountants in Canada through the use of public discourse. In another study, Annisette and Trivedi (2013) argued that "the devaluation of foreign credentials is a real and pervasive problem in Canada which not only threatens the country's image as the model of multiculturalism but for those who see skilled immigration as the key to Canada's economic prosperity" (Annisette & Trivedi, 2013, p. 2). The case of a 2004 merger attempt of accounting associations in Canada witnessed similar boundary protection work to that of the Australian case. Richardson and Jones (2007, p. 153) noted that "the concern most commonly expressed was that the merger would dilute the value of the Chartered Accountant designation either directly through the increase in numbers and consequently the increase in competition within the designation, or indirectly through the dilution of the reputation of the brand". These are examples of "discourse of superiority to create a public image of their members which cast them as superior to other practitioners in the field" (Annisette, 2017, p. 1).

The boundary protection by the Institute members was an attempt to protect their professional identity (Guo, 2012) because boundaries "play a critical role in the process of constructing identities" (Zerubavel, 1991, p. 193) and maintaining them. Guo (2012) examined the recent merger of accounting associations in Canada and found that objections of some CAs were as a result of a potential threat to the professional identities of their status.

In addition to boundary protection work at the individual level, there was an organised boundary protection campaign run by members, which reflected the desire of those members to maintain the exclusiveness model of professional association rather than to accept modification and move closer to the market control strategy. The oral history interviews strengthen the argument that members of the Institute actively became involved in boundary protection both at the individual level and through small organised groups. In his oral history interview, James Dunkley (2014) stated, "I am sure that there was also a group in the Chartered Institute who thought we don't want so many accountants to all become Chartered Accountants". Members of the Institute argued that the "majority of the Society members will have the right to call themselves CAs without necessarily having the broad practical experience and professional qualifications which are demanded by the existing Institute" (Anon, 1969a).

One of the main factors that led to the failure included strong opposition from members of the Institute from Western Australia, as Orr (2014) said:

> The greater opposition seemed to have come from Western Australia. They had published in the Chartered journal all the reasons why they wanted people to vote against it. Their argument was that we worked hard to become Chartered Accountants and they didn't want other people to benefit from it without hard work.

As the next three chapters also show, the younger members of the Institute proved to be a stumbling block in all four cases and the theoretical model applied argues that this was the result of boundary management and boundary protection by members of the Institute. The central argument was articulated as a discourse of superiority, as the Chartered Accountants sought to project a public image that cast them as superior to members of the Society (Annisette, 2017).

The proportion of the existing Institute members to the Society members in the proposed combined Institute would have been about 16 per cent to 84 per cent. In other words, the number of Institute members was 5,488, and with the merger, all the 31,793 members of the new Institute would become CAs (ASA, 1969c; ICAA, 1969). This meant that the Institute members would have had little or no redress regarding decision-making in the future. The campaign led by an anonymous group advocated the membership to cast a "no" vote.

Further evidence of a concerted effort of boundary protection is contained in an open letter written by 14 members of the Institute (including S. B. Denton, who was a member of the South Australian state council of the Institute) to all other members after a 23 September 1969 meeting of members that was held in Adelaide. During that meeting, the unity plan was discussed and debated. The reason for the open letter was to provide a summary of the principal points that had been debated and to which it was claimed no satisfactory answers had been provided. The letter stated that during the meeting most members expressed that they were unhappy about the general council pursuing unity, which, they believed, was being imposed upon them (Anon., 1969b). The letter quoted statements attributed to various members:

> We have not been given the opportunity to vote in favour of the principle of unity. (Anon, 1969b)
>
> Under the method proposed it is impossible to vote 'yes' for the principle of unity without voting 'yes' for a plan which, in detail, shapes our destiny. (Anon, 1969b)

The letter concluded with the following statement: "With this in mind the plan for unity must be re-thought. Members are urged to vote against the present proposals" (Anon, 1969b). The members writing the letter also demanded that there should be a clear distinction between MIPP and those in industry, commerce and government (Anon, 1969b). Hence, the underlying rationale for the merger, specifically that accounting as a profession was to be perceived as equally important in the economy and society in all contexts in which accountants operated, was rejected.

6.4.4 Reactions of Various Stakeholders

The fourth research question of this book relates to the reaction of various stakeholders after the merger attempt failed. As noted in Sect. 5.3, the failure of the merger attempt did not attract significant interest and even newspapers covered it in short descriptive detail only. Orr (2014) substantiated the reactions of parties outside the profession and said that governments did not put any pressure on the idea of unity and added that other stakeholders, including those in the commercial world, "didn't take much real interest in the merger until it happened and failed. They were generally disappointed. But I don't remember seeing any outburst from any sections of commercial world".

6.5 Conclusion

This chapter has examined the first attempt to merge the Society and the Institute. This merger attempt was a unique development in the Australian accounting profession because each body had been set up based on different organisational strategies. Since the formation of both bodies, there has not been significant cooperation regarding accounting standards, research, the education of accountants, and communication with the government on matters affecting the profession and representation of the profession at the international level. The professional challenges and legitimacy crisis of the 1960s forced the bodies to engage in joint work and finally work out a merger plan. This chapter has also shown that the long-term objective of both bodies was a complete occupational closure by gaining registration for accountants.

The merger discussions commenced informally at the request of the Institute president and then became formal through the formation of the unity committee, which drew all its members from the national councils of both bodies. Although the final vote indicated that the Society members overwhelmingly supported the move, criticism of the merger process was expressed by the Tasmanian branch of the Society, which cited a lack of disclosures. Despite public confidence, the merger attempt failed because of a lack of sufficient support from the Institute members.

Chapter 7 of this book considers the second merger attempt, which was planned for the longest period and was one of the most rigorous processes among all four merger attempts.

References

Anderson, C. W. (1967). *Report of general registrar of general council on international congress of accountants dated 3 November 1967 by C. W. Anderson.* Submitted for Executive Committee meeting on 13 November 1967, ASA, Melbourne, 1–19.

Anderson, M., Edwards, J. R., & Chandler, R. A. (2005). Constructing the 'well qualified' chartered accountant in England and Wales. *The Accounting Historians Journal, 32*(2), 5–54.

Annisette, M. (2017). Discourse of the professions: The making, normalizing and taming of Ontario's foreign-trained accountant. *Accounting, Organizations and Society, 60*, 37–61.

Annisette, M., & Trivedi, V. U. (2013). Globalization, paradox and the (un) making of identities: Immigrant chartered accountants of India in Canada. *Accounting, Organisations and Society, 38*(1), 1–29.
Anon. (1964a, March 19). Registration sought by Vic. Accountants. *Financial Review*, p. 7.
Anon. (1964b, April 21). Accountants should be registered. *Mercury*, p. 8.
Anon. (1964c, July). The Institute and Society meet in conference. *The Australian Accountant*, p. 358.
Anon. (1965a, February). Joint action within the profession *The Australian Accountant*, p. 61.
Anon. (1965b, June 4). Accountancy research. *Morning Herald*, p. 8.
Anon. (1965c, January 20). Research for better practice or public relations. *Australian Financial Review*, pp. 2–3.
Anon. (1966, May). Integration of the Australian Society of Accountants and the Australasian Institute of Cost Accountants. *The Australian Accountant*, pp. 240–241.
Anon. (1967a, July 27). Accountants to aim at amalgamation. *The Age*, p. 9.
Anon. (1967b, July 27). Accountants may merge. *Courier Mail*, p. 6.
Anon. (1968a, 3 July). Accountants bodies may unite. *The West Australian*, p. 8.
Anon. (1968b, July). Announcement. *The Australian Accountant*, p. 7.
Anon. (1968c, October). Institute news. *The Chartered Accountant in Australia*, p. 403.
Anon. (1968d, July 6). Accountants urge more information. *The West Australian*, p. 8.
Anon. (1968e, December). Unification of profession proposed in India. *The Australian Accountant*, p. 697.
Anon. (1969a). A plan for the unity of the accountancy profession in Australia; Contra: A case against (circulated on behalf of a representative group of Chartered Accountants to the members of the Institute of Chartered Accountants in Australia), August 1, pp. 1–17.
Anon. (1969b). An open letter to members of the Institute of Chartered Accountants in Australia (South Australian Branch), October 20.
Anon. (1969c, November). Unity of the profession. *The Chartered Accountant in Australia*, p. 27.
Anon. (1969e, December 9) Accountants merger off. *The Australian*, p. 5.
Anon. (1969f, December 9). Accountants' merger defeated. *The Sydney Morning Herald*, p. 7.
Anon. (1969g, December 9). Accounting merger vetoed by Institute. *Australian Financial Review*, p. 8.
Anon. (1969h, September). Unity proposals submitted to members. *The Australian Accountant*, p. 394.

Arndt, M., & Bigelow, B. (2005). Professionalizing and masculinizing a female occupation: The reconceptualization of hospital administration. *Administrative Science Quarterly, 50*, 233–261.

Australian Bureau of Statistics. (1968). Australian demographics statistics.

Australian Society of Accountants and the Institute of Chartered Accountants in Australia. (1967). Eighth conference of representatives of The Institute of Chartered Accountants and the Australian Society of Accountants held in Sydney on December 6, 1967 (1–21). ASA Melbourne and ICAA Sydney.

Australian Society of Accountants and The Institute of Chartered Accountants in Australia. (1968a). Ninth Conference of representatives of The Institute of Chartered Accountants and the Australian Society of Accountants held in Melbourne on March 22–23, 1968 (1–18). ASA Melbourne and ICAA Sydney.

Australian Society of Accountants and The Institute of Chartered Accountants in Australia. (1968b). Tenth Conference of representatives of The Institute of Chartered Accountants and the Australian Society of Accountants held in Sydney on June 4–5, 1968 (1–21). ASA Melbourne and ICAA Sydney.

Australian Society of Accountants and the Institute of Chartered Accountants in Australia. (1969). *Report of Joint Meeting of Education Committees*. ASA Melbourne and ICAA Sydney, 1–19.

Australian Society of Accountants. (1965). *Annual report*. Melbourne, Australia.

Australian Society of Accountants. (1966a). *Accounting principles and practices discussed in reports of company failures*.

Australian Society of Accountants. (1966b). *Minutes of meeting of General Council held on 7–8 November* (1–23). Surfers Paradise.

Australian Society of Accountants. (1967a). *Minutes of meeting of Executive Committee held on 17 February 1967a* (1–20).

Australian Society of Accountants. (1967b). *Minutes of meeting of General Council held on 1–4 May 1967at Hobart* (1–21).

Australian Society of Accountants. (1967c). *Minutes of meeting of Executive Committee held on 13–14 June* (1–11).

Australian Society of Accountants. (1967d). *Executive committee report presented to the general council on 13 November*.

Australian Society of Accountants. (1967e). *Annual report*. Melbourne, Australia.

Australian Society of Accountants. (1967f). *Annual report*. Melbourne, Australia.

Australian Society of Accountants. (1967g). *Executive committee report presented to the General Council on 13 November* (1–16).

Australian Society of Accountants. (1968a). *Annual report*. Melbourne, Australia.

Australian Society of Accountants. (1968b). *Report of Executive Committee submitted by J. G. Orr (Chairman) on behalf of executive committee to the general council on 30 October* (20–35).

Australian Society of Accountants. (1969a). *Report of Executive Committee submitted by L. P. Crockett (Chairman) on behalf of executive committee to the general council on 12 June* (1–19).
Australian Society of Accountants. (1969b, August 1). *President's letter to members*. Melbourne, Australia.
Australian Society of Accountants. (1969c). *Minutes of meeting of general council held on May 19–21* (1–22).
Australian Society of Accountants. (1969d). *Annual report*.
Australian Society of Accountants. (1969e). *Minutes of meeting of General Council held in Melbourne November 13–14* (1–16). Melbourne, Australia.
Australian Society of Accountants. (1969f). *Report of executive committee submitted by L. P. Crockett (Chairman) on behalf of executive committee to the general council on 14 October 1969d* (17–30).
Australian Society of Accountants. (1970). *Annual report*. Melbourne, Australia.
Australian Society of Accountants and the Institute of Chartered Accountants in Australia. (1969). *Report of Joint Meeting of Education Committees*. ASA Melbourne and ICAA Sydney, pp. 1–19.
Boscoe, L. G. (1969, November). Letters to the editor. *The Australian Accountant*, p. 522.
Braddock, L. A. (1965). Future education policy of the society, report submitted by L. A.
Burrows, G. (1996). *The foundation: A history of the Australian Accounting Research Foundation 1966–91*. Australian Accounting Research Foundation.
Carnegie, G. D. (1993). The Australian Institute of Incorporated Accountants (1892–1938). *Accounting, Business and Financial History, 3*(1), 61–80.
Carnegie, G. D. (2009). The development of accounting regulation, education and literature in Australia, 1788–2005. *Australian Economic History Review, 49*(3), 276–301.
Carnegie, G. D., & Edwards, J. R. (2001). The construction of the professional accountant: The case of the Incorporated Institute of Accountants, Victoria (1886). *Accounting, Organisations and Society, 26*(4/5), 301–325.
Carnegie, G. D., & O'Connell, B. T. (2012). Understanding the responses of professional accounting bodies to crises: The case of the Australian profession in the 1960s. *Accounting Auditing and Accountability Journal, 25*(5), 835–875.
Carnegie, G. D., & Parker, R. H. (1999). Accountants and empire: The case of co-membership of Australian and British accountancy bodies, 1885 to 1914. *Accounting, Business & Financial History, 9*(1), 77–102.
Carnegie, G. D., Edwards, J. R., & West, B. P. (2003). Understanding the dynamics of the Australian accounting profession: A prosopographical study of the founding members of the Incorporated Institute of Accountants,

Victoria, 1886 to 1908. *Accounting, Auditing & Accountability Journal, 16*(5), 790–820.

Cash, K. (1997). Social epistemology, gender and nursing theory. *International Journal of Nursing Studies, 34*(2), 137–143.

Clarke, F., Dean, G., & Oliver, K. (2003). *Corporate collapse: Accounting, regulatory and ethical failure* (2nd ed.). Cambridge University Press.

Craig, H. F. (1963, May). Registration of accountants—Presidential address. *The Australian Accountant,* 235–237.

Dunkley, J. (2014). Interview with James Dunkley on 26 April.

Edwards, J. R., Carnegie, G. D., & Cauberg, J. (1997). The Incorporated Institute of Accountants, Victoria (1886): A study of founders' backgrounds. In T. E. Cooke, & C. W. Nobes (Eds.), *The development of accounting in an international context: A festschrift in honour of R. H. Parker* (49–67).Routledge.

Edwards, J. R., Dean, G., Clarke, F., & Wolnizer, P. (2013). Accounting academic elites: The tale of ARIA. *Accounting, Organisations and Society, 38*(5), 365–381.

Fournier, V. (2000). Boundary work and the (un) making of the professions. Professionalism, boundaries and the workplace, 67.

Gavens, J. J. (1990). A historical perspective of integration of the Australian accounting profession. In R. H. Parker (Ed.), *Accounting in Australia: Historical essays* (pp. 381–407). Garland.

Gibson, E. A. (1970, January 8). Accounting histrionics. *Financial Review*, p. 7.

Gieryn, T. F. (1983). Boundary-work and the demarcation of science from non-science: Strains and interests in the professional ideologies of scientists. *American Sociological Review, 48*(6), 781–795.

Gieryn, T. F. (1995). Boundaries of science. In S. Jasanoff, G. E Markle, J. C Petersen, & T. Pinch (Eds.), *Handbook of science and technology studies* (393–443). Sage.

Gieryn, T. F. (1999). *Cultural boundaries of science: Credibility on the line.* University of Chicago Press.

Graham, A. A. (1972, May). The profession in Australia: Problems and developments. *The Chartered Accountant in Australia*, 4–14.

Grbic, N. (2010). 'Boundary work' as a concept for studying professionalization processes in the interpreting field. *Translation and Interpreting Studies, 5*(1), 109–123.

Guo, K. H. (2012). Understanding why and how some chartered accountants object to the proposed merger of the three accounting professions in Canada. *Accounting Perspectives, 11*(2), 111–130.

Gynther, R. S. (1967). *Practising accountants in Australia.* Queensland University Press.

Harriman, P. G. (1968). Letter to the editor. *The Chartered Accountant in Australia,* September, 1969, October issue, 27.
Irving, H. R. (1966). Report on professional awards for accountants (designation of CPA) submitted on behalf of the Executive Committee by President, The Australian Society of Accountants. 7 October 1966, 1–27.
Keohane, R. O., & Milner, H. V. (Eds.). (1996). *Internationalization and domestic politics*. Cambridge University Press.
Lamont, M., & Molnár, V. (2002). The study of boundaries in the social sciences. *Annual Review of Sociology, 28*(1), 167–195.
Lee, T. A. (2010). Consolidating the public accountancy profession: The case of the proposed Institute of Chartered Accountants of Great Britain, 1988–9. *Accounting History, 15*(1), 7–39.
Linn, R. (1996). *Power, progress and profit: A history of the Australian accounting profession*. Australian Society of Certified Practising Accountants.
Little, J. K. (1968, July). The profession and its public accountability. *The Chartered Accountant in Australia,* pp. 150–161.
Lloyd, J. (1966, March 1), Accountancy in turmoil—State control to raise standards? *The Australian*, p. 66.
Macdonald, K. M. (1985). Social closure and occupational registration. *Sociology, 19*(4), 541–556.
Macdonald, K. M. (1995). *The sociology of the professions*. Sage.
Macdonald, K. M., & Ritzer, G. (1988). The sociology of the professions: Dead or alive? *Work and Occupations, 15*(3), 251–272.
McEwen, D. J. (1967, August 2). Letter to the editor. *Financial Review*, 11.
Milner, D. (1996). Children and racism: Beyond the value of dolls. In P. W Robinson (Ed.), *Social groups and identities: Developing the legacy of Henri Tajfel* (249–68). Butterworth Heinermann.
Nancarrow, S. A., & Borthwick, A. M. (2005). Dynamic professional boundaries in the healthcare workforce. *Sociology of Health & Illness, 27*(7), 897–919.
Niezen, M. G. H., & Mathijssen, J. J. P. (2014). Reframing professional boundaries in healthcare: A systematic review of facilitators and barriers to task reallocation from the domain of medicine to the nursing domain. *Health Policy, 117*(2), 151–169.
O'Neill, H. G. (1969, November). Letter to editor dated October 9, 1969. *Chartered Accountant in Australia*, p. 19.
Orr, J. G. (1969, May 9). Australian Society of Accountants: Statement on unity proposals. *The Australian Accountant*, p. 214.
Orr, J. G. (2014). Interview with Geoff Orr on May 17.
Parker, R. H. (1986, November). Accounting in Australia. *The Australian Accountant,* pp. 85–87.

Parker, R. H. (1989). Importing and exporting accounting: The British experience. In A. G. Hopwood (Ed.), *International pressures for accounting change* (pp. 7–29). Prentice-Hall.

Parker, R. H. (2005). Naming and branding: Accountants and accountancy bodies in the British Empire and Commonwealth, 1853–2003. *Accounting History, 10*(1), 7–46.

Parry, R. W. (1969, June). Unity discussions. *The Chartered Accountant in Australia*, 1076.

Richardson, A. J., & Jones, D. B. (2007). Professional 'brand', personal identity and resistance to change in the Canadian accounting profession: A comparative history of two accounting association merger negotiations. *Accounting History, 12*(2), 135–164.

Sands, J. E. L. (Undated, Public Accountant and Secretary), Untitled, Letter to the Secretary of West Australian Division of Australian Society of Accountants.

Savage, E. W. (1969). The plan for unity: Stage II—The vote in principle. A letter to the members by the president of Institute, E. W. Savage dated November 5, 1969, 1.

Shackleton, K. & Walker, S. P. (2001). *A future for the accountancy profession: The quest for closure and integration, 1957–1970*. Institute of Chartered Accountants of Scotland.

Shackleton, K., & Walker. S. P. (1998). *Professional reconstruction: The coordination of the accountancy bodies, 1930–1957*. Edinburgh, Scotland: Institute of Chartered Accountants of Scotland.

Swedlow, B. (2007). Using the boundaries of science to do boundary-work among scientists: Pollution and purity claims. *Science and Public Policy, 34*(9), 633–643.

Sykes, T. (1998). *Two centuries of panic: A history of corporate collapses in Australia*. Crows Nest, Australia: Allen & Unwin.

The Institute of Chartered Accountants in Australia. (1965). *Annual report*. Australia.

The Institute of Chartered Accountants in Australia. (1966). *Annual report*. Australia.

The Institute of Chartered Accountants in Australia. (1967). *Annual report*. Australia.

The Institute of Chartered Accountants in Australia. (1968). *Annual report*. Australia.

The Institute of Chartered Accountants in Australia. (1969). *Annual report*. Australia.

The Institute of Chartered Accountants in Australia. (1970). *Annual report*. Australia.

Vatter, W. J. (1964a). *Survey of Accountancy Education in Australia*, sponsored by the Australian Society of Accountants, the Institute of Chartered Accountants and the Australasian Institute of Cost Accountant.
Vatter, W. J. (1964b, August). Survey of accountancy education in Australia—Report of Professor W. J. Vatter. *The Australian Accountant,* pp. 429–460.
Walker, S. P. (1991). The defence of professional monopoly: Scottish chartered accountants and 'satellites in the accountancy firmament' 1854–1914. *Accounting, Organisations and Society, 16*(3), 257–283.
Worley, W. R. (1967). Report of Central Public Accountants Committee, Australian Society of Accountants, submitted on 10 April, 1967 by Chairman W. R. Worley.
Zeff, S. A. (1973, March). Forging accounting principles in Australia. *Society Bulletin,* p. 14.
Zerubavel, E. (1991). *The fine line: Making distinctions in everyday life*. The University of Chicago Press.

CHAPTER 7

The Second Attempt to Unite the Dominant Professional Accounting Associations

7.1 Introduction

This chapter examines the second merger attempt, which the Institute and the Society mounted in the early 1970s, having released the first draft proposal in 1976. After the failure of the first attempt, in 1969, both bodies re-initiated merger discussions within about six years (ICAA, 1975, p. 9). The discussions on matters of mutual interest continued even after the failure of the first attempt (ASA, 1970). This book's examination of the process and strategies adopted by both professional bodies reveals that the process followed to develop the proposals for the second merger attempt and undertake a members' vote was the most rigorous among all the four merger attempts.

The merger proposal was overwhelmingly supported by the membership of the Society, but the Institute failed to deliver the minimum vote required to enable a merger to proceed. The outcome was that 90.1% of the Society's members voted in favour of the merger, while only 56.5% of the Institute's members supported it (ASA, 1981; ICAA, 1981; Linn, 1996, p. 194).

This chapter is structured into five sections. The second section provides the background to the mounting of the second merger attempt. Discussions include those on the failed attempts by the Society to create a separate category for its MIPP, joint works performed by both bodies, the relationship of both bodies with the Institute of Affiliate Accountants

J. Sidhu et al., *Understanding the Sociology of the Accounting Profession*,
https://doi.org/10.1007/978-981-99-1572-9_7

(IAA) and an analysis of the financial results of both bodies. A comparison of the membership of both bodies and the declining trend of the Institute's members engaged in public practice are also part of the second section. The third section examines the integration, or merger attempt, including attempts by the leadership of both bodies to gain members' support. It also provides a brief overview of the post-failure scenario and the response to it by both bodies. The fourth section provides an analysis of the findings relating to the second merger attempt and responses to the research questions. The last section concludes this chapter.

7.2 Background

Similarly to the first merger attempt, in the case of the second merger attempt, the Institute approached the Society to commence discussions on matters of mutual interest. This was the second attempt by the Institute to modify its traditional strategy of linking exclusivity with its membership strategies. Later sections of this chapter explain the chronology of events from the initial approach to the failure of the second merger attempt. This section examines events and activities that may have created circumstances favourable to the mounting of this attempt.

In the early to mid-1970s, another series of corporate collapses occurred, owing to which accountants and auditors faced criticism once again (Henderson, 1997). After the failure of the first merger attempt, the Society formed a subcommittee of its general council in 1970 to review the organisation of the Society. This subcommittee also reviewed the Society's mission and objectives, the relationship between the general and divisional councils, and the means by which the maximum possible services could be rendered to members on the most efficient and economic basis (ASA, 1970). The Society declared that the basic objective of the organisation was to "conduct a professional body of accountants in a manner which will assist its members to best serve the community" (ASA, 1970, p. 1). The Society also paid special attention to developing professional qualifications for members, advocating that trained support staff aid accountants, providing greater facilities for continuing education, reviewing the profession's research and technical work, and providing advice to state and federal governments on legislation changes affecting the profession (ASA, 1970).

Further, the Society focused on improving relationships with other professional accounting bodies at both national and international levels, outlining the professional and ethical responsibilities of accountants, enhancing the public image of accountants, achieving statutory recognition of the profession and meeting the special needs of public, government, managerial and farm accountants (ASA, 1970). As per the plans, in achieving these objectives, the Society was to perform most of the work independently but, wherever practicable, would seek the cooperation of the Institute. These efforts of the Society appeared to be aimed at securing status for its members, which, thus far, it had not achieved owing to the failure of the first merger attempt, and would have resulted in enabling its members to gain the higher status associated with the title of CA.

The Society's annual report of 1971 refers to the ongoing debate about raising the profile and status of its members (ASA, 1971). For example, some entry requirements for Society membership were changed. The Society phased out its examination system for accountants who had achieved a degree or diploma from a university or college of advanced education if the subjects taken had covered the basic requirements of the Society (ASA, 1971). In fact, this had occurred even before the first merger attempt. Further, it was indicated that members should seek continuous training and education to upgrade their skills. The Society's executive committee determined that it was most important to project an image of the Society of quiet efficiency and first-class service to members (ASA, 1971). The Society took these steps to upgrade its members' status after the first merger attempt had failed.

The Institute and the Society were concerned about the image of public accountants. In September 1971, *The Chartered Accountant in Australia* published a message from the Institute's general council in response to certain advertisements that appeared in newspapers seeking recruitment for accountants. *The Australian Accountant* reprinted this message in its October 1971 edition. The Institute and the Society were concerned about the use of certain terms in the education criteria of those advertisements. The required criteria for target candidates were "unqualified", "partly qualified" or "nearly qualified". In 1975, a message from R. F. Munro, executive director of the Society, appeared in *The Australian Accountant*. Munro (1975b) cautioned aspiring accountants about such advertisements, particularly regarding the use of terms that reflected badly on the status of accounting as a profession. Munro (1975b) also held a view that such advertisements misrepresented facts regarding gaining membership in professional bodies, especially in the case of the Society.

In a joint message dated 9 May 1974, G. W. Burg (president of the Society) and E. H. Burgess (president of the Institute) stated that both bodies were considering ways of protecting the public from those persons who called themselves accountants but had not acquired adequate professional qualifications. Among other steps, state registration and statutory recognition of the profession were on their agenda (Anon., 1974). This discussion demonstrates that despite the failure of the first merger attempt in 1969, the spirit of cooperation between the two bodies remained alive. Factors such as protecting the image of the profession and raising the status of Society members led both bodies to restart merger discussions.

7.2.1 *The Society Failed to Give Status to Its Members in Public Practice*

The Institute had followed an approach of listing its MIPP as principals in a separate category. Documentary evidence does not show when this practice started, since archival materials used for examining the first merger attempt do not mention it. This practice created a sub-boundary between the Institute members involved in public practice and those who were not in public practice (Arndt & Bigelow, 2005; Gieryn, 1983; Lamont & Molnár, 2002). The Society made a similar attempt to create a separate category for its MIPP in November 1974 when its general council accepted a plan to establish an approved list of principals in public practice with effect from 1 July 1976. This was an attempt by the Society to demarcate its own members based on the nature of their professional work by creating a sub-boundary. However, it was challenged by Ian Proctor a British Petroleum accountant, himself an MNIPP, who brought a motion against this change. The motion was supported by 57% of members, while less than 20% of the Society's members cast their vote (McKeon, 1975a). E. S. Robinson (1975), a member of the Society, opposed the introduction of such a list and wrote in a letter to The Australian Financial Review stating that such list would create an apparently elite class of accountants (Robinson, 1975).

Another letter, by P. J. Wood, echoes similar views that Society's first duty was to its total membership, not to work for the effective upgrading of some at the expense and downgrading of others (Wood, 1975). Hence, the Society's MNIPP engaged in boundary protection and defeated attempts at demarcating MIPP and MNIPP (Fournier, 2000; Gieryn, 1983; Persson, 2010). However, this did not stop the Society's

MIPP with dual membership from only using their title associated with membership of the Institute (Irving, 1966).

When Proctor launched his opposition, the Society's and the Institute's leaders believed that the defeat of the Proctor resolution was crucial to the success of the move to integrate the two bodies (McKeon, 1975b). Ian Vassie, federal treasurer of the Society, supported the idea of establishing a separate list for public practitioners (McKeon, 1975b). Failure to establish a list of MIPP meant that the attempt by the Society to create a special status for MIPP did not succeed (McKeon, 1975a; Wood, 1975). Consequently, the Society accepted the idea of merging with the Institute (Anon., 1976b), although, as discussed earlier in this chapter, various other factors played a key role in creating circumstances to mount the second merger attempt.

In later years, the Society expressed that the growing complexity and variety of professional affairs was a matter of concern (ASA, 1977). It also expressed a concern about the increasing criticism and scrutiny of companies' financial affairs from different sections of the community and the associated criticism of the accounting profession. The Society recognised that its challenges included upgrading the skills of members, and the organisation and structure of the profession, which needed re-examination to meet such challenges (ASA, 1977). The next section provides a summary of joint works undertaken by both bodies, which played a favourable role in the mounting of the second merger attempt.

7.2.2 Joint Work

Soon after the failure of the first merger attempt, a joint standing committee comprising members of the respective executive committees of each body was formed to consider matters of mutual interest (ASA, 1970). Various subcommittees were also formed to avoid duplication of efforts, to discuss educational policies and professional development and to discuss ways of speaking with one voice on professional matters with both the Commonwealth and the state governments. A joint committee specifically examined ways to achieve statutory recognition of the profession. Changes were also made to the qualifying examinations (ASA, 1970). In 1971, an improved liaison was established between the ARF, the Institute and the Society (ASA, 1971).

Further, in 1972, both bodies extended cooperation into the areas of joint accounting pronouncements and related affairs of the IAA

(ASA, 1972). The Legislative Review Committee of the Society worked closely with the Parliamentary and Laws Committee of the Institute. The Accounting Principles Committee also consulted the Institute regularly on the form and content of accounting pronouncements. In addition, the Audit Practice Committee worked closely with a similar committee of the Institute (ASA, 1972). The outgoing president of the Society D. P. Williams said in his message that the relationship between the Institute and the Society reached its peak in 1972 when both bodies jointly hosted the Tenth International Congress of Accountants (Williams, 1973).

The Society reported that 1974 was a year of cooperation with the Institute, which included major achievements, such as the restructuring of the ARF and the formation of many joint committees (ASA, 1974). Working jointly, the Institute and the Society had established satisfactory lines of communication with both national and state governments (ICAA, 1975). This strengthened the idea of speaking with one voice with governments. In 1974, the Society's general council approved the Professional Orientation Year (POY), which applied to all provisional members who wanted to advance to the associate status from 1 April 1976 (Henderson, 1975). Both bodies worked closely on matters affecting the accounting profession and this created favourable conditions to recommence merger discussions. The role of the Society to invigorate the IAA by assisting financially and otherwise is discussed in the next section, including the importance of having a professional body such as the IAA, as projected by both bodies.

7.2.3 The Institute of Affiliate Accountants

As a result of the failure of the first merger attempt, the Society failed to achieve professional elevation for its members by merging with the Institute and thereby did not gain the Chartered Accountant title for members. Consequently, the Society supported the creation of a subprofessional accounting category. This was an attempt to elevate the status of the Society members by creating a professional category of lower professional standing than that of the Society members.

The subprofessional body was the IAA. The Society gave administrative support to the IAA by letting its properties to the IAA and by publishing news about the IAA in the Society's journal (ASA, 1970). The IAA and its progress were regularly mentioned even in the 1971 annual report (ASA. 1971). For example, the financial statements of the Society showed the

IAA as an expense category in the income statement. In 1970, the Society spent $AU12,500 on the IAA, which rose to $AU45,476, $AU60,073 and $AU70,090 in 1979, 1980 and 1981, respectively.

The Society was keen to create a subprofessional category, and this was evident in the 1972 annual report, which mentioned that the development of a second tier of professional category would assist in raising the status of Society members:

> As it is the policy of the Society to raise the status of its members, it will be appreciated that the development of a second tier to undertake many of the routine duties and responsibilities in the financial field within Commerce, Industry, Government and Public Accounting will allow the professional accountant to devote more attention to the higher levels of management. (ASA, 1972, p. 6)

By 1980, the membership of the IAA reached 4,000. The Institute also supported the IAA by providing advice and appointing observers on the IAA council. The Institute was in agreement with the Society regarding the creation of a second-tier professional accounting body to undertake routine tasks (ICAA, 1980).

7.2.4 *Financial Situation of Both Bodies*

This subsection compares the financial results of both bodies. Table 7.1 provides the Society's total income and surplus from 1970 to 1981.

The Society experienced four good years when its surplus was more than 6% of its revenue. For six years, the Society suffered a deficit, including a low point in 1980 at −7.63% of the total income. Despite suffering deficits in 1979, 1980 and 1981, the Society spent $AU45,476, $AU60,073 and $AU70,090, respectively, on the IAA, and $AU125,768, $AU156,206 and $AU160,151, respectively, on the ARF. The costs of integration attempt reported in 1980 and 1981 were $AU223,935 and $AU34,385, respectively. Table 7.2 presents the financial results of the Institute from 1970 to 1981.

For the same period, 1970–1981, the Institute's financial situation was much better than that of the Society. It incurred a deficit in only three years of that period and, generally, despite the surplus being low, did not suffer a deficit in other years. In 1979, 1980 and 1981, the Institute spent $AU81,000, $AU198,408 and $AU128,966, respectively, on ARF.

Table 7.1 Financial results of the Society 1970–1981

SN	*Year*	*Revenue/income ($AU)*	*Deficit/surplus ($AU)*	*Deficit/surplus (%)*
1	1970	777,686	89,966	11.57
2	1971	774,090	23,541	3.04
3	1972	947,863	102,598	10.82
4	1973	974,468	(18,707)	−1.92
5	1974	1,290,194	(42,503)	−3.29
6	1975	1,873,575	86,293	4.61
7	1976	1,679,516	211,930	12.62
8	1977	2,277,991	(28,238)	−1.24
9	1978	2,732,549	177,886	6.51
10	1979	3,115,410	(37,120)	−1.19
11	1980	3,548,949	(270,931)	−7.63
12	1981	4,163,494	(53,729)	−1.29

Source Annual reports, ASA 1970–1981

Table 7.2 Financial results of the Institute 1970–1981

SN	*Year*	*Revenue/income ($AU)*	*Deficit/Surplus ($AU)*	*Deficit/surplus (%)*
1	1970	285,618	8,791	3.08
2	1971	305,720	(17,489)	−5.72
3	1972	428,406	41,813	9.76
4	1973	450,113	153,945	34.20
5	1974	466,678	(59,007)	−12.64
6	1975	777,954	53,510	6.88
7	1976	1,911,146	80,231	4.20
8	1977	2,273,808	(95,672)	−4.21
9	1978	2,959,466	55,427	1.87
10	1979	3,328,134	56,858	1.71
11	1980	3,740,656	23,781	0.64
12	1981	4,711,678	64,055	1.36

Source Annual reports, ICAA 1970–1981

Unlike the Society, the Institute did not financially support operations of the IAA.

Table 7.3 Comparison of the Institute's and the Society's revenue

SN	*Year*	*Society income*	*Institute income*	*Society income/Institute income*
1	1970	777,686	285,618	2.7
2	1971	774,090	305,720	2.5
3	1972	947,863	428,406	2.2
4	1973	974,468	450,113	2.2
5	1974	1,290,194	466,678	2.8
6	1975	1,873,575	777,954	2.4
7	1976	1,679,516	1,911,146	0.9
8	1977	2,277,991	2,273,808	1.0
9	1978	2,732,549	2,959,466	0.9
10	1979	3,115,410	3,328,134	0.9
11	1980	3,548,949	3,740,656	0.9
12	1981	4,163,494	4,711,678	0.9

Source Annual reports, ASA 1970–1981

As shown in Table 7.3, the financial results of both bodies reveal an interesting trend in the years under study, that is, 1970–1981. The Society's income was more than twice the size of the Institute's until 1976 when the Institute registered nearly two and a half times the income growth and overtook the Society's income for the first time. For the four years of 1978–1981, the Institute's income was consistently higher than that of the Society.

7.2.5 Membership of Both Bodies

Tables 7.4 and 7.5, respectively, show the statewide membership and the percentage of statewide membership of the Institute for the period under study, that is, from 1970 to 1981. During the 12-year period, the membership share of New South Wales declined, while Victoria's share increased little. The decline in New South Wales' share of the total membership of the Institute was around 11 percentage points. The population share of New South Wales was 36% in 1970, and by 1981, it had fallen slightly to 35% (ABS, 1992). This demonstrates that New South Wales was over-represented in the Institute's membership by around 19% in 1970 and 9% in 1981. Conversely, all other states, including Victoria, were under-represented in the total membership of the Institute. The population share of Victoria in the total Australian population was 23%

in 1970 and 27% in 1981, while its share in the total membership of the Institute was 22% and 22.53% in 1970 and 1981, respectively. The data reveal that membership of the Institute was concentrated in New South Wales. However, during the 12-year period under study, the membership share of New South Wales declined and was replaced with other states and overseas memberships.

Table 7.6 provides a comparison of MIPP and MNIPP and shows a decline in the proportion of MIPP. For the 11-year period from 1971 to 1981, the proportion of MIPP steadily decreased, with a total fall of 6.5 percentage points. MIPP were further divided into categories: those working as principals and as employees. MIPP as principals registered an eight percentage point decrease from 1970 to 1981. Chapter 2 of this book highlighted that the boundaries of the Institute were created based on the notion that public practice was a superior vocation and that the Institute mainly represented MIPP. However, as Table 7.6 shows, during a 11-year period, the share of the Institute's MIPP as a proportion of the total members decreased by around 6.5 percentage points. This decreasing proportion indicates that the argument used to create the Institute's boundaries, namely that it was a professional body mainly representing MIPP, became weaker. Hence, the organisational strategy of the Institute was in a continuum of modifications because boundaries are dynamic structures that keep changing (Annisette & Trivedi, 2013; Brodkin, 1998; Gieryn, 1983; Ignatiev, 1995).

Tables 7.7 and 7.8 provide a comparison of the Society membership from 1970 to 1981 across various states and their respective membership percentages. Victoria's membership of the Society was 8–9 percentage points over-represented in relation to its share of the population of Australia for this period. This reveals that a regional focus in the professionalisation of accounting from the last decades of the nineteenth century and the early 1900s was still somewhat prevalent, since Victoria was the home state of the Society. However, New South Wales was neither under- nor over-represented in the membership compared with its population share. In the case of the Institute, membership share of New South Wales and Victoria declined from 77% in 1970 to 66% in 1981, revealing that in comparison, the Society had more representation from the rest of the states for all the years under study.

However, the Institute's membership was primarily concentrated in the two states of New South Wales and Victoria throughout the 1970s, and in 1981, these two states still dominated it. The combined population of

Table 7.4 Statewide membership of the Institute

SN	*State*	*1970*	*1971*	*1972*	*1973*	*1974*	*1975*	*1976*	*1977*	*1978*	*1980*	*1981*
1	New South Wales	3,146	3,253	3,415[a]	3,286	3,357	3,529	3,702	4,097	4,346	4,919	5,238
2	Queensland	489	505	531	570	591	652	734	819	893	1,043	1,133
3	South Australia	368	366	401	469	534	573	592	666	709	803	850
4	Tasmania	113	113	121	127	128	148	151	156	162	185	190
5	Victoria	1,269	1,303	1,425	1,557	1,585	1,718	1,867	2,077	2,236	2,576	2,690
6	Western Australia	368	382	424	467	498	558	586	642	701	787	850
7	Overseas	–	–	–	427	526	645	723	816	875	989	990
8	Total	5,753	5,922	6,317	6,903	7,219	7,823	8,355	9,273	9,922	11,305	11,941

[a]Includes overseas members

Source Annual reports, ICAA 1970–1981

Table 7.5 Statewide membership of the Institute (%)

SN	*State*	*1970*	*1971*	*1972*	*1973*	*1974*	*1975*	*1976*	*1977*	*1978*	*1980*	*1981*
1	New South Wales	54.68	54.93	54.06	47.6	46.5	45.11	44.31	44.18	43.8	43.51	43.87
2	Queensland	8.5	8.53	8.41	8.26	8.19	8.33	8.79	8.83	9	9.23	9.49
3	South Australia	6.4	6.18	6.35	6.79	7.4	7.32	7.09	7.18	7.15	7.13	7.12
4	Tasmania	1.96	1.91	1.92	1.84	1.77	1.89	1.81	1.68	1.63	1.64	1.59
5	Victoria	22.06	22	22.56	22.56	21.96	21.96	22.35	22.4	22.54	22.79	22.53
6	Western Australia	6.4	6.45	6.71	6.77	6.9	7.13	7.01	6.92	7.07	6.96	7.12
7	Overseas	0	0	0	6.19	7.29	8.24	8.65	8.8	8.82	8.75	8.29
8	Total	100	100	100	100	100	100	100	100	100	100	100

Source Annual reports, ICAA 1970–1981

Table 7.6 Membership classification of the Institute (%)

SN	*Member category*	*1971*	*1972*	*1973*	*1974*	*1975*	*1976*	*1977*	*1978*	*1979*	*1980*	*1981*
1	Members in practice as principals	50.54	50.47	48.49	49.2	48.75	46.87	44.56	44.94	43.45	42.48	42.53
2	Members employed in practice	21.58	22.78	26.14	25.3	26.6	27.43	27.42	26.43	25.26	24.38	23.08
	Total members in public practice	72.12	73.25	74.63	74.5	75.35	74.3	71.98	71.37	68.71	66.86	65.61
3	Members not in practice	27.88	26.75	25.37	25.5	24.65	25.7	28.02	28.63	31.29	33.14	34.39
	Total	100	100	100	100	100	100	100	100	100	100	100

Source Annual reports, ICAA 1971–1981

Table 7.7 Statewide membership of the Society

SN	*Year*	*New South Wales*	*Victoria*	*Queensland*	*South Australia*	*Western Australia*	*Tasmania*	*ACT*[a]	*Overseas*	*Total*
1	1970	11,315	10,146	3,288	2,894	2,749	632	–	2,133	33,157
2	1971	12,013	10,627	3,426	3,013	2,947	653	–	2,268	34,947
3	1972	11,692	11,041	3,548	3,123	3,102	687	851	2,407	36,541
4	1973	11,983	11,638	3,626	3,370	3,176	709	935	2,563	38,000
5	1974	12,339	12,037	3,524	3,262	3,535	730	1,039	2,829	39,295
6	1975	12,358	12,154	3,551	3,206	3,562	1,068	720	2,901	39,520
7	1976	13,148	13,127	3,857	3,285	3,797	721	1,195	3,152	42,282
8	1977	13,133	13,376	3,936	3,292	3,848	747	1,224	3,133	42,689
9	1978	13,170	13,667	3,950	3,265	3,848	759	1,232	5,971	45,862
10	1979	13,413	14,121	4,049	3,264	3,940	766	1,254	3,270	44,077
11	1980	13,679	14,543	4,160	3,320	4,014	794	1,273	3,365	45,148
12	1981	14,061	15,022	4,375	3,322	4,195	803	1,292	3,492	46,562

[a]The ACT division was formed in May 1972

Source Annual reports, ASA 1976–1981

Table 7.8 Statewide membership of the Society (%)

SN	*Year*	*New South Wales*	*Victoria*	*Queensland*	*South Australia*	*Western Australia*	*Tasmania*	*ACT*[a]	*Overseas*	*Total*
1	1970	34.13	30.60	9.92	8.73	8.29	1.91	0.00	6.43	100
2	1971	34.37	30.41	9.80	8.62	8.43	1.87	0.00	6.49	100
3	1972	32.00	30.40	9.75	8.57	8.49	1.88	2.33	6.59	100
4	1973	31.53	30.63	9.54	8.87	8.36	1.87	2.46	6.74	100
5	1974	31.40	30.63	8.97	8.30	9.00	1.86	2.64	7.20	100
6	1975	31.27	30.75	8.99	8.11	9.01	2.70	1.82	7.34	100
7	1976	31.10	31.05	9.12	7.77	8.98	1.71	2.83	7.45	100
8	1977	30.76	31.33	9.22	7.71	9.01	1.75	2.87	7.34	100
9	1978	28.72	29.80	8.61	7.12	8.39	1.65	2.69	13.02	100
10	1979	30.43	32.04	9.19	7.41	8.94	1.74	2.85	7.42	100
11	1980	30.30	32.21	9.21	7.35	8.89	1.76	2.82	7.45	100
12	1981	30.20	32.26	9.40	7.13	9.01	1.72	2.77	7.50	100

[a]The ACT division was formed in May 1972
Source Annual reports, ASA 1976–1981

these two states was 59% of the Australian population in 1970 and 62% in 1981. This finding demonstrates that the early trends of regionalism were not so prevalent because the number of professional bodies had reduced to three. However, the impact of early regionalism could still be observed as far as membership of the Institute was concerned, with the concentration in New South Wales. The following sections discuss how the second merger attempt failed mainly because of opposition from Western Australia, indicating a regional revolt against the leadership of the Institute with membership concentrated mainly in New South Wales and Victoria.

7.3 The Merger Proposal

In the case of the first merger attempt, the leadership of the Institute took the initial step to initiate merger discussions, which has been discussed in Chapter 6. In the case of the second merger attempt, the Institute again approached the Society to initiate integration discussions in 1974 (ASA, 1981). This was the second attempt by the Institute leaders to modify its traditional strategy of being an exclusive organisation and to make changes in organisational boundaries (Annisette & Trivedi, 2013; Brodkin, 1998; Gieryn, 1983; Ignatiev, 1995), whereas the Society members had already supported changes to its traditional strategy of market control in the case of the first merger attempt. Further, the literature shows that changes in boundaries are supported by individuals in lower-status groups (Lamont & Molnár, 2002).

The 1975 annual report of the Institute mentioned:

> At the November 1974 meeting the National Council unanimously approved a recommendation from its Forward Planning Committee that an approach be made to the Australian Society of Accountants suggesting that discussions should be held to determine whether a basis existed for full integration of the profession in Australia. (ICAA, 1975, p. 9)

This proposal was addressed and approved in February 1975 at a meeting of the general council of the Society (Anon., 1976b). Both bodies together formed an Integration Sub-committee (ISC) in 1975 (ICAA, 1975). A financial journalist commented that a key factor behind the Institute taking the first step was financial (McKeon, 1975c). However, data presented in Table 7.2 does not show that the Institute was in any major financial crisis.

A former president of the Society G. W. Bottrill[1] commented on merger talks and wrote that the executive committees of both bodies were regularly meeting for a full and frank discussion to ensure that there was a single voice representing the accountancy profession in Australia (Bottrill, 1975). The presidents made a statement that it was unanimously decided by their respective councils to reopen discussions on the integration of the two organisations (Bottrill, 1975). It was also mentioned that integration could only succeed if it was on "fair and proper terms" and if members had given enthusiastic support (Bottrill, 1975). According to the Society's President Rex Thiele (1975), the unity of both bodies was also a step towards achieving statutory recognition.

Following the approval of both councils, letters dated 17 March 1975 were sent to the members of both bodies by the respective presidents disclosing the decision to restart integration discussions (Bottrill, 1975; ICAA, 1975). In his letter, G. W. Bottrill wrote that after jointly hosting the Tenth International Congress of Accountants in Sydney with the Institute, a close working relationship had emerged between the two bodies (Bottrill, 1975). The Institute's annual report also mentioned that both councils agreed that before developing any plan, the views of members should be sought in members' meetings and through sending a letter (Bottrill, 1975; ICAA, 1975). McKeon (1975c) of *The Australian Financial Review* commented on the idea of members' meetings:

> The meetings will allow the councils of both bodies to assess rank and file sentiments and so avoid the problems involving the last formal unity move in 1969. If the rank and file indicates it does not want integration, the matter will be deferred indefinitely. (p. 11)

On 9 May 1975, the executive director of the Society R. F. Munro wrote to members referring to a series of meetings of members to gain opinions on the idea of merger (Munro, 1975a). These meetings were held throughout Australia in capital cities and several country towns between

[1] G. W. Bottrill was vice-president of the Society during the first merger attempt in the late 1960s and president in 1974.

June and August 1975.[2] According to the Institute's annual report, these meetings were valuable and proved useful to guide the ISC about the opinions of members in relation to the potential merger (ICAA, 1975). This was an additional step through which both bodies made an attempt to study the mood of their members in relation to support for the merger. In particular, for the Institute, this was an attempt to overcome the issue of detachment of its leaders from its members, which had led the Institute members to engage in boundary protection work in the case of the first merger attempt (Fournier, 2000; Keohane & Milner, 1996; Milner, 1996). By taking its members into confidence, the Institute made an attempt to avoid circumstances that would lead to further boundary protection work by its members. Attendance ranged from 20 to 200 members (Anon., 1976a).

Apart from attending meetings to express their views on a merger, members were also requested to present their opinions on the idea of merger by sending in letters. Out of 191 letters received, only three were against the merger (Munro, 1975a). Munro (1975a) also mentioned that both bodies had decided not to publish members' letters in their respective journals. As a result, other than the claims by the professional bodies, no independent evidence exists to show how many letters were in favour of merger and how many were against it. Examining the vote outcomes, as shown in later sections of this chapter, support from the Institute and the Society members, even when combined, was not even close to 98.5%. McKeon (1975c) indicated that both bodies were cautious about merger discussions, stating:

> The Institute and the Society Councils want to avoid embarrassment and will launch a referendum on the matter only if integration is sure to succeed. (p. 11)

Hence, members' opinions were requested in meetings and by letters. In September 1975, the Institute and the Society issued a progress report on merger discussions following the actions taken since sending out the

[2] The first meeting was planned at AMP Theatre, 535 Bourke Street, Melbourne on 18 June 1975 (Munro, 1975a). Further meetings were planned as follows: Sydney, 23 July 1975; Adelaide, 14 August 1975; Perth 15 August 1975; and Brisbane 30 July 1975 (Munro, 1975b).

letters dated 17 March 1975. Both bodies also outlined the objectives of integration (Anon., 1975). These were:

- to demonstrate, nationally and internationally, that there is in Australia one profession of accounting, speaking with one voice
- to enhance the technical standards of members in all fields, and the ability of the profession to serve the community
- to obtain optimum utilisation of the human, financial and other resources of the profession, by avoiding duplication of activities, services and administration
- to establish uniform ethical standards for the profession enforced through common investigation and disciplinary procedures
- to provide all members with greater opportunities to benefit from association with accountants in fields other than their own; to encourage and facilitate the interchange of ideas and experience between accountants in commerce, the government and public practice and the academic field to their mutual benefit
- to strengthen the status of accountants by having one strong professional organisation and to dispel the confusion in the public mind caused by different professional designations each claiming its own status (Anon., 1975).

The presidents of both bodies submitted a report to the ISC on letters received from members about their opinion on the idea of merger and on views expressed by members in meetings held throughout Australia. The ISC also considered various operational and procedural issues in the period leading to integration and after integration. The ISC formed an opinion that it should proceed with the objective of producing a draft proposal for the integration of the profession (Anon., 1976a). A finding of members' meetings was also that there were several misconceptions held by members of both bodies, even at the highest levels. To assist in overcoming this issue, some exploratory "position" papers were prepared and exchanged among committee members of both bodies (Anon., 1976a). In addition, many background papers were prepared on topics related to relevant procedures and operations if integration were to proceed (Anon., 1976a). Based on reviews of members' meetings and their opinions reflected through letters, it was decided in 1975 to defer the plan for integration. It was also decided to conduct further discussions with members before proceeding with the integration plan (ICAA, 1975). The 1975 annual report of the Institute reported that based on members' views the integration plan would be postponed, even though, as previously mentioned, both bodies had received 191 letters of which only three were against the proposed integration attempt. Thus, claims by the bodies seem to be self-contradictory. An article was published by McKeon (1975b) in *The Australian Financial Review* in October 1975 that provided further information on integration progress.

Following this deferment, the views of members were reviewed again and their opinions were included in the integration process. This review followed the development of an exposure draft containing 10 proposals for integration, which was released on 14 July 1976 (ASA & ICAA, 1976). This was the first version of the proposals that led to the second merger attempt. The exposure draft was released at a press conference in Sydney, which was attended by the president of the Society R. H. Henderson, the president of the Institute J. H. Jamison and the chairperson of the ISC, P. C. E. Cox (ICAA, 1976). A highlight was the proposed name, specified as "the Australian Institute of Chartered Accountants", with the basis of incorporation being the Royal Charter. In the proposed united body, practical accounting experience was mandatory for three years in one or more areas of commerce and industry, the government or public practice (ASA & ICAA, 1976).[3]

Institute members actively opposed various aspects of the exposure draft. The ISC continued to work on those aspects during 1976 and drafted alternatives to those proposals to which there was active opposition. No further information was provided regarding which aspects were not acceptable (ICAA, 1976). Unlike the 1969 merger, this time, both bodies first issued the exposure draft for members' comments before issuing the final proposals (Anon., 1976c). Members were asked to provide written comments on the proposal by 24 September 1976 (Anon., 1976d). *The Australian Accountant* summarised the gains from integration as follows:

> Integration will enhance our ability to provide improved services for our members at reasonable cost, eliminate existing duplication of activities and

[3] This requirement was a departure from the Institute's current requirement of practical work experience under a public practitioner.

> problems of communication between two bodies, make it easier for outside bodies to deal with the profession and the profession with outside bodies, and enhance the profession's status (Anon., 1976a, p. 394).

The Institute had arranged for the IPC to address members at different branches, but attendance was very low, which the president of the Institute termed as disappointing (ICAA, 1976).

7.3.1 *Further Progress on Merger*

Along with the progress on merger discussions, the Society and the Institute continued to represent jointly the Australian accounting profession overseas, including at the Eleventh International Congress of Accountants held in Munich, Germany, on 11–14 October 1977 (ASA, 1977). During that year, the ARF made eight tax-related submissions and 12 submissions related to other matters on behalf of the Society and the Institute to various governments (ASA, 1977). Therefore, these submissions at least made joint representations on behalf of both accounting bodies. Additionally, both bodies continued to arrange joint seminars on professional matters. For example, on 7 August 1979, both bodies organised a one-day seminar in Victoria on public accounting (Anon., 1979a).

As the years passed, both bodies published joint accounting statements and contributed to the debate about integration. For example, the Society in its 1977 annual report stated that the increasing complexity of the affairs of the profession provided a powerful case for integration. The discussion was also around substantial duplication of work which was avoidable if there was one unified body (ASA, 1977). As discussed in Chapter 6, discursive claims by both bodies had changed in an attempt to foster a public image of Society members being equal, or at least not significantly inferior, to Institute members. This contrasted with the Institute's traditional discourse, which was marked by claims of superiority, and enabled the Society to call on Institute members to adopt a long-term view on integration:

> Members should weigh carefully the long-run advantages of a unified professional body against what seem to them to be sacrifices. Members should understand that no desirable goal is attained without some cost. (ASA, 1977, p. 10)

When one compares the second integration attempt with the first, the development process of the integration proposals of the former involved detailed and lengthy steps, including ongoing consultations with members. Both bodies continued to work on developing proposals that took into consideration the objections of members on the 1976 draft proposal (ASA, 1978, p. 6). The ISC of the Society and the Institute met frequently during 1977 and considered the first draft merger proposal released in 1976 (ASA, 1977).

The Society president reported that in early 1978, the ISC of the joint standing committee of the Society and the Institute had produced the next draft version of integration proposals. These proposals were submitted to divisional and state councils of both bodies. A professional accounting firm undertook a survey to study the support for these proposals by members of both bodies. The national councils of both bodies made an assessment that, based on this survey, the merger was unlikely to achieve acceptance from the requisite number of members of the two bodies. Details of the survey were not reported and documents that were accessed did not provide further details beyond what was reported in the annual report. The Society president accepted that this outcome slowed down the impetus for integration and he called 1978 a disappointing year for the integration of both bodies (ASA, 1978, p. 6). Just as details of the minutes of meetings of the ISC were not available, further details, such as when and why merger discussions were put on hold or slowed down, were not available. The only other sources of information related to this outcome were annual reports or other documents available in public archives.

After the setback in 1978, discussions resumed in the following year, and the Society's annual report noted that during 1979, the general council of the Society and the national council of the Institute reaffirmed their commitment to the principle of integration (ASA, 1979). It is not clear what triggered this change. Both councils also agreed that it was necessary to put integration proposals to the members of both bodies as soon as possible (ASA, 1979). To do so and to speed up the process, J. D. Norgard, chairperson of the Australian Broadcasting Commission, was appointed as independent chairperson of the IPC, which was a new committee.

The president of the Society mentioned that the Society was committed to unity and believed that accounting was a single profession; therefore, integration was necessary (ASA, 1979). The formation of the IPC was termed a new phase in integration discussions by the Institute. The aim of forming the IPC was to create a favourable opinion among members of both bodies for the integration. The target vote deadline was 30 November 1980 (ICAA, 1979). Even in the early stages of IPC meetings, it was clear that the initial draft proposals were unlikely to be accepted by members and that significant changes in the integration proposals were needed. Issues of contention were the entry requirements for joining the integrated body, the conditions for granting practising certificates and the constitution and composition of councils (Anon., 1981j; Hale, 1981; Kelly, 1981c).

Table 7.9 provides details of the IPC and its members, and 10 members represented both bodies with equal representation from the Institute and the Society. The IPC comprised the presidents and executive directors of the two bodies, together with three other nominated members from each organisation. In the first 18 months of formation, the IPC used the 1976 proposals as a starting point and reviewed all proposals, assisted by qualitative and quantitative market surveys and the views of subcommittees in every state (Anon., 1981a).

The annual report of the Institute mentioned that even after nearly a decade of first forming various joint committees, a strong bond and cooperation existed between both bodies and that many joint activities initially started in the early 1970s continued (ICAA, 1979). Further, the 1980 annual report of the Institute mentioned that the joint standing committee was an instrument for coordinating joint policy matters (ICAA, 1980). It appears that these arguments were presented to support the merger discussions, which were progressing very slowly.

Table 7.9 Final Integration Policy Committee

SN	*Name*	*Designation*	*SN*	*Name*	*Designation*
1	J. D. Norgard (Chairperson)	Chairperson	7	V. A. Prosser	Institute nominee
2	R. L. Cotton	Society nominee	8	H. L. Spencer	Society nominee
3	W. G. Phillip (Vic)	Institute nominee	9	G. A. Vincent	Society nominee
4	P. D. Agars	Institute nominee	10	A. W. Graham	Society nominee
5	D. G. Neilson	Institute nominee	11	A. G. Brown	Institute nominee
6	P. J. Lanigan	Society nominee			

Source Anon. (1981a)

In his discursive claims in favour of merger, the president of the Institute W. G. Phillip wrote in the 1980 annual report that the Institute was not rich in physical assets and was facing many challenges. He made specific discursive claims in favour of integration:

> During the last five years a relatively small group of members have worked hard to develop a proposal which provides for the Institute to merge with the Australian Society of Accountants. At the time of writing these notes the decision of members regarding the proposal is not known. (ICAA, 1980, p. 3)

The president of the Society P. J. Lanigan wrote an editorial in July 1980 about the integration moves. Lanigan (1980) stated:

> The greatest single hurdle to integrate is to be found in the different membership patterns of the two bodies. The typical member of the Institute combines high technical standards with substantial practical experience in general public accounting—and is naturally cautious about any membership change that might possibly erode his special status in the profession. On the other hand, our own members have the advantage of belonging to a great organisation which is already integrated in the sense that its 45,000 members include most of the accountants in business and government, as well as many thousands working in private practice. (p. 355)

The Society reaffirmed its public support for integration, stating in its annual report that:

> At a time when suggestions have been made in several countries that there may be a case for government intervention and statutory control of the accountancy profession by formal enactment of accounting standards where the public interest is involved—accountants in Australia can still afford the doubtful luxury of two organisations duplicating the vital functions of regulating the profession. (ASA, 1980, p. 7)

The president of the Society stated that over the years, efforts to achieve integration had not been successful because of the difficulty of devising an integration formula that would be sufficiently attractive to the members of both bodies to win the required special majority of the votes in each organisation (ASA, 1980).

In 1980, the next version of draft proposals was circulated to members and an intensive informational program was undertaken to ensure that members were fully aware of the issues involved (ICAA, 1980). After the circulation of proposals to members, both bodies had decided that the formal vote would not be taken until there was a reasonable chance of its acceptance. The next subsection provides details of the national survey of their members conducted by both bodies to determine the level of support for the proposed merger.

7.3.2 Australian National Opinion Poll Survey

The Australian National Opinion Poll (ANOP), a market research company, was appointed in August 1980 to conduct, first, an initial study incorporating qualitative assessment of members' views concerning draft proposals and, second, a quantitative study of members of both bodies regarding support for the draft proposal. The sample size was 500 Society and 1,000 Institute members. The technique used was the telephone survey (Anon., 1981h). The survey findings provided valuable input to the IPC; the integration proposal booklet was developed from ANOP's August 1980 survey and was published on 10 March 1981 (Anon., 1981h). The survey indicated that there was sufficient support for integration from Society members and reasonable support from Institute members, which fell short of the required two-thirds majority[4] (ICAA, 1980). Following this, many changes to the proposals were made at the national council meetings of both bodies and at the meetings of the joint standing committee held on 3 and 4 August 1980. After this, the IPC refined the integration proposals.

In May 1981, the ANOP was again appointed to design and carry out a major quantitative study to explore the level of support for merger and to reveal any remaining problem areas. The sample size was 1,500 members drawn from both bodies: no further details were provided on the members surveyed belonging to each body separately. The method was a telephone survey completed between late May and 8 June 1981 (Anon., 1981i, p. 483). The poll indicated that only 56% of the Institute members supported the merger. After this, both bodies decided to defer the integration poll (Kelly, 1981b). It was also decided that further

[4] The required majority for passing the unity proposals in the case of the Institute was two-thirds and in the case of the Society was 75% (Lanigan, 1980, p. 355).

modifications to the plans and further consultations with members were necessary to achieve the required majority. By the end of 1980, proposals were refined in light of the members' reactions (ASA, 1980).

Vic Prosser (1981) also wrote in the May edition of the Institute's journal in an attempt to convince young Professional Year (PY) graduates to support the integration. Further, in the Integration Forum (see Sect. 7.3.3) the IPC wrote that although support for integration was increasing, if votes were taken, it was unlikely that the required two-thirds majority support would be achieved (Anon., 1981j). Moreover, the ANOP survey revealed that the majority of CAs wanted a distinction between members in practice and members not in practice (Hale, 1981). After the June survey, a further survey was conducted by the ANOP in October, which showed that 66% of the Institute members were in favour of merger, while 90% of the Society members favoured it (Kelly, 1981c; Uren, 1981).

7.3.3 Integration Forum and Attempts to Gain Support

In a joint message in February 1981, the president of the Society P. J. Lanigan and the president of the Institute W. G. Phillip promoted the integration to the members. They also started an Integration Forum in the Society and the Institute journals covering opinions, discussions and views of members and other commentators on the merger proposals. This continued until a vote was undertaken. The Integration Forum was initiated to take feedback from members and make necessary changes to proposals.

The first Integration Forum appeared in the February 1981 issues of journals of both bodies, which summarised the development of the integration proposals. The first Integration Forum also provided details of changes in the aims and objectives of the Institute (Anon., 1981a). Both bodies recognised their common interest by agreements to work together, which included work on the ARF as well. The International Accounting Standards Committee had country-based representation, and both bodies agreed to have joint nominations. Policy matters were dealt with by a joint standing committee comprising executive committee members of the two bodies. Further, both bodies established special committees in each state with the responsibility of providing a two-way communication channel to members. These committees arranged meetings of members throughout Australia. One of their responsibilities was to receive critical comments on the exposure draft and pass it to the IPC (Anon., 1981a). The Integration Forum also mentioned that the issue of integration not only affected the members of both bodies but it was of great interest to the financial and business community, to State and Federal Governments, and to educators (Anon., 1981a).

The Integration Forum of the Institute's journal of May 1981 published around 10 letters from members, which were received after the release of final integration proposals. Of these letters, only one was against the merger. At the June 1981 Integration Forum, the IPC discussed the adoption of the title CPA replacing CA, but a view was taken that CPA would not be acceptable to the Institute members and the idea was dropped (Anon., 1981e). Barnes (1981 p. 572), an associate member of the Society, wrote that in his view integration was unlikely to succeed because larger accounting firms were not approached to issue statements in support of the integration. Further, Barnes (1981) expressed his opinion that the Institute's leaders were also not decisively in favour of integration.

Although both bodies were moving ahead with merger discussions, they did not fully cooperate with each other on all matters. The *Accountancy Age* reported on 26 September 1980 that the Institute had failed to publish a tax practice statement for the third time because the Society had refused to support it at every attempt (Anon., 1980). In October 1981, for the first time, a joint meeting of the national councils of both the Society and the Institute was held in Sydney. It was decided unanimously at this meeting to put the issue of integration to a postal ballot of members (ASA, 1981; Crook & Brolly, 1981). In early November 1981, Price Waterhouse (PW) joined the public discourse in support of merging the two bodies. PW's senior partner R. G. Lee said that integration was in the best interests of both the profession and the public (Anon., 1981f). Lee added that a united profession could develop technical and ethical standards more strongly (Anon., 1981f).

Before the appointment of Norgard, the IPC was known as the ISC and was headed by a member of the Institute, namely P. C. E. Cox. Norgard was appointed because he was independent of both bodies (McKenon, 1979). Cox's letter dated 10 December 1981 appeared in *The Australian Financial Review* and criticised the merger proposals in their final form before they went to a vote. Cox (1981) said that he was a fellow of the Institute and a member of the council of the Institute in 1969 when the first merger attempt had failed. He was president of the Institute and was chairperson of the ISC from the time of its formation before being removed so that J. D. Norgard could be appointed as chair. Cox (1981) also mentioned that he had advocated in 1979 that the Institute withdraws from integration talks before he was removed:

> I deplore what I perceive as a degradation of the Institute by our National Council with their attempt to integrate the Institute with the Australian Society of Accountants regardless of the consequences to the Institute. (p. 7)

In response, a letter appeared in *The Australian Financial Review* on 15 December 1981, which attempted to neutralise Cox's criticism (Agars & Neilson, 1981). The July edition of the Integration Forum published a classification of the members of the proposed integrated body. There would be 28% MIPP and the rest would be MNIPP. In the July 1981 edition of the Integration Forum, letters from the Society members were published and all members were in favour of a merger attempt (Anon., 1981g).

A letter from the former registrar of the Western Australian state division of the Institute H. M. Kitson was published in the Society's journal, demonstrating strong support for the merger (Anon., 1981g). The publication of a letter from the Institute's former Western Australian registrar could be viewed as a way of assuring Society members and others that the Institute's leadership, whether current or former, was in favour of merger.

The August Integration Forum in the Society's journal expressed a concern by the IPC that the integration proposal may fail and that failure could be caused by the fact that many members would vote against unity without even reading the proposals (Anon., 1981i). The August edition published letters from members, but it is noteworthy that all these letters were from Institute members and all were in favour of the unity attempt (Anon., 1981i).

7.3.4 *Final Moves*

On 1 March 1981, the integration proposals were again sent to members of both bodies for their comments and opinions. These proposals included a letter by the IPC chairperson Norgard (1981). The integration proposals included letters from both presidents. The proposals mentioned four focus areas for the merger:

- development of the status of the profession with the general public, business and government and the educational requirements
- regulation of the accountancy profession
- the profession's technical and ethical standards
- the optimum organisation of the profession (ASA & ICAA, 1981, p. 9).

The proposal offered detailed explanations of the above four issues. On the issue of status development, the fear of loss of status by the Institute members was acknowledged:

> It has been suggested that some Institute members fear that they will lose status by surrendering the exclusive use of the term "Chartered Accountant". The counter view is that this is a small and short term price to pay for the longer term benefits that integration will bring to all accountants. (ASA & ICAA, 1981, p. 9)

The public claims by leaders of the professional bodies were countering discursive claims by the Institute members. The argument of sameness was a central plank and any loss of status was termed as a short-term cost when compared with the long-term benefits. The linguistic claims included that technical standards were issued jointly by both bodies and that the ethical standards of both bodies were also identical (ASA & ICAA, 1981, p. 12). Hence, these linguistic claims were used to promote the merger.

The leaders expanded discursive arguments to foster a merger, linking it to the issue of regulation of the profession:

> Government, both State and Federal, will continue, in the interests of their members—the general public—to exercise control over the profession through legislation. The profession needs to have a strong voice with governments. The strength will come more easily from one professional body. (ASA & ICAA, 1981, p. 11)

The name of the proposed body in the original 1976 proposals was retained: "the Australian Institute of Chartered Accountants". There were two categories of members, Associate Chartered Accountant (ACA) and

Fellow Chartered Accountant (FCA). The basis of incorporation was Royal Charter (ASA & ICAA, 1981, p. 15). The admission requirements were the completion of an approved degree or diploma at an approved university or college of advanced education. Within both memberships, there would be two streams, public practice and general practice. Experience requirements included three years' work with MIPP or general practice based on members' choice and completion of a professional program for a relevant stream (ASA & ICAA, 1981, p. 16). All members aiming to enter public practice would be required to obtain a public practice certificate (ASA & ICAA, 1981, p. 18). Further, it was proposed that in the first two years following the date of integration, the national council of the proposed body was to be elected by and from regional councils, so that its composition would be one-third MIPP, one-third members in general practice, and the remaining one-third members from either category (ASA & ICAA, 1981, p. 21).

Thus, it was boundary construction work to ensure that there was at least one-third representation of MIPP on the national council. Arndt and Bigelow (2005) found similar boundary construction in the case of US hospital administration work, which is a female-dominated occupation. The processes were constructed to ensure male dominance in senior positions in hospital administration roles. Similarly, in the merger proposal, inclusionary processes were created to ensure the presence of MIPP in the national council. Table 7.10 shows that MNIPP would comprise 72% of the total members of the merged accountancy body, which means based on a simple majority, the national council could be controlled by a majority of members in general practice.

The national council of the proposed body would be selected based on quotas for each state, as shown in Table 7.11.

Table 7.12 shows changes in the designation of the Society members and the proposed status upgrade of Senior Associate to FCA.

Table 7.10 Classification of members in the integrated body

Category	*Public practice*	*General practice*	*Government*	*Other*	*Total*
Number	16,102	28,172	7,584	5,010	56,868
Per cent	28	50	13	9	100

Source Anon. (1981g)

Table 7.11 National council representation in the integrated body

Regional Council	*In public practice*	*In general practice*	*In any category*	*Total*
NSW	2	2	1	5
VIC	2	2	1	5
QLD	1	1	1	3
WA	1	1	1	3
SA	1	1	1	3
ACT			2	2
TAS			2	2
Total	7	7	9	23

Source ASA and ICAA (1981, p. 21)

Table 7.12 Status upgrade for the Society members

The Society	*New body*
Associate (AASA)	Associate Chartered Accountant (ACA)
Senior Associate (AASA (Snr.))	Fellow Chartered Accountant (FCA)
Fellow (FASA)	Fellow Chartered Accountant (FCA)
Life member	Life member Chartered Accountant
Honorary	Honorary member Chartered Accountant

Source ASA and ICAA (1981, p. 24)

In the proposed titles shown in Table 7.12, there was a clear status upgrade for the Society members who were senior associates. Under the proposed titles, they were designated as becoming FCAs (ASA & ICAA, 1981, p. 24), which was an upgrade of status from being a senior associate member (Lamont & Molnár, 2002) (Table 7.13).

To pass the integration proposal, a two-thirds majority of a special meeting of the Institute was required. In the case of the Society, the requirement was 75% of members voting in favour of change (ASA & ICAA, 1981, p. 27). An anonymous associate member of the Society, wrote in the Integration Forum of September 1981 making a strong case for integration and argued that it would be a tragedy if the current integration proposals were rejected (ASA & ICAA, 1981).

Table 7.13 Comparative membership of the Society and the Institute (As of 31 December 1980 [3,500 members overlap])

	The Society		*The Institute*	
	Number	*Per cent*	*Number*	*Per cent*
Public practice as principals	5,417	12.0	5,003	42.7
Public practice as employees	2,889	6.4	2,793	23.8
Total public practice	8,306	18.4	7,796	66.5
Government	7,584	16.8		
Commerce/industry/others	24,795	54.9	3,377	28.8
Academic	1,409	3.1		
Retired	3,053	6.8	548	4.7
Total Non-public practice	36,841	81.6	3,925	33.5
Total	45,147	100	11,721	100

Source ASA and ICAA (1981, p. 26)

The final integration proposals were released on 15 November 1981 with the return of a postal ballot by 21 December 1981. Peter Agars (1981), president of the Society, expressed a fear that based on the ANOP final survey, some members might not vote in favour of integration. The release of the final integration proposals attracted criticism from the Institute members in Singapore who strongly opposed the move by both bodies. Eight hundred accountants in Singapore were members of Australian bodies, of whom about 720 were Society members and 97 were Institute members[5] (Anon., 1981b). After the release of the final proposals, both the Society and the Institute received letters from their members expressing their opinions regarding the merger. Both the Society and the Institute claimed that 90% of members were in favour of the integration (McKenon, 1981). According to Chong (1981), the officials of the Institute believed the membership was divided, with a possible slight majority in favour of integration. Fearing that integration might fail, the president of the Institute stated on 27 April 1981 at the New South Wales Congress of the Institute that, he urged members to take the long-term view and not the short-term view of matters which affect them personally (Kelly, 1981a).

[5] Presumably around 17 were members of both bodies.

After the ballot closed on 21 December 1981 and members had voted, the results were announced on 8 January 1982 in a joint press release by the Society President P. D. Agars and the Institute President D. G. Neilson. The results of the members' poll revealed that the councils of the two bodies had not been empowered to proceed with integration. The membership of the Society overwhelmingly supported the merger proposal, but the Institute failed to deliver the minimum vote required to enable a merger to proceed. In the case of the Society, 90.1% of members supported the merger attempt with a response rate of 65%, while in the case of the Institute, 56.5% of members supported the move with a response rate of 74% (Anon., 1982a; ASA, 1981; ICAA, 1981; Miles, 1982). The outcome was similar to the ANOP June survey, which showed 90% of the Society members and 56% of the Institute members in support of the merger attempt (Anon., 1981k). The ANOP survey of September, which showed that the Institute members' support had risen from 56% to 66%, was questioned and its validity challenged (Anon., 1982b).

The Society president said that, it was regrettable that members of the Institute did not take advantage of the opportunity and the privilege of merger with the Society (ASA, 1981). In the aftermath of the failure, the Society promptly started a reassessment of the scope and direction of the Society objectives to meet their needs and challenges. After extensive consultation, a document titled "Forward Plan" was prepared (ASA, 1981). Peter Agars stated that members had a strong feeling that after the failure of integration, positive steps were necessary to maintain the Society's leadership in the profession (ASA, 1981).

Following the failure, the executive director of the Society Geoff Vincent said that cooperation with the Institute of Chartered Accountants in Australia would continue and rather it would be enhanced in many areas (ASA, 1981). According to Vincent, the Society was also paying special attention to the professional development of its members (ASA, 1981). The national council reported that 90.1% of Society members supported the integration, which demonstrated members' understanding of the significance of issues and their recognition of the importance of a unified profession (ASA, 1981).

The co-regulation of the profession was a new development in 1981. The newly formed National Companies and Securities Commission held meetings with the Society and the Institute to form an Accounting Standards Review Board. This enabled the avoidance of outright government regulation (ASA, 1981).

Further, Neilson (Institute President) said that some Chartered Accountants had indicated they feared their interests would be swamped by the bigger membership of the Society while others were unwilling to share the title "Chartered Accountant" (Crook & Brolly, 1982, p. 7). He also expressed that from 1969s first integration attempt, the support from the Institute members rose to 56.5% in 1981 from 41.8% in 1969 (Crook & Brolly, 1982). Neilson also said that the two bodies would work to achieve the objectives of integration without the corporate integration itself (Crook & Brolly, 1982, p. 7). He added:

> In the future, I think we will be working closely together in matters such as education, ethical rulings and professional conduct. But there would be no plans for another referendum in the next few years although I would hope that we could have a merger in some years. (Crook & Brolly, 1982. p. 7)

After the failure of the integration attempt, the Society issued a press release on 8 January 1982 stating, as Australia's largest professional accountancy body, the Society had forecasted major changes to its entry standards and to the continuing education of its members (ASA, 1982). The press release stated its appreciation of the Society members for supporting the integration attempt and regretted that, despite the Institute council's first step towards unity, members did not support the proposal. The Society outlined four key areas of work for the future: technical competence of members, professional image and voice, organisation and management of the Society and the ethical standards of members (ASA, 1982).

McKenon (1982, p. 43) reported

> While pursuing the cause of integration publicly, many officials and councillors were privately pursuing the interests of their body. In the professional standards area there were disagreements. The Institute decided to issue standards on tax practice, independence and quality control. The Society stepped back from applying its imprimatur.

Crook (1982) also downplayed the status of Society members, stating that Institute members would not want an association with "riff-raff" and praised the PY program of the Institute, saying that it was a difficult program and many people had repeatedly failed it. Those who passed and become CAs deserved to be called KCMG: Kindly Call Me God (Crook, 1982, p. 7).

The next section provides responses to the research questions and conducts an analysis of the findings using a theoretical framework.

7.4 Discussion and Analysis

Two significant findings emerge from this chapter: (1) the traditional organisational strategies of both bodies were modified and (2) there was a successful protection of the Institute's boundaries by its members and, consequently, the preservation of the different organisational strategies of each body. These respective findings are presented in conjunction with four of the five research questions of this study.

7.4.1 Reasons for Mounting the Merger Attempt

The first research question is "What were the reasons for mounting the second merger attempt between the Society and the Institute?" The three types of reason were first, reasons that jointly affected the Institute and the Society and second and third, reasons specific to each body.

Several common reasons assisted in mounting the second merger attempt. There was a challenge to professional accountants' status in 1971, when a series of advertisements appeared in newspapers seeking accountants. Target candidates of the advertisement were individuals without accreditation from either of the two bodies (Anon., 1971). Then, there were challenges to the legitimacy of the profession when, in the early to mid-1970s, a series of corporate collapses resulted in the criticism of accountants and auditors (Henderson, 1997). These factors contributed to the mounting of the second merger attempt; the legitimacy crisis was a common factor between the first and second merger attempts, as Carnegie and O'Connell (2012) found in their study, which referred to the first merger attempt. Both bodies were also aware of government intervention and statutory control to regulate the accounting profession in several other countries (ASA, 1980, p. 7). All these factors provided strength to the idea of a second merger attempt.

In addition, both bodies claimed that statutory recognition of the accounting profession could be achieved by using the stronger lobbying power that a united body would have (Thiele, 1975). J. D. Norgard, who was chairperson of the Australian Broadcasting Commission and an independent chairperson of the IPC, joined the public discourse in favour of the merger. Norgard (1980) wrote in September 1980 that the integration of the profession was important as it would enable accounting bodies "to speak up with one voice, loud and clear". This argument had been used in the case of the first merger attempt (Anon., 1968; Gynther, 1967, p. 290), but was represented in the second merger attempt. In response to an interview question about the reasons for again attempting a merger, Miller said:

> Because the leaders of the professional bodies were great people of foresight, ethics and vision. They thought in a small country like Australia it was counter-productive to have competing resources with two bodies so it occurred to the leaders of both bodies that it should be singular. (2015)

The society had its own reasons for mounting the second merger attempt. As mentioned in Chapter 5, many of the Society's MIPP did not disclose their membership with the Society and, because they held joint membership, they only disclosed their membership with the Institute when conducting their public practice. The Society was concerned that its members did not have a generic title similar to CAs (ASA, 1967). As discussed in Sect. 5.2, to overcome such issues, the Society attempted in 1976 to create a separate list for its MIPP to endow them with special status compared with the Institute's members (Anon., 1976b). This motion was voted down, with opposition from 57% of voting members (McKeon, 1975a). Therefore, the attempt to create a sub-boundary between its members, similar to the approach adopted by the Institute, failed and demarcation of the Society's members based on their involvement in public practice did not succeed (Fournier, 2000; Gieryn, 1983; Lamont & Molnár, 2002; Persson, 2010). This provided incentives to accept the Institute's offer for merger discussions.

Reasons that were specific to the Institute included changing the composition of its membership profile. Over the years, the share of the Institute's members involved in public practice was on decline. Yet, the Institute was formed by granting a Royal Charter to 28 accountants in public practice (ICAA, 1969), which means the very formation of that body was based solely on MIPP. However, gradually the proportion of MNIPP increased and the boundaries formed around MIPP shifted to that of the elite professional title of CA. For example, in the period of

11 years from 1971 to 1981, the proportion of MIPP steadily decreased, with a total fall of 6.5 percentage points (ICAA, 1971–1980), which meant that the exclusivity status of the Institute was gradually becoming weaker, which provided additional leverage to its leaders for presenting arguments in favour of the merger.

Geoff Neilson, who was president of the Institute at the time of the merger attempt, provided some insights on what the leadership of the Institute believed while proposing changes in their traditional strategies. Neilson stated:

> I think the Institute generally felt at a national level the merger was desirable. Competition between two bodies was not good for Australia. We were part of the global accounting profession and once united it would be very significant body in terms of numbers. So I think the motivation was to have a united accounting profession in Australia, which was a very significant part of the world accounting profession. The feeling was very strong in the National Council. The main motivation was to form a significant world-class professional accounting body. (Neilson, 2015)

For decades, the Institute leadership had claimed to be exclusive, but the statement by Neilson (2015) indicates that they were prepared to alter their exclusivity strategy.

In their study of the healthcare profession, Nancarrow and Borthwick (2005, p. 897) argued:

> The healthcare professions have never been static in terms of their own disciplinary boundaries, nor in their role or status in society. Healthcare provision has been defined by changing societal expectations and beliefs, new ways of perceiving health and illness, the introduction of a range of technologies and, more recently, the formal recognition of particular groups through the introduction of education and regulation. It has also been shaped by both interprofessional and profession-state relationships forged over time.

In summary, changes in context, external pressures, challenges to professional titles, legitimacy crisis and internal changes led to this move, which shows that boundaries are dynamic structures (Gieryn, 1983; Nancarrow & Borthwick, 2005).

7.4.2 *Strategies Adopted by Both Bodies in the Merger Attempt*

The second research question was linked with strategies adopted by the Society and the Institute in mounting the second merger attempt that was centred around modifying traditional strategies of "'exclusiveness' versus market control" adopted by both bodies (Macdonald & Ritzer, 1988, p. 257). To achieve successful modification of their organisational strategies, the bodies initiated many joint activities. Only a year after the failure of the first merger attempt, a joint standing committee comprising members of the respective executive committees of both bodies was formed to consider matters of mutual interest (ASA, 1970). Both bodies continued to issue statements projecting the merger attempt, which was a way of gaining support from their members. For example, the Society argued, "the increasing complexity of the affairs of the profession provides a powerful case for integration" (ASA, 1977, p. 10).

Both bodies had jointly established satisfactory communication lines with various state and federal governments representing the profession (ICAA, 1975). Many joint submissions to various governments on legal and tax matters were also made (ASA, 1977). These actions were based on arguments for the ability to speak effectively with one voice with governments and eventually assisted leaders of both bodies to present the case for merger. As mentioned previously, joint actions included representation at the Eleventh International Congress of Accountants held in Munich, Germany, on 11–14 October 1977 (ASA, 1977). To gain support from members, both bodies issued a few joint letters written by their presidents. This included sending a joint letter to members informing them about the decision to restart merger discussions (Bottrill, 1975; ICAA, 1975). In the case of the first merger attempt, the Institute took the initiative for merger, and this was also the case in the second merger attempt (ASA, 1981).

Chapter 5 and earlier sections of this chapter have addressed that boundaries in the Australian accounting profession were initially created around MIPP with the formation of the Institute in 1928, which had adopted an exclusivity strategy by gaining a Royal Charter (Anderson et al., 2005; Carnegie et al., 2003; Carnegie & Parker, 1999; Edwards et al., 2013; Macdonald & Ritzer, 1988; Parker, 2005). Similarly, the Scottish accountancy bodies had sought to adopt exclusivity in Royal Charters (Lee, 1995, p. 51) which "was a deliberate act to publicly separate Chartered Accountants from other accountants". The Society had adopted an alternative organisational strategy linked with market control (Macdonald & Ritzer, 1988), while in the British context, the Society of Incorporated Accountants in England had adopted the market control strategy targeting a broad membership base both in public and private sectors (Lee, 1995).

Contrary to their traditional approach, in the case of the second merger attempt, both bodies were modifying their traditional strategies (Annisette & Trivedi, 2013; Edwards et al., 2005; Macdonald & Ritzer, 1988, p. 257). The Institute had made some changes in 1973 when in the Supplementary Royal Charter, its objectives were amended to remove the imputation that its sphere of activity was largely public practice (Anon., 1981a). The Society's Annual Report of 1971 refers to the ongoing debate about raising the profile and status of the Society members (ASA, 1971). A joint statement issued by both bodies as part of the first exposure draft, which was released in August 1976, indicated a departure from traditional strategies. It contained a statement issued by both presidents that "we believe that integration is a natural and logical culmination of the development of accountancy in Australia" (ASA & ICAA, 1976, p. 8). A month after the release of the first draft proposals *The Chartered Accountant in Australia* summarised the rationale for the merger:

> The accountancy profession is under increasing public scrutiny and it is likely that pressure for greater accountability by the profession itself will increase. A pooling of the talent, initiative and resources of our joint memberships will strengthen the profession to meet this challenge, whereas if both bodies were to continue as separate organisations our respective standing and influence could well diminish. (ASA, 1976, p. 94)

This rationale clearly departed from a discourse of superiority and showed a shift from the earlier claims of the Institute. However, despite leaders of the profession engaging in a discourse of sameness of both bodies, it was estimated that a major section of the Institute members did not support the merger with the Society (Anon., 1979b). With this assessment in mind and to convince the members, the Institute's executive director, Vic Prosser, made public claims that "approximately 30 percent of our members are [were] not currently in practice at all—but occupy positions in commerce, industry, government, academic bodies or elsewhere" (1979, p. 13). Further he added that "one of the real strengths of the Institute is its diversity of membership" (Prosser, 1979, p. 13). This public discourse was used as a strategy to assist in strengthening the case for modifying the traditional boundaries of the Institute.

According to Gracia and Oats (2012, p. 308), "Boundaries are ubiquitous in modern social life and the work of creating and maintaining boundaries is particularly evident within professions, their regulation and operations". Over time, an exclusionary discourse can change to include individuals who were earlier excluded. The leaders of the Institute changed their discursive arguments from exclusivity to that of forming a larger body that would have exclusive status because of its size, yet have more control over the market for accounting services. In a similar situation, the racial boundaries of "white" identities were expanded over time in the US. Initially, it excluded Irish and Jews; however, with the expansion of "white" identity, Irish immigrants (Ignatiev, 1995) and Jews (Brodkin, 1998), who were earlier cast as racial "non-whites", were included as "white" (Annisette & Trivedi, 2013).

Both bodies learned from the failure of the first merger attempt and made a few changes in their approach to plan and execute the second merger. A major change was consultation with members on the idea of merger at meetings conducted throughout Australia (Anon., 1976a; Munro, 1975a). Members who could not attend meetings were asked to express their opinions by sending letters (Munro, 1975a). Neither body disclosed the contents of letters to the other (Munro, 1975a), which indicates a selective disclosure. Further, both bodies regularly issued statements and reports on the progress of merger (Anon, 1975). This was a strategy to keep members involved and to gain their support.

In 1979, J. D. Norgard, chairperson of the Australian Broadcasting Commission, was appointed as independent chairperson of the IPC. Various surveys were conducted by the ANOP (Anon., 1981h) to assess the level of support for the merger attempt. This was a different approach from the first merger attempt. Major discussions on the merger were undertaken at national and general council levels and between councils and the unity committee, which was a common strategy between the first and second merger attempts. The expansion of organisational boundaries and the inclusion of a larger number of the Society members were projected with various public arguments, such as the one presented by W. G. Phillip:

> Whatever the ultimate results will be, I firmly believe that it will be in the best long term interests of the accounting profession if the two major

> bodies could merger to become a more forceful group in the community. The pressures of today from governments, special interest groups, large corporations and others are such that we must not provide opportunity for the profession to be divided. (ICAA, 1980, p. 3)

Phillip continued his discourse by arguing that to retain the status of a profession, all sectional groups of people working in public practice, the government, academia or in commerce needed to work together, putting aside their sectional interests (ICAA, 1980). This was particularly important to maintain and improve respect and support from the community (ICAA, 1980). Phillip also added that in recent years, there were "increasing expectations of leadership from senior politicians" (ICAA, 1980, p. 3). During the final stages of the integration process, in March 1981, the proposals were again sent to members of both bodies for their comments and opinions. The proposals mentioned that "The Society members in particular will benefit from the more clearly defined professional and ethical standards that are embodied in these proposals" (ASA & ICAA, 1981, p. 4). Hence, the discursive claims show that both bodies had modified their traditional organisational strategies.

7.4.3 *Reasons for Merger Attempt Failure*

The third research question concerns factors that contributed to the failure of the second merger attempt. On similar lines as indicated in the fifth chapter, there are two angles in the analysis when responding to the third research question. A major reason for the failure was the detachment of the Institute leaders from the members (Lee, 2010; Shackleton & Walker, 2001). A second consequential reason was that the Institute members engaged in boundary protection because the leadership could not convince them of the claimed benefits associated with the proposed merger (Fournier, 2000; Gieryn, 1983; Persson, 2010). The overwhelming support of changes in professional boundaries from the Society members is also discussed.

As shown in Chapter 5, the reasons for the first merger attempt's failure were similar to those for the second. However, in the case of the second merger attempt, both bodies tried certain strategies to reduce the chances of failure. The then vice-president of the Society, John Miller, spoke about the leaders of both bodies moving ahead with their plan for changes in traditional boundaries while the Institute members were opposing this strategy. Miller (2015) added some other dimensions as well:

> Key factors were the failure of Chartered leaders to understand how deeply the younger members felt about the Professional Year. There was no strategy to cope with those feelings. Charter leaders sadly didn't do the research; therefore, they were not able to take any corrective actions. There was a geographical thing. Australia is a big country with a small population. The charter was very much Sydney centric. In Perth and Brisbane there was a feeling of resent that this was driven by head office. I think votes were quite bad in Perth and Queensland as a result. So I think the Chartered Institute leaders who were essentially accountants and business people didn't understand marketing and the need to really find out what their members wanted.

John Miller shifted the burden of failure to the Institute leaders. *The Age* reported on 6 October 1979, "The merger has always been backed by the chiefs of the two bodies but has run into strong grass-roots opposition, especially in the Institute" (Anon., 1979b, p. 3). The Institute leaders had realised that a significant portion of its members did not agree with them on the issue of merger and support from members was weak. To assess the level of support, ANOP was appointed and surveys were conducted in March and May 1981, which showed that support from the Institute members was insufficient. The March 1981 survey results showed that support for the merger from the Institute members was short of the required two-third majority (ICAA, 1980) while the May 1981 survey results showed that support for the merger from the Institute members was only 56% (Kelly, 1981b). In the case of the accounting profession in the UK, Lee (2010) and Shackleton and Walker (2001) found the detachment of leaders a reason for the failure of various merger attempts.

After the first merger attempt, it was clear that the Institute members did not support the merger move. To overcome that issue, the Institute had arranged for the IPC to address members at different meetings, but attendance was very low, which the president of the Institute termed disappointing (ICAA, 1976). Even at the early stages of IPC meetings, it was clear that the initially prepared draft proposals were unlikely to be accepted by members and that significant changes in integration proposals were needed. Issues of contention were entry requirements for joining the integrated body, conditions for granting practising certificates and the constitution and the composition of councils (Anon., 1981j; Hale,

1981; Kelly, 1981c). According to Lanigan (1980, p. 355), the greatest single hurdle to integrate was the different membership patterns of the two bodies, which was mainly between MIPP and MNIPP, or in other words, changes in the then-established boundaries of both professional bodies, which had been moulded by their respective histories.

A difference from the first merger attempt was that steps were taken to overcome members' objections. After the May 1981 ANOP survey, which showed a low level of support from the Institute members, the merger vote was deferred (Kelly, 1981b). During the period when the integration poll was postponed, the proposals were amended in July 1981 with a view to increasing support from the Institute members. The three main changes were first, granting fellow status to all Institute members who had been members for at least 10 years or had completed the PY of study and had been members for three years (Hale, 1981); second, all existing Institute or Society members who had been members for 10 years and had been principals and/or employees in public practice for three years would qualify for a public practice certificate; and third, other members transferring to public practice were required to complete 12 months in the employment of a public practice certificate holder (Kelly, 1981c). One other amendment was the reduction of the period to become a fellow after completing PY from 10 years to three (Anon., 1981j). This was mainly to assist in overcoming the opposition of younger members of the Institute (Hale, 1981) and to counter boundary protection by the Institute members. In addition, leaders of both bodies jointly initiated an Integration Forum in February 1981 in the official journals of both bodies.

The second merger attempt failed because of successful boundary protection by Institute members (Fournier, 2000; Persson, 2010). Their argument was that the "merger could lead to a dilution of entrance requirements to the Institute" (Anon, 1981b, p. 9). In the June 1981 edition of *Integration Forum*, W. S. Kierath, a member of the Institute, objected to the unity attempt and particularly to having two types of membership: members with public practice experience and members with no public practice experience or training. Kierath (1981) argued that the merger could be between public accountants of the Institute and the Society but merger between all members of both bodies was unacceptable to the Institute members.

From these discursive claims, it is clear that some Institute members were not in favour of changes in the boundaries of the professional association and engaged in boundary work to protect the boundaries of their Institute. According to Lamont and Molnár (2002, p. 168), boundaries "are an essential medium through which people acquire status and monopolize resources". Any changes to boundaries are likely to lead to boundary protection (Fournier, 2000; Persson, 2010). Evidence of boundary protection is found in the comments of McKenon (1981, p. 9) who stated:

> Out in the accounting world there is opposition to integration, especially among NSW members of the Institute. In 1969, when integration proposals were last placed before members, the younger NSW members of the Institute voted strongly against them.

McKenon (1981, p. 9) further stated:

> In recent months there have been signs that the 1969 Institute resistance remains roughly the same. A straw poll conducted late last year by Australian National Opinion Poll indicated support of about 56 percent.

At the June 1981 Integration Forum, the IPC engaged in public discourse stating that for the previous 10 years, the education policies of both bodies were identical, with each body requiring the candidates to obtain an approved degree or diploma at an approved university or college of advanced education (Anon., 1981e). Most letters published in the June 1981 edition of *Integration Forum* in the Society's journal were from Institute members and were generally in favour of the merger. These letters included a letter from R. N. H. Denton, FCA and former president of the Institute from 1978 to 1979. Further, a letter from C. J. Hurford, MP, Shadow Minister for Industry and Commerce, appeared, which was also in support of the merger of the two bodies. Hurford (1981, p. 354) claimed that "while we are divided, standards suffer, if this continues, governments will find it necessary to intervene in the regulation of accounting to a far greater extent than hitherto in order to protect the interests of the public". These are examples of steps taken by both bodies and especially by the Institute to gain support from its members to vote in favour of the merger attempt and to thereby counter boundary protection.

There is further evidence of attempts to counter the boundary protection work. On 1 May 1981, W. G. Phillip wrote a three-page letter to members as the Institute president. Phillip (1981) particularly referred to younger members opposing the integration. In his discursive claims, Phillip (1981) tried to remove fears that only a small portion of the Society members would be eligible to receive a public practice certificate. His views were based on the fact that nearly 3,500 of the Institute members were also Society members. This formed around 30% of the Institute membership. Further, he argued that after integration the public practice certificate would be issued only after passing the Institute's PY program. Phillip (1981) concluded his letter by saying that

> Integration will give us one body, one voice and the opportunity to improve our educational standards and professional competence of all members. In short, it will give us a stronger and better profession and that must be of great benefit to all accountants – and especially younger ones.

In June 1981, Norgard stated that if members were not willing to take the long-term view then the integration prospects would be problematic (Anon., 1981d). In December 1981, Norgard stated that "the concern I have is that some accountants might not read the documents and may vote with what I might call a referendum approach" (Anon., 1981h). Norgard also indicated that the first attempt in 1969 failed because of the opposition of young members of the Institute (Anon., 1981h).

There was strong support for the merger attempt from the Society members. Goodall (1981), an AASA, strongly supported the merger and claimed that the public image of the profession would improve. Goodall (1981) wrote, "my only complaint is why has it taken so long?" Hegan (1981), another AASA, also strongly favoured the merger between the two bodies, while Mullen (1981), also an AASA, stated that the ability to speak with one voice on accountancy matters was a major advantage of a united profession. The overwhelming support of 90.1% of Society members and its reasons have been argued its reasons have been argued in earlier chapters, which indicated that individuals in lower-status groups accept changes in traditional strategies and boundaries readily (Keohane & Milner, 1996; Milner, 1996). Usually, for lower-status groups, if changes to boundaries lead to status upgrade, then that becomes group mobility (Lamont & Molnár, 2002). Therefore, the failure of the second merger attempt is attributed mainly to boundary protection work by Institute members as a response to the proposed modification of the strategy of exclusivity. The boundary protection by many of the Institute members was an attempt at protecting "professional identity" (Gieryn, 1983; Guo, 2012).

There are numerous examples of linguistic claims by Institute members opposing the merger (Annisette, 2017). The August 1981 issue of the Institute's journal published letters from ACAs. Most of these letters voiced strong opposition to the merger proposals. Shorrock (1981), who was a recent PY graduate, stressed:

> As a member who recently passed the Professional Year programme, I am disappointed that the integration proposals do not recognise the enormous amount of time and energy involved in completing a year that had a dramatic effect on not only myself but also on my wife and family. At this stage I am not prepared to vote for a proposal which would grant equal status to those members of the Society who have undertaken only a twenty-hour professional orientation programme. (1981, p. 19)

Shorrock's (1981) discursive arguments are also evidence of boundary protection. J. H. Barber, an ACA, noticed some prejudice and wrote to the editor of the Institute journal:

> Every single letter against the issue was accompanied by the editor's comments explaining away any points raised. I feel this severe form of prejudice should be avoided. (1981, p. 14)

In his claims, Hines (1981, p. 355), an ACA, expressed a fear of dilution of the Institute members' powers and argued that in the integrated body with 12,000 Institute and 45,000 Society members, "Chartered Accountants will exercise about one-fifth of the total voting rights". Hines (1981, p. 355) also commented that "the Society's educational entry requirements are not comparable with those of the Institute". Hines (1981) compared the PY program of the Institute with the Society's 40 hours of attendance at non-examinable professional development courses. Further, he said that candidates who fail the PY of the Institute join the Society because of the lower level of its entry requirements (1981). Hines (1981) made a reference to a statement of the president of the Institute from the March 1981 edition of the Institute's journal in which it was argued that a united profession had better prospects of gaining the registration of accountants at the federal level. Hines (1981) criticised this reason to push for unity. Therefore, the discursive arguments of the Institute members opposing the merger attempt was a way of demarcating themselves from the Society members in the same way as scientists apply for boundary work in their profession: "their attribution of selected characteristics to the institution of science (i.e. to its practitioners, methods, stock of knowledge, values and work organisation) for purposes of constructing a social boundary that distinguishes some intellectual activities as 'non-science'" (Gieryn, 1983, p. 782).

Miller (2015) explained why younger members of the Institute were against the merger:

> Basically, the view among the Chartered Accountants' younger people was that the Professional Year was very demanding and appropriate. The Society's professional orientation program was considered a bit inadequate and I tended to agree with them. But the important thing is that I knew and I was also very confident that the younger people at the Institute would not be supporting the merger. When I told the joint Executives of both bodies that I didn't think that it would succeed they were very upset with me. I said I am giving you my first hand market research. I said that we were going to have a big problem and sadly I was right and all my colleagues were wrong. I had the view that the merger would fail.

Another example of public discourse opposing the merger is an anonymous young CA who criticised the integration plan and stated, "your proposals seem to be based on the totally false premise that all accountants can be considered as one. But this is not true—we serve different purposes" (Anon., 1981c, p. 18). This member also criticised the argument that members should consider long-term gains and wrote "You talk of long term aims. Does this mean we disregard the present?" (Anon., 1981c, p. 18). This suggests that the sentiments among some young members were quite strong, and they eventually did preserve the boundaries of the Institute.

Further evidence of boundary protection includes a young member of the Institute who anonymously wrote, "We as the Institute members will be overruled by the Society's members—are their members so dedicated to such standards as the Institute lays down?" (Anon., 1981c, p. 18). These discursive arguments and strategies are aligned with literature that shows that with the change of context, where traditional strategies of the Institute changed, members acted to defend the status quo and engage in boundary protection (Fournier, 2000; Keohane & Milner, 1996; Milner, 1996). In his work, Gieryn (1983, p. 792) argued that "boundary-work excludes rivals from within by defining them as outsiders with labels such as 'pseudo', 'deviant', or 'amateur'". The arguments of the Institute members seeking to protect their professional boundaries were thereby analogous to those observed by Gieryn (1983).

On 7 December 1981, Austin Donnelly (1981), a former president of the Queensland division, former general councillor and a member of the Institute for 34 years, wrote a letter to *The News* opposing the merger. Although archival materials show that it was predominantly the younger members who opposed the merger, Donnelly's (1981) opposition is evidence of boundary protection by experienced members, including those who formerly held leadership positions in the Institute.

A group of CAs opposing the merger published a public notice on 2 December 1981 in *The Financial Review*. The notice mentioned that unity was unrealistic because both bodies did not represent all accountants in Australia and because an integrated profession was not evident in many other countries. It also rejected the argument that a united body would have a single voice on matters of mutual interest by arguing that both bodies were already working jointly. The notice also mentioned that the image of CAs would not improve with the inclusion of the Society members (Anon, 1981j).

The response of Miller in his oral history interview aids an understanding of the reasons for the strong boundary protection attempts from Western Australia. When John Miller was asked about the opposition faced by Institute members from Perth and Brisbane and whether regional tensions[6] were still playing a role, he responded:

> Yes, in Australia there is a cultural difference between the west and the east and even between north and south. Back in my professional practice I was advised to be very careful what you do and say in Perth and Brisbane. The chartered institute led from Sydney did not understand personality differences. The reasons are beyond accounting and go back to Federation. There is a long history of this. Western Australia was a reluctant party in

[6] As Poullaos (1994) stated, despite the formation of the Federation, regionalism was quite strong and differences between states were at various levels, such as climate, natural resources, laws, infrastructure and custom duties. Even with the formation of a united Commonwealth "the tensions which held up Federation did not disappear" (Poullaos, 1994, p. 51).

> the 1901 Federation of Australia. Several times they threatened not to join and subsequently they have threatened to secede. So Western Australia have always had a bit of an issue with the east. I think politics and Aussie [social] rules are now changing a bit, but Western Australia and Queensland are very big states. They are huge states. They don't socially and politically respond well to directions from Canberra or Melbourne and Sydney. You can see this not only in accounting but also in business and politics. (2015)

Thus, John Miller added the dimension of regional pride and tensions to the other key reasons for opposition to the merger given by younger people. The interview response received from the Institute president at the time of the failure of the second merger attempt reaffirmed this. In a response to questions about potential causes that led to the failure of the second merger attempt, Geoff Neilson stated:

> We felt it came down to individuals. Two reasons I think. One, members from Western Australia. Some individuals in Western Australia were always a problem for any part of the integration. The second reason would be PY. The recent Professional Year graduates who were mainly younger members felt that their hard won reputation was going to be diluted if the merger had gone ahead. (2015)

Susan Crook, *The Age* business writer, wrote "many Chartered Accountants breathed a sigh of relief with the failure of vote on the proposed integration of Australia's two accounting bodies" (1982, p. 7). There is evidence of the Society's members opposing boundary protection by the Institute members. Peter Privitelli, who was a provisional member of the Society, wrote a letter to the editor of the Society journal in October 1979 and mentioned:

> I know for a fact that there are several Institute members who regard themselves as a separate and superior cult to those members belonging to the Society, merely because there are fewer members belonging to the Institute. (1979, p. 655)

In summary, the key reason for failure of the second merger attempt was the successful boundary protection by the Institute members (Fournier, 2000; Gieryn, 1983; Persson, 2010).

7.4.4 Reactions of Various Stakeholders

The fourth research question is linked to the reactions of various stakeholders[7] to the proposals for unification and their subsequent failures. Similar to the first merger attempt, the failure of the second merger attempt did not attract significant interest from stakeholders. The press covered the outcome in a descriptive way only. Based on archival data, only PW, a major accounting firm and a key stakeholder, came out strongly in support of the merger attempt in November 1981. PW's senior partner R. G. Lee called for support of the integration because it was in the best interest of the public and the profession (Anon., 1981f). The Integration Forum of June 1981 reported a letter from C. J. Hurford, Shadow Minister for Industry and Commerce, which was also in support of merger of the two bodies (Hurford, 1981). However, larger accounting firms were not taken into confidence nor asked to make any public statements in support of a merger (Barnes, 1981). In an interview about the role of the government as a stakeholder, Miller said (2015) "no pressure at all from the government. Pressure on government was from us to protect the term accountant".

Regarding whether there was any pressure from governments, as stakeholders, on both bodies to merge, Geoff Neilson stated that:

> Yes, I believe there was but I can't be specific about this. When we used to lobby with governments they would occasionally say why don't you two get together. So I think that was obvious. But we never heard that as a word but it was pretty evident that it was the case. (2015)

Thus, existence as two separate bodies would seem to have had implications for their ability to speak with governments; however, there was no active pressure from governments on the bodies to merge. It appears that some stakeholders were supportive of the merger attempt. Documentary evidence did not reflect responses from other stakeholders.

When John Miller was asked about the reactions of various stakeholders to the failure of the merger attempt, he stated:

> The government was very neutral. The governments might have welcomed the merger but didn't put any pressure. The big charter firms were very

[7] Stakeholders include members of each professional body, the government, policymakers, accounting firms and investors.

> much for the merger because their clients were mostly members of the Society. There were good marketing reasons for big firms to support the merger and they supported it very strongly. The academicians were generally for the merger. It was the small practitioners in Perth and Brisbane that made merger difficult.

The response indicates that attempts to change the traditional strategies of both bodies and the failure of these because of boundary protection were deemed an internal affair of the accounting profession. This failure did not attract much external reaction. Similar to the first merger attempt, stakeholders outside the accounting profession did not respond to the failure. Documentary evidence does not provide much detail to explain the reasons for this poor response.

7.5 Conclusion

This chapter considered the second merger attempt, which was planned for the longest period. The process was also one of the most rigorous among all the four merger attempts. Both bodies had applied the lessons learned from the failure of the first merger attempt to execute the second merger attempt. The integration proposals were initially prepared in 1976 when, at the invitation of the Institute's national council, the Society's national council initiated formal merger discussions (ASA & ICAA, 1976; ICAA, 1975, p. 9). Between 1975 and 1976, the ISC, which consisted of members of both bodies, met frequently to develop the first draft of merger proposals (ICAA, 1976). This was followed by a series of meetings of members to seek their opinions and feedback on merger discussions (Anon., 1976c).

After these meetings and after receiving feedback from members, it was agreed that significant refinements to the proposals were necessary before acceptance could be achieved. By 1979, a further set of integration proposals was prepared. Both councils agreed that the ISC had performed everything that could reasonably be expected of it and they resolved to adopt a new approach, which led to the formation of the IPC under an independent chairperson J. D. Norgard (Anon., 1981a). The IPC prepared the final merger proposals, which were put to members of each body for voting in 1981 and were defeated by the Institute members, as was the case with the first merger attempt.

In addition to the process for the development of proposals, consultation with members for the second merger attempt was more carefully planned and each body was more cautious of not repeating the outcomes of the first merger attempt. In the first instance, members were asked to comment on the idea of merger via letters and in person at members' meetings, which has been discussed in the earlier parts of this chapter (Anon., 1976c). After this consultation process, the bodies released the first draft of integration proposals. It took about four years to develop the initial proposals. Members were consulted via letters, comments to editors of journals of both bodies and in meetings of members. The initial proposals were amended on different occasions. After working on developing proposals for a few years, it became apparent in the late 1970s that support from Institute members was still insufficient to pass the resolution (ASA, 1978).

In fact, the chair of the IPC preparing the integration proposals, P. C. E. Cox, who was representing the Institute at the committee, bluntly called for disbanding of any further discussion. Cox was removed from his post and an independent chair of the IPC was appointed (McKenon, 1979). Both the Society and the Institute conducted a survey of its members to read their mood (Anon., 1981h, 1981i, 1981k; Hale, 1981; Kelly, 1981c; Uren, 1981). Both bodies also slowed down merger discussions, restarted them the following year and held a joint national council meeting. Finally, after the longest process among all four merger attempts, the merger vote was taken in 1981 (Agars, 1981). However, boundary protection work by the Institute members resulted in failure of the second merger attempt, preserving the existing boundaries. The next chapter considers the third merger attempt.

References

Australian Bureau of Statistics. (1992). Australian population.

Agars, P. D. (1981, December). An interview with the president. *The Australian Accountant*, pp. 723–724.

Agars, P. D., & Neilson, D. G. (1981, December 15). Accounting merger proposals clarified. *Financial Review*, p. 7.

Anderson, M., Edwards, J. R., & Chandler, R. A. (2005). Constructing the 'well qualified' chartered accountant in England and Wales. *The Accounting Historians Journal, 32*(2), 5–54.

Annisette, M. (2017). Discourse of the professions: The making, normalizing and taming of Ontario's foreign-trained accountant. *Accounting, Organizations and Society, 60*, 37–61.
Annisette, M., & Trivedi, V. U. (2013). Globalization, paradox and the (un)making of identities: Immigrant chartered accountants of India in Canada. *Accounting, Organisations and Society, 38*(1), 1–29.
Anon. (1968, July). Announcement. *The Australian Accountant*, p. 7.
Anon. (1971, October). Status of accountants. *The Australian Accountant*, p. 420.
Anon. (1974, July). Joint message by G. W. Bottrill (President of Society) and E. H. Burgess (President of Institute). *The Australian Accountant*, p. 455.
Anon. (1975, October). Structure of the profession in Australia. *The Chartered Accountant in Australia*, pp. 17–18.
Anon. (1976a, August). Integration: News and notes. *The Australian Accountant*, p. 394.
Anon. (1976b). *General council annual report 1975*, p. 7.
Anon. (1976c, July 15). Accountants try again for merger. *The Australian*, p. 7.
Anon. (1976d, July 15). Figures men have a say. *Sun*, p. 8.
Anon. (1979a, July). Joint activities—Victoria. *The Chartered Accountant in Australia*, p. 79.
Anon. (1979b, October 6). Climactic vote. *The Age*, p. 3.
Anon. (1980, September 26). Australian row hits integration. *Accountancy Age*, p. 8.
Anon. (1981a, March). Integration forum. *The Australian Accountant*, pp. 90–93.
Anon. (1981b, April 10). Accountants' rift Singapore. *Financial Review*, p. 9.
Anon. (1981c, May). Integration forum, Letter by a concerned young chartered accountant. *The Chartered Accountant in Australia*, pp. 17–18.
Anon. (1981d, May 30–June 5). Man in the middle. *Business Review*, p. 28.
Anon. (1981e, June). Integration forum. *The Australian Accountant*, pp. 350–356.
Anon. (1981f, November 17). PW says yes to merger. *Sun*, p. 9.
Anon. (1981g, July). Integration forum. *The Australian Accountant*, pp. 438–443.
Anon. (1981h, December 5). NSW key to poll. *Business Review*, p. 9.
Anon. (1981i, August). Integration forum. *The Australian Accountant*, pp. 480–484.
Anon. (1981j, December 2). Notice to accountants—Vote no to integration. *Financial Review*, p. 255.
Anon. (1981k, September). Integration forum. *The Australian Accountant*, pp. 481–483.

Anon. (1982a, January/February). No to integration. *The Australian Accountant*, p. 5.
Anon. (1982b, May 15–21). Neilson on non-integration. *Business Review Weekly*, p. 53.
Arndt, M., & Bigelow, B. (2005). Professionalizing and masculinizing a female occupation: The reconceptualization of hospital administration. *Administrative Science Quarterly, 50*, 233–261.
Australian Society of Accountants. (1967). *Minutes of meeting of Executive Committee held on 17 February 1967* (pp. 1–20). Melbourne, Australia.
Australian Society of Accountants. (1970). *Annual report*. Melbourne, Australia.
Australian Society of Accountants. (1971). *Annual report*. Melbourne, Australia.
Australian Society of Accountants. (1972). *Annual report*. Melbourne, Australia.
Australian Society of Accountants. (1974). *Annual report*. Melbourne, Australia.
Australian Society of Accountants. (1976). *Annual report*. Melbourne, Australia.
Australian Society of Accountants. (1977). *Annual report*. Melbourne, Australia.
Australian Society of Accountants. (1978). *Annual report*. Melbourne, Australia.
Australian Society of Accountants. (1979). *Annual report*. Melbourne, Australia.
Australian Society of Accountants. (1980). *Annual report*. Melbourne, Australia.
Australian Society of Accountants. (1981). *Annual report*. Melbourne, Australia.
Australian Society of Accountants. (1982, January 8). *ASA to change* [Press release, Ray Andrews–Director of Public Affairs, Australian Society of Accountants].
Australian Society of Accountants and Institute of Chartered Accountants in Australia. (1976, July). *A draft proposal for integration of Australian Society of Accountants and the Institute of Chartered Accountants in Australia* (pp. 1–28). Exposure draft.
Australian Society of Accountants and Institute of Chartered Accountants in Australia. (1981, March 1). *Draft proposals for the integration of the accountancy profession in Australia* (pp. 1–20). Australian Society of Accountants and the Institute of Chartered Accountants in Australia.
Barnes, J. C. (1981, September). Integration forum. *The Australian Accountant*, pp. 571–572.
Bottrill, G. W. (1975, April). Integration of the accountancy profession in Australia. *The Australian Accountant*, p. 131.
Brodkin, K. (1998). *How the Jews became white folk and what that says about race in America*. Rutgers University Press.
Carnegie, G. D., Edwards, J. R., & West, B. P. (2003). Understanding the dynamics of the Australian accounting profession: A prosopographical study of the founding members of the Incorporated Institute of Accountants, Victoria, 1886 to 1908. *Accounting, Auditing & Accountability Journal, 16*(5), 790–820.

Carnegie, G. D., & O'Connell, B. T. (2012). Understanding the responses of professional accounting bodies to crises: The case of the Australian profession in the 1960s. *Accounting Auditing and Accountability Journal, 25*(5), 835–875.

Carnegie, G. D., & Parker, R. H. (1999). Accountants and empire: The case of co-membership of Australian and British accountancy bodies, 1885 to 1914. *Accounting, Business & Financial History, 9*(1), 77–102.

Chong, F. (1981, April 21). Accountants to decide in August. *Sun*, p. 9.

Cox, P. C. E. (1981, December 10). Letter to the editor. *Financial Review*, p. 7.

Crook, S. (1982, January 11). More that meets the eye in accountants' failure to merger. *The Age*, p. 7.

Crook, S., & Brolly, M. (1981, October 27). Accountants to vote on merger soon. *The Age*, p. 13.

Crook, S., & Brolly, M. (1982, January 8). Accountants deny their urge to merger-again. *Morning Herald*, p. 7.

Donnelly, A. (1981, December 7). Accounting move opposed—Letters to the finance editor. *The News*, p. 8.

Edwards, J. R., Anderson, M., & Chandler, R. (2005). How not to mount a professional project: The formation of the ICAEW in 1880. *Accounting and Business Research, 35*(3), 229–248.

Edwards, J. R., Dean, G., Clarke, F., & Wolnizer, P. (2013). Accounting academic elites: The tale of ARIA. *Accounting, Organisations and Society, 38*(5), 365–381.

Fournier, V. (2000). Boundary work and the (un)making of the professions. In *Professionalism, boundaries and the workplace* (p. 67). Routledge.

Gieryn, T. F. (1983). Boundary-work and the demarcation of science from non-science: Strains and interests in the professional ideologies of scientists. *American Sociological Review, 48*(6), 781–795.

Goodall, R. L. (1981, June). Integration forum. *The Australian Accountant*, pp. 350–356.

Gracia, L., & Oats, L. (2012). Boundary work and tax regulation: A Bourdieusian view. *Accounting, Organizations and Society, 37*(5), 304–321.

Guo, K. H. (2012). Understanding why and how some chartered accountants object to the proposed merger of the three accounting professions in Canada. *Accounting Perspectives, 11*(2), 111–130.

Gynther, R. S. (1967, July). The future of the accountant—And the accountant of future. *The Australian Accountant*, pp. 373–382.

Hale, B. (1981, August 6). Accountants merger plan amended to win support. *The Australian*, p. 8.

Hegan, W. J. (1981, June). Integration forum. *The Australian Accountant*, pp. 350–356.

Henderson, R. H. (1975, January/ February). Introduction of the professional orientation year. *The Australian Accountant*, 5.
Henderson, S. (1997). The expectations gap and the Australian accounting profession. *Accounting Forum, 21*(2), 175–188.
Hines, R. D. (1981, June). Integration forum. *The Australian Accountant*, pp. 350–356.
Hurford, C. J. (1981, June). Integration forum. *The Australian Accountant*, pp. 350–356.
Ignatiev, N. (1995). *How the Irish became white*. Routledge.
Irving, H. R. (1966, October 7). Report on professional awards for accountants (designation of CPA) submitted on behalf of the Executive Committee by President. *The Australian Society of Accountants*, pp. 1–27.
Kelly, K. (1981a, April 28). ICA President comes down on the side of amalgamation. *Financial Review*, p. 3.
Kelly, K. (1981b, August 6). Amalgamation issue on hold. *Financial Review*, p. 9.
Kelly, K. (1981c, October 13). Poll favours integration of Institute and Society. *Financial Review*, p. 10.
Keohane, R. O., & Milner, H. V. (Eds.). (1996). *Internationalization and domestic politics*. Cambridge University Press.
Kierath, W. S. (1981, June). Integration forum. *The Australian Accountant*, pp. 350–356.
Lamont, M., & Molnár, V. (2002). The study of boundaries in the social sciences. *Annual Review of Sociology, 28*(1), 167–195.
Lanigan, P. J. (1980, July). Integration-when? *The Australian Accountant*, p. 355.
Lee, T. A. (1995). The professionalization of accountancy: A history of protecting the public interest in a self-interested way. *Accounting, Auditing & Accountability Journal, 8*(4), 48–69.
Lee, T. A. (2010). Consolidating the public accountancy profession: The case of the proposed Institute of Chartered Accountants of Great Britain, 1988–9. *Accounting History, 15*(1), 7–39.
Linn, R. (1996). *Power, progress and profit: A history of the Australian accounting profession*. Australian Society of Certified Practising Accountants.
Macdonald, K. M., & Ritzer, G. (1988). The sociology of the professions: Dead or alive? *Work and Occupations, 15*(3), 251–272.
McKeon, A. (1975a, April 4). Accountants in disarray. *Financial Review*, p. 2.
McKeon, A. (1975b, April 9). Top accountants back reforms. *Financial Review*, p. 4.
McKeon, A. (1975c, June 9). Accounting bodies to sound out rank-and-file attitude to union. *Financial Review*, p. 11.

McKenon, A. (1979, October 5). Norgard picked to aid profession's integration. *Financial Review*, p. 10.

McKenon, A. (1981, April 10). Integration on the boil. *Business Review*, p. 9.

McKenon, A. (1982, January 16–22). Unity breakdown will lead to rivalry. *Business Review Weekly*, p. 43.

Miles, P. (1982, January 8). Accountants' merger fails. *The Sun*, p. 12.

Miller, J. (2015). *Interview with John Miller on February 27.*

Milner, D. (1996). Children and racism: Beyond the value of dolls. In P. W. Robinson (Ed.), *Social groups and identities: Developing the legacy of Henri Tajfel* (pp. 249–268). Butterworth Heinermann.

Mullen, T. G. (1981, June). Integration forum. *The Australian Accountant*, pp. 350–356.

Munro, R. F. (1975a, June). Integration. *The Australian Accountant*, p. 255.

Munro, R. F. (1975b, March). Qualification requirements of the Australian Society of Accountants. *The Australian Accountant*, p. 63

Nancarrow, S. A., & Borthwick, A. M. (2005). Dynamic professional boundaries in the healthcare workforce. *Sociology of Health & Illness, 27*(7), 897–919.

Neilson, G. (2015). *Interview with Geoff Neilson on February 20.*

Norgard, J. D. (1980, September). Integration: The position to date. *The Australian Accountant*, p. 527.

Norgard, J. D. (1981). *Letter to member of Society and Institute dated March 1, 1981.*

Parker, R. H. (2005). Naming and branding: Accountants and accountancy bodies in the British Empire and Commonwealth, 1853–2003. *Accounting History, 10*(1), 7–46.

Persson, A. (2010). Soldiers and secretaries: Gendered boundary work in the Swedish Armed Forces. *Scandinavian Journal of Management, 26*, 166–175.

Phillip, W. G. (1981). *Letter to Institute members as President, May 1.*

Privitelli, P. (1979, October). Unity of the profession. *The Australian Society of Accountants*, p. 655

Poullaos, C. (1994). *Making the Australian chartered accountant*. New York. NY: Garland.

Prosser, V. (1979, September). Talking point: A note from the Executive Director. *The Chartered Accountant in Australia*, p. 13.

Prosser, V. (1981, May). Talking point: A note from the Executive Director. *The Chartered Accountant in Australia*, p. 15.

Robinson, E. S. (1975, April 18). Accounting elitism. *Financial Review*, p. 11

Shackleton, K., & Walker, S. P. (2001). *A future for the accountancy profession: The quest for closure and integration, 1957–1970*. Institute of Chartered Accountants of Scotland.

Shorrock, W. R. (1981, August). A recent PY graduate's view, Integration Forum. *The Chartered Accountant in Australia*, p. 18.

The Institute of Chartered Accountants in Australia. (1969). *Annual report*. Sydney, Australia.
The Institute of Chartered Accountants in Australia. (1971). *Annual report*. Sydney, Australia.
The Institute of Chartered Accountants in Australia. (1972). *Annual report*. Sydney, Australia.
The Institute of Chartered Accountants in Australia. (1973). *Annual report*. Sydney, Australia.
The Institute of Chartered Accountants in Australia. (1974). *Annual report*. Sydney, Australia.
The Institute of Chartered Accountants in Australia. (1975). *Annual report*. Sydney, Australia.
The Institute of Chartered Accountants in Australia. (1976). *Annual report*. Sydney, Australia.
The Institute of Chartered Accountants in Australia. (1977). *Annual report*. Sydney, Australia.
The Institute of Chartered Accountants in Australia. (1978). *Annual report*. Sydney, Australia.
The Institute of Chartered Accountants in Australia. (1979). *Annual report*. Sydney, Australia.
The Institute of Chartered Accountants in Australia. (1980). *Annual report*. Sydney, Australia.
The Institute of Chartered Accountants in Australia. (1981). *Annual report*. Sydney, Australia.
Thiele, R. (1975, July). Editorial. *The Australian Accountant*, p. 321.
Uren, D. (1981, October 13). Merger of accountants gathers more support. *The Age*, p. 10.
Williams, D. P. (1973, May). Message from outgoing president. *The Australian Accountant*, p. 11.
Wood, P. J. (1975, April 15). Elite group accountants. *Financial Review*, p. 9.

CHAPTER 8

The Third Attempt to Unite the Dominant Professional Accounting Associations

8.1 Introduction

This chapter explains the third merger attempt, which, as in the case of each of the other merger attempts, had its own distinctive nuances. Unlike the first two merger attempts, where unity committees or integration committees were established, in the case of the third merger attempt most merger-related decisions, as will be shown, were taken by the presidents of both bodies. The context that led to the mounting of the third merger attempt had some commonalities with that of the first merger attempt. Similar to the first merger attempt, external pressures and developments created favourable conditions for mounting the third merger attempt. The developments affecting the accounting profession included corporate collapses, rising unemployment, economic recession and one of the biggest stock market crashes during the period under study, namely, between the late 1960s and the late 1990s (McMahon, 2007; Wright, 2008).

This chapter has four sections. The next section provides details on the background to the third merger attempt, including developments post-second-merger attempt. Joint work by the two bodies on matters of mutual interest, the membership and financial positions of both bodies and a time-specific corporate crisis are also discussed. The third section provides details of the merger talks, which took place in two stages. The first round of merger talks started when the Institute president made a

J. Sidhu et al., *Understanding the Sociology of the Accounting Profession*,
https://doi.org/10.1007/978-981-99-1572-9_8

unilateral offer in June 1989 to the Society's members to join the Institute, provided they had accumulated 10 years of experience. This created friction between the two bodies, and they initiated some formal merger talks. However, those talks were scrapped after a few months. The second round of merger talks started a year later in September 1990. The third section also examines the post failure context of the merger attempt. Finally, the fourth section provides a discussion and analysis using the theoretical frameworks applied in this thesis and provides responses to the four research questions within the context of the third merger attempt.

8.2 Background

After the failure of the second merger attempt, the president of the Institute issued a statement about the postfailure position, stating that:

> There has been considerable publicity given to the intention to work closely with the Society, and it seems that there has also been an expectation by some members of immediate changes flowing from that decision. (Anon., 1982)

In line with this statement, the Institute decided to prepare long-term plans for joint work using the overall objectives stated in its charter (Prosser, 1982c). The executive director of the Institute, Vic Prosser, wrote that both bodies decided to put integration aside (1982c). After the failure of the second merger attempt, the Institute concentrated on growing its membership since its membership grew by an average of 5.9% per annum from 1982 to 1991 (ICAA, 1982–1991), while the corresponding figure for the Society was 3.3% (ASA, 1982–1991). One of the strategies for increasing membership was centred around making the PY more popular among students. Vic Prosser wrote:

> Chartered Accountants lead the accountancy profession in providing business, governments and individuals with a wide range of financial and management services—for which they have the highest professional training and experience. (1986, p. 4)

To achieve targets of expansion and increase the membership base, the Institute even created a full-time position of Director of Marketing and

Public Relations to coordinate marketing and to enhance the professional reputation of CAs and the Institute (Prosser, 1986, p. 4).

In his oral history interview dated 27 February 2015, the then president of the Society John Miller, who was the incoming president after the failure of the second merger attempt, provided details of the Society's alternative plans in the post failure context. This plan was termed "Plan B" or "Forward Plan" for the 1980s, which gave special attention to organisation and management, integrity and independence, technical competence and professional image and voice (Agars, 1982). As a result of pursuing this alternative plan, the Society made numerous structural changes and streamlined its decision-making processes (ASA, 1982). John Miller wrote that the Society made both financial and organisational progress in 1982. Although the Society had become aggressive in projecting itself as the main accounting association with a series of advertisements and other campaigns, it had kept the options of working jointly with the Institute where necessary. The annual report of 1982 mentioned about maintaining a strong relationship with the ICAA where it was in the interests of the community and members (ASA, 1982).

After the failure of the second merger attempt, the Society adopted the professional title of Certified Practising Accountant (CPA) under the "Professional Schedule" issued in March 1983 for its members (ASA, 1983, p. 2). The CPA title was approved by members in March 1984 at the annual general meeting (AGM) of the Society. The president of the Society J. E. Tomlinson referred to the adoption of the CPA title by members as a historic vote which started a new era of technical excellence and professionalism (ASA, 1984). This adoption was a major development for the Society since its members previously lacked a professional title, especially when compared with the Chartered Accountant title of the Institute members. The Society's adoption of the professional title CPA was an attempt to draw boundaries around its membership, in the way Institute boundaries had settled around membership of that body. This was a step towards exclusivity associated with the branding of a professional service. The change was not against the traditional strategy of market control that the Society had adopted, but did mark an attempt to define its boundaries more precisely.

Other major developments included the preparation of a draft *Accountants and Auditors Bill* which had provisions to reserve use of title accountant to members of professional bodies only (ASA, 1983, p. 2). A comparative example is medical and legal profession where it is not possible for anyone with certain claims to skills to call themselves as doctor or lawyer. However, use of term accountant is not protected. The preparation of this draft Bill was an unsuccessful attempt to create legal boundaries around the term "accountant" (Gieryn, 1983, 1995, 1999; Gieryn et al., 1985) and formalise differences between accountants and non-accountants (Grbic, 2010). Similar unsuccessful attempts were made in the UK (Macdonald, 1985; Walker & Shackleton, 1995).

In 1982, Vic Prosser wrote that the Society, the Institute and the ARF had made submissions to the National Companies and Securities Commission for gaining legislative backing for accounting standards (Prosser, 1982a). In May 1982, the Institute and the Society made a joint submission to the National Companies and Securities Commission seeking statutory backing for its accounting standards (Prosser, 1982b). In 1984, Miss S. Bonnici became member number 50,000 of the Society (ASA 1984). In 1986, the Society celebrated the centennial of the founding of its earliest predecessor body, the IIAV (ASA, 1986). From these developments, it can be argued that both bodies were planning to move forward independently and the spirit of unity that was observed soon after the failure of the first merger attempt was now missing.

8.2.1 *Joint Work*

Although another merger attempt was not on their agendas during the 1980s, both bodies were involved in several joint activities. Such joint activities included joint international representation at the International Federation of Accountants, at the International Accounting Standards Committee and at the Confederation of Asian and Pacific Accountants (ASA, 1984). On the home front, joint work was in relation to the ARF, the joint standing committee and the Australian Taxation Research Foundation (ASA, 1984). In 1986, the Institute and the Society jointly hosted the eleventh Conference of the Confederation of Asian and Pacific Accountants in Melbourne (ASA, 1986). The Society and the Institute established a joint task force (JTF) in 1988 to study issues and problems faced by students in relation to the funding of accounting education by governments. The presidents and executive directors were meeting four times per annum in the joint standing committee to discuss matters of mutual interest (Sharpe, 1983). These joint activities were centred on domestic matters affecting the profession and international representation of the Australian accounting profession.

8.2.2 *Membership of Both Bodies*

This section compares and discusses membership of the Society and the Institute. Table 8.1 provides a comparison of membership of both bodies from 1982 to 1991.

Table 8.1 shows that in the case of the Institute, the share of MNIPP progressively increased during this period. Between 1978 and 1981 the number had increased from 28.6 to 34.4% (ICAA, 1982). The rate of Society members involved in public practice was at 21.45% in 1982 (ASA, 1982), which grew to 21.93% in 1987 (ASA, 1987). In 1990, MIPP were 22.07% (ASA, 1990). Table 8.2 compares MIPP and MNIPP of both bodies for years 1981 and 1987.

Table 8.1 Members of the society and the institute 1982–1991

Years	*Society members*	*Institute members*	*Institute MNIPP (%)*
1982	46,681	12,673	35.4
1983	49,549	13,389	36.5
1984	51,942	14,284	37.3
1985	52,759	15,042	38.9
1986	53,608	15,710	40.2
1987	54,536	16,327	43.3
1988	56,103	17,526	43.5
1989	57,453	18,609	43.7
1990	59,582	19,775	44.1
1991	62,465	21,219	44.3

Source ICAA, 1982–1991 and ASA, 1982–1991

Table 8.2 Comparison of the Society's and the institute's MIPP and MNIPP in 1981 and 1987

	The institute				*The society*			
	1981	*Per cent*	*1987*	*Per cent*	*1981*	*Per cent*	*1987*	*Per cent*
Public practice	7,796	66	9,265	57	8,306	18	11,960	22
Not in public practice	3,925	34	7,062	43	36,841	82	42,576	78
Total	11,721	100	16,327	100	45,147	100	54,536	100

Source Henderson (1988, p. 6)

Analysis of the data presented in Tables 8.1 and 8.2 shows that the difference between membership size of the Institute and the Society registered a decline during the period under study. In 1982, the Society membership number was 3.7 times that of the Institute. This number decreased to 2.9 in 1991, revealing that the membership growth of the Institute was faster than that of the Society. The average rate of membership growth between 1982 and 1991 was 3.3% for the Society, while it was 5.9% for the Institute. Table 8.2 also reveals that while the Society's level of MNIPP was at 78% in 1990, the Institute registered 44.3%. The historical construction of the boundary between the two organisations was based on the perceived superior status of professional accounting work undertaken in public practice (Gieryn, 1983; Grbic, 2010). Table 8.1 demonstrates that the share of Institute members engaged in public practice was showing a declining trend. This meant that the traditional basis of boundary construction was getting weaker; that is, fewer Institute members were engaged in public practice. However, although the gap between the MNIPP of the two bodies was becoming smaller, it was still a significant gap. After initial boundary construction around MIPP, the Institute boundaries had settled around membership of that body.

Henderson (1988) presented a paper at the Annual Congress of the ASA held in April 1988 in Adelaide. Among many other comparisons, he presented a table that compared MIPP and MNIPP in 1981 and 1987 for both the Society and the Institute. Henderson (1988) found that between 1981 and 1987, the Institute's MIPP had dropped by 9 percentage points while the Society's MIPP had increased by 4 percentage points. In 1989, out of the total membership of the Institute only 56% were MIPP and 44% were MNIPP (Boreham, 1989). Henderson (1988) also argued that the profession was becoming more uniform and it was the right time for both bodies to unite.

8.2.3 Financial Position

Table 8.3 provides details of the income and deficit or surplus of the Society from 1981 to 1991. The highest surplus was in 1982 at 15.98% of the annual revenue or income, while the worst years were 1981 and 1990. Between 1981 and 1991, the average surplus of the Society was at 4.28%. From 1981 to 1985, the Society spent a total of more than

$AU500,000 on supporting the IAA.[1] This was a considerable expense, especially in 1983, 1984 and 1985 when the Society's surplus was not significantly high. In 1981, the Society incurred a deficit but in all other years its financial result was in surplus.

The Society had provided full administrative support to the IAA since 1972, and the IAA was shown as an expense category in the Society's income statements (ASA, 1984, p. 4).

Table 8.4 provides details of the financial results of the Institute from 1981 to 1991. With the exception of 1990, when the Institute incurred a loss, it reported surpluses in all other years. However, similar to the Society, the level of surplus fluctuated across these years but registered an upward trend after 1984 with the exception of 1991. The average surplus as a percentage of total annual revenue or income between 1981 and 1991 was 2.74%.

Table 8.3 Income and deficit/surplus of society (1981–1991)

Year	*Revenue/income ($AU)*	*Deficit/ surplus ($AU)*	*($AU)*	*Deficit/surplus (%)*
1981	4,163,494	(53,729)	IAA expense 70,090	−1.29
1982	5,488,494	876,975	IAA expense 86,857	15.98
1983	5,778,260	398,992	IAA expense 130,111	6.91
1984	7,615,840	551,025	IAA expense 195,388	7.24
1985	10,893,000	372,000	IAA expense 88,000	3.42
1986	17,169,000	498,000		2.90
1987	19,131,000	656,000		3.43
1988	21,719,000	836,000		3.85
1989	26,000,000	623,000		2.40
1990	28,652,000	208,000		0.73
1991	34,312,000	519,000		1.51
	Average surplus (%)			4.28

Source ASA, 1981–1991

[1] The name of this body was changed to National Institute of Accountants in 1988. To avoid confusion, this chapter continues to refer to this body as IAA throughout the discussion.

Table 8.4 Income and deficit/surplus of institute (1981–1991)

Year	*Revenue/income ($AU)*	*Deficit/surplus ($AU)*	*Deficit/ surplus (%)*
1981	4,711,000	64,000	1.36
1982	5,264,000	62,000	1.18
1983	5,948,000	88,000	1.48
1984	6,294,000	53,000	0.84
1985	7,285,000	153,000	2.10
1986	8,413,000	268,000	3.19
1987	10,328,000	406,000	3.93
1988	11,592,000	647,000	5.58
1989	15,430,000	838,000	5.43
1990	18,649,000	(312,000)	−1.67
1991	20,217,000	1,348,000	6.67
	Average surplus (%)		2.74

Source ICAA, 1981–1991

8.2.4 Professional Branding

As mentioned, in addition to the two major bodies the IAA had a presence as a third body in Australian accounting. The IAA had grown to 7,300 members in 1988 and had its own plans for expansion. The Institute and the Society filed a legal case against the IAA[2] and demanded that IAA members should not be counted as part of the accounting profession, but Justice Hempel dismissed this claim as inadmissible on the grounds that it was a matter of inference from any factual material that might be presented to court as to what comprised "the profession" (Walker, 1988, p. 95). Further, neither body could prove in court with documentary evidence their claims of IAA members having lower standards (Walker, 1988). This episode provided a potential motivation for the merger of both bodies to counter the rising influence of the IAA. It also represented a failed joint attempt at boundary construction by both bodies around the term "accountant" using state-sanctioned restrictions. By seeking to do so, they intended to exclude IAA members initially and then all other individuals involved in accounting work who were not members of either of these two bodies. However, this attempt to create legal boundaries

[2] The case was fought in December 1987 between the Australian Society of Accountants and the Institute of Chartered Accountants, the plaintiffs, and the IAA and the Commissioner for Corporate Affairs, the defendants.

around who could be referred to as an "accountant" or as part of "the profession" did not succeed.

The Society was conscious of the need to improve the professional brand and image of its members and the accounting profession in general. Its attempts included a substantial volume of advertising and promotional campaigns targeting its professional title of CPA. The Society claimed that such campaigns were successful in raising and maintaining the profile and public awareness of both the Society and the profession (ASA, 1987). Conversely, Vic Prosser wrote about the Institute's attempts to improve the brand and image of the Chartered Accountant title (Prosser, 1987). In 1988, the president of the Society, Elizabeth Alexander, also pointed out that the Society needed to improve its visibility and standing, citing objectives of the Society that included the aspiration of high professional standing for its members.

The 1988 annual report of the Society stated that its mission, which was adopted from the Memorandum of Association of 1952, was "To support, protect and advance the character, status and interests of the accountancy profession generally and particularly of accountants being of the Society" (ASA, 1988, p. 4). To achieve this mission, it mentioned five main objectives, which were technical competence, integrity and independence, professional image and voice, community service and organisation and management. The third objective, "professional image and voice", was described thus: "to enhance the standing of accountants in the community". Elizabeth Alexander indicated that a merger with the Institute was not on the Society's agenda at that point in time:

> There are many challenges facing the Society. Each of these provides us with a great opportunity to grow stronger and to further ourselves as the pre-eminent accounting body in Australia and one of the leading accounting bodies in the world. (ASA, 1988, p. 7)

This message also shows that the Society was aiming at gaining exclusivity or, in other words, stepping away from its traditional strategy of market control.

In 1988, the Society's executive director Michael F. McKenna reviewed the organisational and management structure of the Society (ASA, 1988, p. 8). In his plan for 1989, McKenna also aimed at increasing interest among existing members to join the CPA program and to target new members towards gaining CPA membership (ASA, 1988, p. 9). From these actions, it can be argued that the Society was working towards improving its profile and image. One way to achieve this was to improve the public standing of its professional title CPA to provide its members with a comparative advantage against Institute members, who had the Chartered Accountant title.

8.2.5 *Financial Crisis and Corporate Collapses*

Before the mounting of the third merger attempt, global share markets suffered a severe downturn on 19 October 1987. This became known as Black Monday, which saw the worst share market collapses since 1929. The impact on the Australian stock market was much bigger and the market took longer to recover than those of other countries. By the end of 1987, Australian shares had crashed by 50%, whereas the US markets had fallen by only 35% (McMahon, 2007). This demonstrates that the stock market crash, which started outside Australia in the US, affected Australian capital markets significantly. This also contributed to the financial crisis of the early 1990s, as summarised by Ian Macfarlane, the governor of the Reserve Bank from 1996 to 2006. Macfarlane (2006) argued that:

> A number of well-known businesses that had been bought by highly geared acquirers had to be sold in distressed circumstances and two of the Big Four private banks incurred losses and had to be recapitalised.

Macfarlane (2006) further stated that the recession had started in the September quarter of 1990 and had lasted until the September quarter of 1991. During the recession, Australian gross domestic product fell by 1.7%, employment fell by 3.4% and the unemployment rate rose to 10.8%. Similar to all recessions, it was a period of disruption and economic distress. It was particularly deep in Victoria, where a disproportionate share of the financial failure occurred. Employment in Victoria fell by 8.5% compared with a fall of 2.1% for the rest of Australia. Macfarlane (2006) stated that it was Australia's "deepest post-war recession". Macfarlane (2006) further stated that numerous financial institutions failed around Australia, including the State Bank of Victoria, the State Bank of South Australia, the Teachers Credit Union of Western Australia and the Pyramid Building Society, as well as several merchant banks, a mortgage trust and a friendly society. In 1990, Victoria's Pyramid Building

Society collapsed with debts in excess of $AU2 billion (Macfarlane, 2006). According to Wright (2008), the State Bank of South Australia, owned by the Government of South Australia, collapsed in 1991 with a debt of $AU3 billion.

Gottliebsen (1990) addressed the issue of an ethical crisis faced by the accounting profession using the case study of the failure of Rothwells Merchant Bank and the sentencing of Laurie Connell. Gottliebsen (1990, p. 14) cited Rothwells' investigator Malcolm McCusker, who criticised the auditors of Rothwells, KMG Hungerfords:

> As appears from the evidence [the auditor] was fully aware that Rothwells was being used by Connell for very extensive borrowing during the year. The auditor saw no ledger cards or computer print outs relating to any of the debts.

McCusker also criticised Rothwells' accounting treatment of doubtful incomes, which were recorded as income in the statements. With such high-profile corporate collapses, the accounting profession was facing a serious problem and the proposed merger of both associations occurred at the right time (Gottliebsen, 1990).

Section 8.2 provided a snapshot of circumstances that assisted in creating conditions favourable to the mounting of a further merger attempt. Section 8.3 discusses the subsequent merger talks, merger vote and its outcome.

8.3 Merger Talks

The merger talks took place in two rounds. The first started when the Institute president made a one-sided decision on 2 June 1989 and invited Society members with 10 years or more experience to apply for Institute membership. This step was criticised by the Society and, as a result, the Institute withdrew this offer. The second started in September 1990, which eventually led to a merger vote but did not attract sufficient support from Institute members. The next subsections discuss these two merger talks and their eventual failure.

8.3.1 *First Merger Talks*

The earliest discursive evidence of a renewed focus on unity comes from an editorial in *Accountancy Week,* which published a statement by Clyde Dickens, president of the Society, from his address to the Victorian State Congress. Dickens said that it was most regretful that there were two separate bodies with similar ideals (Thomas, 1987). During the same period, the officials of the Institute expressed their concern that unification of both bodies was not possible younger members of the Institute were convinced (Thomas, 1987). Dickens wrote further about the issue of the unification of the two bodies in the 1987 annual report. Dickens also mentioned that the issue was not new and that a united body was more effective in running the operations of the profession and in exerting influence over governments.

In addition, Dickens continued his discursive argument and mentioned that the reasons for previous failures were unfavourable comparisons made between the Society's orientation to the work place program and the Institute's Professional Year (ASA, 1987). He also claimed that the CPA program was extremely effective and efficient in selecting members from eligible graduates and in orientating them to the work place. Dickens further added that whether a merger with the Institute proceeded or not, the Society was planning to increase its lobbying power with the government and with influential people (ASA, 1987, p. 3). He made the first formal proposal for merger of the two bodies at the bi-annual meeting of joint committees of the Institute and the Society held in early 1988 (Anon., 1988). Dickens made an ambitious proposal to proceed with a postal ballot by the end of 1988 (Anon., 1988). However, in the case of this third merger attempt, evidence shows that while the Society president made public statements about a merger, formal talks were unable to proceed. In other words, the high-status group, that is, the Institute, had to agree to make changes in its organisational boundaries, and unless its leadership showed interest, a merger proposal could not proceed. This proved correct when the Institute made a unilateral decision and its President Peter Middleton announced on 2 June 1989 via a press release that the national council of the Institute had decided to initiate discussions with the Society to achieve a peak accountant body in Australia (Middleton, 1989a). This was a membership strategy to strengthen the Institute that then led to formal merger discussions.

The Institute's proposal had the following terms:

- the Institute to be the vehicle for the creation of the peak body;
- the retention of a Royal Charter;
- the Institute's name to remain unchanged;
- the designation "Chartered Accountant" to be the only ongoing professional designation;
- the immediate admission to membership of the Institute as CAs of all Society members with at least 10 years' Society membership;
- the accommodation of all other categories of the Society members with appropriate pathways to full membership (Prosser, 1989, p. 22).

Peter Middleton also had a meeting with Joe Abraham, the then president of the Society, on 1 June 1989 at which they discussed the proposal of the Institute. Commenting on the Institute's one-sided merger proposal, Nick Burton Taylor, former president of the Institute, said in his oral history interview:

> The Institute made a pre-emptive offer to the Society under Peter Middleton's Presidency, which was essentially for the Society to fold into the Institute. It was a far more aggressive approach that was more in all honesty a takeover proposal than a merger proposal. It was, not surprisingly... resoundingly rejected by the Executive and then the Council of the Society. (2016)

Joe Abraham said that the Institute's move was a surprise and its campaign was largely directed to increasing its own membership (McKnight, 1989a, p. 43). This proposal was unacceptable to the Society because it would discriminate against most of its members and it had argued that merger could only be accepted on equal terms, as the Society president said in a press release on 3 June:

> It must be clearly understood that such a merger can only take place on the basis of recognition of the equality of qualifications and professionalism of the members of both bodies. (Abraham, 1989c, p. 1)

Anticipating opposition from certain factions of the Institute, the president wrote to the PY candidates and graduates assuring them that the unity of profession was in the best interests of the profession (Middleton,

1989b). Those Society members who did not meet the requirement of the specified length of experience in years were to be placed in a separate category of "provisional members" until they completed a separate PY program that would enable them to become full members (McKnight, 1989a). The conditions of the Institute had implications regarding the rights of the Society members under the Institute's proposal. For example, the associate members would only be able to vote on matters affecting them, which meant the rights of some of the Society members would be eroded (Kohler, 1989). Gieryn (1983) argued that boundaries are dynamic structures that change with the context, and the proposal from the Institute president to only include the Society members with a specified length of experience in years showed that the Institute leaders were proposing changes in the boundaries of the Institute. As argued earlier in this thesis, the boundaries of the Institute were based on membership of that body. This move was also a modification of the traditional strategy of exclusiveness, which the Institute had adopted since its formation. This was not a complete transition, as the inclusion of Society members was based on a condition that would still exclude many members who did not meet the requirement. However, this proposal would create sub-boundaries between the Society members who were eligible for full membership of the Institute and those who were not and would be labelled as "provisional members".

On 3 June 1989, David McKnight (1989a) wrote in the *The Sydney Morning Herald* that the proposal was prepared hastily, which took Joe Abraham by surprise. Paul Luker wrote in *The Age* of 3 June 1989 that the ICAA had stunned its sister professional organisation (1989a, p. 4) with its proposal. The Society's executive director Michael McKenna said the Society did not like the approach Institute took. It was cheeky and unfortunate, but a positive sign towards unification (Bowerman, 1989a). The presidents of the Institute and the Society met on 7 June 1989 when the Society president made it clear that the Institute's proposal in its current form was unacceptable to them (Abraham, 1989d). Abraham (1989d) commented that genuine merger talks must be held rather than unification on the basis of one body inviting members to join the other body. The initial proposal of the Institute only needed a simple majority of its members to be approved, compared with the 66.67% which would be required for a full merger with the Society (Porter, 1989). There was no discussion on the remaining Society members. The Society saw the proposal as a bid to weaken its organisation because it would only accept more senior Society members as eligible for membership (Luker, 1989b). This was termed a "reverse takeover" bid by the Institute (Murrill, 1989a).

In June 1989, the national council of the Society met and discussed the proposal by the Institute president regarding the specified length of experience in years (Anon., 1989a). The national council discussed two options, including a counteroffer to the Institute members to join the Society. The second and preferred option was to:

> ... work towards the creation of a unified body as is the Society's policy, and as sought in the ICAA proposal, on the basis that it is fair, equitable and acceptable to the Society members. (Anon., 1989a, p. 3)

The policy regarding the mooted merger of the two associations as adopted by the national council of the Society was released on 19 June and was covered by the media. It suggested a discussion of the merger proposal with the Institute (Anon., 1989b; Porter, 1989; Luker, 1989b). The Institute's response to the Society's 19 June counterproposal was positive and Peter Middleton expressed satisfaction that the Society had the desire to discuss merger issues, but the Institute was not prepared to engage in merger talks if the merger involved the loss of its charter (Murrill, 1989a, p. 25). Moreover, the high-status group tended to reject changes in its boundaries that posed a threat to their status (Keohane & Milner, 1996). Following these developments, the presidents of the Society and the Institute, Joe Abraham and Peter Middleton respectively, along with senior representatives of both bodies met on 20 June and issued a joint statement that there was a firm basis for achieving unity of the profession (ASA & ICAA, 1989).

Senior executives of both bodies, which included presidents and executive officers, met a few times in June and July of 1989 and these were noted as almost daily discussions (Dunstan, 1989). On 27 June, they made an announcement that both bodies were planning to set a timeline to achieve a merger (Dunstan, 1989). Ryan (1989) stated that the Society planned that by 31 July 1989 both bodies would reach an agreement regarding a merger proposal. This would be followed by gaining approval from the national councils by August so that voting on merger could be held after November 1989, with a target date for achieving a merger set for 1 January 1990 (McKnight, 1989b).

In July 1989, Peter Middleton wrote to Institute members providing them with updates of the merger discussions (Middleton, 1989c). In July 1989, the Institute issued a pamphlet explaining the benefits of merger to gain support from its members. According to this document, in a combined body, MIPP would drop to 29% and MNIPP would be 71% (ICAA, 1989a). Both bodies maintained merger talks during August 1989, and it was decided that talks would be furthered based on an initial proposal from the Institute, which had the condition of a specified length of membership for Society members joining the Institute as members. The name of the proposed body was the Institute of Chartered Practising Accountants (Murrill, 1989b). The location of the head office of the new body was likely to be Sydney because the Australian Securities Commission was also based in Sydney (Anon., 1989c). The Institute was seeking other interested Society members with less than the specified length of experience in years to complete its PY program, which took up to four years to complete (Murrill, 1989b). These incidents indicate that the starting point for merger discussion was changes in the traditional strategies of the Institute and the Society, which were based on exclusiveness and market control, respectively (Macdonald & Ritzer, 1988). In various mergers of the British accounting associations, changes in organisational strategies and professional boundaries were often the starting point for initiating merger discussions (Walker & Shackleton, 1995). The case of the third merger attempt was similar to the UK context, and serious merger talks started only when both bodies agreed to change their traditional strategies.

8.3.2 *First Merger Talk Failure*

By the end of August, merger discussions were on the verge of breakdown and the main issue of contention was the inclusion of Society members with insufficient experience based on the rules specified. The Institute did not want to include these members in the merged body, while the Society was firm that these members should be included (Anon., 1989c; Murrill, 1989c). In August 1989, the Institute president wrote a letter to the Society president asking that the Society give up the CPA title if it wanted to see merger discussions go ahead. However, at the heart of the deadlock were the 9,000 Society members who did not have at least 10 years of experience and the 5,500 "grandfathered CPAs" who did not have any formal qualification when they were granted the CPA upon its introduction. These members also had less than 10 years of experience. The Institute did not want these 14,500 members to become members of the merged body without gaining further qualifications (Bowerman, 1989b). This shows that although changes were proposed using the traditional strategies of the Institute, which were based on exclusiveness (Macdonald & Ritzer, 1988), the Institute leaders did not want to fully relax the boundaries constructed around the membership of that body or, in other words, around the right to use the title CA. They aimed to do that by controlling who could use the professional title Chartered Accountant and only allowing Society members with the specified length of experience in years to join the Institute if the merger was successful. Therefore, this was a model that would create sub-boundaries within the membership of a single large body, which would include a large membership of the Society divided using a boundary drawn on specified length of experience in years (Gieryn, 1983). This was an attempt to separate Society members into "superior" and "inferior" categories, based on a specified length of experience (Jasanoff, 1995, p. 53).

On 7 September 1989, the Society formally informed the Institute about its decision to break off merger discussions. The Society also issued a formal press release announcing that merger talks had failed (Abraham, 1989a). In his statement, Joe Abraham said that he was very disappointed that both bodies had been unable to achieve a unified accountancy body on a basis that was fair, equitable and acceptable (Abraham, 1989b). Institute President Peter Middleton expressed disappointment over the Society's decision to terminate merger discussions and said that the Institute was prepared to reopen discussions based on current proposals (Anon., 1989d; Luker, 1989c; McKnight, 1989c).

After the merger talks had been terminated, the Institute added to the public discourse in a letter to its members on 11 September 1989 outlining the reasons for the failure of the initial merger talks. This letter also made it clear that the Institute was not prepared to dilute the quality of the Institute's PY program and its services (Middleton, 1989d). After the breakdown of the merger, Professor Murray Wells of the University of Sydney criticised the Institute, stating that the Institute's young Turks still believed they were superior (Dobbie & Boreham, 1989, p. 125). Professor Wells further commented that the Institute's proposal of a virtual takeover of the Society was not a good idea. Professor Bill Birkett of the University of New South Wales agreed with Professor Wells

(Dobbie & Boreham, 1989). These are evidence of discursive arguments in support of the merger from outside the profession (Annisette, 2017).

In their usual discursive arguments, the CAs would claim their professional title was of higher quality than the CPA; however, Mary Hines, Director of Financial Services recruiting with Morgan & Banks, provided a counter-discursive claim on the PY program of the Institute:

> They [Institute members] believe they have the higher qualification because of the Professional Year. But an employer doesn't care whether the accountant is one or the other, as long as they are professionally qualified. (Dobbie & Boreham, 1989, p. 125)

She further said:

> The Institute has always seen itself as elitist but the employers do not. When a client is seeking a well-qualified accountant for a middle-management job, they want the best person for the job, and that isn't necessarily someone from the Institute. (Dobbie & Boreham, 1989, p. 125)

After the failure of merger talks, the Society published full page advertisements in newspapers entitled "Strong words from 57,091 Australian Accountants". The advertisements were placed in eight national newspapers to create awareness about the CPA professional brand and to attract future members. It included claims that the Society was the body that represented the real strength of the Australian accounting profession and that no other accounting body even came closer to its strength (Murrill, 1989d). This decision was perceived as a step by the Society to pursue its own agenda and initiatives away from a merger (Middleton, 1989e).

In November 1989, the Society developed a proposal to change its name to the Australian Society of Certified Practising Accountants (ASCPA). Joe Abraham said that more than half of the Society members were CPAs, and hence, the name change was logical (Lewis, 1989). It was estimated that in 1990, 60% of the Society members held the title of CPA (Eastwood, 1990a). The name change proposal was successful because Society members overwhelmingly supported it (Eastwood, 1990c).

On 6 November 1989, Peter Middleton issued a media release about the failure of merger talks, which came two months after the Society issued a media release to formally announce that it had withdrawn from merger discussions (Middleton, 1989e). Middleton (1989e) expressed disappointment that the Society had withdrawn from discussions in September 1989. However, Middleton (1989e) also mentioned that just before withdrawal of talks every effort had been made by the Institute to bring the Society back to the discussion table to resolve the remaining hurdles. Middleton (1989e) also mentioned that the Institute was prepared to discuss modifications in proposals but, as discussed earlier, the Society had withdrawn from discussions. The 6 November 1989 statement by the Institute president formally scrapped the first merger talks.

8.3.3 Second Merger Talks

In September 1990, nearly a year after they had broken down in 1989, merger discussions started again (Briggs, 1991). The documentary evidence does not show a clear trigger. The early evidence of a second round of merger talks can be observed from the statement of the Society President Ken Eastwood in his October 1990 message, which was published in *The Australian Accountant*. In this message, the name of the proposed new body was the Institute of Chartered Accountants and Certified Practising Accountants in Australia (Eastwood, 1990d).

The rationale for merger was provided as follows:

- a greater ability to contribute to the financial and economic policy of Australia;
- an ability to provide higher level of service to the community;
- a stronger voice with government, particularly in the fields of education, taxation, business and finance;
- stronger professional, ethical and accounting standards;
- an improved ability to self-regulate the profession;
- an improved level of professional development;
- an improved capability to conduct research into relevant areas of accounting and finance;
- an enhanced opportunity to gain statutory recognition of the professional status of accountants (Eastwood, 1990d, p. 5).

Ken Eastwood and the Institute President Gerry Allen finalised the unity proposal. The final decision regarding voting on unification was entrusted to the national presidents, deputy presidents and executive directors of both bodies (Eastwood, 1990e). This means that, unlike for the first two merger attempts, the bodies did not establish a unity committee.

During 1990, significant progress was made on the issue of unification. The joint merger proposals were released and sent to members in December 1990 (Anon., 1990b; ASCPA & ICAA, 1990). In the 1990 annual report of the Society, it was also mentioned that the final proposal distributed to members was a compromise, but that it provided a firm basis for unification (ASA, 1990). Both bodies hired Worthington DiMarzio, a market research firm, to conduct a survey on the viability of unification. Research found that support from Institute members was not sufficient for the proposals to succeed, although with significant efforts, it was expected to rise to 67%, which was just more than the two-thirds required for majority support (Anon., 1990a, p. 109).

Along with the release of merger proposals, a two-page pamphlet was circulated to members presenting key benefits of and strong arguments for unification of the profession. Key arguments for unification were greater resources, cost effectiveness and the ability to speak with one voice. The date for the return of the ballot was 20 March 1991 by 5 pm (ASCPA, 1991). The merger date was proposed as 1 July 1991. The united body would have four categories of members, namely ACA, CA, Associate CPA and CPA. According to the arrangement, fellows and other members of both bodies who had attained at least 10 years of aggregate membership of the two bodies were entitled to describe themselves either as a CPA or CA. The use of both titles by the same member was prohibited (ASCPA & ICAA, 1990). The merger proposals also stated that:

> Members with under 10 years' full membership will be able to use only the designation of the body of which they were a member, until they reach 10 years' full membership. (ASCPA & ICAA, 1990, p. 5)

Although it was a compromise from the earlier position where all Society members would become CAs, Eastwood (1990d) was confident that the united body would be able to modify the titles.

As per the proposals, the initial national council would consist of 36 members, 18 from each body, but would be reduced at a later stage to 19. The size of divisional councils and representation in the proposed national council of the merged body was as follows in Table 8.5.

Table 8.5 Proposed divisional and national councils of the merged body

SN	*State*	*Size of divisional council*	*Representation in national council*
1	New South Wales	15	6
2	Victoria	15	5
3	Queensland	12	2
4	South Australia	12	2
5	Western Australia	12	2
6	Tasmania	9	1
7	ACT	9	1

Source ASCPA (1992, p. 4)

Going forward with this merger plan, both bodies conducted joint market research and the findings suggested that Society members' support of the unification was strong. However, some sections of the Institute members needed more convincing about the benefits of a united profession. They believed that their professional standards were higher than those of the Society members and did not want to see these diluted through merger (Eastwood, 1990f). Ken Eastwood said that if merger was to succeed, then it was necessary that members overcame their ingrained prejudices and approached unity with an open mind and real commitment. Eastwood (1990f) also wrote in his December 1990 message in *The Australian Accountant* that the CPA program was a high-quality one and it shared a common syllabus with the PY program of the Institute. According to Eastwood (1990f), the proposed new body would combine the best features of both bodies. In March 1991, Eastwood further argued the case for a merger, citing reasons such as duplication of activities and waste of resources. Similar to his message in December, Eastwood (1991) compared the CPA program and the PY program of the Institute and claimed that they had the same standards. However, in a letter to the editor of *Charter*, Henry Leong, another Institute member, did not agree that the Society had similar education standards for its members compared with the PY of the Institute (1991). Further, Leong (1991) feared that the Society members would outnumber the Institute members in the united body.

Nick Burton Taylor wrote a letter to members on 11 December 1990 and announced that unification discussions at formal and informal levels had been taking place for 18 months. Taylor (1991) mentioned that for the entire period since discussions began, a series of meetings had taken place between the two bodies. The Institute also had discussions with members and members' groups across Australia on the issue of a future merger attempt. Taylor (1991) also wrote that the proposal was a compromise in some organisational respects. Taylor (1991) also assured that members would be kept informed and that special meetings would be arranged to allow members to express their opinions. He further indicated that amalgamations of accounting bodies had been part of the evolution of the accountancy profession in Australia.

In a message to the Institute members, Taylor (1991) pointed out that both bodies were involved in many joint projects, such as formation of the ARF, joint accreditation of tertiary education courses and joint representation of the profession. Taylor (1991) further wrote that despite much cooperation on many fronts, both bodies were facing issues in relation to the unification. Among the challenges faced by the profession, there were pressures from the Society and business community to improve the standing of the accounting profession, its reputation and the development of accounting standards. According to Taylor (1991), a unified profession could achieve such improvements more effectively and he asked members to support the creation of one accounting body.

The date of a general meeting for passing a special resolution related to the merger of both bodies was fixed for 22 March 1991 (Anon., 1991a). The Institute issued a joint briefing paper outlining the rationale and benefits of unity. The rationale also included financial benefits at the micro and macro levels. Macro-level benefits included the cost reduction of running a single marketing campaign for a united body compared with the dual campaigns run separately by the two bodies. Collective benefits also included the improved ability to push for wider recognition of the term "accountant" to strengthen the case for self-regulation with minimal government interference in the profession. Other benefits included the improved journal and library resources of the united body, better services for members and high-quality postgraduate training in different areas of employment. The ability to influence government decisions through increased lobbying powers was also mentioned as a potential benefit. The briefing paper stated:

> Senior politicians and public servants have stated on many occasions that the development of laws affecting accountants and business in Australia would be much simpler and more effective with a unified accounting profession. (ICAA, 1991c)

The Institute ran a special campaign entitled “The colleague to colleague campaign”. This campaign was internally known as a “proxy-gathering” campaign. The colleague to colleague campaign was reliant on the influence of members on their colleagues and the Institute published a message for those collecting proxies asking that when collecting proxies it should be checked that they are completed and despatched promptly (ICAA, 1991e). Nick Burton Taylor requested influential members participating in this campaign to write letters to at least 100 members requesting them to vote for unification. Other members were encouraged to use letters rather than telephone calls when running this campaign. Contrary to initial suggestions of contacting 20–30 members, the colleague to colleague campaign briefing paper suggested that each member participating in this campaign should contact 10 members advocating a “Yes” vote to unification. The divisional and state councils were requested to identify such individuals who exerted influence among members. There was a separate strategy to contact partners and members of the largest 15 accounting firms to gain their support (ICAA, 1991e).

The campaign kit also included a list of potential questions and answers (Q&A) that Institute members were likely to ask. The Q&A document had a message from the Institute’s national council: “Having decided that unification of the Institute and the Society is highly desirable, Council is urging members to support the proposal” (ICAA, 1991b, p. 3). The Q&A document stated that if the proposed unification attempt failed, further attempts would not be considered. Supplementary materials with the campaign kit also mentioned the expected cost of unification for the Institute, which was about $AU20 per member (ICAA, 1991b). There were also details about the Professional Entry Programme (PEP), which would replace the Institute’s PY program and the CPA programs of both bodies. The unification proposal claimed that the PEP would incorporate the best features of both programs (ASCPA & ICAA, 1990). Post-unification, from January 1992, all new registered graduates would be entered through the PEP and this would move professional standards to a higher level. One question addressed representation on the national council of the new body. The period between unification to the AGM of

1992 was proposed to be a transitional period during which there would be equal representation of members of both bodies. However, after that, representation would be proportionate to membership (ICAA, 1991b). This meant that former members of the Society could control the national council.

The proxy gathering campaign attracted criticism of members. As one of the Institute members, Tim Blue from the accounting firm Robert Morrison Darwin, pointed out:

> They [the Institute] are not only aggressively marketing unification and stifling dissent but also will be conducting the vote by way of appointing proxies, where individual members are identified on their ballot, as against using a secret ballot. This is a constitutional referendum and not a shareholders' meeting. This [ballot] methodology does not inspire the confidence of ICAA members, nor does it reveal to the public the balanced professionalism the ICAA must maintain if it is to have any relevance in the Australian community. (1991b, p. 60)

Blue (1991b, p. 60) further argued that:

> It seems that the big firms are pushing hard for unification in the hope that one large accounting body will be able to counter any attempt by the federal government to regulate the profession.

As discussed earlier, aside from Blue's (1991b) comment, many other reasons led both bodies to start merger talks. The method adopted in proxy gathering did not ensure the anonymity of voters and members could be identified, including those voting "No". Blue (1991b) further stated that fear of being identified as someone who voted "No" and probably against the advice of their employers was not the right thing.

Executive chairperson George Bennett of Australia's largest accounting firm KPMG Peat Marwick supported the merger. This firm prepared a document for circulation to its staff outlining its position in support of the merger. It included discursive arguments to eliminate duplication and reduce costs (Lewis & Lawson, 1991). George Bennett (Blue, 1991a, p. 60) articulated other discursive claims, including that many politicians were in favour of the merger and had demonstrated their support for unification by lobbying senior members of the Institute. Graham Walters, a partner at KPMG Peat Marwick, explained the official argument of his firm in supporting the merger as follows:

> Unification is in the best interests of the Australian business community and the profession. Too much time is spent debating the details of unification rather than concentrating on the need for unification and achieving that end. (Walters, 1991, p. 76)

Other discursive claims included damage to the reputation of the accounting profession at international levels because of high-profile corporate failures (Eastwood, 1990b). In addition to KPMG Peat Marwick, other accounting firms that openly supported merging included Ernst & Young and Arthur Andersen & Co (Bowerman, 1991c). Bruce Knowles, chairperson of Ernst & Young, and John Burrows, national managing partner of Arthur Andersen & Co., openly supported the merger (Bowerman, 1991c). Moreover, the media commented that in comparison with previous mergers, the third merger had received considerable support from some of the largest Chartered Accountant firms, government and business leaders (Minter, 1991).

Blue (1991b, p. 6) quoted Vic Prosser's discursive argument in support of a merger and quoted the issue of political pressures for a merger:

> In business and political circles, there is an overwhelming belief that a divided profession damages our efforts to resolve successfully the major issues on which we must face governments. My experience shows how dangerous it is for one organisation to give one point of view to government, business and the media, while the other organisation presents a different picture. Over the years we've tried to minimise government regulation by working with Canberra and state governments. To a great extent this has been successful, but increasingly we find our representations in Canberra and the states have been hampered because the Institute and the Society are often approached separately by the government on issues. Often public servants and politicians use our separate identities to undermine our submissions and arguments.

Blue (1991b, p. 61) also summarised various arguments supporting the merger, as quoted directly below.

> The case for:
>
> - The profession will speak with one voice in industry, commerce and government.
> - Whichever are the more demanding professional standards are the ones that will be adopted by the merged organisation. Enforcement

of higher standards will be vigorous, with consistent controls placed over the whole profession.

- The Institute members will enjoy increased representation in commerce.
- Unification will end the anomaly of two organisations providing duplicate services, and will release resources for use on professional issues.
- Annual savings of between $AU3 million and $AU5 million can be made through greater efficiencies.
- Subscriptions will be lower and better controlled.
- This is the last chance for unification. The alternative is costly and counter-productive competition.
- Better resources [will be available] for postgraduate training.
- Marketing campaigns [can be conducted] for the whole profession rather than competing against each other.

The arguments in favour of merging show that the Institute was modifying its traditional strategy of exclusiveness. As argued earlier, in addition, there was also an attempt to redraw the boundaries of the Institute.

8.3.4 Merger Proposal, Vote and Failure

The final merger proposal was dated December 1990, which was less than three months before the vote was undertaken. A joint message from both presidents was printed on page 1 of the proposal:

> We are aware of the increasing demands being placed on us and on our colleagues in virtually every area of professional activity. A united body would, we believe, give the profession more effective representation to government, to business and industry organisations, to educational and other institutions as well as to the general community. (ASCPA & ICAA, 1990, p. 1)

The Institute needed a 66.67% vote in favour of the merger and the Society a 75% vote in favour to make the proposal successful (Lewis, 1991a). The official rationale for unity was summarised as follows:

> A unified body will be better resourced with a greater ability to meet the very significant challenges facing the accountancy profession. It will speak with one voice to industry, commerce, Government, and the community

> at large. It will be more cost effective in delivering improved services to members and in ensuring enhanced technical and professional standards. (ASCPA & ICAA, 1990, p. 10)

In the merger proposal that he had favoured about 19 months earlier on 2 June 1989, Peter Middleton had suggested the inclusion of all the Society members with at least 10 years' experience as full members, that is, as CAs, of the merged body and the accommodation of all other members with pathways provided to gain full membership (Prosser, 1989). These discussions broke down when the Society withdrew from discussions on 7 September 1989 (Abraham, 1989a). However, the final merger proposals of December 1990 were very similar to those Peter Middleton had suggested on 2 June 1989. The documentary evidence does not reveal anything about why the Society agreed to the same proposal that it had rejected initially. Table 8.6 provides a comparison of existing professional titles of both associations and the proposed professional titles in the merged body as per the new proposal.

This was a proposal to create sub-boundaries between "us" and "them" (Gieryn, 1999; Lamont, 1992, 2000) by bringing changes to the Institute and Society boundaries. It was an attempt to modify the boundaries of the professional title of the Institute, namely CA, by relaxing them. However, in this instance there was a proposal to draw sub-boundaries between the Society members having professional experience of a specified number of years, which was at least 10 years. Thus, in the redrawn boundaries, the Society members without such experience would be excluded from holding the Chartered Accountant title. Society

Table 8.6 Comparative professional titles

SN	*ASCPA*	*ICAA*	*Merged body*
1	The Australian Society of Certified Practising Accountants	The Institute of Chartered Accountants in Australia	Institute of Chartered Accountants and Certified Practising Accountants in Australia
2	Fellow CPA	Fellow CA	Fellow CPA or Fellow CA
3	CPA > 10 years	ACA > 10 years	CPA or CA
4	CPA < 10 years		CPA
5		ACA < 10 years	CA

Source ASCPA and ICAA (1990, p. 10)

members with the specified length of experience in years would gain elevation of their professional status since they were given a choice to use either the CPA or the Chartered Accountant title. Gieryn (1983) pointed out that boundaries are continuously drawn and redrawn. If the proposal succeeded, it would create differences between the former members of the Society as well, especially those who would adopt the title CA, while others could only use the CPA title.

The merger announcement was made in January 1991 and attracted wide media coverage (Anon., 1990b; Clafton, 1991; Howard, 1991). The research conducted by both bodies in advance of the merger showed that support from the Institute members would not be sufficient for the merger proposal to pass (Bowerman, 1991a). In a response to this projected outcome, Society President Ken Eastwood's discursive argument was that if there was an indication that the support from the membership was both sufficient then vote should be delayed until more support could be secured (Bowerman, 1991a). However, Nick Burton Taylor had a different viewpoint and said that the chances of successfully merging the two bodies had improved since Christmas of 1990. Taylor added that there was a beat of optimism among the Institute members that wasn't around before Christmas (Bowerman, 1991a).

The Institute produced a video featuring well-known people, such as BHP Chief Brian Loton, Opposition Spokesman John Howard and former corporate regulator Henry Bosch. This video was an attempt to influence Institute members to vote in favour of the merger attempt. Vic Prosser wrote an article in *New Accountant* advocating a "Yes" vote for the merger. Prosser (1991a) used various rationales, including the current inability to speak with one voice to the government, businesses, other professions, educators and the general community. The presidents of both bodies made statements in the public discourse in an attempt to convince members of their respective bodies. Nick Burton Taylor said that:

> If the vote fails, the two bodies will move into more competitive positions. A negative vote will effectively translate into our members saying they wish to remain separate identities and this separateness would then have to be developed by each accounting body. (Howard, 1991, p. 10)

Ken Eastwood was appreciative of the fact that the Society members had overwhelmingly supported the previous two mergers. Eastwood argued:

> In the first vote in 1968, 88.5 per cent of the Society members voted in favour of the merger. In 1981, 90 per cent voted yes. On both occasions, the Institute members blocked the merger. This time we expect about 85 per cent of Society members to agree. While this is easily in excess of the 75 per cent we need to accept the merger proposal, it seems the longer it goes, the more reluctant our members are to join forces. (Howard, 1991, p. 10)

In February 1991, the Institute conducted a survey of its members to examine support for the merger of the two bodies (Lewis & Lawson, 1991). The survey found that 49% of Institute members were in support of the merger compared with 85% support among Society members. Both bodies had planned to conduct 100 meetings with members to gain support for the merger proposal during four weeks in late February and March (Lewis & Lawson, 1991). The survey involved telephone discussions with 800 members of the Institute and the Society, and it revealed that support from the Institute's New South Wales members was insufficient (Anon., 1991f). The viewpoint of Vic Prosser appeared again in *New Accountant* on 7 March 1991. Prosser (1991b) projected a strong case for the merger and repeated the arguments mentioned several times in this discussion already. Prosser (1991b, p. 22) stated that the chairperson of the Australian Securities Commission, Tony Hartnell, supported the merger calling it in the best interest of the profession and the public.

Ken Eastwood wrote a message for Institute members in its journal, *Charter*. Eastwood (1991) made a final attempt to persuade them to vote for the merger proposals. Eastwood (1991) argued that they should consider the long-term benefits to the profession, improvements in standards of training and professional services and the possibility of gaining statutory recognition as a united body. Another example of public discourse was a message from 12 individuals that appeared in *The Financial Review* on 1 March 1991 in support of the merger proposal. These individuals included managing directors, chief executive officers (CEOs) and the director general of the Department of the Premier of New South Wales (Anon., 1991e). The message referred to the challenges faced by the Australian economy, the future role of the accounting profession in the business community and the ability of a united profession to face such challenges (Anon., 1991e).

An article appeared in *New Accountant* on 21 February 1991 (Anon., 1991d) that presented the views of a dissident group from Perth, with

Kim Bradbury, principal of a small public practice in Perth, as its spokesman. The dissidents expressed concerns about the potential decline in professional standards in the postmerger period in the event of a successful merger; their discursive arguments were based on the fact that the majority of the Society members had not undertaken a postgraduate program that was equivalent to the Institute's PY program (Anon., 1991d). Further, the dissidents also argued that the Institute did not recognise the Society's CPA program as equivalent to its PY program (Anon., 1991d). The information presented in Table 8.7 was used by dissidents from Perth who argued that in the new body, the Society members would dominate democratically, "would swamp" the Institute members and would be in a strong lobbying position (Anon., 1991d, p. 18).

As discussed above, the dissidents also said that having two specialised bodies meant healthy competition. Moreover, two bodies were not easy for the government to control, unlike one body (Anon., 1991d). The dissidents also downplayed the argument of cost savings and criticised a lack of a detailed report on such claims (Anon., 1991d). However, some Society members commented on a campaign run by the Perth-based CAs against the merger, stating that the claims of higher professional standards and arguments that Society members would bring those standards down showed an element of sheer arrogance in Institute members.

Table 8.7 Membership of the ASCPA, ICAA and new body

SN	*Member category*	*ASCPA (Before integration)*	*ICAA (Before integration)*	*After new body*	*New share (%)*
1	Institute members		20,000	20,000	25
2	Fellow CPAs	8,000		8,000	10
3	CPAs, more than 10 years of membership	16,000		16,000	20
4	CPAs, less than 10 years of membership	8,000		8,000	10
5	Voting associates	17,000		17,000	22
6	Non-voting associates	10,000		10,000	13
7	Total	59,000	20,000	79,000	100

Source Anon. (1991d, p. 18)

On 18 February 1991, Ken Eastwood wrote a letter to Institute members outlining the benefits of a merger. Along with this letter, a notice for an AGM was issued, during which the merger proposal would be put to the members' vote. The AGM took place on 22 March 1991 at the Society's head office in Melbourne at 5 pm (Eastwood, 1990a). Before the voting, a two-hour discussion and debate was held on the merits of the merger during the AGM of the Institute. Most opposition at this meeting came from younger members of the Institute (Briggs, 1991). The Society had already passed the merger vote before the Institute vote and 94% of its members voted in favour of the third merger attempt (Briggs, 1991). The third merger attempt narrowly missed achieving the Institute's required 66.67% vote in favour, falling short by just 400 votes (Porter, 1991). There was another important factual detail regarding the Institute vote. Institute members who had practising certificates were entitled to have two votes, while most of the young Institute members, who were vocally against the merger, had one vote (Anon., 1991g). If every member had been given one vote, then merger would have failed by an even wider margin (Anon., 1991g). After the failure, the Society president predicted that the fourth attempt might not happen for another 10 years (Porter, 1991). However, history has shown that the fourth and last merger attempt was mounted following the shortest gap between any two mergers and was put to the vote inside a period of seven years.

8.3.5 Post Third Merger Attempt Failure

After the failure of this third attempt at unification, Society President B. J. Waldron mentioned:

> I was very pleased to see the strong support members gave to the Society's campaign to unify the profession. It was, therefore, disappointing that the Institute was unable to deliver a positive vote albeit by a small margin. (ASA, 1992, p. 5)

Waldron also said that after the merger failure, the Society had adopted a firm development strategy, keeping issues of cooperation open between the two bodies. He thanked Society members for their support and criticised the lack of support by Institute members:

Waldron (1991a, p. 5) argued that the society was strong professionally, numerically and financially, and added that the Society did not need to look back at a lost opportunity; rather, it should focus on its strengths and the challenges of the future. Waldron (1991a) concluded that the Society would continue to cooperate with the Institute in vital areas, such as accounting standards, accreditation of tertiary institutions and international representation of the Australian accounting profession. After the third merger attempt failed, Waldron's discursive arguments reiterated that the Society was a professional body with high standards and it was the right time to capitalise on its strengths, especially after the failure of the third merger attempt (Waldron, 1991b, 1991c). Waldron (1991c) informed members that the national council of the Society was still in favour of a single national body.

Nick Burton Taylor also said that the Institute had considered strategies in case the merger proposal failed, and that it was now time to examine them (Minter, 1991; Thomas, 1991). The Institute was considering future membership growth after the failure. In the 1990s, the membership of the Institute grew by 66% and PY enrolments increased strongly as well. For example, PY enrolments in 1990 were 28% more than that in the previous year. Taylor called for members to reinforce their strong commitment to professional standards. Thus, both bodies had plans to move forward in the wake of the failure.

8.4 Discussion and Analysis

This section provides responses to the research questions, within the context of the third merger proposal. Two significant findings emerge from this chapter: (1) the traditional organisational strategies of both bodies were modified (2) and there was a successful protection of the Institute's boundaries by its members and, consequently, the preservation of the different organisational strategies of each body. These respective findings are discussed in conjunction with four of the five research questions of this study.

8.4.1 Reasons for Mounting the Merger Attempt

The first question was related to the reasons for mounting the third merger attempt between the Society and the Institute. In other words, the first question was based on finding reasons that led to changes in the traditional organisational strategies of both bodies.

Some overriding common reasons existed for mounting the third merger attempt. Graeme McGregor (2015) explained how the merger attempt was mounted: "I think it started informally. Also fair to say the Institute was seen [to be] keener than the Society. I think they perceived the threat from the Society". Both bodies had lost a legal case against the IAA, having perceived a threat from that body that motivated the two bodies to unite in their case against it.

Nick Burton Taylor also provided a response to this question from the Institute's perspective:

> There were the standards setting costs and the perception that increased costs, complexity and financial obligation was on the way with the development of those standards and secondly it was a time of very introspective views on professional discipline. It was the time of a number of corporate failures; we had Bond Corp and a number of high profile failures where the auditor was somewhat of a scapegoat. We saw that there was pressure on the standards setting side, public pressure of perception which should be tidied up in terms of a common voice on professional obligations and role that auditors played in corporate world and in the society. We felt a compelling need and particularly on the taxation side of things, to have a common voice and so all of those things compelled to make a case for unification. It was never ever seen as a defensive move it was always seen as a constructive, professional building, national building opportunity. (2016)

From Taylor's statement and other evidence, it can be argued that a professional crisis and challenges from the IAA forced the bodies to take the decision to go ahead with a merger that would lead to modification of traditional strategies of exclusiveness and market control, which were the respective strategies of the Institute and the Society (Macdonald & Ritzer, 1988, p. 257). Additionally, on 19 October 1987, share markets around the world faced the biggest collapse since 1929. Just before the third merger attempt, Australia went into an economic recession with gross domestic product falling by 1.7% and the unemployment rate rising. Several financial institutions had failed and had debts of billions of dollars (Macfarlane, 2006), and the accounting and auditing professions were criticised by government investigators (Gottliebsen, 1990). Peter Agars, deputy president of the International Federation of Accountants and a former president of the Society at the time of the second merger attempt, commented on the corporate collapses, linking them to the accounting profession. Agars said, "In general, the profession is perceived to be partially to blame for the inadequate or late disclosure of the problem of companies and financial institutions" (Bowerman, 1991e, p. 2). For both bodies, these factors further motivated merger talks.

Graeme McGregor also provided reasons for mounting the third merger attempt in his interview:

> I think continuation of good relations that developed at the senior level of both bodies. We worked successfully at the senior level in something like the Joint Committees where Presidents, Deputy Presidents of each body worked together on key issues. We had a shared responsibility in the Australian Accounting Research Foundation which set the accounting standards at the time. We alternated the chair of that between the two bodies. At the senior level we could feel the sense of having one powerful body in Australia that spoke with one voice. Through the joint standing committees, we had a common view on most items but every now and then different messages would go out particularly to our politicians. And each body had its own agenda, the Institute had started the process seeking to limit the liability of auditors. Particularly after the corporate crashes where auditors were held liable. At the upper level there was a strong feeling that we should merge. (2015)

McGregor (2015) further said, "Clearly an overriding reason to merge was the thought of speaking with one voice. There was also duplication of efforts at the State and National level". When asked whether there were any perceived financial benefits from the merger, McGregor (2015) said:

> It was seen as an advantage by both bodies because a larger membership would have carry-on benefits for higher income and lower cost from lower administration needs. But it was not the overriding reason. It was really carried by a belief that it was silly to have two bodies with the same objective, as one body would be listened to better.

Certain reasons were specific to the Society. In March 1983, the Society adopted the title CPA for its members (ASA, 1983). It aimed to lift the professional profile of its members, with its president reporting that a professional marketing firm, Box Emery & Partners, had been hired to assist in projecting the image of the Society in public and professional domains (Alexander, 1988a). The objective was to create a brand name for its members so that they could enjoy benefits accruing from the professional status enjoyed by the Institute members holding the title of

CA. Australian accountant Elizabeth Alexander made many attempts to create interest among members to gain the CPA qualification and reaffirmed the Society's objective to improve its national image and visibility in messages that appeared throughout 1988 in different editions of the Society's journal (Alexander, 1988a, 1988b, 1988c).

Meanwhile, slightly earlier than the Society, the Institute had also been working on strengthening its brand and improving the public profile of its members (ICAA, 1987). These activities show that the Society was moving away from its traditional strategy of market control and aiming to achieve exclusive status for its members. A proposal to merge with the Institute was an easier way to achieve such status and alter the boundaries of the accounting profession. Professional boundaries are the result of past struggles (Cash, 1997), through which professionals distinguish themselves from the others (Gieryn, 1983). From oral history interviews, it appears that the merger attempt was a proactive step taken by both bodies to meet emerging challenges posed by economic recession, corporate collapse and professional threats from the IAA as well to gain the ability to speak with one voice. It can be argued that leaders of both bodies decided to modify boundaries, and in particular, leaders of the Institute offered to modify the arguments of superior occupational status that distinguished their members from Society members (Cash, 1997; Gieryn, 1983).

8.4.2 *Strategies Adopted by Both Bodies in the Merger Attempt*

The second research question was linked to strategies adopted by the Society and the Institute for mounting the third merger attempt. McGregor (2015) revealed that, mostly, the presidents took decisions, where:

> Face to face discussions and agreements were made between presidents of each body but of course both of us kept our national councils informed. And I must say that there were voices that didn't necessarily support the idea of a merger.

Before the Society came on board to discuss the merger attempt, the Institute president had tried to attract the most senior members of the Society, which was more of a "takeover proposal than a merger proposal" (Taylor, 2016). However, this strategy failed when the Society president made it clear that such an attempt was unacceptable (Abraham, 1989d). For the third merger attempt, the bodies did not form a unity committee and decisions were taken mainly by the national presidents, deputy presidents and executive directors of both bodies (Eastwood, 1990e). Similar to other mergers, neither body conducted market research to study the mood of members regarding the merger proposal (Anon., 1990a). To influence Institute members, a video featuring well-known individuals was created, including BHP Chief Brian Loton, opposition Spokesman John Howard and a former corporate regulator Henry Bosch (Boreham, 1991). Both bodies convinced various corporate managing directors, CEOs, the director general of the Department of the Premier of New South Wales and the chairperson of the Australian Securities Commission Tony Hartnell to openly support merger (Anon., 1991e; Prosser, 1991b). To exert pressure on members to support the merger attempt, both bodies had opted not to go for a secret ballot (Bowerman, 1991d). To convince members, Nick Burton Taylor (1991) wrote in February 1991 that both bodies were facing many challenges and it was important that they work together. As mentioned earlier, the challenges included corporate collapse, the stock market crash and associated issues confronting the profession (Macfarlane, 2006; McMahon, 2007).

Charter published letters written by Institute members to the editor before the merger vote on 22 March 1991. Leong (1991) stated that there were many voices against the merger, including young accountants from Perth, which contradicts the fact that almost all published letters favoured the merger move or were not critically against it (Leong, 1991). Another strategy adopted by the Institute to gain more support from its members was the colleague to colleague campaign. The objective of the campaign was "to maximize the vote to approve unification" (ICAA, 1991b, p. 4). The process included creation of a proxy gathering network of members to advocate the unification of both bodies (ICAA, 1991b). These members were expected to contact 20 to 30 other members and ask their intentions regarding voting (ICAA, 1991b).

In such meetings, if the views expressed by members were positive, the next step was to encourage them to attend the special general meeting. If the views were neutral, the next step was to explain the benefits of unification and ask members to vote as soon as possible. If the members expressed objections to the merger attempt, the strategy was to discuss relevant issues briefly and, if their objections reduced evidently, to encourage them to attend the special general meeting and vote as soon as possible. If their views did not change, the discussion was terminated. This campaign was structured with three individuals in charge of running the network, Allen Blewitt, Bill Tuck and Helen Dickinson (ICAA, 1991b). This was a defence mechanism anticipating boundary protection work where boundary protection included attempts to preserve the boundaries of the Institute (Fournier, 2000). The CPA library resources provided access to the Institute's presentation kits for this research, which were prepared for use at the meetings of members. Such kits included some compelling reasons for a unification attempt:

> Each of us is well aware of the daunting problems confronting the business community and, indeed, the Australian economy as a whole. (ICAA, 1991d, p. 6)

> Members of our profession are being attacked because of their involvement in some of the more prominent corporate failures. (ICAA, 1991d, p. 6)

> Following the 1989 unification initiative, a group of well-respected members of the Institute and the Society began informal discussions on the best way of proceeding with unification of our profession. They believed then—and are even more convinced now—that unification of the profession is an opportunity we dare not let slip. (ICAA, 1991d, p. 6)

> The complex development of our profession has helped to produce the present situation where many people outside the profession are confused about our different designations and professional expertise. (ICAA, 1991d, p. 7)

These arguments were used to convince Institute members to support the merger attempt. However, the attempt failed, which is examined in the next subsection.

8.4.3 *Reasons for the Merger Attempt Failure*

There are two angles in the analysis when responding to the third research question. First, there was detachment between leaders and Institute members (Lee, 2010; Shackleton & Walker, 2001). Second, Institute members engaged in boundary protection work and preserved the existing boundaries. Within this response, overwhelming support to changes in professional boundaries from the Society members is also discussed.

The third research question explored key factors that contributed to the failure of the third merger attempt. In his oral history interview, Graeme McGregor (2015) outlined reasons for the failure, and said:

> I can say that the key people who sold the idea were the Presidents and Deputy Presidents, most discussions took place with them. There was a problem with the younger Institute members who recently completed the Professional Year program. They thought they were giving up hard earned advantage. I was told that it was really a group of younger people from the southern suburbs of Sydney who were very strongly against the merger. They were influencing other younger people which is why it failed.

When asked if something else could have been done by both bodies to gain support for the merger attempt, Graeme McGregor (2015) said:

> As I said before we carried the vote, they did not. I believe we should have taken more time and should have done more marketing and instead of sending letters to members more face to face interaction would have helped. It would have helped rank and file members. I don't think it would have swayed [the] vocal group in the Institute in Perth because they had a very strong view. The CPA program was only in [its] formative stages and had been going for only five years. They still thought it was mickey mouse that included distance learning through Deakin University.

Nick Burton Taylor gave reasons for the failure, especially talking about the Perth campaign:

> I think we failed at the executive level and executive leadership level in convincing the executives of the Western Australian branch of the merits of merger. The executive there gave tacit approval for the dissenting voice and whilst that was laudatory at one level, it gave credibility to a dissenting voice which then I think grew to a level that cost us a successful outcome. So, I think we failed at the organisational level to have our own team as believers, the executive team particularly in Western Australia, and that led into pockets of natural dissent and as you are aware in Western Australia there is a traditional animosity to things federal and things imposed via national structures so that has to be handled very carefully and I think we allowed that gap to exist and then that gap was exploited by the opponents of unification. (2016)

Taylor further added:

> Of course, there were traditional reasons around a brand which had been in existence very successfully for 60 years as to why change and so that resistance that's involved in all of these sort of referenda, that was a pocket that was always going to be there and they remained. (2016)

These statements indicate the detachment between leaders and members of the Institute, which led members in Perth to go against the former's decision. The dissenters included senior members, such as Tony Connolly, a partner in Pannell Kerr Forster, Perth, who argued, "We're being treated like little boys [sic] by the executive of both bodies" (Anon., 1991b, p. 7).

Connolly was also critical of the fact that the Institute had proposed that the voting in relation to the merger was to be at a special meeting in Sydney on 22 March 1991 and not by postal ballot (Anon., 1991b, p. 7). Nick Burton Taylor said that after the failure of the 1981 merger, the proxy system was included in the charter of the Institute. Although he preferred a postal ballot, the legal department had suggested the use of proxy or in person voting (Bowerman, 1991d). According to Bowerman (1991d), both the Institute and the Society were claiming that if a third attempt failed, this was the last chance to merge the two bodies because after significant expense and efforts neither body would be able to make another attempt. Clearly, this discursive claim did not prove correct because a fourth attempt was mounted within seven years.

John Greeve, a Chartered Accountant from West Perth, expressed strong support for the "No Vote" campaign in a message to *The Financial Review* editor, which was published on 12 March 1991. Greeve (1991) compared the \$AU9,000 cost of the "No Vote" campaign against the \$AU500,000 spent by the Institute on mounting the merger attempt. Greeve (1991) held the Institute's national executive accountable for not releasing details of surveys and PW research and commented that it was likely that those reports showed that Institute members were against the merger. On the issue of the merger, Greeve (1991, p. 7) further commented, that the grass roots members of the Institute were at odds with the leadership. This discussion and reaction of the Institute members via letters, organised campaigns and otherwise shows that leaders of the Institute did not understand the members' mood and were detached from members (Lee, 2010; Shackleton & Walker, 2001).

In a letter to the Institute's journal *Charter*, Graham Edmonds, a Partner of Mann Judd, criticised the merger and stated that "unification, particularly the promoted "compromise" will, paradoxically, be self-descriptive". Edmonds also downplayed the proposed advantages of a merger and specifically criticised the notion of the purported benefits of "speaking with one voice" (Edmonds, 1991, p. 8). However, Vic Prosser responded to Edmonds and stated that:

> Those of us who deal frequently with Government have been repeatedly assured that unification will lead to a more efficient and effective relationship between the profession and government and its instrumentalities. (1991a, p. 8)

An Institute national councillor, Bruce Riley, who claimed to have support from two other councillors, joined the public discourse against the merger. Riley expressed that he had fairly strong reservations as to whether the merger would produce the big picture benefits cited (Anon., 1991b).

Frank P. Cornelius, an Institute member, wrote a letter to the editor of *The Financial Review*, which was published on 26 February 1991. Cornelius (1991) criticised the national executive of the Institute for proceeding with the merger vote and for spending $AU1 million, even though an Institute survey showed support from members for a merger being at less than 50%. Cornelius (1991) also criticised the voting process, which did not involve a secret ballot. Bowerman (1991c) analysed the situation during the last few weeks before the merger vote of 22 March and reported strong opposition and criticism of the Institute's executive, including the expenditure of $AU500,000 for the merger proposal.

Next, boundary protection by Institute members is discussed. In a letter to *The Financial Review* editor published on 13 March 1991, Deborah Garlick (1991, p. 7), a CA from Perth, expressed a concern that with the proposed merger of two bodies many CAs such as her "were going to lose recognition as fully qualified Chartered Accountants". Garlick's (1991) statement was consistent with arguments of "No Vote" proponents who had made similar claims regarding loss of professional status if the merger attempt succeeded (Anon., 1991d; Blue, 1991b, p. 61). In a letter to the editor of *The Financial Review* on 15 March, Charles Sugar, a member of the Society, attempted to respond to Deborah Garlick's letter, claiming that unity of the profession should be above personal loss of status (Sugar, 1991). On 14 March 1991, eight days before the merger vote of 22 March, an article by Steve Lewis published the claims of the Perth-based antimerger group. Lewis (1991b, p. 2) wrote, that a group of Chartered Accountants campaigning against the merger of two accounting professional bodies were claiming victory, one week before voting closes in the controversial election.

Anthony Hardwick, a member of the Institute, wrote in *The Australian* on 15 March 1991 that six of the largest national accounting firms were supporting the merger so that they could increase their lobbying power with the government. Hardwick (1991) asked all members to vote "No" to the merger proposal. The returning officer of the Institute, Vic Prosser, gave a statement on 14 March 1991 that, per his estimates, almost 67% of Institute members had voted in favour of the merger (Lewis, 1991b). According to Prosser, he was forced to make this announcement after the Perth-based group propagated confusion by claiming that 80% of votes cast were against the merger (Lewis, 1991b).

Noake (1991, p. 7), an associate member of the Institute, criticised the merger attempt and the argument that a merger would enable the profession to speak with one voice to governments and regulators and stated that the bases for a merger were not sound. Some Institute members wrote letters to editors raising various queries. Robert Morrison, an Institute member from Darwin, expressed concerns via a letter to the editor of *The Financial Review* over the lack of information available to Institute members about the merger, including with respect to the financial position of both bodies. Other letters also criticised the merger and commented that it would be unreasonable to expect Institute members to accept dilution of their hard-earned professional titles (Anderson, 1991; Fisher, 1991). The Society and the Institute had differences of opinion on the postunity condition of offering their programs overseas. The Institute was against offering chartered accounting programs outside Australia, but for the Society, overseas students were the third-largest group after students from New South Wales and Victoria (Ryan, 1991).

Boundary protection was a well-coordinated campaign by a group of Institute members in Perth (Anon., 1991c). Apart from Kim Bradbury, other members were Frank Cornelous, Brad McVeigh, Joe Pier and John Greeve (Anon., 1991c). This group published an advertisement in *The Financial Review* on 5 March 1991 urging Institute members to "vote no to the merger". This advertisement listed 15 members and their phone numbers, including that of Kim Bradbury. The advertisement also included a sentence that referred to the support extended by accounting firms for the merger attempt, stating that this was individual vote as a member, not that of a firm (Anon., 1991f). These are examples of public discourse against the merger attempt (Annisette, 2017). Bradbury further said:

> Members of ICA in Perth believe we have a commercial advantage; why should we give it away? There has been an enormous amount of rushing around ... the ICA executive is just trying to force people to accept it. (Bowerman, 1991b, p. 2)

Bradbury also revealed the group's strategy to oppose the merger move, which centred on a collective campaign against the merger, including issuing personal contacts, mail-outs and some press advertisements (Bowerman, 1991b). The arguments against the merger attempt were very strong and were an attempt at boundary protection by members. Blue (1991b, p. 60) also wrote that:

> The strongest opposition from the Institute members seems to be among recent graduates of the Professional Year, who feel their blood, sweat and tears might be wasted in a merger with the Society.
>
> The case against:
>
> - Professional standards will be compromised.
> - The term 'Chartered Accountants' will be devalued in the market place with a corresponding loss of marketability.
> - The Institute will be placed under the control of the Society majority.
> - 'One voice' will simply mean one less voice.
> - The present position of cooperation between the ICA and the ASCPA on vital issues is preferred—two heads are better than one.
> - One body is easier for the government to control.
> - The much-touted economies of scale are a myth. They have never been verified and in the majority of cases only represent a downgrading of facilities.
> - The way in which the current vote is being carried out represents an erosion of democratic principles.
> - The size of the new body means it is less personal—'big is not beautiful'.
> - Amalgamation may lead to a loss of benefits of reciprocal membership enjoyed by the Institute members. (Blue, 1991b, p. 61)

The Perth group of Institute members demanded the resignation of Nick Burton Taylor if the merger failed. They also criticised the Institute's national executive for not funding a "No Vote" campaign. They sent letters to all the Institute members, a strategy funded by second-tier accounting firms from Perth, including PKF, Hendry Rae Court, Bentleys, Ferrier Hodgson and Nelson Parkhill (Bowerman, 1991c). Such were the boundary protection strategies adopted by Institute members (Fournier, 2000; Persson, 2010). In their studies of race-based social boundaries, Perry (2002), McDermott (2006) and Wray (2006) found similar arguments used by members of the perceived high-status group to protect their boundaries. For example, their studies found that white people maintained their ethnic boundaries by disassociating themselves from black people by labelling the latter as inferior. The dissident members of the Institute used similar arguments, for instance, that after integration, the public would no longer be able to rely to the same extent on those standards previously expected of Chartered Accountants (Anon., 1991d). Hence, they labelled Society members as having lower professional standards, which has been an approach used in race-based boundaries (McDermott, 2006; Perry, 2002; Wray, 2006).

8.4.4 Reactions of Various Stakeholders

The fourth research question concerns the reactions of various stakeholders[3] to the proposals for unification and their subsequent failures. McGregor (2015) said in his interview that there was no reaction to the merger from the government, stating that:

> It was bit reverse. We had lobbied outside people to come out publicly to support a merger to show that there was widespread public support for merger. I think they didn't care and they had higher priorities.

Australia's largest accounting firms KPMG Peat Marwick, Ernst & Young and Arthur Andersen & Co. openly supported the merger (Bowerman, 1991c). However, Graham Edmonds, a Partner of Mann Judd, CAs from Brisbane, criticised the merger attempt (Edmonds, 1991, p. 8). After the failure, Professor Murray Wells of the University of Sydney and Professor

[3] Stakeholders include members of both professional bodies, the government, policy-makers, accounting firms and investors.

Bill Birkett of the University of New South Wales criticised members who voted against the proposal (Dobbie & Boreham, 1989).

Responding to a question by the researcher on the reactions of stakeholders, Taylor (2016) contributed a perspective of people who were involved in the merger attempt:

> There was a feeling of spent energy because a lot of people put a lot of energy in[to] the whole process but to be honest the B team had done a pretty good job of coming up with some plans to really come out of the box sparring and that's what happened and so it was an interesting observation of human behaviour. You sort of finish a book and you get to the last chapter which is quite exciting and you put it down and close your eyes and think wow that's a great book and then you look around the room for a minute and then someone else pushes a book in front of you. You start reading the new book and your mind travels to the new book and that's exactly what happened.

Hence, in Nick Burton Taylor's view, there was not much reaction to the failure and both bodies moved to the next chapters. The last research question for this study focused on the long-term ramifications of the unsuccessful merger attempt for the Australian accounting profession, and on this matter Nick Burton Taylor responded:

> Well I think it enhanced the process of accounting standards moving into the government and international control. We influenced the international accounting standards through various appointments and everything but we lost as a profession the domestic influence on the sort of standards that we once might have had. (Taylor, 2016)

Thus, one of the long-term ramifications was that the profession lost control over the process of setting standards.

8.5 Conclusion

This chapter examined the third merger attempt. Similar to the first two attempts, it failed because the Institute members voted against the proposed merger. Both bodies had developed an ongoing understanding about the need to work together, which was kept alive before and after the mounting of the third merger attempt. As Chapters 6 and 7, which examined the first and second merger attempts, respectively, have shown, the traditional strategy of the Society was modified and it moved from market control towards exclusivity, an approach observed across all four merger attempts. A similar, related issue was the lack of a recognised professional title for Society members, which was a matter of concern for the Society leadership, as evidenced from archives before the mounting of the first merger attempt. After the failure of the second merger attempt, the Society adopted the CPA title in March 1983, which made it possible for its members to have an exclusive professional title. This was part of Plan B, which was adopted by the Society after the failure of the second merger attempt, along with many other changes in its structure and operations. Moreover, the IAA membership was growing, which posed a professional challenge to both bodies, forcing them to engage in merger discussions.

The membership size difference decreased between 1982 and 1991, the period under study for the third merger attempt. During this period, the Institute's membership grew at double the rate of the Society membership. In addition, the financial position of both bodies fluctuated. The stock market crash and corporate collapses added background context to the mounting of the merger attempt. The third merger attempt had a unique development in that the president of the Institute made a unilateral decision to invite senior members of the Society to apply for membership of the Institute. Although this step attracted a backlash, it did lead to the initiation of merger talks. It was rejected by the Society but by September 1989, this offer had sparked interest and a first attempt to initiate merger discussions was filed within three months. It took one more year to restart the merger discussions of September 1990. By December 1990, both bodies had issued the merger proposals (ASCPA & ICAA, 1990).

As in the first two attempts, the third merger attempt talks were initiated by the Institute. The third attempt also failed, but it was not to be the last attempt and one more unsuccessful merger attempt was made, which is examined in Chapter 9.

References

Abraham, J. (1989a, September). Unification update. *The Australian Accountant*, p. 6.

Abraham, J. (1989b, November). President's report. *The Australian Accountant*, p. 9.

Abraham, J. (1989c, June 2). *ASA welcomes Institute response* [Press release, President, Australian Society of Accountants], p. 1.
Abraham, J. (1989d, June 7). *Towards a unified profession* [Press release, President, Australian Society of Accountants], p. 1.
Agars, P. D. (1982, January/February). The way ahead. *The Australian Accountant*, pp. 14–16.
Alexander, E. (1988a, September). From the president. *The Australian Accountant*, p. 8.
Alexander, E. (1988b, October). From the president. *The Australian Accountant*, p. 7.
Alexander, E. (1988c, September). From the president. *The Australian Accountant*, p. 11.
Anderson, P. (1991, March 20). Aim to be more efficient. *Financial Review*, p. 8.
Annisette, M. (2017). Discourse of the professions: The making, normalizing and taming of Ontario's foreign-trained accountant. *Accounting, Organizations and Society, 60*, 37–61.
Anon. (1982, February). Integration will not proceed. *The Chartered Accountant in Australia*, pp. 2–3.
Anon. (1988, March 25). Unite or forget, accountancy hotline. *Business Review Weekly*, p. 8.
Anon. (1989a, June 19). *A unified profession.* Policy of the Australian Society of Accountants adopted by National Council, pp. 1–4.
Anon. (1989b, June 29). Accountants merger plan released. *The West Australian*, p. 4.
Anon. (1989c, August). Merger plan runs into trouble. *World Accounting Report*, p. 11.
Anon. (1989d, September 8). Accountants fail to form umbrella organization. *The Advertiser*, p. 10.
Anon. (1990a, November). Unity doubt. *Business Review Weekly*, p. 109.
Anon. (1990b, December). Merger plan revealed. *Business Review Weekly*, p. 101.
Anon. (1991a). Explanatory memorandum. *The Australian Society of Accountants and the Institute of Chartered Accountants in Australia.*
Anon. (1991b, January/February). Merger update. *Chartac*, p. 7.
Anon. (1991c, February 13). *Unification: The case against integration of the accountancy profession. A campaign run against unification*, pp. 1–2.
Anon. (1991d, February 21). The unification debate: The house divided. *New Accountant*, p. 18.
Anon. (1991e, March 1). For unity of accountants. *Financial Review*, p. 3.
Anon. (1991f, March 5). Chartered accountants vote no to merger. *Financial Review*, no page.

Anon. (1991g, April 3). Accounting for the merger decision. *Financial Review*, p. 1.
Australian Society of Accountants. (1982). *Annual report*. Melbourne, Australia.
Australian Society of Accountants. (1983). *Annual report*. Melbourne, Australia.
Australian Society of Accountants. (1984). *Annual report*. Melbourne, Australia.
Australian Society of Accountants. (1985). *Annual report*. Melbourne, Australia.
Australian Society of Accountants. (1986). *Annual report*. Melbourne, Australia.
Australian Society of Accountants. (1987). *Annual report*. Melbourne, Australia.
Australian Society of Accountants. (1988). *Annual report*. Melbourne, Australia.
Australian Society of Accountants. (1989). *Annual report*. Melbourne, Australia.
Australian Society of Accountants. (1990). *Annual report*. Melbourne, Australia.
Australian Society of Accountants. (1991). *Annual report*. Melbourne, Australia.
Australian Society of Accountants. (1992). *Annual report*. Melbourne, Australia.
Australian Society of Accountants and the Institute of Chartered Accountants in Australia. (1989). *Accountancy bodies commit to joint body* [Joint press release, June 21], p. 1.
Australian Society of Certified Practising Accountants and the Institute of Chartered Accountants in Australia. (1990, December). *Unification Proposal, jointly issued by both bodies*, pp. 1–16.
Blue, T. (1991a, March 6). The state of union. *Australian Business*, pp. 60–61.
Blue, T. (1991b, February 27). Below the line: Accountancy. *Australian Business*, p. 60.
Boreham, T. (1989, December 8). ICA's Allen wants a year of healing. *Business Review Weekly*, pp. 123–124.
Boreham, T. (1991, February, 9). Members get the hard sell on unification. *Business Review Weekly*, pp. 77–79.
Bowerman, R. (1989a, June 15). War clouds over ICA unity proposal. *New Accountant*, p. 4.
Bowerman, R. (1989b, September 7). ICA letter reveals offer to drop CPA title in unity bid. *New Accountant*, p. 1.
Bowerman, R. (1991a, January 23). Improved prospects for unity proposal. *New Accountant*, pp. 1–2.
Bowerman, R. (1991b, January 23). ICA group steps up opposition. *New Accountant*, p. 2.
Bowerman, R. (1991c, March 7). Last chance for unification: ICA voter looks perilously close. *New Accountant*, p. 1.
Bowerman, R. (1991d, March 7). ICA: Unity cost an investment for the future. *New Accountant*, p. 6.
Bowerman, R. (1991e, March 7). Somewhere, accountants lost their way. *New Accountant*, p. 2.
Briggs, L. (1991, March 23–24). Third time unlucky for accounting merger vote. *The Weekend Australian*, p. 12.

Cash, K. (1997). Social epistemology, gender and nursing theory. *International Journal of Nursing Studies, 34*(2), 137–143.
Clafton, S. (1991, 15 January). Accounting bodies to vote on merger, again. *The Age*, p. 10.
Cornelius, P. F. (1991, February 21). Accountants not informed on merger. *Financial Review*, p. 5.
Dobbie, M., & Boreham, T. (1989, September 15). Rays of hope after merger talks fail. *Business Review Weekly*, pp. 123–125.
Dunstan, B. (1989, June 28). Negotiators close to merging profession. *Financial Review*, p. 10.
Eastwood, K. (1990a, April). A statement from the president. *The Australian Accountant*, p. 7.
Eastwood, K. (1990b, May). From the president. *The Australian Accountant*, p. 5.
Eastwood, K. (1990c, June). From the president. *The Australian Accountant*, p. 5.
Eastwood, K. (1990d, October). From the president. *The Australian Accountant*, p. 5.
Eastwood, K. (1990e, November). From the president. *The Australian Accountant*, p. 5.
Eastwood, K. (1990f, December). From the president. *The Australian Accountant*, p. 5.
Eastwood, K. (1991, February 18). Letter from president to members. *Australian Society of Certified Practising Accountants*, pp. 1–2.
Edmonds, G. (1991, February). Unification letters—A letter to the editor. *Charter*, pp. 8–9.
Fisher, B. (1991, March 20). Titles concern accountants. *Financial Review*, p. 8.
Fournier, V. (2000). Boundary work and the (un)making of the professions. In *Professionalism, boundaries and the workplace* (p. 67).
Garlick, D. (1991, March 13). Accountant merger worry: A letter to the editor. *Financial Review*, p. 7.
Gieryn, T. F. (1983). Boundary-work and the demarcation of science from non-science: Strains and interests in the professional ideologies of scientists. *American Sociological Review, 48*(6), 781–795.
Gieryn, T. F. (1995). Boundaries of science. In S. Jasanoff, G. E. Markle, J. C. Petersen, & T. Pinch (Eds.), *Handbook of science and technology studies* (pp. 393–443). Sage.
Gieryn, T. F. (1999). *Cultural boundaries of science: Credibility on the line*. University of Chicago Press.
Gieryn, T. F., Bevins, G. M., & Zehi, S. C. (1985). Professionalization of American scientists: Public science in the creation/evolution trials. *American Sociological Review, 50*(3), 392–409.

Gottliebsen, R. (1990, September). Accounting's crisis of ethics. *Business Review Weekly*, pp. 14–15.
Grbic, N. (2010). 'Boundary work' as a concept for studying professionalization processes in the interpreting field. *Translation and Interpreting Studies, 5*(1), 109–123.
Greeve, J. (1991, March 12). Merger murmurs: A letter to the editor. *Financial Review*, p. 7.
Hardwick, A. (1991, March 15). Accounting for status quo. *The Australian*, p. 8.
Henderson, M. S. (1988, April). *Towards unification of the Australian accounting profession.* Paper presented at the Annual Congress of the Australian Society of Accountants held in April 1988 at Adelaide (pp. 1–15).
Howard, P. (1991, March 10). Accountants need to make up merger. *Sunday Age*, p. 10.
Jasanoff, S. (1995). *Science at the bar: Law, science, and technology in America.* Harvard University Press.
Keohane, R. O., & Milner, H. V. (Eds.). (1996). *Internationalization and domestic politics*. Cambridge University Press.
Kohler, A. (1989, November 8). Accountants wrangle puts sense on the debit side. *Australian Financial Review*, p. 19.
Lamont, M. (1992). *Money, morals, and manners: The culture of the French and American upper-middle class*. University of Chicago Press.
Lamont, M. (2000). *The dignity of working men: Morality and the boundaries of race, class, and immigration*. Harvard University Press.
Lee, T. A. (2010). Consolidating the public accountancy profession: The case of the proposed Institute of Chartered Accountants of Great Britain, 1988–9. *Accounting History, 15*(1), 7–39.
Leong, H. (1991, February). Letter to editor. *Charter*, p. 59.
Lewis, S. (1989, November 1). Name-calling in accountants' war. *Financial Review*, p. 21.
Lewis, S. (1991a, January 29). Accountants try another path to merge professional bodies. *Financial Review*, p. 6.
Lewis, S. (1991b, March 15). ICA claims win in accountants' move to merge. *Financial Review*, p. 3.
Lewis, S., & Lawson, M. (1991, February 21). Accountants still reluctant to merge. *Financial Review*, p. 5.
Luker, P. (1989a, June 3). New ICA proposal to merger with ASA. *The Age*, p. 4.
Luker, P. (1989b, June 20). Accountants split over merger terms. *The Age*, p. 17.
Luker, P. (1989c, September 8). Accountancy merger plan called off, for time being. *The Age*, p. 18.

Macdonald, K. M. (1985). Social closure and occupational registration. *Sociology, 19*(4), 541–556.
Macdonald, K. M., & Ritzer, G. (1988). The sociology of the professions: Dead or alive? *Work and Occupations, 15*(3), 251–272.
Macfarlane, I., (2006, December 2). The real reasons why it was the 1990s recession we had to have—Business. *The Age*. Retrieved August 18, 2015, from Theage.com.au.
McDermott, M. (2006). *Working-class white: The making and unmaking of race relations*. Berkeley, CA: University of California Press.
McGregor, G. (2015). Interview with Graeme McGregor on December 14.
McKnight, D. (1989a, June 3). Accountants again discuss merger. *The Sydney Morning Herald*, p. 43.
McKnight, D. (1989b, August 2). Accountant merger deadline goes quietly. *The Sydney Morning Herald*, p. 7.
McKnight, D. (1989c, September 8). Accountants fail to agree in merger talks. *The Sydney Morning Herald*, p. 11.
McMahon, S. (2007, 13 October 13). Two days that shook the world. *Herald Sun*. www.heraldsun.com.au/businessold/two-days-that-shook-the-world/story-e6frfh4f-1111114631654
Middleton, P. (1989a, June 2). *Statement by Peter Middleton, president*. The Institute of Chartered Accountants in Australia.
Middleton, P. (1989b, June 3). *Letter from president to professional year candidates and professional year graduates*. The Institute of Chartered Accountants in Australia.
Middleton, P. (1989c, July 17). *Letter from president to members*. The Institute of Chartered Accountants in Australia.
Middleton, P. (1989d, September 11). *Letter from president to members*. The Institute of Chartered Accountants in Australia, pp. 1–4.
Middleton, P. (1989e, November 9). *Accountancy unification discussions abandoned*. A media release by President of The Institute of Chartered Accountants in Australia, pp. 1–3.
Minter, E. (1991, March 23). Rebel group blocks accountancy merger. *The Age*, p. 7.
Murrill, M. (1989a, June 20). ASA takes the initiative with merger proposal. *Financial Review*, pp. 17 and 25.
Murrill, M. (1989b, August 14). Professional bodies have merger problems. *Financial Review*, p. 18.
Murrill, M. (1989c, August 25). Merger talks are at make or break point. *Financial Review*, p. 17.
Murrill, M. (1989d, September 27). Merger failure sets rival bodies chasing members. *Financial Review*, p. 13.
Noake, M. (1991, March 18). Image of the single voice. *Financial Review*, p. 7.

Perry, P. (2002). *Shades of white: White kids and racial identities in high school.* Duke University Press.
Persson, A. (2010). Soldiers and secretaries: Gendered boundary work in the Swedish Armed Forces. *Scandinavian Journal of Management, 26*, 166–175.
Porter, I. (1989, June 20). Accounting groups to attempt merger again. *The Advertiser*, p. 9.
Porter, I. (1991, March 23). Third time unlucky for accounting merger bid. *The Advertiser (Business Edition)*, p. 2.
Prosser, V. (1982a, May). Talking point. *The Chartered Accountant in Australia*, p. 6.
Prosser, V. (1982b, May). Talking point. *The Chartered Accountant in Australia*, p. 6.
Prosser, V. (1982c, June). Talking point. *The Chartered Accountant in Australia*, p. 8.
Prosser, V. (1986, September). Talking point. *The Chartered Accountant in Australia*, p. 4.
Prosser, V. (1987, August). Talking point. *The Chartered Accountant in Australia*, 4.
Prosser, V. (1989, September). The failure of the merger. *New Accountant*, p. 22.
Prosser, V. (1991a, February). Unification disadvantages will fade with time. *New Accountant*, p. 8.
Prosser, V. (1991b, March). This might be the last chance for unification. *New Accountant, 7*, 22.
Ryan, M. (1989, June 29). Countdown begins as ASA, ICA try to put differences aside. *New Accountant*, pp. 1–3.
Ryan, M. (1991, March 21). Unity poses questions for accountancy educators. *New Accountant*, p. 3.
Shackleton, K. & Walker, S. P. (2001). *A future for the accountancy profession: The quest for closure and integration, 1957–1970.* Edinburgh, Scotland: Institute of Chartered Accountants of Scotland.
Sharpe, M. (1983). President's overview. *Annual report.* The Australian Society of Accountants, pp. 2–3.
Sugar, C. (1991, March 15). Unity above status. *Financial Review*, p. 8.
Taylor, N. B. (1991, February). A message from the President. *The Chartered Accountant in Australia*, p. 3.
Taylor, N. B. (2016). Interview with Nick Burton Taylor on March 18.
The Australian Society of Certified Practising Accountants. (1991). Explanatory Memorandum, Document circulated to members, No date, pp. 1–8.
The Institute of Chartered Accountants in Australia. (1984). *Annual report.* Sydney, Australia.
The Institute of Chartered Accountants in Australia. (1982). *Annual report.* Sydney, Australia.

The Institute of Chartered Accountants in Australia. (1983). *Annual report*. Sydney, Australia.
The Institute of Chartered Accountants in Australia. (1985). *Annual report*. Sydney, Australia.
The Institute of Chartered Accountants in Australia. (1986). *Annual report*. Sydney, Australia.
The Institute of Chartered Accountants in Australia. (1987). *Annual report*. Sydney, Australia.
The Institute of Chartered Accountants in Australia. (1988). *Annual report*. Sydney, Australia.
The Institute of Chartered Accountants in Australia. (1989a, July). *One voice: Partners in a stronger profession*. Issued by National Council, pp. 1–4.
The Institute of Chartered Accountants in Australia. (1989b). *Annual report*. Sydney, Australia.
The Institute of Chartered Accountants in Australia. (1990). *Annual report*. Sydney, Australia.
The Institute of Chartered Accountants in Australia. (1991a). *Annual report*. Sydney, Australia.
The Institute of Chartered Accountants in Australia. (1991b, 18 January). *Colleague to colleague campaign*, pp. 1–10.
The Institute of Chartered Accountants in Australia. (1991c, 31 January). *Briefing paper: Benefits of unification*.
The Institute of Chartered Accountants in Australia. (1991d, 31 January). *Members meeting: Presentation program*, pp. 1–10.
The Institute of Chartered Accountants in Australia. (1991e, 31 January). *Commentary on colleagues to colleague campaign*, pp. 1–7.
Thomas, C. (1991, March 23), Accounting merger bid voted out. *Herald Sun*, 7
Thomas, T. (1987, November 13), Old rivals review push for merger. *Accountancy Week*, p. 153.
Waldron, B. (1991a, April). From the president. *The Australian Accountant*, p. 5.
Waldron, B. (1991b, May). From the president. *The Australian Accountant*, p. 5.
Waldron, B. (1991c, July). From the president. *The Australian Accountant*, p. 7.
Walker, B. (1988, February). Accountants at war. *Australian Business*, pp. 94–95.
Walker, S. P., & Shackleton, K. (1995). Corporatism and structural change in the British accountancy profession, 1930–1957. *Accounting, Organisations and Society, 20*(6), 467–503.
Walters, G. (1991, March). Unification of the accounting profession. *Company Director*, p. 76.

Wray, M. (2006). *Not quite white: White trash and the boundaries of whiteness*. Duke University Press.

Wright, J. (2008, May 29). *Top 10 Financial moments that shaped SA*. ABC South Australia. Australian Broadcasting Corporation (ABC). Retrieved August 18, 2015, from Blogs.abc.net.au.

CHAPTER 9

The Last Attempt to Unite the Dominant Professional Accounting Associations

9.1 Introduction

This chapter examines the fourth and last merger attempt, which was mounted by the Society and the Institute in 1998, in a relatively brief time after the third merger attempt. From the commencement of initial discussions about a merger, which took place between the presidents of the two bodies, to the point of the merger vote, the period was the shortest among all four merger attempts. Similar to the first three merger attempts, the fourth merger attempt failed because of insufficient support from Institute members. After the failure of the third merger attempt, both bodies and their leaders had reaffirmed their stand to work jointly on matters of mutual interest (Taylor, 1991c). The idea for the fourth merger attempt was formed at a meeting between the Institute President, Rob Ward, and the Society President, Denis Cortese, during the International Accounting Congress in Paris in 1997. According to Boymal (2016), it was Rob Ward who initiated the idea of again attempting a merger and he drove the early discussions. Therefore, in the case of all four merger attempts, it was the Institute that initiated the merger discussions. Within a few months, the merger discussions led to the finalisation of a merger proposal, for which voting was held on 14 December 1998.

This chapter is structured in five sections. The next section provides the background context to the fourth merger attempt, along with a discussion of the scenario after the failure of the third merger attempt and how

J. Sidhu et al., *Understanding the Sociology of the Accounting Profession*, https://doi.org/10.1007/978-981-99-1572-9_9

both bodies reacted and adopted different strategies. It also includes a discussion on joint work, the financial position of both bodies and their membership levels. Section 9.3 discusses the merger attempt, including the background and the timeframe. It also provides details of the efforts made by members of the Institute who opposed the merger attempt. Section 9.4 provides an overall discussion and analysis of the fourth merger attempt. Summarising and concluding comments are provided in the final section.

9.1.1 Background and Context

The failure of the third merger attempt, which went to the vote on 22 March 1991, forced both bodies to adopt alternative strategies and issue statements to support their decision to go ahead with the merger. For example, the Society adopted a new mission statement and the Institute president called for more cooperation between the two bodies (ASA, 1992; Taylor, 1991c) since the merger had failed owing to a lack of sufficient support from Institute members. In his monthly message in *Charter*, Nick Burton Taylor, the president of the Institute, referred to the merger failure and the challenges facing the profession, including external pressures, which meant that both bodies needed to work cooperatively on matters of mutual interest. Taylor (1991c) wrote in one such message:

> Following the unification vote in March, I advised our membership that both the ICA and the ASCPA have a responsibility to support the accountancy profession and that we must place strong emphasis on how best to meet our future community obligations. In the light of the continuing debate and the attempt to allocate blame for corporate collapses it is imperative that the accountancy bodies cooperate with each other for the good of the profession to ensure a common approach and truly effective liaison with government in addition to the maintenance of standards. (Taylor, 1991c, p. 66)

In addition, Taylor wrote that the Institute had a record intake of PY candidates in 1991 (Taylor, 1991b, p. 59). He used this to present the case that the Institute would be able to achieve its own strong membership growth. Further, in the same edition of the Institute's journal, Taylor argued that 45 per cent of Institute members were not in public practice, which reflected the diversity of the Institute's membership base (Taylor, 1991b). This discourse was used to defend the decision to seek a merger with the Society, which had a larger share of its total membership not involved in public practice.

Following the failure of the third merger attempt, the president of the Society, Brian Waldron, pointed out that although he was disappointed with the outcome, he was not looking back. Waldron stated that Society had put many significant new initiatives on hold which could go ahead after merger had failed (Cohn, 1991). One of those initiatives was adopting a new mission statement, which was "to lead the Australian accounting profession" (ASA, 1992, p. 1). In addition, the objectives of the Society as a professional accounting body were revised as follows:

- **Intellectual capital**: To use the intellectual capital of members and promote research to advance the knowledge base of the profession
- **Professional growth**: To facilitate the maintenance and development of member competencies throughout their professional careers
- **Integrity**: To maintain the highest level of professional standards and integrity of members in the interest of the community
- **Representation**: To represent the profession in the community
- **Organising and management**: To ensure that the Society's structure and management meet the needs of members in a rapidly changing environment (ASA, 1992, p. 1)

Another response to the failure of the third merger attempt was the increased emphasis on the quality of services offered by CPAs and the establishment of 10 specialist centres of excellence to offer support to members. These centres aimed to enhance the public credibility and authority of CPAs and the Society as a professional association (ASA, 1992). In summary, the new objectives indicated that the Society was aiming to provide leadership within the profession in its own right; the idea of another merger seemed unrealistic. These objectives were quite comprehensive and covered many aspects.

A key development was that the Society recorded a 21 per cent increase in enrolment for membership compared with the 1991 figures. In addition to the official journal of the Society, *The Australian Accountant*, a new journal, *Financial Forum*, was initiated. An ASCPA *Guide to Financial Services* and a *Members Handbook* were also published in 1991 (ASA,

1992). The Society also reviewed its organisational structure and identified three key areas based on the report of the Structural Review Task Force, namely, membership services, utilising the intellectual capital of members and continuing professional development (Cohn, 1991, p. 20). The next section discusses developments within both bodies between the third and the fourth merger attempt.

9.1.2 *Society and Institute Developments*

In 1993, the Society completed 40 years of operation since its formation from the merger of three accounting bodies in 1953 (ASA, 1993). It reported that in 1993, it organised 900 seminars, conferences and workshops attended by 40,000 members accumulating more than 200,000 hours in professional development activities. The significant amount of professional development hours offered was owing to an annual requirement of 20 hours of professional development for every member (ASA, 1993).

The Institute also made progress in different areas, including developing a new strategic plan, a new mission statement and a new logo among other initiatives. In 1992, the Institute finalised its strategic plan for 1992–1996, which was approved by its national council in October 1991 (ICAA, 1992). This plan was finalised after the failure of the third merger attempt. The new plan had various objectives, such as establishing the Institute as the leader of the Australian accounting profession, forming new strategic alliances and achieving financial strength. Building relationships with external stakeholders, including state and federal governments, was also identified as a key priority (ICAA, 1992).

The Institute's mission was finalised as follows:

> To be the pre-eminent professional accountancy body in Australia by providing leadership and by maintaining an environment in which Chartered Accountants meet the highest quality of professional standards and thereby positively influence the national economic well-being of Australia. (ICAA, 1992, p. 2)

In 1994, the Institute commenced offering its PY program overseas, with Hong Kong being the first overseas location. This was known as the Professional Year Offshore (ICAA, 1994). In July 1995, the PY Offshore program commenced in Singapore and Malaysia as well (ICAA, 1995).

In 1994, the Institute launched the CA logo for the first time, which was designed to strengthen the profile and positioning of CAs with business and the community. In April 1994, the Society admitted member number 70,000. Around 8,000 of its total members were in Asia, which made it one of the biggest overseas professional accounting bodies in that region (ASA, 1994). The official journal of the Society, *The Australian Accountant*, exceeded publication of 79,000 copies per month in 1994 (ASA, 1994). In 1995, the Society started CPA Online, an online service for its members. The national council approved the formation of the Asian division of the Society (ASA, 1995), which was established in 1996 and afforded representation on the national council of the Society. In 1996, the Indonesian branch of the Society was also established. Another development in 1996 included the Society hosting a month-long tour of 20 Chinese officials from the Chinese Institute of Certified Public Accountants (ASA, 1996).

The 1996 annual report of the Society provided details of its organisational and operational structure, including 60 national and divisional committees, which together had 450–500 meetings throughout that year; additionally, 200 technical discussion groups were organised (ASA, 1996). In 1996, the Society reported that public awareness of the CPA professional title was 74 per cent, a rise from 63 per cent in 1994 and 55 per cent in 1993 (ASA, 1996, p. 33). By 1997, such awareness had reached 76 per cent (ASA, 1997). Further, in 1996 the Society organised congresses in Hong Kong, Papua New Guinea and Europe. The Hong Kong congress was one of the most successful and attracted more than 400 attendees (ASA, 1996, p. 34). By 1996, the Society had opened branches in Europe, Hong Kong, Indonesia, Malaysia, New Zealand, Papua New Guinea and Singapore (ASA, 1996, p. 35). In 1997, the Society established its branch in Fiji. Additionally, as membership numbers grew, the Society appointed a Director of Members Services and a Director of Intellectual Capital (ASA, 1997). The Society also reviewed and restructured its operations to ensure that customers were the main focus and services for members were improved. Further, the Society's business plan was revised, with new objectives clearly focused on enhancing members' competitive advantage and professional status (ASA, 1997, p. 5). In the explanations related to its objectives, the Society added that it expected its members to be well trained, up-to-date experts who had high levels of education and who participated in ongoing professional development (ASA, 1997).

In 1997, the Society signed an agreement with the Capital University of Economics and Business in Beijing, which made it possible for Chinese students to study Deakin University's Master of Professional Accounting program in China, which incorporated the CPA program. The Society was the first international body to enter into such an agreement with the Chinese Institute of Certified Public Accountants (ASA, 1997). In 1997, the Society prepared 88 submissions to various governments, including making representations to the Australian Tax Office on matters affecting the profession (ASA, 1997). The CPA Online system was offering online services for its members to access 300,000 catalogues from the library, including, for instance, news affecting the profession, employment opportunities and tax rulings (ASA, 1997). In 1997, the Society arranged 1,222 events in Australia and Asia on issues related to the accounting profession (ASA, 1997). Both bodies were making significant developments and advances in their own right. The next section provides an overview of their joint work on matters of mutual interest.

9.1.3 Joint Work

In addition to making progress on different fronts separately, both bodies continued their mutual work on common matters affecting the profession. The Institute president wrote in his message that the Society and the Institute were extending cooperation in several areas, including the quality review process that each body conducted for its own organisation (Taylor, 1991c). The 1992 annual report of the Society provided greater details of areas of joint work, which included accounting standards, international representation, education and other areas of mutual interest, such as a campaign to limit the liability of auditors (ASA, 1992). In 1992, the Society and the Institute revised the terms of their joint standing committee, adding four compulsory meetings of the combined executive committees in one year to facilitate cooperation and understanding between the two bodies (ICAA, 1992). In his annual message, the president of the Society briefed members about joint work with the Institute concerning the setting of accounting standards (ASA, 1993).

In 1993, the Institute reported in its annual report that both bodies were extending the cooperative efforts that were put in place in 1992. The joint standing committee included the full executive committees of both bodies and it met every three months, both formally and informally in an open forum (ICAA, 1993). The joint standing committee was responsible for ensuring the adoption of a joint approach on matters of importance to the accounting profession, including areas such as accounting standards, international affairs, limitation of auditor's liability, quality control, accounting education and many other technical matters (ICAA, 1993).

In 1994, the Society and the Institute together established the Urgent Issues Group (UIG) initiative. According to the Society's 1994 annual report, the UIG would "seek to anticipate problems affecting financial reporting practices in Australia and to provide timely guidance on interpretation of existing accounting standards and guidance on the treatment of emerging issues" (ASA, 1994, p. 15). In 1995, the Society and the Institute agreed to work on a policy for the harmonisation of national accounting standards with the international accounting standards. Both bodies also agreed that while working on such harmonisation, no compromise would be made to the Australian standards. It was agreed that accounting standards would be prepared in such a way that they met domestic needs as well as achieved automatic compliance with international standards (ASA, 1995). The Society and the Institute continued to fund the Australian Accounting Research Foundation (ASA 1996). In 1996, the Society developed and released CPA Vision 2020. This vision document identified eight key "member values" to address: status, competitive advantage, skills currency, information support, representation, personal growth, career progression and fellowship (ASA, 1996).

9.1.4 Membership and Financial Situation

Table 9.1 provides details of the Society's membership and depicts its growth from 1991 to 1998.

In 1992, 81 per cent of Society members were male and 19 per cent were female. Victoria represented 31 per cent of total members while New South Wales represented 28 per cent of members, followed by the other states (ASA, 1992, p. 16). Victoria's share of Australia's national population was 25.5 per cent; hence, the state was over-represented in the membership of the Society by about 6 percentage points. In contrast, the population of New South Wales was 34 per cent of the Australian population (ABS, 1992), revealing that of New South Wales was under-represented in terms of its membership share by 6 percentage points. In 1992, MIPP and MNIPP of the Society accounted for 21 per cent and 69.5 per cent of its total members, respectively, with retired members at 9.5 per cent (ASA, 1992, p. 16). The share of members in Victoria

Table 9.1 Society membership

SN	*Year*	*Members*	*Growth (%)*
1	1991	62,465	
2	1992	65,539	4.92
3	1993	68,929	5.17
4	1994	73,460	6.57
5	1995	77,721	5.80
6	1996	81,082	4.32
7	1997	84,116	3.74
8	1998	86,881	3.29

Source ASA Annual Report, 1991–1998

fell to 29 per cent in 1994 and that of New South Wales to 27 per cent, reflecting increased membership from other states and overseas. The share of female members increased to 22 per cent in 1994, while MIPP was also at 22 per cent (ASA, 1994, p. 18).

By 1995, there were 10,000 Society members based in Asia, which led to the development of the Asian division. Victoria's membership share of the Society fell to 28 per cent in 1995, and female membership represented 24 per cent. The MIPP portion was steady at 22 per cent (ASA, 1995). The annual report of 1996 showed that 23 per cent of the Society's 81,082 members were below the age of 30, while 52 per cent of members were aged less than 40 years (ASA, 1996). In 1997, of the total membership of the Society, the share of Victoria was 27 per cent and that of New South Wales was 26 per cent. Female members constituted 27 per cent of the total membership, while MIPP was at 22 per cent (ASA, 1997, p. 17). In 1998, 29 per cent of the Society members were female, which reveals a trend of increased representation of females in the accounting profession; the same year showed 19 per cent MIPP, which was a decrease from 1997 when MIPP represented 22 per cent (ASA, 1998 p. 14). In 1999, female members rose to 30 per cent, CPAs were 47 per cent and MIPP fell to 17 per cent. Further, 23 per cent of members were below 30 years of age and 51 per cent below 50 (ASA, 1999b, p. 29). Overall, membership of the Society increased, as shown in Table 9.1, but the share of MIPP decreased, which presented further strength to the arguments of the Institute members who opposed a merger with a body that mainly represented MNIPP.

Table 9.2 provides details of the Institute's membership and depicts its growth from 1991 to 1998.

Table 9.2 The institute members

SN	*Year*	*Members*	*Growth (%)*
1	1991	21,219	
2	1992	22,633	6.66
3	1993	24,011	6.09
4	1994	25,350	5.58
5	1995	27,240	7.46
6	1996	29,403	7.94
7	1997	29,798	1.34
8	1998	30,868	3.59
9	1999	32,429	5.06

Source ASA (1991–1999), ICAA (1991–1999)

In 1992, 44 per cent of the Institute members were from New South Wales, while 24 per cent of its members were from Victoria (ICAA, 1992, p. 22). As stated above, Victoria had a 25.5 per cent share and New South Wales a 34 per cent share of the Australian population (ABS, 1992). This shows that Victoria was slightly under-represented in terms of its share in the total membership of the Institute, while New South Wales was over-represented by 10 percentage points. In 1992, 19.5 per cent of members were below 30 years of age, while 55 per cent of members were below 40 years. MIPP represented 32 per cent of the total membership, employees in public practice 23 per cent and the remaining 45 per cent comprised MNIPP (ICAA, 1992, p. 23). The numbers of MIPP of the Institute and employees in public practice are comparable with the Society's MIPP because that figure also consisted of employees in public practice. For example, as discussed earlier in this chapter, the Society's MIPP were 21 per cent in 1992, but this figure also included employees in public practice. Conversely, MIPP and employees in public practice combined in the case of the Institute was 55 per cent.

According to the Institute's 1998 annual report, by that year the female share in the Institute's membership was 20.5 per cent (ICAA, 1998). In 1999, theInstitute's MIPP decreased to 46 per cent from 55 per cent in 1992. This number included both principals and employees in public practice (ICAA, 1999). This means that by the time the fourth merger attempt was mounted, for the first time the Institute did not have a majority of MIPP. It is reasonable to expect that this might have created a more favourable circumstance for the Institute's members to support a merger with the Society. However, the outcome shows that not even the

Table 9.3 The society revenue and Surplus/Deficit

Year	*Revenue/Income ($AU)*	*Deficit/surplus ($AU)*	*Deficit/Surplus (% of Revenue)*
1991	34,312,000	519,000	1.51
1992	36,230,000	656,000	1.81
1993	39,420,000	1,024,000	2.60
1994	42,141,000	1,217,000	2.89
1995	44,227,000	(944,000)	−2.13
1996	45,759,000	(2,734,000)	−5.97
1997	51,835,000	2,962,000	5.71
1998	56,391,000	2,542,000	4.51
1999	64,874,000	2,003,000	3.09

Source ASA (1991–1999)

MNIPP supported a merger. The Society also had higher female representation at 30 per cent in 1999; as aforementioned, female membership of the Institute was 20.5 per cent in 1998.

Table 9.3 shows the Society's revenue and the total surplus or deficit in dollars and as a percentage of revenue for the years 1991 to 1999.

Between 1991 and 1994, during a four-year period, the Society earned a moderate surplus and the surplus increased slowly. However, the next two years saw the Society record a deficit of $AU944,000 in 1995 and a deficit in excess of $AU2.7 million in 1996. David Boymal was treasurer of the Society in 1997 and discovered the reasons behind this staggering deficit. In his oral history interview, he stated:

> The CPAs [Society] had got themselves into some financial difficulty. Well, it wasn't long-term financial difficulty, they had a bad year, which was a result of mismanagement and I then was Treasurer in the year that we had to put things right. The CPA would get commissions arising from whenever an insurance bit [contract] was sold or a computer was sold or anything else from a service provider to a member which is introduced by the CPA. The marketing manager hadn't lined up those commissions and they were accounting the year before for anticipation to receiving commissions and the commissions weren't forthcoming because they'd messed it up.

Table 9.4 The institute revenue and Surplus/Deficit

Year	*Revenue/Income ($AU)*	*Deficit/Surplus ($AU)*	*Deficit/Surplus (% of Revenue)*
1991	22,265,000	1,348,000	6.05
1992	23,430,000	1,485,000	6.34
1993	24,827,000	1,095,000	4.41
1994	26,727,000	207,000	0.77
1995	29,623,000	586,000	1.98
1996	32,838,000	1,937,000	5.90
1997	34,844,000	1,394,000	4.00
1998	38,275,000	1,178,000	3.08
1999	41,256,000	1,135,000	2.75

Source ICAA (1991–1999)

Over the next three years, the financial situation of the Society improved; it recovered from the financial problems and registered a surplus of 5.71, 4.51 and 3.09 per cent of revenue in 1997, 1998 and 1999, respectively.

Table 9.4 shows the Institute's revenue and total surplus or deficit in dollars and as a percentage of revenue for the years 1991 to 1999.

Between 1991 and 1993, the Institute's financial situation was quite strong, while 1994 and 1995 registered a surplus of only 0.77 and 1.98 per cent of revenue, respectively. However, in 1996, the surplus was 5.9 per cent, while after that there was a steady decrease in the size of the surpluses, in both dollar and percentage terms, despite revenue increasing in each year. In 1997, 1998 and 1999, the surplus was at 4.0, 3.08 and 2.75 per cent of the total revenue, respectively. Overall, for the period covered by the two tables, the Institute's financial results were much better than the Society's. The average surplus of the Institute was 3.9 per cent of revenue, while the comparable figure of the Society was only 1.6 per cent. The next section discusses the merger attempt process and its outcome.

9.2 Merger Attempt

The earliest mention of the fourth merger attempt was in Brian Waldron's report to members in September 1991, which stated National Council at its August meeting in Canberra passed a resolution to reaffirm the Society's support for a single body to represent the profession (Waldron,

1991a). However, despite this early discursive argument in support of another merger attempt, the actual formal discussion and initiation of a merger attempt did not occur until much later. The documentary evidence shows that it was early in 1998 when both bodies started formal talks about the merger attempt. This is verified by articles in accounting journals that covered the public announcements (Anon, 1998f, 1998j, 1998m). David Boymal, president of the Society at the time of fourth merger attempt, affirmed this in his oral history interview of 8 February 2016. By 1996, both organisations were engulfed in a branding war. As one of the articles published in *Charter* mentioned:

> The branding war was the cause of great angst in the past two years. It escalated with the very public brawl between the Institute and the Society in July 1996 over the strengths and weaknesses of the CPA program and the ICA Professional Year. (Anon, 1998l, p. 7)

The initial informal discussions started on the initiative of Rob Ward with Denis Cortese during the International Accounting Congress in Paris in 1997. Ward argued that the merger proposal had emerged by default because of the increasing number of joint projects being undertaken by both bodies, including work on the registration and regulation of auditors (Anon, 1998l). Ward stated that the bodies had already made 57 joint submissions to the government, which demonstrated a capacity over the past few years to formulate a common position (Farnham, 1998). This fact shows that in the views of both bodies and their leaders the traditional boundaries were blurring and both bodies were open to negotiating and redrawing them (Allen, 1997). After an initial discussion in Paris, both presidents agreed that a merger was a good idea but neither made any comment on the prospect of merger talks in any form until a formal approach was made by the Institute to the Society for serious merger discussions (Anon, 1998l).

Both presidents then tested support for another merger attempt during meetings of the state councils of both bodies for one month. By means of a media release on 18 March 1998, both organisations made a public announcement regarding the formation of a JTF to finalise details on a proposal for a merger between them (Anon, 1998j, 1998k; Dowling, 1998; Lawson, 1998a). The JTF had seven members: four from the Society and three from the Institute. This team spent six weeks developing the proposals (Farnham, 1998). The joint standing committee representing both bodies endorsed the plan to explore opportunities for greater cooperation and the possibility of a merger to create a new professional association (Farnham, 1998). After attending the World Accounting Congress in Paris in 1997, Ward stated:

> Accounting bodies overseas fail to understand why Australia has two main accounting bodies given the size of its marketplace. Two organisations in a country of this size competing against each other is a waste of resources; we can leverage better together. (Anon, 1998l, p. 7)

This was a discursive claim to build ground before the merger announcement was made so that members of both bodies did not receive a surprise. The comment also indicates that the Institute was modifying its traditional strategy of exclusivity, which was a firm basis for gaining the Royal Charter and elite status for its members (Macdonald & Ritzer, 1988). In March, Boymal wrote in the *Australian CPA* that the joint negotiating team of both bodies had finalised a merger proposal for members' consideration (Boymal, 1998a). As per the proposals, the combined national council would comprise members of the state and national councils of both bodies. From the date of merger, the size of the state and the national councils would be reduced through an annual election in the next four years.

The key elements of the merger proposal included:

- formation of a new professional body of 110,000 members to be called the Institute of Chartered Professional Accountants of Australia
- option to CPAs and CAs to adopt the new designation of Chartered Professional Accountant (CHPA) or use two designations, including the old designation
- development of a new common professional entry program based on the revised CPA program and the Institute's PY program after the year 2000, while ensuring international recognition for the new program, especially in the US, the UK and Asia
- equal representation for existing institutions in a transitional governance structure, which would be phased out within four years
- restriction on increase of CPA membership fees above the inflation level and reduction of CA membership fees to the level of CPA

membership fees by July 1999, with the progressive reduction of current CA Public Practice fees in three years (Anon, 1998b)

Farnham (1998) stated that a key feature of the current proposal, and a difference with previous proposals, was that the current member designations would be retained. The rationale behind allowing members to keep both titles was to attract more members to vote in favour of the proposed merger proposal (Thomas, 1998a). The JTF met for the first time on 27 March 1998 with the objective of starting work on the draft merger proposal, which was later released in July 1998 for members' voting. The merger proposal was named "Project Newpro". This name was chosen to assist in effectively selling the idea of merger to the members of both bodies. At this meeting, it was decided to take a further six weeks to finalise the merger proposal and for the voting to be undertaken in September 1998 (Anon, 1998l). In fact, in a single meeting, most decisions were taken. The merger proposals had a preliminary period from 1 July to 11 August 1998 when members were asked to send feedback either by calling a special telephone line (1300 366 999) or via Internet, email or the websites of both organisations (Anon, 1998b). Both organisations held briefing sessions throughout Australia and at overseas locations to allow members to express their views and ask questions (Anon, 1998b).

During May 1998 in an interview with the *Australian CPA*, Boymal responded to a question about how the fourth merger proposal was different from the earlier merger proposals. Boymal stated that the plan was to bring the two organisations together through the establishment of a new professional body, which both memberships would join (Anon, 1998a). Boymal added that both organisations were planning to move quickly on the fourth merger attempt (Anon, 1998a). The merger, in fact, was not a merger of two bodies, but involved the bringing together of two separate organisations with their different titles. So, unlike the first two merger attempts where all the Society members and in the case of third merger attempt Society members with more than 10 years' experience could adopt the CA title in the event of an agreed merger, the fourth merger proposition had additional leverage.

As the boundary management literature shows, the fourth merger attempt proposal was not altering the traditional boundaries of both bodies completely; rather, new boundaries were drawn and expanded (Allen, 2001). The original boundaries between the Institute and Society members would blur in the case of the fourth merger attempt. The negotiated boundaries would keep a distinction between those members of the new organisation who would continue to call themselves CA, CPA or CHPA. This was the result of negotiated boundaries between the two bodies, which were proposed to be redrawn from around two titles to around three titles (Carmel, 2006). In a study of health professionals, Carmel (2006) found that when boundaries within an intensive care unit blurred, new boundaries at the organisational level, especially between senior nurses and junior doctors, emerged. Similarly, after the proposed merger, the boundaries between the CAs and CPAs would blur, but new boundaries would be negotiated with the new title of CHPA.

The fourth merger attempt attracted support from some high-profile personalities as well. This included John Shanahan, the Deloitte Touche Tohmatsu audit partner, who stated that the merged body could push to have a financial reporting panel in Australia, similar to the UK. The accounting profession was facing challenges from the legal profession, and the financial reporting panel would assist in solving the jurisdictional disputes between accounting and legal professionals with regard to the corporation law (Anon, 1998l). During late March and April, Institute members were asked to send their views on the idea of the proposed merger and the Institute received 40 merger-related messages via letters, emails and website submissions. An overview of members' reactions was presented in an article that stated the letters suggested the joint merger task force had a long way to go before it succeeded in wooing enough Institute members to vote "Yes" (Anon, 1998m).

In July 1998, the preliminary merger proposal was sent to the members of both bodies seeking their reactions to the actual proposal. It was sent in a booklet form titled "*Towards a new era—Preliminary Proposal for the creation of a new Accounting Body for Australia*". This was followed by four rounds of quantitative research involving 4,000 members of both bodies, who were surveyed by telephone interview between May and September 1999 (ICAA, 1999). Worthington DiMarzio performed this research. The surveys included an equal number of members from both bodies (Anon, 1999b). After a few rounds of surveys of members, and especially the Institute members, it was estimated that support for the merger was at just more than 50 per cent. This led to a potential delay in the merger vote, which was originally planned for October 1999 (Gettler, 1998a). After the preliminary period, the national council of the Society met on 10 August and analysed the outcomes of the joint market research, which had shown that support from the Institute members had increased; however, it was still not sufficient for a merger to succeed. Therefore, it was decided to meet again in September and decide whether to go ahead with the vote (Anon, 1998c). This allowed the Institute to promote further the merger proposal to its members to increase the prospects of success (Anon, 1998c, 1998g). One of the four preliminary research surveys involving 1,400 Institute members showed that support for the merger attempt was insufficient for it to be likely to be able to proceed (Thomas, 1998c). Speaking of the survey of members, David Boymal, president of the Society and Rob Ward, president of the Institute jointly stated:

> We were determined not to proceed to a vote without a strong indication of its likely success. It is very pleasing, therefore, to see that research has indicated that it has the necessary majority support. (Anon, 1998o, p. 1)

Both bodies also released a joint media statement about the decision to delay the merger discussions with members (ASA & ICAA 1998c). The media release mentioned:

> While CPAs are clearly in support of a merger, there is still a relatively large proportion of Chartered Accountants who have moved from 'no' to 'undecided' indicating that the advantages of merging are being recognised but that more time is needed to cement a 'yes' vote. The National Councils have agreed to extend by one month the time for promoting the benefits of the merger so that in the best interests of the profession the merger is given a good chance of succeeding. (ASA & ICAA, 1998c, p. 1)

Earlier, Boymal had changed the discourse and made it clear that going ahead with a vote and failing was worse than not going ahead with vote. Boymal further added:

> Neither party wants egg on its face from being rebuffed by the other. Last time each body turned its back on the other and went back into the bunkers, leaving little cooperation in place. This time, if voting is aborted we will each be able to continue joint planning and activities. (Thomas, 1998a, p. 84)

According to Boymal, it was better to abort the discussion and continue to work in a coordinated manner than go ahead with a potential to fail, which could also have a negative impact on the relationship between both bodies (Thomas, 1998a).

The 1999 annual report of the Institute claimed that by the last round of research the number of members indicating that they would vote yes was in excess of the two-thirds majority required for the proposal to succeed (ICAA, 1999). The same section of the Institute's annual report also claimed that during this period the number of members who were opposed to merger and were planning to vote "No" had dropped to half (ICAA, 1999), while an earlier round of market research showed that 61 per cent planned to vote "Yes" (Anon, 1999a, p. 12). It was claimed that the more information members received from the Institute, the more likely they would be to not vote against the merger (ICAA, 1999). The last round of research showed that 92 per cent of members of the Institute were planning to vote, with 68 per cent supporting the merger (Anon, 1999b, p. 12). After the last round of research, the Society decided to make a public announcement on September 17 about going ahead with the vote on the proposed merger.

Despite these encouraging surveys, the executive director of the Institute, Stephen Harrison, stated the vote was impossible to predict (Leon, 1998b). Leon (1998b, p. 36) noted that members of the Institute in the past had claimed that the Society's postgraduate course was no match for the Institute's PY standards of eligibility for public practice. Hence, the differences in education standards had proved a stumbling block in previous merger attempts (Leon, 1998b). However, Ward continued to work to convince members of the Institute to vote in support of the merger attempt. Ward made strong discursive arguments:

> The new body will equip members to compete in the global arena of business. It will enable them to stay in front of the change process and advances in technology, increasing competition from other professions and specialisation, and will address the diverse needs of emerging member groups. Key benefits such as improved resources for researching; developing and delivering better targeted services to members; strong local and global brand positioning; and a more powerful voice with government and in the community. Members in commerce who now vie with MBAs and economists for the top finance spots will also benefit from higher recognition, a stronger brand and programs more keenly targeted to their areas of special interest than is possible with two separate bodies. (cited in Anon, 1998i, p. 12)

Ward summarised multiple benefits of a merger, and identified a factor that was absent from previous merger attempts: the competition that accountants faced from other professions, such as law, economics and management (Wildman, 1998). Some Institute members had concerns about the dilution of quality in the Institute's PY program. Responding to such concerns, Ward, who was also a former National Education Committee chairperson, stated:

> As a PY graduate and a past chairman of the New South Wales and National Education Committees, I was naturally keen to ensure that the very best education programme was proposed for the new body. In fact, the new education programme, which will kick off in January 2001 after a two-year transition period, will represent current best practice so that international recognition and reciprocal membership rights are not only retained but enhanced. The new programme will be benchmarked against the highest standards of international recognition. (Anon, 1998i, p. 12)

With this public discourse, Ward tried to convince members who were arguing that the education standards of the Society were lower than those of the Institute. Meanwhile, the Institute's deputy President, Rob Atkinson, presented further convincing arguments to members stating that members could use two designations and explaining that in the marketplace, people tend to differentiate by performance and reputation, not by designation. Atkinson also added that those who had completed the PY would always enjoy its standing as an industry benchmark (Anon, 1998i, p. 12).

Finally, the deadlines for merging the two bodies were planned as follows:

- September to October: All final details relating to the explanatory statements were to be completed with relevant legal details related to the merger proposal.
- Late October: A meeting of members was to be convened to vote on the merger proposal.
- Early November: An explanatory statement, including details on merger proposals, was to be sent to members.

- Early December: A special general meeting of members would be called to approve or reject the proposal (Anon, 1998d).

The categories of members in the merged body would be Fellow Chartered Professional Accountant (FCHPA), Chartered Professional Accountant (CHPA) and associate accountant (AA) (Anon, 1998d). Although both bodies were engaged in the merger discussions, the Society launched its new television ad campaign in June 1998 to promote the CPA program, which was in direct competition with the Institute's PY program (Anon, 1998i). In 1998, the Institute released its Visions 2020 paper, which considered the future of the Institute and provided guidance to members for future skill building, so that they could boost their client base. This plan was to go ahead with its implementation if the merger failed (Anon, 1998i).

In the November edition of the *Australian CPA*, Boymal put forward three broad advantages of a merger, which comprised (1) a better ability to face competition, (2) more resources particularly in the area of intellectual capital and education (3) and better opportunities for marketing and branding of one recognised designation (Boymal, 1998b).

9.2.1 Opposition to the Merger Attempt

A group of Institute members from Perth and New South Wales formed a committee to oppose the merger attempt. The committee was called the Opposing View Committee (OVC). Dennis Robertson, a partner with Sydney firm Weston Woodley and Robertson, was the OVC spokesman. The OVC claimed that the merger attempt was not in the best interests of Institute members and that it would severely dilute the voice of MIPP (Anon, 1998e). This was an attempt at boundary protection, in the same way that the medical profession engaged in boundary management to protect professional boundaries (Allen, 1997, 2001; Hunter, 2005). The OVC engaged in an organised public discourse to oppose the merger. Their claims were related to discourse of superiority of CAs (Annisette, 2017). Robertson argued that the Institute's MIPP would comprise only 11–12 per cent of the merged body and they would have little say or representation in the affairs of the new organisation (Anon, 1998e).

The OVC was informally called the "No Case" committee and their proposals were termed the "No Case". The OVC proponents believed that since the failure of the third merger attempt in 1991, the Society had not upgraded its education standards and it demanded that the Institute should support the OVC case equally by bearing the cost of mail to all members (Thomas, 1998d). This request was initially denied but later the Institute agreed when OVC members threatened with court action. Harvey Pickup, a partner in a small practice of three partners and 10 staff in West Perth and a member of the No Case committee stated:

> The proposal is a sell-out, particularly of younger practice and commerce members' hard-won Chartered designation and market premium. The 'yes' case is long on rhetoric and short on facts; it's all big-picture and blue-sky compared with the tangible disadvantages. We are much better organised than in the cases of previous merger voting proposals, with good networks across Australia. When we put the issues to members, many who might have been passive 'yes' voters change their minds. (Thomas, 1998d, p. 116)

The process of merger discussion and vote was brief because of the time span of nine months, which was short compared with those of the previous three merger attempts. This meant that members were not given significant opportunities to express their opinions. However, various media articles reported on interviews with members, especially the "No Case" proponents (Bufflinl, 1998; Caruana, 1998). A young female CA Susan Carter stated:

> The ASCPA has suffered losses in the last years. Why would any CA consider themselves better serviced? On a straight financial analysis, we can't see how we would be better serviced by a bigger body. Also, while the chartered designation may not be important for the Big Five—they don't even call themselves accountants anymore—there is competition between CAs and CPAs in small firms in the commercial world. (Bufflinl, 1998, p. 4)

Meanwhile, West Australian CA Frank Cornelius[1] stated the Institute was basically giving away its goodwill free of charge to the much larger and not as well placed Society (Bufflinl, 1998). He also criticised the merger attempt stating that he believed that thousands of Institute members

[1] Frank Cornelius was also a member of the Institute's national council and a partner in the Perth-based accounting firm Barrington Partners. In addition, Cornelius was chairperson of the Western Australia State Division of the Institute.

did not want merger (Anon, 1998s). A spokesperson for OVC Richard Saunders had a short article published in the November edition of the Institute's journal. Saunders wrote:

> Every aspect of the merger proposal (including the vote) has been rushed. As a result, serious and legitimate concerns of many Chartered Accountants and business people have been either ignored or inadequately addressed by the proponents of the merger. Complacency and inaction (not voting) by those members who have concerns about the merger may lead your Institute down the irreversible path to merger with the ASCPA.

A. T. Harris, an FCA from West Perth, wrote a letter to the editor of *The Australian Financial Review* opposing the merger:

> Having experienced membership of both the Institute of Chartered Accountants in Australia and the Australian Society of Certified Practising Accountants, it is disappointing that in the seven years since the last merger attempt the ASCPA has not endeavoured to match the ICAA's Professional Year standard of eligibility for public practice. The Australian business community is subject to national and international pressures never before experienced, and the accounting profession in general should recognise the important role played by the ICAA in setting the highest standards of public practice and behaviour, comparable to anywhere else in the world. A merger for the sake of size may erode those standards. The public wrangling and division is proof enough that the merger may not work. It should be strongly resisted. (1998, p. 22)

A young CA from Victoria Darren Stafford wrote a letter to the editor of *Charter*. Stafford commented on the proposed merger with discontent and wrote:

> Being a recent graduate of the PY program and a current group leader, I find it, at the risk of sounding an intellectual snob, unfair that I, who have been subjected to 18 months of rigorous study of the program, should be put on the same level as someone who has completed five 'multiple choice' exams, which, according to my investigations, can all be completed within a three-month timeframe!. (1998, p. 8)

Stafford (1998) added another point, stating that in the new proposed body even the members of the Society could call themselves CHPA, while he would prefer the title of CA. However, the risk was that the public would perceive him as a lesser form of accountant (Stafford, 1998). These examples of strong public discourse against the merger attempt show that the Institute members were protecting their professional identity based on distinguishing themselves from members of the Society (Annisette, 2017).

9.2.2 Merger Process

Both bodies prepared a common presentation kit to convince members to support the merger proposal. The presentation had eight slides, an eight-minute video, speaking notes and a copy of the preliminary proposal (ASA & ICAA, 1998a). The kit also included the suggested format for presentations, which started with a welcome, followed by the video, the slide presentation of about six minutes and a presentation of about five minutes by the proponents of No Case. This was to be followed by a discussion of 20 minutes or more (ASA & ICAA, 1998a). The kit also provided the details of No Case and pointed out:

> We are obliged to present a balanced case to members. The national councils of the ICAA and ASCPA are in full support of the proposal but we know there will be members who oppose some aspects. Please provide any representative of the No Case who wishes to speak with an introduction and ample time (say 5–6 minutes to put their case). (ASA & ICAA, 1998a, p. 2)

The benefits to members from the merger of the two bodies were listed as follows, with arguments that the merged body would have more resources and capabilities to achieve them:

- status and recognition
- education and training
- global recognition
- standards
- advocacy
- marketing
- intellectual capital (ASA & ICAA,1998b, pp. 4–5)

The draft merger proposal included various arguments for representation of the Australian accounting profession by a single body, starting with the ability to provide better marketing of the services provided by accountants. Further, it noted that the combined resources of both organisations would provide intellectual resources to develop new products and services, which members could offer to their clients in a rapidly changing business environment. Stronger advocacy on behalf of the profession was also a key argument advanced, especially when dealing with Australian governments and representing the national accounting profession at the international level. Competition from the non-accounting profession was given a greater emphasis (ASA & ICAA, 1998c). The proposal stated:

> Our profession is also under threat from outside. The demand for services traditionally provided by accountants is increasingly being met by competitors from outside the profession. In 5–10-years' time the current level of competition from lawyers, economists, engineers, business consultants and information specialists will be far greater than today. All accountants, whether CAs or CPAs, need a single powerful body representing their interest in this more open and competitive environment. (ASA & ICAA, 1998c, p. 2)

9.2.3 Merger Proposal Vote

Early in November 1998, the merger proposal was sent to members of both bodies. In an article in *The Age*, Leon (1998a) stated that the proposed body, the Institute of Chartered Professional Accountants in Australia, would protect and promote the professional path of accountants more effectively by bringing the two bodies together. This was a descriptive comment that provided the basic details of the merger arrangement. The Institute members voted on the merger proposal at a meeting in Sydney on 14 December, while the Society members voted in Melbourne on the same day. The closing date for sending proxies was 4 pm on 11 December (Anon, 1998d, 1998h). The merger vote was covered briefly by press all over Australia (Leon, 1998c). The result was that out of those members who voted, only a minority 41 per cent of Institute members voted in favour of the merger, while in the Society, 90 per cent of members voted in favour of the merger attempt (Gettler, 1998b). The Institute reported in its 1999 annual report that "Just over 6,000 members voted in favour, while nearly 9,000 voted against with just over 50% voted in total" (ICAA, 1999, p. 4).

Institute President, Rob Atkinson was not looking back at the failure of this fourth merger attempt and was hopeful about working with the Society on matters of mutual interest.

9.3 Discussion and Analysis

This section provides responses to the research questions. Two significant findings emerge from this chapter: (1) the traditional organisational strategies of both bodies were modified (2) and Institute members were once again successful in protecting the Institute's boundaries and, consequently, the different organisational strategies of each body were preserved. These respective findings are discussed in conjunction with four of the five research questions of this study.

9.3.1 Reasons for Mounting the Merger Attempt

The first research question concerned the reasons for mounting the fourth merger attempt between the Society and the Institute. In other words, the first question was based on identifying reasons that led to changes in the traditional organisational strategies of both bodies. Boymal summarised the reasons for mounting the fourth merger attempt, which included arguments such as:

> Having one body speak on behalf of the profession, rather than two bodies. Remove competition in recruiting people to the profession. Reduce promotional costs that focused purely on recruiting people to one or the other brand. (2016)

One of the arguments for mounting the merger attempt was a perceived threat of competition from the legal, economics and other professions (Thomas, 1998b, 1998c; Wildman, 1998). Similar to the earlier three merger attempts, the first step for the fourth merger attempt was also taken by the Institute; Boymal endeavoured to explain why:

> The CPAs were spending a huge amount of money on marketing and the Institute was therefore required to react or respond to that and so they too must have been spending huge amounts. When you say huge amounts I mean many millions of marketing to counter the very strong marketing of the CPAs. That may have been the financial incentive, but I think more

likely the institute having seen that bad result of the CPAs in the two years prior, probably saw it as a once in a lifetime opportunity to make an approach to the CPAs when they thought the CPAs were financially weakened and therefore may have been more obliged or forced to respond. So, I think it was more opportunistic than the chartered themselves being under pressure. They thought the CPAs were under pressure and I think that's why they made the approach.

As discussed in Sect. 9.2.3 and presented in Table 9.3, the Society suffered deficits of $AU944,000 and $AU2.7 million consecutively in 1995 and 1996. In his oral history interview, Boymal argued that the Institute leaders thought that this was their opportunity to approach the Society. Additionally, both bodies engaged in ongoing joint work. This included work done by the joint standing committee on matters affecting the accounting profession, such as standards setting, international representation of the Australian accounting profession (ICAA, 1993) and the establishment of the UIG (ASA, 1994). Ward had argued that the merger attempt was a logical progression as both bodies were involved in many joint projects and had made 57 joint submissions (Anon, 1998l; Farnham, 1998).

9.3.2 *Strategies Adopted by Both Bodies in the Merger Attempt*

The second research question concerns strategies adopted by the Society and the Institute in each of the four merger attempts. First, unlike in the previous mergers, the Society leaders were not very enthusiastic initially. Boymal stated, that if there were signs in preliminary polling that the vote may be too close to call, as occurred in 1991, the Society would abort the process (Thomas, 1998a). This was based on the fact that the first three merger attempts were overwhelmingly supported by members of the Society, but all these three merger attempts were voted down by members of the Institute. Boymal further stated:

> There were many reservations on the CPA side because of the past failures and, it's really ironic but we stated to the Institute, we would only proceed if polls indicated that it was going to work. (2016)

This shows that for the first time in merger negotiations, the Society set some conditions to avoid facing a similar situation to that faced during the first three merger attempts. Both bodies formed a JTF with seven members, four from the Society and three from the Institute, to develop merger proposals. As discussed earlier, both bodies jointly produced a video supporting the "Yes" case, featuring different accountants who were involved in a range of professional accounting work, such as a partner in the Big Five audit firms, a suburban public practitioner, a commercial accountant, an office bearer involved in government work and a young member (Thomas, 1998b).

To convince members to support the merger attempt, a joint newspaper advertisement was placed in papers across Australia along with an open and brief letter containing the names of 31 leading accounting professionals, including the former presidents of both bodies, Professor Philip Brown, Professor Murray Wells and David Crawford (the national chairperson of KPMG) (Thomas, 1998b). The aim of the advertisement and letter was to send a message, especially to Institute members, that the fourth merger attempt had widespread support from different sections of accounting professionals involved in many types of accounting work (Gettler, 1998a).

Other strategies adopted by both bodies included gaining support from institutions and well-known personalities. For example, the Big Five firms came on board to support the merger attempt (Boymal, 2016). To introduce the issue of merger, Ward stated that a country of Australia's size did not need two organisations competing for resources (Anon, 1998l, p. 7). The deputy president of the Society, Rob Atkinson, dismissed claims that the merger was driven by the Big Five firms and argued that members involved in all types of accounting work were driving the merger (Anon, 1998i, p. 12). This appears to have been a strategy to gain members' support because the outcome of the vote showed that these were claims made only by leaders of the Institute. Similarly, Ward made attempts to sell the merger to members claiming that a single professional body would have greater resources to meet the challenges of technology and globalisation.

To develop members' interest in supporting the merger attempt, the Institute initially ignored the OVC demands. The group then threatened court action, which caused the Institute's leadership to change its strategy from completely ignoring the demands to acknowledging the existence of the active and organised opposition to the merger attempt by the Institute members (Anon, 1998e). The draft merger proposal was used to argue the merger case by citing reasons of better service quality, lobbying power and international representation (ASA & ICAA, 1998c). These strategies were used to gain support for changes in traditional strategies and for changing the boundaries of the Institute, which were based on membership of that body.

Although the aim was to convince members of the Institute to support the fourth merger attempt, the merger proposals in fact ensured that except for the existing members of the Institute, no new members could call themselves CAs, which was an issue of contention. So, members of the Society could either use the new title CHPA, standing for Chartered Professional Accountant, or CPA, or use both the new and the old designations. In other words, unlike previous attempts, in the event of a successful merger vote, Society members would not use the title CA. Similarly, Institute members could use their existing title of CA or the new title. This strategy was used to gain support from members of the Institute.

9.4 Reasons for Merger Attempt Failure

There are two aspects in the analysis when responding to the third research question. First, there was detachment between leaders and members of the Institute (Lee, 2010; Shackleton & Walker, 2001). Second, the members of the Institute engaged in boundary protection work and sought to preserve the existing boundaries.

Boymal stated that the key reason for failure was that young members did not support the merger, which shows the detachment of the leadership from members. Boymal (2016) stated:

> I think it's probably fair to say that they [CAs] put in much more hours to get their qualification than the CPA member. So the Institute people, particularly the young people who had just done the course had come to their own conclusion that they had put in a lot harder work than had sort of the equivalent CPA member and therefore they were better and the Institute had been promoting in its marketing this whole idea that it was the superior accounting body, it had the most stringent education and the others weren't anywhere near it in quality.

Historical reasons that had led to the formation of two bodies initially and then led to the failure of the first three merger attempts also contributed to the failure of the fourth merger attempt. In most cases, archival documents available for both bodies did not contain information about

Table 9.5 Institute members voting "Yes" (%)

Years of Membership	*NSW*	*VIC*	*QLD*	*SA/NT*	*WA*	*TAS*	*ACT*	*Total*
0–5	26.6	35.6	29.8	34.5	19.5	43.9	45.1	28.6
6–10	32.3	45.5	42.8	42.9	24.2	62.2	63.2	36.8
11–15	39.7	52.7	52.3	47.3	36	70.6	63.4	44.4
16–25	45.8	55.6	54.5	58.1	46.4	70.4	53.3	52.9
26 +	49.9	59.3	54.5	58.1	46.4	70.4	53.3	52.9
Total	37.9	48	43.9	48.1	30.2	61.9	54.3	40.6

Source Anon (1999b, p. 12)

detailed voting patterns. However, the Institute had recorded voting patterns based on states and age of membership for the fourth merger attempt, as presented in Table 9.5.

Table 9.5 provides an analysis that shows that members who had shorter periods of membership showed less support for the merger proposal, while the highest support was among members who had more than 11, 16 or 26 years of membership. The lowest overall support for the merger was from Western Australia, while the second lowest was from New South Wales. This outcome of the vote and strong opposition from Institute members in Western Australia and New South Wales was also reflected in the views of the Institute members presented via letters and arguments of organised campaigns, which were run mainly in Western Australia against the proposed merger (Anon, 1998m; Harris, 1998; Stafford, 1998). Boymal (2016) also stated that the new president of the Institute was not as enthusiastic as the previous president:

> Look I suppose in truth the enthusiasm of Rob Ward wasn't with the next president [Rob Atkinson]. I think with all things like that it has to come from the top, it has to come from the leadership and if the leadership gives any indication of not being enthusiastic then it sorts of feeds. I was enthusiastic but my counterpart in the Institute was nowhere near as enthusiastic as Rob Ward. Although they kept going with it and the CPAs kept putting pressure on them... they painted themselves into a corner—I think a corner that was hard for them to extract themselves from. So it ended up that I... more by default than anything else, ended up being the main pusher of it.

Hence, Boymal highlighted that lack of strong leadership to advocate the Institute's view was a reason for the failure of last merger attempt. Boymal

(2016) identified another factor around the competitive advantage of having the CA title:

> There was one other factor though and that is something that we hadn't quite appreciated and it was probably more apparent in Western Australia than elsewhere. If you're in a country town and you've got your shingle up that says Bill Smith Chartered Accountant and his competition there is with Arthur Jones CPA... for both of them the distinguishing feature is Chartered Accountant. We hadn't quite appreciated just how deep this feeling was. I think the point that I made though which is that the value of the designation from a competition point of view in smaller towns.

Proponents of the OVC believed that the actions and process adopted for mounting the merger attempt were too fast and that the concerns of many members of the Institute were ignored (Saunders, 1998, p. 3). This was one of the reasons that had unsettled a portion of the Institute members. The arguments of the Institute members included claims that the education standards of the Society were inferior (Harris, 1998). After the failure, Boymal stated, "the problem is that the rank-and-file membership of the Institute and its leadership don't think as one and it is therefore difficult … when they talk and can't deliver" (Gettler, 1998b, p. 15). Hence, detachment of the leadership of the Institute from its members was one of the reasons for failure.

A New South Wales state councillor of the Institute, Saunders, also broke ranks and went public against the decision of his council. Saunders stated, National Council had spent over $AU1 million of members' money trying to force them to accept a minority position in new accounting body (Thomas, 1998d). This points to a detachment of leaders from members of the professional bodies, which was also visible in Britain where a central reason for various unsuccessful merger attempts was the detachment of office bearers of professional associations from rank and file members. Such detachment could be fatal, given that the ultimate authority to approve any merger scheme would vest with the members (Shackleton & Walker, 2001).

The Institute President Rob Atkinson wrote:

> While no clear answer is available as to why the result differed from the predicted outcome, the late appearance of the case against merger clearly swayed many to change their minds. The complex and lengthy documentation required by law to be sent to members was undoubtedly another

> detracting factor. I thank those who participated in the debate, took the time to vote and volunteered their views. (ICAA, 1999, p. 4)

This reveals that the Institute leaders failed to understand the mood of members accurately. As with the other three merger attempts, the leaders could not convince members of the virtue of the proposed merger and also did not realise that most members were against the proposed merger, which led them to engage in boundary protection work. Atkinson acknowledged in his statement that the leadership misread the level of support offered by the Institute members (Leon, 1998a).

9.4.1 *Reactions of Various Stakeholders*

The fourth research question concerned the reactions of various stakeholders[2] to the proposals for unification and their subsequent failures. The fourth merger attempt attracted support from big accounting firms and other well-known individuals, such as the CEO of Arthur Andersen Chris Knoblanche, who stated:

> We run the risk of looking naive to our market place if we can't get to a position where we understand what we are as a profession and represent that in a united, consistent manner. (Bufflinl, 1998, p. 4)

Another major supporter of merger, Professor Ken Leo, Head of Accounting at Curtin University, identified that young Institute members who had recently gained qualification would contribute to the failure of the merger attempt. In fact, he was right (Anon, 1998a). Professor Terry Heazlewood, Head of the School of Finance at Charles Sturt University in Wagga Wagga, stated accounting departments in Australian universities would find life much easier dealing with one large accounting body (Anon, 1998a). Heazlewood further added that a single body would mean each university would not need two staff members acting as representatives of either body (Anon, 1998a, p. 2).

When Boymal (2016) was asked about the reaction of stakeholders after the failure of merger attempt, he stated:

[2] Stakeholders include members of both professional bodies, the government, policymakers, accounting firms and investors.

> There was no reaction. The big firms I think were attracted with the reduction in the subscriptions because if you're not spending so much on marketing then you should expect some reduction in subscriptions and the big firms were in the habit of paying the membership subscription of all of their staff. So there was a reasonable amount of cost involved to the big firms and so that's why the management were in favour but, they quite obviously couldn't get their younger employees [to support the proposal] and understandably if their employees weren't paying their subscriptions then that wasn't enough of an incentive.

The failure of the merger attempt was covered by the press (Caruana, 1998; Gettler, 1998b; Lawson, 1998b; Leon, 1998a). Clearly not pleased with the outcome, the Institute's national President, Atkinson stated, it appeared the proponents of the "no" case had pitched their case on emotional grounds that the status of Chartered Accountants was at risk (Leon, 1998a). This was an attempt to modify the traditional strategies of the Institute, which were based on exclusiveness, being the underlying strategy on which the boundaries of Institute were initially constructed. Hence, when such boundaries were threatened, members engaged in boundary protection. Ultimately, it was the members who would make the final decision about whether to accept the move for merger or not. While leaders of the Institute failed to fully understand the sentiments of members, it was likely that merger would fail. Frank Cornelius, an opponent of merger and member of the Institute's national council, pointed out that there were many reasons that members of the Institute had rejected the merger, the most important being lower education standards of the Society members. Cornelius added that the Institute members were fearful of the erosion of their prized CA designation (Lawson, 1998b): in other words, the exclusive status associated with the title of CA that was developed over many decades and around which boundaries were constructed. Members of the Institute did not want to change those boundaries.

9.5 Conclusion

This chapter examined the fourth merger attempt, which was the last attempt to consolidate the Australian accounting profession. The failure of the last of the four merger attempts ended efforts across a period of four decades by the leaders of the Society and the Institute to instigate a merger. As this chapter shows, the period between initial discussions on the fourth merger and the final vote was the shortest among all four mergers. From initial discussion to merger vote, the whole process was completed within nine months, between March and December 1998.

The fourth merger attempt was unique because the merger discussions started informally between the presidents of both bodies in Paris. The Society had experienced three merger attempt failures and its leadership was not as keen as it had been in earlier merger attempts. The president of the Society openly admitted that they would like to discontinue merger discussions rather than face another failure (Thomas, 1998a). The merger vote was also extended in August one of the many surveys conducted found that there was not enough support from members.

Similar to the other three attempts, the merger discussions for the fourth attempt were initiated by the Institute and were accepted by the Society. Young members, especially from Western Australia, led a structured opposition. For this merger attempt, the Institute retained details in its voting result documents of the length of membership in years and the pattern of support for the merger. This evidence shows that younger members and those with the shortest length of membership in the Institute showed the lowest level of support for the merger attempt. The next chapter provides a comparative analysis of all the four merger attempts.

References

Allen, D. (1997). The nursing-medical boundary: A negotiated order? *Sociology of Health and Illness, 19*(4), 498–520.

Allen, D. (2001). *The changing shape of nursing practice*. Routledge.

Annisette, M. (2017). Discourse of the professions: The making, normalizing and taming of Ontario's foreign-trained accountant. *Accounting, Organizations and Society, 60*, 37–61.

Anon. (1998a, May). New national president: David Boymal. *Australian CPA*, pp. 18–19.

Anon. (1998b, August). Merger: The key points. *Australian CPA*, p. 18.

Anon. (1998c, September). Merger: Continuing progress. *Australian CPA*, p. 20.

Anon. (1998d, October). Merger: Moving on the vote. *Australian CPA*, p. 14.

Anon. (1998e, November). Members to vote on merger proposal. *Accountant*, p. 7.

Anon. (1998f, April). Australian bodies make wedding plans—again. *Accountant*, p. 2.

Anon. (1998g, September). Aussie merger put on hold. *Accountancy,* p. 10.
Anon. (1998h, April). Education—still the stumbling block. *Chartac,* p. 2.
Anon. (1998i, August). Positive response to initial merger proposals. *Charter,* p. 12.
Anon. (1998j, March 18). Accountants' olive branch. *The Daily Telegraph*, p. 8.
Anon. (1998k, June). And speaking of the merger. *Chartac,* p. 33.
Anon. (1998l). A merger codenamed 'Newpro'. *Chartac Accountancy News, 22*(265), 1, 68.
Anon. (1998m, April 10). Merger latest. *Chartac Accountancy News*, p. 2
Anon. (1998o, December 5). Bringing a merger to book. *Australian Financial Review*, p. 6.
Anon. (1999a). Summit convened after merger plans abandoned. *Charter, 70*(1), 12.
Anon. (1999b, April). Research failed to predict merger result. *Charter, 70*(2), 12.
Australian Bureau of Statistics. (1992). Australian population.
Australian Society of Accountants and The Institute of Chartered Accountants in Australia. (1998a). Towards a new era—preliminary proposal for the creation of a new accounting body for Australia, letter accompanying presentation kit, no date, 1–2.
Australian Society of Accountants and The Institute of Chartered Accountants in Australia. (1998b). Accounting merger—decision delayed, August 11, 1.
Australian Society of Accountants and The Institute of Chartered Accountants in Australia. (1998c). Preliminary proposal for the creation of a new accounting body for Australia, no date, 1–9.
Australian Society of Accountants. (1992). *Annual report*. Melbourne, Australia.
Australian Society of Accountants. (1993). *Annual report*. Melbourne, Australia.
Australian Society of Accountants. (1994). *Annual report*. Melbourne, Australia.
Australian Society of Accountants. (1995). *Annual report*. Melbourne, Australia.
Australian Society of Accountants. (1996). *Annual report*. Melbourne, Australia.
Australian Society of Accountants. (1997). *Annual report*. Melbourne, Australia.
Australian Society of Accountants. (1998). *Annual report*. Melbourne, Australia.
Australian Society of Accountants. (1999). *Annual report*. Melbourne, Australia.
Boymal, D. (1998a, July). Merger proposal finalized. *Australian CPA*, p. 3
Boymal, D. (1998b, November). Merger: Yes or no. *Australian CPA*, p. 4.
Boymal, D. (2016), Interview with David Boymal on February 8.
Bufflinl, F. (1998, November 30). It's time to take everything into account. *Australian Financial Review*, p. 4.
Carmel, S. (2006). Boundaries obscured and boundaries reinforced: Incorporation as a strategy of occupational enhancement for intensive care. *Sociology of Health & Illness, 28*(2), 154–177.

Caruana, L. (1998, December 15). Accountants' 2 into 1 won't go. *The Australian*, p. 3.

Cohn, C. (1991, May). Profile: Brian Waldron: New ASCPA national president. *Australian Accountant*, pp. 20–21.

Dowling, J. (1998, March 18). Competing accountancy bodies in merger talks. *Courier Mail*, p. 11.

Farnham, C. (1998, March). ASCPA, ICAA merger mooted. *Australian CPA*, p. 11.

Gettler, L. (1998a, August 13). Accounting bodies put off push for merger. *The Age*, p. 3.

Gettler, L. (1998b, December 12). Merger numbers fall well short. *The Age*, p. 13.

Harris, T. A. (1998, November 16). Merger could ruin standards. *Australian Financial Review*, p. 22.

Hunter, B. (2005). Emotion work and boundary maintenance in hospital-based midwifery. *Midwifery, 21*(3), 253–266.

Lawson, M. (1998a, March 18). Accountants try for merger. *Australian Financial Review*, p. 14.

Lawson, M. (1998b, December 15). Accountants give a resounding 'nay' on merger plan. *Australian Financial Review*, p. 12.

Lee, T. A. (2010). Consolidating the public accountancy profession: The case of the proposed Institute of Chartered Accountants of Great Britain, 1988–9. *Accounting History, 15*(1), 7–39.

Leon, G. (1998a, December 15). Merger numbers fall well short. *The Age*, p. 3.

Leon, G. (1998b, December 14). Accountants vote on merge. *Sydney Morning Herald*, p. 36.

Leon, G. (1998c, November 17). Deja vu for accountants. *The Age*, p. 5.

Macdonald, K. M., & Ritzer, G. (1988). The sociology of the professions: Dead or alive? *Work and Occupations, 15*(3), 251–272.

Saunders, R. (1998, November). Winners and losers. *The Bulletin,* p. 3.

Shackleton, K. & Walker, S. P. (2001). *A future for the accountancy profession: The quest for closure and integration, 1957–1970*. Institute of Chartered Accountants of Scotland.

Stafford, D. (1998, December). Letter to the editor—Proposed merger with ASCPA. *Charter,* p. 8.

Taylor, N. B. (1991b, August). Message of president. *Charter,* p. 59.

Taylor, N. B. (1991c, October). Message of president. *Charter,* p. 66.

The Institute of Chartered Accountants in Australia. (1992). *Annual report*. Australia.

The Institute of Chartered Accountants in Australia. (1993). *Annual report*. Australia.

The Institute of Chartered Accountants in Australia. (1994). *Annual report*. Australia.

The Institute of Chartered Accountants in Australia. (1995). *Annual report*. Australia.

The Institute of Chartered Accountants in Australia. (1997). *Annual report*. Australia.

The Institute of Chartered Accountants in Australia. (1998). *Annual report*. Australia.

The Institute of Chartered Accountants in Australia. (1999). *Annual report*. Australia.

Thomas, T. (1998a), Merger vote doubt, *Business Review Weekly*, April 13, p. 84.

Thomas, T. (1998b, July 13). Merger research begins. *Business Review Weekly*, p. 83.

Thomas, T. (1998c, August 17). Vote delayed to ensure yes. *Business Review Weekly*, p. 102.

Thomas, T. (1998d, November 23). Merger vote under way. *Business Review Weekly*, p. 116.

Waldron, B. (1991a, April). From the president. *The Australian Accountant*, p. 5.

Wildman, T. (1998, August). The merger principle: A means to meet challenges. 17.

CHAPTER 10

Similarities and Differences Across All Merger Attempts

10.1 Introduction

This chapter provides a comparative view of the four merger attempts, primarily considering the similarities and differences that affected failure of the merger attempts. This comparative view is provided to enable viewing these attempts from a macro perspective. A common theme across all merger attempts was that the leaders of the Institute presumably believed that their membership would support the merger proposal or could at least be persuaded to do so. However, the votes revealed, except perhaps for the third merger attempt where the voting was very close, that this presumption was seriously in error. This has been characterised as a detachment of the Institute leaders from its members (Lee, 2010; Shackleton & Walker, 2001).

While many common themes exist across each of the merger attempts, there are also some differences. For example, the process adopted to mount the merger attempts was different across the four merger attempts. In the case of first two merger attempts, subcommittees of members of both bodies were formed to consider the matter and draft the final proposals. However, for the last two merger attempts, most decisions were taken by the senior leadership, especially the presidents of the two organisations. The process of initiation of merger discussions was also different in each case. A common theme in this process was that the Institute presidents initiated all merger attempts.

J. Sidhu et al., *Understanding the Sociology of the Accounting Profession*,
https://doi.org/10.1007/978-981-99-1572-9_10

Second section of this chapter provides of key research questions across all four merger attempts. Section 10.3 provides a brief discussion of similarities and differences across the four merger attempts. This includes joint work and joint activities undertaken by both bodies from the early 1960s to the time of the final merger attempt and the period immediately after its failure. Across a period of more than three decades, cooperation between the two bodies on matters of mutual interest was a key common theme. The trend also shows that gradually both bodies were getting closer to each other while responding to professional challenges and opportunities. This section also examines a challenge that the Institute faced during the period under investigation, namely, the profile of its membership. The last section concludes this chapter.

Another common factor related to the required majority to pass the merger attempt proposals. For a merger proposal to succeed, the Institute needed the support of a two-thirds majority of members. Across all four merger attempts, the Institute members voted well below this threshold, apart from the third merger attempt that almost succeeded. However, a different voting method was used in that case, which boosted the votes of Institute members in favour of the merger attempt. In the case of the Society, the minimum requirement was 75 per cent of members voting in favour of change, which did not turn out to be an issue for any of the four merger attempts.

Apart from these common factors, there were differences as well. For example, the process adopted to mount the merger attempts was different across the four merger attempts. In the case of first two merger attempts, subcommittees of members of both bodies were formed to consider the matter and draft the final proposals. However, for the last two merger attempts, most decisions were taken by the senior leadership, especially the presidents of the two organisations. The process of initiation of merger discussions was also different in each case. A common theme in this process was that the Institute presidents initiated all merger attempts. Some other such factors are analysed in the following sections.

According to Carnegie and Napier (2012), there is significant potential for the study of accounting developments from a comparative international perspective. However, comparative accounting history also has the potential to expand into the study of accounting history across a period in a comparative social, economic and political context, such as the four unsuccessful mergers studied in this project. This is the focus of the current chapter. Section 10.2 provides a comparative analysis of responses to the four research questions, examining common themes and any differences. Chapters 6 to 9 covered the first to fourth merger attempts respectively, with a focus on the individual merger cases. This chapter provides a macro and overall analysis of the four merger attempts. In other words, this chapter has a comparative accounting history focus (Carnegie & Napier, 2002).

10.2 Comparative Analysis of Responses to the Four Research Questions

The first research question was "What were the reasons for mounting the merger attempts between the Society and the Institute?" According to Gieryn (1983), boundaries are dynamic structures that can be modified as a response to crisis and internal change and supporters of the merger proposals emphasised arguments such as the ability to speak with one voice, increased lobbying power, international representation, cost reduction and raising standards of education (Gieryn, 1983; Nancarrow & Borthwick, 2005). The reasons for mounting the four merger attempts can be summarised as deriving from external pressures and internal motivations. External pressures included the legitimacy crisis faced by the Australian accounting profession, which was a key factor across the first three merger attempts. For the first merger attempt, a legitimacy crisis had resulted from a series of corporate failures in the early to mid-1960s (Carnegie & O'Connell, 2012). Similarly, during the second merger attempt, a legitimacy crisis emerged in the early to mid-1970s after a spate of corporate collapses, specifically in the mining and finance sectors (Henderson, 1997). Before the mounting of the third merger attempt, the share market crash and related economic recession and corporate collapses once again led to a legitimacy crisis for the accounting profession (Gottliebsen, 1990; Macfarlane, 2006; Taylor, 2016). These circumstances were not visible during the fourth merger attempt, especially as the whole process lasted for a period of nine months only. These conditions indicate that a period of crisis and challenges may precipitate attempts to change professional boundaries, as creating and maintaining boundaries is particularly evident within professions, their regulation and operations.

Various internal motivations for the leaders of both bodies included the ability to speak with one voice as a united single body; a resultant incentive linked with unity was increased lobbying power in dealing with various state and federal governments (Gottliebsen, 1990; Henderson, 1997; Macfarlane, 2006; Taylor, 2016). The international representation of the Australian accounting profession by a single body was also an argument regularly presented by leaders of both bodies. Apart from these factors, other motivations included reduction in costs and in the resources being allocated to rival marketing campaigns by both bodies. Raising of the status of professional accountants was a key motivation for at least the Society leaders, but both bodies agreed on the need to raise the overall standards of accountants' education (Gottliebsen, 1990; Macfarlane, 2006; Taylor, 2016).

Research shows that relaxing a strategy of exclusiveness by allowing more members to join a professional association can enable greater market control (Macdonald & Ritzer, 1988, p. 258) and this has been quite visible in merger attempts. With the shift of focus from exclusivity to growth-oriented organisations allow more individuals to join with less strict entry requirements. This approach enables them to expand their membership base and thereby gain a greater degree of market control. A dominant common theme across all merger attempts was that a single body would have the ability to speak with one voice and thereby have stronger lobbying power (Anon, 1968b; Miller, 2015; Taylor, 2016; Thiele, 1975). The second merger attempt projected an important requirement for accounting bodies "to speak up with one voice, loud and clear" (Norgard, 1980). For the third merger attempt, the lobbying power of a united body was described as "an overriding reason to merge", along with avoiding duplication of effort and waste of resources (McGregor, 2015). Competition between the two bodies, resulting in duplication of efforts, and cost reduction factors were common across the second, third and fourth merger attempts (Boymal, 2016; Neilson, 2015). Therefore, intra-professional rivalry may lead to changes of context, which makes professional boundaries more susceptible to amendments (Nancarrow & Borthwick, 2005). These factors, whether they were internal to the bodies or driven by external forces, led to proposed changes in the professional boundaries of both bodies, which were considered potentially dynamic and flexible by leaders of both bodies (Gieryn, 1983; Nancarrow & Borthwick, 2005).

Question 2 was "What strategies were adopted by the Society and the Institute in each of the four merger attempts?" An analysis of this question across the four merger attempts shows that the mergers were mounted on the basis of modifying the traditional organisational strategies around "exclusiveness versus market control" (Macdonald & Ritzer, 1988, p. 257). Hence, changes to traditional organisational strategies were key changes proposed by both bodies across the four merger attempts. The Society was aiming at status upgrade and, thereby, modification of its traditional strategy of market control linked primarily with membership growth (Anon, 1976b; Irving, 1966). The upgrade of professional status of its members was viewed as a key motivation to merge with a perceived higher-status organisation, namely, the Institute (Anon, 1976b; Irving, 1966; Miller, 2015).

For the Institute, conversely, the portion of its MIPP was in decline, which meant the arguments of exclusiveness were becoming weaker (MIPP declined from 72 per cent in 1969 to 46 per cent in 1999) (ICAA, 1969, 1999). Contrary to its historical foundations based solely on MIPP, this share was now not enough to claim that the Institute was an organisation of public practitioners. The reasons for the mergers analysed in question one show that the leaders of the Institute were prepared to sacrifice some of the exclusive status of their members, which then led to the proposed changes in professional boundaries (Gieryn, 1983). Across all four merger attempts, the language of the Institute leaders shifted from the traditional emphasis on exclusivity in favour of inclusivity, as illustrated by the following statement: "accountancy is one undivided profession of which public practice is but one segment" (Savage, 1969, p.1). Earlier, the Institute leaders would emphasise differences, but they changed their language during the merger attempts in favour of statements such as "Unity is strength. The status of each individual accountant is related to the status and strength of the profession" (Anon, 1991b, p. 7). This change in language used, switching between claims of exclusivity and inclusivity, is explained by Gieryn (1983), who argued that demarcation is based on certain narratives.

Question 3 was, "What key factors contributed to the failure of each merger attempt?" The overall reasons for failure were common across the four merger attempts. They included the detachment of the leaders from Institute members (Lee, 2010; Shackleton & Walker, 2001) and successful boundary protection by the latter. This detachment is reflected in the statements made by members, which showed that some members were quite angry and this prompted others to express their views as well. Ultimately, Institute members demonstrated detachment by voting against its leaders' recommendations (Lee, 2010; Shackleton & Walker, 2001).

Richardson and Jones (2007) found that successful mergers of accounting associations are the result of modification of boundaries by which members of the perceived higher-status associations agree to adjust their self-image to accommodate changes relating to organisational strategy (Richardson & Jones, 2007). This was not the case for the four merger attempts because they all failed owing to insufficient support from Institute members. Across the four merger attempts, the Institute leaders failed to understand that members were not prepared to accept changes in professional boundaries to the extent necessary for a merger to proceed. The evidence shows that Institute members were detached from leaders across all four merger attempts (Lee, 2010; Shackleton & Walker, 2001), which was also reflected in public discourse by the former. For example, "We're being treated like little boys" (Anon, 1991b, p. 7), leading to the claim that "the rank-and-file membership of the Institute and its leadership don't think as one" (Gettler, 1998b, p. 15). These sentiments illuminate detachment to the extent that Institute members were quite angry at its leadership for proposing the four merger attempts. It is acknowledged, however, that the third merger attempt came close to succeeding.

Research shows that any changes to professional boundaries may precipitate resentment from members of the perceived higher-status organisations (Fournier, 2000), who may then deploy defence strategies to protect their preferred boundaries (Keohane & Milner, 1996; Milner, 1996). The common pattern across the four merger attempts is that the younger Institute members, and especially those from Western Australia, were instrumental in opposing all four mergers: see Orr (2014); McKenon (1981) and Miller (2015); Bowerman (1991b), McGregor (2015) and Taylor (2016) and Boymal (2016) for more details in this regard on the first, second, third and fourth attempts, respectively. This means those members were generally more detached and participated in boundary protection activities much more than others.

During the first merger attempt, Institute members engaged in discursive arguments that expressed sentiments such as "we are the persons to make the decision not General Council" (Anon, 1969b). Such statements reveal that some members did not consider themselves bound to follow the recommendations of the organisation's leaders (Lee, 2010; Shackleton & Walker, 2001). Boundary protection work for the first merger attempt was achieved with such discursive arguments as the claim that Institute members had worked hard to become CAs and did not want other people to benefit from the same title without the same hard work (Orr, 2014). In other words, the boundary protection was an attempt to protect the professional identity (Guo, 2012) constructed by the Institute around exclusiveness (Zerubavel, 1991).

For the second merger attempt, the leaders of the Institute again did not successfully read the mood of their members; as Miller (2015) stated, there was a "failure of Chartered leaders to understand how deeply the younger members felt". In addition to individual boundary protection work, the members engaged in organised boundary protection work, which was also the case for the first merger attempt (Anon, 1981j). For the third merger attempt, which almost succeeded, boundary protection was a well-coordinated campaign by a group of the Institute's younger members in Perth (Anon, 1991c), who even extended their discourse through published advertisements calling for Institute members to vote "No" to the merger attempt (Anon, 1991c). Therefore, the opposition by this group to boundary changes was more structured and formal and hence more effective.

The fourth merger attempt failed because of similar reasons, and members conducted the boundary protection work at a more organised level. The campaign committee was officially called the OVC, and its discursive argument was that the proposed merger was against the interests of Institute members and would dilute the voice of its MIPP because the new body would have a significant majority of MNIPP (Anon, 1998e). This was also an attempt to protect the status of MIPP and their resultant access to resources, such as higher income (Lamont & Molnár, 2002). Therefore, consistent with Gieryn (1983), the Institute members constructed labels to distinguish themselves from the Society members and successfully defended the boundaries across the four merger attempts.

The boundary protection work by the Institute members was an attempt to protect their professional identity (Guo, 2012), because boundaries "play a critical role in the process of constructing identities" (Zerubavel, 1991, p. 193) and in maintaining them. The members of the Institute repeatedly stated that the standards of Society members were lower than that of the Institute (Boymal, 2016; Miller, 2015; Orr, 2014). Boundary protection work often involves use of exclusionary labels, such as "'pseudo', 'deviant', or 'amateur'" (Gieryn, 1983 p. 792). Across the four merger attempts, the Institute members used similar labels for the Society members to oppose the merger attempts, referring to their "lower technical ability to deal with people" (Orr, 2014) and that the "merger could lead to a dilution of standards" (Anon, 1981b, p. 9) owing to lower education standards of the Society members (Leong, 1991). The demarcation between members of the Institute and the Society was based on these arguments in a similar way as scientists have used boundary work (Gieryn, 1983) and how Canadian trained accountants distinguished themselves from "foreign" trained accountants (Annisette, 1999; Annisette & Trivedi, 2013).

Question 4 was concerned with the reaction of various stakeholders after the merger attempts had failed. The analysis across the four merger attempts shows that the attempts to change the traditional organisational strategies of both bodies (Macdonald & Ritzer, 1988) and their failure resulting from successful boundary protection (Fournier, 2000; Gieryn, 1983; Persson, 2010) were essentially deemed to be an internal affair of the accounting profession. The failure of the merger attempts did not attract significant public interest, as the lack of evidence shows for the first two merger attempts (Anon, 1981f; Barnes, 1981; Neilson, 2015; Orr, 2014). After the failure of the almost-successful third merger attempt, commenting on the reaction of stakeholders, especially the governments, McGregor (2015) stated that "they didn't care and they had higher priorities". The fourth merger attempt attracted big accounting firms and other influential individuals to support the move (Bufflinl, 1998). This shows that the Big 4 were foreseeing benefits resulting from a single body linked with better control over the market and lobbying power. However, in relation to the reaction of stakeholders after the failure, Boymal (2016) believed that "There was no reaction". Hence, the findings do not provide much context for a detailed discussion in response to the fourth research question.

10.3 Similarities and Differences Across the Four Merger Attempts

This section identifies similarities and differences across the four merger attempts. Although each merger attempt was a unique scenario, various similarities and differences exist among these as regards the reasons for attempting a merger, contexts, merger processes and reasons for ultimate failure. The comparative analysis across the four merger attempts adds further value to the findings and relevance of this study.

10.3.1 Joint Work

Among other common issues observed across the four merger attempts is the issue of significant joint activities and cooperation on matters of common interest. Since both bodies started discussions on matters of mutual interest, a first joint committee was established in 1965 (Anon, 1965a) and this trend continued, despite the failure of the first merger attempt. The formation of the ARF was a significant joint achievement before the first merger attempt (Burrows, 1996; Carnegie & O'Connell, 2012). Therefore, before the first merger attempt was mounted, joint work on common issues had already started about four years earlier. A key development included joint conferences of the two bodies (Carnegie & O'Connell, 2012), and eight suc1968ah conferences were held between March 1967 and October 1968 (ASA & ICAA,). The formal unity committee emerged from these conferences after June 1968, which took all key decisions related to the first merger attempt (ASA & ICAA, 1968a).

After the failure of the first merger attempt, and to mount the second merger attempt, a joint standing committee with members from the executive committees of both bodies was formed to work on matters affecting the interests of both bodies. Under the auspices of this committee, different subcommittees were also formed (ASA, 1970). Both bodies also regularly consulted in relation to their submissions to various governments (ASA, 1972). A major joint work before the second merger attempt was the hosting of the Tenth International Congress of Accountants in Sydney in 1972 (Williams, 1973). Both bodies jointly established satisfactory communications with the federal and state governments (ICAA, 1975).

Before the third merger attempt, cooperation between the two bodies had increased to include joint activities on matters of accounting and auditing pronouncements, international representation and government submissions. The joint standing committee, which included the presidents and executive directors of both bodies, was meeting four times a year (Sharpe, 1983). After the failure of the third merger attempt and before the fourth merger attempt was mounted, the joint activities between the two bodies continued apace. In 1992, both bodies revised the terms of the joint standing committee with four compulsory annual joint meetings of the entire executive committees to facilitate cooperation and understanding on matters of mutual interest (ICAA, 1992). The UIG was established by both bodies in 1994 to address emerging issues faced by the accounting profession (ASA, 1994, p. 15).

Although all four merger attempts failed, both bodies continued to work together on matters affecting the profession, from right before the first merger attempt and throughout the period under investigation.

10.3.2 Decrease in the Institute's Members in Public Practice

A common trend relating to the four merger attempts was that the Institute's MIPP were declining as a proportion of its total membership. The Institute's Royal Charter was granted to 28 public accountants in 1928 (ICAA, 1969), and its predecessor organisation was the ACPA, that is, a national association of public accountants. At the time of the first merger attempt, 72 per cent of the members of the Institute were MIPP (ICAA, 1969). After the failure of the first merger attempt in 1972, this figure remained at 72 per cent but it then declined in 1981 to 65.6 per cent of the membership (ICAA 1971–1981). Therefore, during a period of 11 years, the proportion of MIPP declined by 6.5 percentage points.

In 1987, the Institute's MIPP fell further to 57 per cent (Henderson, 1988, p. 6), and by 1992, it had fallen to 55 per cent (ICAA, 1992, p. 23). By 1999, the Institute's MIPP were in a minority, comprising just 46 per cent of the membership. This gradual decrease in the Institute's MIPP was used as an argument by leaders of the Institute to support the idea of a united and more broadly based merged body. For example, in arguing in favour of a merger the then Institute president, Savage (1969, p. 1), stated that "accountancy is one undivided profession of which public practice is but one segment" (Savage, 1969, p. 1). Meanwhile, Phillip, who was the Institute president at the time of the second merger attempt, stated that sectional groups working in public practice, the government and academia or in commerce needed to work together, putting aside their sectional interests (ICAA, 1980). Taylor (1991b) argued that the Institute's 45 per cent MNIPP showed the strength of the diversity of its membership. The increasing share of MNIPP was used as an argument to convince members of the Institute, even in the case of the fourth merger attempt (ICAA, 1998).

10.3.3 Official Rationale and Objectives

The mergers of professional associations in Australia were mounted as proactive steps to protect the professional legitimacy of the profession resulting from sudden corporate failures, as in the case of the first three mergers at least, to promote and develop the professional brand and to enhance the lobbying power of the profession (Anon, 1976a; Gottliebsen, 1990; Henderson, 1997; Macfarlane, 2006; Taylor, 2016). Mergers of professional associations typically lead to modification of traditional strategies, resulting in changed professional boundaries as a response to professional crisis and internal changes (Gieryn, 1983; Nancarrow & Borthwick, 2005). Such factors generally influence the decision to mount mergers of professional accounting associations (Richardson & Jones, 2007). In the context of British accounting profession mergers, modification of organisational strategies of exclusivity versus market control has been an initiating factor for merger discussions (Walker & Shackleton, 1995). This section compares the official rationale and objectives of the four merger attempts by examining the commonality of internal motivations and responses to professional crisis.

The official rationale for the first merger attempt was projected in a jointly issued merger proposal. It stated:

> The integration of these two organisations to form one body, comprising some 35,000 members drawn from all sectors of the profession, is a natural and logical culmination of the development of accountancy in Australia. It will strengthen the ability of our profession to meet the many challenges facing its members and facilitate effective action to develop and enforce the standards of accounting appropriate to the rapid economic expansion of Australia. (ICAA & ASA, 1969, p. 2)

This rationale concentrated on long-term gains for the accounting profession, proposing permanent changes in the boundaries of the professional accounting associations. As a result, the professional boundaries drawn around the membership of the Institute would shift with the formation of one large body with a Royal Charter (Gieryn, 1983; Lamont & Molnár, 2002). Similar to the stated rationale and objectives of the first merger attempt, the official rationale for the second merger attempt also addressed the challenges that the profession was facing. The rationale for the merger was stated as follows:

> The accountancy profession is under increasing public scrutiny and it is likely that pressure for greater accountability by the profession itself will increase. A pooling of the talent, initiative and resources of our joint memberships will strengthen the profession to meet this challenge, whereas if both bodies were to continue as separate organisations our respective standing and influence could well diminish. (ASA, 1976, p. 9)

The official rationale for the third merger attempt also drew upon the challenges faced by the profession as a key point to argue the case. The ability to speak with one voice and cost-effective operations resulting from one organisation were some other strong arguments. As quoted earlier in sections, the official rationale of unity was summarised as follows:

> A unified body will be better resourced with a greater ability to meet the very significant challenges facing the accountancy profession. It will speak with one voice to industry, commerce, Government, and the community at large. It will be more cost effective in delivering improved services to members and in ensuring enhanced technical and professional standards. (ASCPA & ICAA, 1990, p. 10)

For the fourth and last merger attempt, the rationale also included issues such as the need to raise the professional status of accountants, and to recognise and raise education and training standards in the profession. A stronger lobbying power resulting from a single body was also a key argument (ASA & ICAA, 1998c). Across the four merger attempts, there were more common themes than differences, which included raising the professional status of accountants, enforcing accounting standards, stronger lobbying powers and improving the ability to speak with one voice. There were also some differences in the official rationales across the four merger attempts. For example, unity of both bodies was termed as a natural and logical development for the Australian accounting profession during the first merger attempt (ICAA & ASA, 1969). The second merger emphasised that a united profession would better address the accountability of the profession and the benefits of pooling the talents from both bodies, including members and staff.

10.3.4 *Society Members' Strong Support and Institute Members' Opposition*

This subsection examines the overall response from members of both bodies to the merger attempts. Each of the four merger attempts was overwhelmingly supported by the Society members but rejected by Institute members. Society members were going to acquire a higher professional status across all four merger attempts, if successful. As shown in Table 10.1, across all merger attempts, the minimum support from Society members was 88.5 per cent while Institute members' support was low for the first and fourth merger attempts and did not reach a 50 per cent majority. Only the third attempt came very close to success, while all other attempts were far below the set threshold level of support at two-thirds of the vote.

The traditional organisational strategy of the Society had a stronger emphasis on market control than had that of the Institute, which favoured a more exclusive strategy based on MIPP dating back to 1928 (Carnegie et al., 2003; Chua & Poullaos, 1998; Macdonald & Ritzer, 1988). The merger with the Institute would deliver higher status as well as modification to the Society's traditional strategy, because a single body equipped with a well-known and recognised professional title for members to use would be exclusive while also holding significant market control because of its membership size. This helps explain the strong support of the Society's members.

The members of the Institute were asked to accept a modification in the traditional strategy of exclusivity (Carnegie et al., 2003; Chua & Poullaos, 1998; Macdonald & Ritzer, 1988). However, across the four merger

Table 10.1
Comparison of the four merger attempts

Attempt	*Year*	*Members Voting "No" on Merger Proposal (%)*	
		Institute	*Society*
First	1969	58.2	11.5
Second	1981	43.5	9.9
Third	1991	36.0	6.0
Fourth	1998	59.0	10.0

Sources ASA annual reports and ICAA annual reports for 1969, 1981 and 1998. *The Age*, 23 March 1991

attempts, younger Institute members, especially from Western Australia, strongly opposed all the mergers. For example, Shorrock (1981), who was a young recent PY graduate from Perth, commented that he was disappointed that the Institute leaders were ignoring the hard work of its members in gaining membership. He compared education standards of members of the Society and the Institute and rejected the idea of merger. Other examples of discursive arguments against the merger attempts included that of Hines (1981 p. 355), who held similar views: "They have lower technical ability to deal with people and I will not support the merger". Shorrock's (1981) and Hines' (1981) statements are evidence of boundary protection because it appears that some Institute members were not prepared to accept any changes to the boundaries of their body.

Therefore, across all merger attempts there was strong support from members of the Society and insufficient support from members of the Institute and this resulted in all merger attempts failing. The theoretical implications of this outcome are consistent with the findings of previous research that revealed similar trends in terms of reaction from the perceived higher and lower-status groups to proposed changes in social and professional boundaries. Those studies found that whenever changes are proposed to social and professional boundaries to make them more inclusive, such changes attract strong support from members in lower-status groups because such developments lead to their status upgrade (Lamont & Molnár, 2002). However, the individuals in higher-status groups tend to oppose changes in boundaries (Lamont & Molnár, 2002; Milner, 1996). The findings and analysis across all four merger attempts show closely similar outcomes in relation to the strong support for mergers from the Society members, the perceived lower-status group, and opposition to mergers from the Institute members, the perceived higher-status group, with the exception of the third merger attempt. Nevertheless, even then, the Institute support was not enough to effect the merger.

10.4 Conclusion

This chapter examined all the four unsuccessful merger attempts collectively, identifying similarities and differences among them. All four merger attempts failed because of similar reasons, which were discussed in detail in the respective merger chapters and were compared in this chapter. Although the official rationales of all merger attempts did not vary significantly, each merger attempt was a unique case with a different social and economic context that led to the mounting of each merger. Both professional bodies faced different challenges each time. As time passed, the rationales became broader to include issues such as challenges posed to the accounting services market from non-accounting professions and effective international representation of the Australian accounting profession resulting from a united body.

For each of the merger attempts, the leadership making decisions had changed and a structured opposition from the members of Institute involved different players. Hence, some clear differences existed among the four merger attempts, which have been identified and discussed in this chapter. However, many factors and issues were common across all the merger attempts and these also have been discussed in this chapter. Such common factors included continuous opposition from younger members of the Institute, primarily in Western Australia. Despite the failure of the merger attempts, the spirit of cooperation and joint works continued and both bodies were engaged in matters of mutual interest. The Society's members overwhelmingly supported all merger attempts because they saw the opportunity for an upgrade in their professional status, but all merger attempts failed because of insufficient support from Institute members. The rationale and objectives put forward to the members had some similarities across all merger attempts. Following the concluding statements of this chapter, the next and final chapter provides an overall summary of this project and examines the implications of the four unsuccessful merger attempts for the Australian accounting profession.

References

Annisette, M. (1999). Importing accounting: The case of Trinidad and Tobago. *Accounting, Business & Financial History, 9*(1), 103–133.

Annisette, M., & Trivedi, V. U. (2013). Globalization, paradox and the (un) making of identities: Immigrant chartered accountants of India in Canada. *Accounting, Organisations and Society, 38*(1), 1–29.

Anon. (1965a, February). Joint action within the profession *The Australian Accountant,* p. 61.

Anon. (1968b, July). Announcement. *The Australian Accountant,* p. 7.

Anon. (1969b). An open letter to members of the Institute of Chartered Accountants in Australia (South Australian Branch), October 20, Adelaide.

Anon. (1976a, August). Integration: News and notes. *The Australian Accountant,* p. 394.

Anon. (1976b). General council annual report 1975. *Annual Report,* 1975, 7.
Anon. (1981b, April 10). Accountants' rift Singapore. *Financial Review*, p. 9.
Anon. (1981f, November 17). PW says yes to merger. *Sun*, p. 9.
Anon. (1981j, December 2). Notice to accountants—vote no to integration. *Financial Review*, p. 255.
Anon. (1991b, January/February). Merger update. *Chartac*, p. 7.
Anon. (1991c, February 13). Unification: The case against integration of the accountancy profession, A campaign run against unification, 1–2.
Anon. (1998e, November). Members to vote on merger proposal. *Accountant*, p. 7.
Australian Society of Accountants and The Institute of Chartered Accountants in Australia. (1968a). Ninth Conference of representatives of The Institute of Chartered Accountants and the Australian Society of Accountants held in Melbourne on March 22–23, 1968 (1–18). ASA Melbourne and ICAA Sydney.
Australian Society of Accountants and The Institute of Chartered Accountants in Australia. (1998c). Preliminary proposal for the creation of a new accounting body for Australia, no date, 1–9.
Australian Society of Accountants and The Institute of Chartered Accountants in Australia. (1969). *Report of Joint Meeting of Education Committees*. ASA Melbourne and ICAA Sydney, 1–19.
Australian Society of Accountants. (1970). *Annual report*. Melbourne, Australia.
Australian Society of Accountants. (1972). *Annual report*. Melbourne, Australia.
Australian Society of Accountants. (1976). *Annual report*. Melbourne, Australia.
Australian Society of Accountants. (1994). *Annual report*. Melbourne, Australia.
Australian Society of Certified Practising Accountants and The Institute of Chartered Accountants in Australia. (1990). Unification proposal, jointly issued by both bodies, December, 1–16.
Barnes, J. C. (1981, September). Integration forum. *The Australian Accountant,* pp. 571–572.
Bowerman, R. (1991b, January 23). ICA group steps up opposition. *New Accountant*, p. 2.
Boymal, D. (2016), Interview with David Boymal on February 8.
Bufflinl, F. (1998, November 30). It's time to take everything into account. *Australian Financial Review*, p. 4.
Burrows, G. (1996). *The Foundation: A history of the Australian Accounting Research Foundation 1966–91.* Australian Accounting Research Foundation.
Carnegie, G. D., & Napier, C. (2002). Exploring comparative international accounting history. *Accounting, Auditing & Accountability Journal, 15*(5), 689–718.

Carnegie, G. D., & Napier, C. (2012). Accounting's past, present and future: The unifying power of history. *Accounting, Auditing & Accountability Journal, 25*(2), 328–369.

Carnegie, G. D., & O'Connell, B. T. (2012). Understanding the responses of professional accounting bodies to crises: The case of the Australian profession in the 1960s. *Accounting Auditing and Accountability Journal, 25*(5), 835–875.

Carnegie, G. D., Edwards, J. R., & West, B. P. (2003). Understanding the dynamics of the Australian accounting profession: A prosopographical study of the founding members of the Incorporated Institute of Accountants, Victoria, 1886 to 1908. *Accounting, Auditing & Accountability Journal, 16*(5), 790–820.

Chua, W. F., & Poullaos, C. (1998). The dynamics of 'closure' amidst the construction of market, profession, empire and nationhood: An historical analysis of an Australian accounting association, 1886–1903. *Accounting, Organisations and Society, 23*(2), 155–187.

Fournier, V. (2000). Boundary work and the (un) making of the professions. Professionalism, boundaries and the workplace, 67.

Gettler, L. (1998b, December 12). Merger numbers fall well short. *The Age*, p. 13.

Gieryn, T. F. (1983). Boundary-work and the demarcation of science from non-science: Strains and interests in the professional ideologies of scientists. *American Sociological Review, 48*(6), 781–795.

Gottliebsen, R. (1990, September). Accounting's crisis of ethics. *Business Review Weekly*, pp. 14–15.

Guo, K. H. (2012). Understanding why and how some chartered accountants object to the proposed merger of the three accounting professions in Canada. *Accounting Perspectives, 11*(2), 111–130.

Henderson, M. S. (1988, April). Towards unification of the Australian accounting profession, Paper presented at the Annual Congress of the Australian Society of Accountants held in April 1988 at Adelaide (1–15).

Henderson, S. (1997). The expectations gap and the Australian accounting profession. *Accounting Forum, 21*(2), 175–188.

Hines, R. D. (1981, June). Integration forum. *The Australian Accountant*, pp. 350–356.

Irving, H. R. (1966). Report on professional awards for accountants (designation of CPA) submitted on behalf of the Executive Committee by President, The Australian Society of Accountants. 7 October 1966, 1–27.

Keohane, R. O., & Milner, H. V. (Eds.). (1996). *Internationalization and domestic politics*. Cambridge University Press.

Lamont, M., & Molnár, V. (2002). The study of boundaries in the social sciences. *Annual Review of Sociology, 28*(1), 167–195.

Lee, T. A. (2010). Consolidating the public accountancy profession: The case of the proposed Institute of Chartered Accountants of Great Britain, 1988–9. *Accounting History, 15*(1), 7–39.

Leong, H. (1991, February). Letter to editor. *Charter*, p. 59.

Macdonald, K. M., & Ritzer, G. (1988). The sociology of the professions: Dead or alive? *Work and Occupations, 15*(3), 251–272.

Macfarlane, I. (2006, December 2). The real reasons why it was the 1990s recession we had to have—Business. *The Age*. Retrieved 18 August 2015 from *Theage.com.au*.

McGregor, G. (2015). Interview with Graeme McGregor on December 14.

McKenon, A. (1981, April 10). Integration on the boil. *Business Review*, p. 9.

Miller, J. (2015). Interview with John Miller on February 27.

Milner, D. (1996). Children and racism: Beyond the value of dolls. In P. W Robinson (Ed.), *Social groups and identities: Developing the legacy of Henri Tajfel* (249–68). Butterworth Heinermann.

Nancarrow, S. A., & Borthwick, A. M. (2005). Dynamic professional boundaries in the healthcare workforce. *Sociology of Health & Illness, 27*(7), 897–919.

Neilson, G. (2015). Interview with Geoff Neilson on February 20.

Norgard, J. D. (1980, September) Integration: The position to date. *The Australian Accountant*, p. 527.

Orr, J. G. (2014). Interview with Geoff Orr on May 17.

Persson, A. (2010). Soldiers and secretaries: Gendered boundary work in the Swedish Armed Forces. *Scandinavian Journal of Management, 26*, 166–175.

Richardson, A. J., & Jones, D. B. (2007). Professional 'brand', personal identity and resistance to change in the Canadian accounting profession: A comparative history of two accounting association merger negotiations. *Accounting History, 12*(2), 135–164.

Savage, E. W. (1969). The plan for unity: Stage II—the vote in principle. A letter to the members by the president of Institute, E. W. Savage dated November 5, 1969, 1.

Shackleton, K. & Walker, S. P. (2001). *A future for the accountancy profession: The quest for closure and integration, 1957–1970*. Institute of Chartered Accountants of Scotland.

Sharpe, M. (1983). President's overview. *Annual report*, The Australian Society of Accountants, pp. 2–3.

Shorrock, W. R. (1981, August). A recent PY graduate's view, Integration Forum. *The Chartered Accountant in Australia*, p. 18.

Taylor, N. B. (1991b, August). Message of President. *Charter*, p. 59.

Taylor, N. B. (2016). Interview with Nick Burton Taylor on March 18.

The Institute of Chartered Accountants in Australia. (1969). *Annual report*. Australia.

The Institute of Chartered Accountants in Australia. (1971). *Annual report*. Australia.

The Institute of Chartered Accountants in Australia. (1972). *Annual report*. Australia.

The Institute of Chartered Accountants in Australia. (1973). *Annual report*. Australia.

The Institute of Chartered Accountants in Australia. (1974). *Annual report*. Australia.

The Institute of Chartered Accountants in Australia. (1975). *Annual report*. Australia.

The Institute of Chartered Accountants in Australia. (1976). *Annual report*. Australia.

The Institute of Chartered Accountants in Australia. (1977). *Annual report*. Australia.

The Institute of Chartered Accountants in Australia. (1978). *Annual report*. Australia.

The Institute of Chartered Accountants in Australia. (1979). *Annual report*. Australia.

The Institute of Chartered Accountants in Australia. (1980). *Annual report*. Australia.

The Institute of Chartered Accountants in Australia. (1981). *Annual report*. Australia.

The Institute of Chartered Accountants in Australia. (1992). *Annual report*. Australia.

The Institute of Chartered Accountants in Australia. (1998). *Annual report*. Australia.

The Institute of Chartered Accountants in Australia. (1999). *Annual report*. Australia.

Thiele, R. (1975, July). Editorial. *The Australian Accountant*, p. 321.

Walker, S. P., & Shackleton, K. (1995). Corporatism and structural change in the British accountancy profession, 1930–1957. *Accounting, Organisations and Society, 20*(6), 467–503.

Williams, D. P. (1973, May). Message from outgoing president. *The Australian Accountant*, p. 11.

Zerubavel, E. (1991). *The fine line: Making distinctions in everyday life*. The University of Chicago Press.

CHAPTER 11

Learnings from Merger Attempts: Practical and Theoretical Implications

11.1 Introduction

This chapter provides an overall summary of the book, discusses the implications of the failure of the four merger attempts and presents opportunities for further research. This project focused on five research questions, of which four were answered for each separate merger attempt, namely, in Chapters 6–9. The fifth and last research question, which explores the long-term ramifications of the unsuccessful merger attempts, is answered in this chapter.

This chapter has seven sections. Section 11.2 provides a summary of the whole book. Section 11.3 considers the long-term ramifications of the failure of the four merger attempts, and thereby provides a response to the fifth research question. The impact of the failure to merge is discussed in Sect. 11.4 from a public interest perspective. Section 11.5 considers the implications of this study for the theoretical frameworks employed. Limitations and suggestions for further research are discussed in Sect. 11.6. Section 11.7 concludes the chapter and the book.

J. Sidhu et al., *Understanding the Sociology of the Accounting Profession*,
https://doi.org/10.1007/978-981-99-1572-9_11

11.2 Summary of the Book

This book examined the four unsuccessful attempts to unify the Australian accounting profession, covering a period of more than 30 years. The findings of this study were analysed using two complementary theoretical frameworks. The first framework is the "boundary-work" concept of Thomas Gieryn (Gieryn, 1983, 1995, 1999; Gieryn etal., 1985) and Annisette (2017), and the second framework is the "dilemma of exclusiveness versus market control" (Macdonald & Ritzer, 1988, p. 257). Using historical data available in public archives complemented by oral history interviews, this study applied a qualitative research method (Anderson, 2010). The approach used in this study was critical and interpretative, being part of the "new accounting history" paradigm (Fleischman et al., 1996; Miller et al., 1991; Parker, 1999). This section provides a summary of the whole book, drawing on each of the nine previous chapters.

The book began with the introduction and background context to the four unsuccessful merger attempts, including the historical context of the early stages of the professionalisation of accounting in Australia (Carnegie & Edwards, 2001). After the early stages of the professionalisation process, two leading professional accounting bodies finally emerged: the Society and the Institute. This outcome reflected the two distinct organisational strategies adopted by these bodies in terms of MIPP and MNIPP (Carnegie, 2016; Carnegie et al., 2003; Carnegie & O'Connell, 2012), and which encapsulated what Macdonald and Ritzer (1988, p. 257) described as "the dilemma of exclusiveness versus market control". In particular, some accountants, including some leaders of the profession, believed that public practice was a superior domain compared with the roles played by accountants in commerce, industry and the government (Poullaos, 1993).

Thus, and in general terms, public practice was associated with exclusivity, while the diverse and numerous functions of other salaried accounting work provided an opportunity for market influence. These notions had a major effect on the historical structure of the Australian accounting profession (Carnegie et al., 2003). The earliest antecedent bodies of the Society and the Institute were, respectively, the IIAV and the ACPA. The IIAV adopted an inclusive membership strategy, while the ACPA restricted membership to those engaged in public practice (Carnegie et al., 2003; Chua & Poullaos, 1998). These organisational strategies subsequently influenced the long-term strategies of both the

Society and the Institute. The introductory chapter also briefly introduced the literature review, the theoretical frameworks, the four merger attempts, the research methodology, the motivation for the research and its limitations.

Chapter 2 of this study provided the literature review, sourced from two key branches of the accounting literature: historical studies that covered the Australian accounting profession and studies that examined the mergers of professional accounting bodies internationally. Numerous studies were identified that covered historical developments of the Australian accounting profession and which thereby provided background literature to this project (Carnegie, 1993; Carnegie & Edwards, 2001; Carnegie et al., 2003; Carnegie & O'Connell, 2012; Carnegie & Parker, 1999; Chua & Poullaos, 1993, 1998; Gavens, 1990; Gavens & Gibson, 1992; Parker, 1989; Poullaos, 1993, 1994). Chapter 2 provided a detailed account of these studies, identified a gap in the current literature and advanced a case for the study of the attempts to merge the Society and Institute.

Chapter 2 also identified the strategies adopted by professional accounting associations in the past to mount various mergers and common themes among different contexts in these studies. The ability to speak with one voice, increased lobbying power and effective control of the structure and operations of the accounting profession (Richardson & Jones, 2007; Shackleton & Walker 1998, 2001; Walker & Shackleton, 1995, 1998; Willmott, 1986) were some of the common themes evident in actual and attempted mergers of professional accounting associations across Britain and Canada. These themes were also evident in the case of the four Australian merger attempts. A review of this branch of literature identified the need for this Australian study to examine the unique case of four unsuccessful merger attempts.

The research methodology and data collection methods were discussed and explained in Chapter 3. This study used a critical and interpretive research approach, placing it in the paradigm of "new accounting history" (Fleischman et al., 1996; Miller et al., 1991; Parker, 1999). The research method was qualitative, including the collection, analysis and interpretation of data that cannot be reduced to numbers (Anderson, 2010). The primary sources of data were the public archives of CPA Australia, RMIT University library, the State Library of Victoria and other libraries. The oral history interviews conducted complemented the data available in the public archives. The period targeted for this research ranged from the late 1960s to the late 1990s, thus making it a historical accounting study across a period of about 30 years with a key aim to explain the historical context, causes and consequences of events (Bedeian, 1998) such as merger attempts. A critical analysis of the findings, which adds meaning to data found in the archives, and responding to the research questions places the study in the critical and interpretive context (Fleischman et al., 1996) as opposed to a conventional and descriptive context.

The research process had three main steps: collection of data from the available surviving archives, including published official and non-official documents; collection of oral history evidence and the analysis and interpretation of the findings. Various libraries and public archives provided access to documentary data, while interviews with key stakeholders contributed the oral history aspect of the data collection. Documentary data were collected by taking photographs using a high-resolution digital camera. After the data collection for the first merger attempt, data collection for the remaining three merger attempts became more streamlined. The draft notes prepared from documentary sources and the desire to provide comprehensive responses to the study's research questions led to the oral history interviews. Some of the oral history interviews complemented records in the archival materials, while others also contributed new and valuable information to the study.

Chapter 4 of this book articulated the two theoretical frameworks: the "boundary-work construct" of Thomas Gieryn (Gieryn, 1983, 1995, 1999; Gieryn et al., 1985) and "the dilemma of exclusiveness versus market control" (Macdonald & Ritzer, 1988). The boundary-work construct was the main framework used to understand how both bodies positioned themselves historically, leading to a dichotomy of MIPP and MNIPP. These groups had originally emerged as a result of two different organisational strategies adopted by the Society and the Institute. As discussed in Sect. 2.3, although boundaries were originally constructed around the notion of MIPP and MNIPP, the boundaries that finally settled around the membership of each body were somewhat modified, although the Institute maintained stricter entry requirements. Such requirements were accompanied by expectations of higher professional standards from the Institute members. The boundary-work construct has been applied in many studies. However, the most relevant explanations that add meaning to the merger failures examined in this study include the reaction to changes in boundaries by the perceived lower-status groups and higher-status groups (Lamont & Molnár, 2002; Milner, 1996). Individuals in perceived lower-status groups, in this case, the Society, support changes in boundaries if that leads to a status upgrade, while individuals in the perceived higher-status groups, in this case, the Institute, tend to oppose such changes since these are perceived as diluting their status (Lamont & Molnár, 2002).

All four merger attempts involved two types of public discourses: one by leaders of both associations to promote the mergers and the other by Institute members to oppose any merger with the Society (Annisette, 2017). The second framework, the dilemma of exclusiveness versus market control, was applied to understand the historical reasons for the creation of two bodies, with an emphasis on the MIPP and MNIPP dichotomy and the persistence of this tension as a consequence of the failure of all four merger attempts. Within this framework, the study also explained the proposed new business model to be adopted by the new merged body in each of the four cases. The proposed body would be elite because of the possession of a Royal Charter and the historical status related to its title, and it would have effective market control because of the size of its membership.

Chapter 5 considered the first merger attempt between the Society and the Institute mounted in the late 1960s. Since the formation of the Society in 1952, neither body had engaged in much joint work (Zeff, 1973) until they faced a legitimacy crisis in the 1960s because of a series of corporate collapses (Carnegie & O'Connell, 2012). This brought both bodies together to work on matters of mutual interest. Eventually, the Institute made an offer to the Society for merger talks, which was immediately accepted (Orr, 2014). A reason for the enthusiastic response of the Society's leaders was the perceived lower professional status of Society members and their lack of a widely known generic title similar to the title of Chartered Accountant used by Institute members (Irving, 1966). Financial challenges being faced by the Institute may have also provided a motivation for it to seek a merger with the Society (ICAA 1965, 1968).

Both bodies started holding joint conferences, and a formal merger proposal emerged from these conferences (ASA, 1967a). The joint conference group was renamed the "unity committee" in 1968 (ASA & ICAA, 1968a, p. 7). The final merger proposal was released on 1 August 1969 (ICAA & ASA, 1969). The Institute attempted to convince its members to support the proposal by arguing that accounting was one profession, even though the Society mainly represented MNIPP (Anon.,

1969h). This was a modification from the Institute's traditional emphasis on exclusivity, and it thereby sought to permanently change its boundaries. As announced on 8 December 1969 (ICAA 1970, p. 8), the first merger attempt failed because of successful boundary protection work by a sufficient number of members of the Institute (Fournier, 2000; Gieryn, 1983; Persson, 2010), which also indicated a detachment of the Institute's leaders from its members (Lee, 2010; Shackleton & Walker, 2001). However, the merger proposal received an overwhelming positive response from Society members.

Chapter 6 considered the second merger attempt, which was unique in relation to the time spent on the process of developing the merger proposal and the time gap between commencing the merger talks and undertaking the vote, as illustrated in Table 11.1. The initial step for restarting merger discussions was taken by the Institute (ASA, 1981). As with the first merger attempt, a series of corporate collapses and criticism of the accounting profession (Henderson, 1997) provided a motivation for this merger attempt. Additionally, both bodies were concerned with the public image of accounting and the lack of regulation over the use of the term "accountant" (Anon., 1971; Munro, 1975c).

Despite the failure of the first merger attempt, joint work on matters of mutual interest continued (Anon., 1974; ASA, 1970). As discussed in Chapters 5 and 9, the leaders of the Society were concerned that some of its MIPP, who were also members of the Institute, would not disclose their membership and would only use the Institute title. To give the Society's MIPP an exclusive status within that body, it made an unsuccessful attempt to publish a list of its MIPP (McKeon, 1975a). As a direct consequence, the Society readily accepted an offer from the Institute to restart merger discussions (Anon., 1976b). As shown in Table 6.6, the Institute's share of MIPP in total members declined by 6.5 percentage points between 1971 and 1981, providing a motivation for merger. Before releasing the final merger proposal on 15 November 1981, an exposure draft was issued seeking input from members (Anon., 1976c). In 1979, the IPC was formed with an independent chairperson, J. D. Norgard (Anon., 1981a). Both bodies hired ANOP to conduct surveys to study the support for the proposed merger among their members (Anon., 1981h, 1981i; ICAA, 1980). The surveys did not reveal strong enthusiasm for a merger among the Institute members. Therefore, both bodies started an Integration Forum in the journals of both bodies to give members an opportunity to express their views (Anon., 1981a, 1981e).

Table 11.1 Merger process timeline

Attempt	*Initial discussion of merger*	*First public announcement*	*Public release of merger proposal*	*Vote undertaken and failure*	*Total months*
First	June 1967 (ongoing meetings since 1964 and initiated by the Institute)	July 1968	1 August 1969	5 December 1969	30 months
Second	November 1974 (initiated by the Institute)	17 March 1975 (via letters sent to members)	14 July 1976 (first draft) 15 November 1981(final draft)	21 December 1981	73 months
Third	2 June 1989, Institute president invited members of Society with at least 10 years of experience to join the body	2 June 1989	15 January 1991	7 September 1989, first talks failed 22 March 1991, vote failed	21 months
Fourth	March 1998 (initiated by the Institute)	March 1998	July 1998	14 December 1998	9 months

On the completion of voting, the second merger attempt failed, as announced by both presidents in a joint press release on 8 January 1982. Support from the Institute members had increased from 41.8% in the case of the first merger attempt to 56.5% (ASA 1981; ICAA, 1970, 1981). However, this was still insufficient to change the boundaries of the Institute and modify its traditional organisational strategy (Brodkin, 1998; Gieryn, 1983; Ignatiev, 1995). As in the case of the first merger attempt, the merger failed owing to insufficient support from Institute members, while it received overwhelming support from Society members.

The third merger attempt was unique because the initial merger discussions started with the Institute president's hostile takeover bid to attract members of the Society who had completed a specified minimum period of professional experience. Unlike the first two merger attempts where special subcommittees were established, in the case of the third merger attempt most merger-related decisions, as shown in Chapter 7, were taken by the presidents of both bodies. The context that led to the mounting of the third merger attempt had some commonalities with the context that led to the mounting of the first merger attempt. Similar to the first merger attempt, external pressures and internal developments (Gieryn, 1983; Nancarrow & Borthwick, 2005) created favourable conditions for mounting the third merger attempt. For example, in 1987, the capital markets suffered a major downturn. Other issues were corporate collapses, rising unemployment and economic recession (McMahon, 2007; Wright, 2008).

Joint work on matters of mutual interest continued, which included representation at international and government level (ASA, 1984; Sharpe, 1983). The offer of the Institute's president to the Society's members to join the Institute on 2 June 1989 attracted criticism from the Society's leaders. Effective merger discussions started in September 1990 (Eastwood, 1990d) and the final proposal was released in December 1990 (Lewis, 1991a). The third merger attempt failed for reasons similar to the first two merger attempts; that is, successful boundary protection work by a sufficient number of members of the Institute (Fournier, 2000; Gieryn, 1983; Persson, 2010) and detachment of the Institute's leaders from its members (Lee, 2010; Shackleton & Walker, 2001). However, practising members of the Institute had two votes and the merger fell short of being successful by just 200 to 300 votes.

Chapter 8 examined the last of the four attempts to merge Australia's two major professional accounting bodies. Similar to the third merger attempt, the presidents of both bodies undertook most merger-related decisions. After meeting in Paris in late 1997, they initiated merger discussions in early 1998 (Anon., 1998l; Boymal, 2016). Soon after the failure of the third merger attempt, both bodies resumed talks about common issues (ASA, 1992; Taylor, 1991c). On 18 March 1998, they issued a joint media release announcing merger discussions. Although a JTF was formed, major decisions were left to both presidents (Anon., 1998j; Dowling, 1998; Farnham, 1998). A unique element of the fourth merger attempt was that members of both bodies could retain their respective titles or use the new proposed title of “Chartered Professional Accountant” (Anon., 1998b). This was done to attract wider support from Institute members who did not want to share their Chartered Accountant title with Society members (Thomas, 1998a).

In addition to other common reasons for the merger attempt, leverage came from the challenges accountants were facing from a legal profession keen to extend its jurisdiction (Anon., 1998l). As with the second merger attempt, a market research firm, Worthington DiMarzio, was hired to study the level of support among members of both bodies for the merger attempt (Anon., 1999b). Unlike the previous three merger attempts, the Society’s leaders showed less interest and were not keen to go ahead with the vote since the surveys undertaken predicted a low chance of success (Thomas, 1998a). A group of Institute members opposing the merger called themselves the OVC (Anon., 1998e) and they ran a well-organised, well-coordinated campaign. The vote outcome showed the lowest support from the Institute members among all four merger attempts, with only 41% of the Institute’s members voting in favour, while support from the Society’s members was at 90% (Gettler, 1998b). With the failure of the fourth and the last merger attempt, the long-lasting efforts to fully unify the Australian accounting profession have effectively ceased until date. In the two decades since the failure of the fourth merger attempt, the two bodies have not made any further attempts to merge with each other.

Table 11.1 provides a timeline of the four merger attempts, comparing the start of initial merger discussions, the date of the first public announcement, the date of the first public release of merger proposals and, finally, the date on which the merger vote was undertaken. The initial discussion for the first merger attempt took place in June 1967 and within 13 months, the first public announcement was made in July 1968 that both bodies were engaged in merger discussions. It took another year to finalise the proposal, which went to the vote on 5 December 1969: overall, a smooth process without major issues.

The initial discussion for the second merger attempt started in November 1974, and a public announcement was made within a period of four months. Similar to the first merger attempt, the development of the draft proposal took more than a year and it was released on 14 July 1976. The overall process for the second merger attempt was the longest of all four and lasted 73 months; for the first attempt, it was 30 months and it was the second longest. The third merger attempt process was unique in that the merger talks started informally when the Institute president made a one-sided offer on 2 June 1989 to the Society's members with a minimum specified period of experience to apply for Institute membership. Such talks broke down on 7 September 1989. Merger talks started again in September 1990 and were followed by the release of the proposal on 15 January 1991. Within two months, the final vote was undertaken. The merger process for the third merger attempt lasted a period of 21 months.

As discussed in Chapter 8, the fourth merger attempt was the shortest in terms of time spent on the merger process. The discussions started informally between the two presidents in Paris in late 1997. Within a few months, in March 1998, the first public announcement was made, and only nine months elapsed between this announcement and the vote. The time spent on the process shows that the first two attempts took longer because they were the first. The later attempts were, in some ways, building on the earlier attempts and this expedited the process.

Chapter 9 provided a comparative analysis of the four unsuccessful merger attempts, focusing on similarities and differences in the responses to the four research questions within the context of interpretations that were informed by the theoretical frameworks. Across the four merger attempts, one common theme was joint work and cooperation on matters of mutual interest. Before the mounting of the first merger attempt, and despite the subsequent four consecutive failures, both bodies continued to work jointly on issues affecting them. A factor behind all merger proposals was the motivation of the Society's leaders to provide a status upgrade for its members. This was one of the main reasons for accepting the offer for merger discussions before the first merger attempt, as it was for the subsequent merger attempts. The share of the Institute's MIPP was in decline as a percentage of total membership, decreasing from 72% in 1969 (ICAA, 1969) to 46% in 1999 (ICAA, 1999). Therefore, there was a

26 percentage point decline in absolute terms during the 30-year period covered by this study. This was a significant change and signalled that the Institute's profile was moving in the direction of that of the Society, raising the prospect of sufficient commonality to enable a merger.

While the outcome of each of the four merger attempts was the same and each merger attempt failed because of similar reasons, the pre-merger scenarios and circumstances were different in each case. Major external factors included corporate failures, a stock market crash and threats posed to the legitimacy of profession. Across all merger attempts, each proposed merger was projected in the positive light of a single body being able to meet the challenges facing the accounting profession as a whole in a much more effective manner. Other common arguments included the ability to speak with one voice, more effective coordination of operations and the enforcement of better standards. As indicated previously, all merger attempts failed because of insufficient support from members of the Institute, who successfully protected the boundaries of their professional body, with only the third merger attempt coming close to succeeding.

During the first half of the twentieth century, the Australian accounting profession became characterised by a distinctive binary structure. The four merger attempts by the Institute and Society marked an attempt to overcome this divide and achieve unification. Society members overwhelmingly approved all four proposals, with their vote comfortably exceeding the 75% majority this organisation required to enable a merger to proceed, with lowest vote being at 88.5% in the case of first merger attempt. The Institute required only a two-thirds majority, but the vote of its membership fell short of even this threshold, with only the third merger attempt coming close to succeeding. In short, all four merger proposals were strongly supported by the membership of the Society but comprehensively defeated by the membership of the Institute, except for the third merger attempt. These circumstances evidence not only the persistence of efforts to unite the two bodies, but also the persistence of the obstacles that caused all merger proposals to fail.

The next section provides a summary of the analysis of the findings.

11.3 Long-Term Ramifications of the Failure of the Merger Attempts

This section considers the last research question: "What were the long-term ramifications of unsuccessful merger attempts for the Australian accounting profession?" Commenting on the failure of the first merger attempt, Orr stated:

> A united profession would have a higher standing and apart from the standing of the profession there would be tremendous benefits to individual members. Young people who want to enter the profession were confused as to why there were two separate bodies. Why one body would accept them and the other body had different entry requirements. We don't present ourselves as a profession to the general public as much as we should. (2014)

The immediate implications of the failure of the second merger attempt were discussed by John Miller, who stated in an interview:

> The failure would be seen as a bad public image for the Society. So we had developed a Plan B for me as the incoming President. Plan B was designed to be aggressive; to ensure a strong presence in the media. We also launched the professional schedule, which used the CPA brand and introduced compulsory professional development among other things to create the perception of us as professionals. That was all to do with repositioning the Society as an aggressive professional body. (2015)

Thus, the immediate implications of failure were that the Society would lead reforms and engage in a strong marketing campaign that was part of a postfailure Plan B. The impact of the Society's aggressive campaign on the Institute and the profession in general was also explained by the then Institute President Geoff Neilson in his interview. Neilson stated, "The failure led to a strong campaign of advertising. There was a lot of waste of resources because when the Society was advertising the Institute had to advertise" (Neilson, 2015).

After the failure of the third merger attempt, the president of the Institute, Taylor (1991c), referred to the failure in his monthly message in *Charter* and made a point about the challenges faced by the profession:

> Following the unification vote in March, I advised our membership that both the ICA and the ASA have a responsibility to support the accountancy profession and that we must place strong emphasis on how best to meet our future community obligations. I also undertook that the ICA must resist the temptation for easy point scoring where the wellbeing of the profession was concerned. (p. 66)

This shows that the president was keen to work with the Society on common issues. After the failure of the last merger attempt, the Society's annual report of 1998 contained the following statement:

> We believe that the response of Institute members was short-sighted and that it has effectively ensured that another merger attempt is unlikely to ever occur again. Unfortunate though it is, unification of the profession is now off the agenda. Our stature, international connections and world class initiatives only stand to be improved. We expect therefore that the Society's pace of change will significantly accelerate. (ASA, 1998, p. 4)

These claims in the Society's annual report proved to be accurate, and since then, no further merger attempt has been made across a period of 19 years until date. The 1999 annual report of the Society shows its strategic goals with a target date for achievement set for 2004. Some of the key goals included making the Society the best in the region, with a global network and excellent staff (ASA, 1999, p. 1). The mission of the Society was presented as "to position CPAs as leaders in finance, accounting and business advice" (ASA, 1999, p. 1).

In December 1998, the national council of the Institute decided to conduct a significant review of the Institute's strategic plan in the first half of 1999 (Atkinson, 1999). The Institute also informed its members that although the fourth merger attempt had failed, they were still working with the Society on matters of mutual interest. Stephen Harrison the Institute's executive director stated "we must continue to tread the fine line that separates competition and cooperation" (1999, p. 6). Harrison further stated, "We will continue to share common ground with the Society as lobbyists to government and builders of the status quo of the profession" (1999, p. 6) and argued:

> We may be a small and elite body, with extremely high standards and a homogeneous membership restricted only to Chartered Accountants, but

> that doesn't mean we should shut ourselves off from fellow professionals with similar interests and aims.

From these arguments, it is clear that the Institute was keen to continue working on matters of mutual interest.

One of the key reasons for the failure of all four merger attempts was successful boundary protection by a sufficient number of members of the Institute (Fournier, 2000; Gieryn, 1983; Persson, 2010). A key question that arises is why four attempts in all were made despite the failure of earlier merger attempts. From oral history interviews with leaders of both bodies, it appears that the leadership of both bodies had a long-term vision and, with foresight into future challenges facing the profession as a whole, they ultimately mounted four merger attempts. For example, in response to an interview question about the reasons for attempting to merge, John Miller, president of the Society during the second merger attempt, stated:

> Because the leaders of the professional bodies were great people of foresight, ethics and vision. They thought in a small country like Australia it was counter-productive to have competing resources with two bodies. (2015)

Geoff Neilson, who was president of the Institute at the time of the second merger attempt, provided some insights into what the leadership of the Institute believed when approaching the Society for the second merger attempt. Neilson stated:

> I think the Institute generally felt at a national level the merger was desirable. Competition between two bodies was not good for Australia. We were part of the global accounting profession and once united it would be very significant body in terms of numbers. So I think the motivation was to have a united accounting profession in Australia, which was a very significant part of the world accounting profession. The feeling was very strong in the National Council. The main motivation was to form a significant world-class professional accounting body. (2015)

This was a step towards changing arguments related to demarcation of accountants (Gieryn, 1983). For decades, the Institute leadership had claimed exclusivity for the Institute but the statement by Neilson (2015) indicates that they were prepared to alter their exclusivity strategy in the interests of a united accounting profession. In each of the four merger attempts, members of the national and general councils of both bodies had changed, and new presidents were elected who brought with them their vision for the future and encouraged the mergers because they believed that a single body was in the best interests of the profession and, as a consequence, beneficial for the public (Miller, 2015; Orr, 2014; Taylor, 2016). Hence, a key reason for mounting the four consecutive merger attempts was that the successive presidents of both bodies made decisions that they believed would provide long-term benefits to the profession as a whole. It appears that they essentially ignored past failures and were prepared to start afresh. Still, it is a unique case that four merger attempts were mounted with almost the same outcome every time.

11.4 Broader Public Interest Perspectives on the Failure to Unify the Profession

The Society and the Institute traditionally emphasised the "public interest" in terms of their function and reason for being, and their successor bodies continue to do so today. However, little evidence has been found that broader public interest issues were a key consideration in each of the merger proposals. Rather, as has been shown, debate over whether the mergers should proceed seemed to focus on the implications for the accounting profession as a whole, as well as for the two individual bodies and their memberships. However, while it seems that "public interest" was not at the core of any of the four merger attempts, there have been costs associated with the failure to unify the Australian accounting profession. The most obvious of these are the inefficiencies associated with administering two major professional bodies in a country that has a population at the time of writing of only 25 million and the confusion that results from having two professional accounting designations: CA and CPA.

Students continue to ask questions about differences in the two designations and are sometimes confused about whether to seek to become a CA or CPA. The answers to these questions are not simple, and different academics may respond differently. There are other "public interest" costs because conflicting interests between two strong professional bodies add to further confusion. The general public, and accounting students in particular, are also unsure why two bodies exist. The answer to this question, which has been the focus of this book, requires a historical exposition that does not always interest impatient accounting students and the wider public.

A further inefficiency emerges from both bodies engaging in marketing campaigns that aim to win over prospective members, as well as employers and members of the public who are seeking the services of a "qualified" accountant. For many years, the Institute adopted the branding motto of "Number One in Numbers". When the Society introduced the CPA designation, it was promoted as signifying "Not Your Average Accountant". These campaigns can be defended as efforts of professional bodies to distinguish professional accountants from the unqualified, since the term "accountant" in Australia is not subject to any legislative or other enforceable restriction. However, it also seems likely that campaigns of this kind depict an ongoing intra-professional rivalry. The Institute's "Number One in Numbers", for example, could be interpreted as implying that there is an inferior "Number Two" without actually specifying the name of that professional body. Similarly, the CPA slogan was concerned with hierarchical differentiation. In this way, both bodies engage in the typical behaviour of oligopolistic entities: pursuit of market share through expensive marketing and advertising campaigns that are concerned primarily with brand posturing and that deliver limited public benefits.

However, the dynamics of the Australian accounting profession are complex, and it would be wrong to contend that the continuing binary structure simply manifests in inefficiencies born from the triumph of self-interest. Instead, evidence exists that the two bodies compete in ways that do sometimes deliver public benefits. Accounting students, for example, are well served by the educational and career materials that both bodies provide as they seek to attract new members. Similarly, accounting academics benefit from the support, such as sponsorship of academic accounting associations and conferences and the provision of research grants, that each body provides. In addition, both the CA and CPA educational programs are highly regarded, a circumstance that may be at least partly attributable to them being competing alternatives for aspiring accountants. In short, while a monopolistic, or at least hierarchically dominant, association may be the more typical model of a profession, there is some evidence that the duopoly that characterises the Australian accounting profession has delivered some benefits. Whether those benefits exceed the associated costs is a complex issue that lies beyond the scope of the current study.

11.5 Implications for the Application of Theory

The theoretical frameworks adopted in this study, and particularly that of boundary work, were extended in their application to the mergers of professional accounting associations. The original boundary-work research involved ongoing efforts to articulate the nature of scientific endeavour and denigrate activities that did not meet this standard. Therefore, the boundary in question was a boundary between disciplines. In the case of this book, the boundary in question is a boundary between organisations. This makes it a binary divide: the Institute and the Society could either join or remain apart. In the case of the divide between science and non-science, it is more of a continuum. That is, there are some things that are definitely science, such as chemistry, some things that are somewhat scientific, perhaps some alternative health practices, and some things that are categorically non-scientific, such as fortune telling. The basis of the organisational boundaries of both accounting bodies was not as clearly defined as the distinction between "science" and "non-science". Hence, the boundary-work framework is extended to a new context involving mergers of professional accounting associations.

This dispute of demarcation in science was not resolved by a formal process, such as a vote. The accounting profession in Australia is not fully regulated, which exposed this profession to a complex merger process with different levels of hurdles that needed to be cleared. At the first level, the leadership of both bodies needed to agree. At the second, and a more critical level, the ultimate success of any merger proposal depended on the members of both bodies, which is where it failed in each case. The removal of a boundary between two organisations requires a formal process which put the framework to a new test. As the outcomes showed, the nature of this process was difficult in the case of the Institute and the Society. Part of this is the reliance on a voting process: this not only gave every member a "say", but also set a high hurdle in terms of the majority required. If the Institute had required only a simple majority of 50%, the merger would have been easily attained. Similarly, if the decision had just been up to the leadership, merger would have occurred very easily.

In summary, the merger attempts involved organisational boundaries that were always going to be difficult to cross on account of the involvement of the members of the two bodies. It contrasts with other organisational mergers, including corporate mergers, for which leadership can take respective decisions leading to successful mergers. The organisation boundaries were considered flexible by leaders of both bodies, especially by the Institute leaders. A sufficient number of rank and file members of the Institute wanted the boundaries to persist and these stayed resilient with the failure of each merger attempt, apart from in the third merger attempt that was very close to succeeding.

Following Annisette (2017, p. 58), the "discursive realm" associated with "convincing the respective memberships of … merging associations" has been emphasised, that is, the "war of words" over maintaining or moving established boundaries. All four merger attempts were supported by the leaders of both bodies amidst discursive claims of the benefits of "oneness". However, a second and distinctive discourse was also mobilised at the membership level as some CAs asserted their superiority over the Society members. In this way, the merger proposal and accompanying debate were characterised by two competing discourses: the leaders of the profession emphasising themes of commonality and the benefits of unity, while an activist group of CAs promulgated claims of distinctiveness and superiority, and the fear that these qualities would be lost in a merged body. This study applies and extends the framework of Annisette (2017) and offers the boundary-work framework as a path to examining discursive practice within the context of mergers of accounting associations. This represents an alternative to more traditional frameworks, such as closure theories.

The second framework was "the dilemma of exclusiveness versus market control" (Macdonald & Ritzer, 1988, p. 257). Traditionally the Society had favoured a market control strategy (Carnegie, 2016), while the Institute emphasised an exclusiveness strategy (Carnegie & Edwards, 2001; Carnegie et al., 2003), but during the four merger attempts both bodies were moving away from these two extremes of organisational strategies. This shows that the framework also applies to situations in which original strategies are modified over time and are not very rigid. This implies that a binary selection of either exclusiveness or market control is not the only choice that professional organisations may have. The organisational strategies can be modified from being two extremes, that is, either exclusivity or market control, enabling adoption of a more blended approach.

In all four merger attempts, the proposed organisational strategy was a blend of exclusiveness versus market control. The merged organisation would be elite in the sense of being a dominant body with a large membership size, which would assure its market dominance, and subsequently ensure a prominent position among professional associations of any kind in Australia. The merged body would continue to enjoy the status associated with a Royal Charter as has been part of the exclusiveness profile of the Institute. Across the four merger attempts, both bodies had modified their traditional strategies such that they were becoming more similar than distinct. The decrease of the Institute's MIPP as a proportion of total members and the Society's total MIPP being a sizable number meant public accountants from either organisation could access the professional rewards associated with public practice. The notion that the Institute was predominantly an association of MIPP while the Society was predominantly an association of MNIPP was starting to unravel. However, the increasing similarities in the organisational strategies were insufficient for both organisations to merge. Hence, all four merger attempts failed.

11.6 Limitations and Suggestions for Further Research

The first chapter discussed some of the generic limitations of a historical research project. A significant limitation of this study is a lack of access to the minutes of the general and national council meetings of both bodies. Additionally, access to the minutes of the unity and integration committee meetings was also not available. As time passes, the sensitivity of resources and information reduces. Therefore, this limitation poses an opportunity for future research projects. Access to these resources may provide additional explanations for, and insights to, the mounting of the four merger attempts and their failures.

The recent successful merger attempt between the Institute and the New Zealand Institute of Chartered Accountants could become the subject of future studies, in particular, within the context of why the Australian Institute was able to merge with a body from another country after failing four times to merge with a local body.

11.7 Conclusion

Beyond the stark voting outcome that defeated all the merger proposals, some more nuanced observations can be made that provide insights into the nature and causes of Australia's divided accounting profession. First, the fact that all four merger proposals went to the vote reveals that despite some readily discernible differences, the leaderships of the Institute and the Society each saw their traditional organisational strategies as being open to modification, resulting in the development of formal merger proposals for deliberation by members of both bodies before voting on the merger proposition. That is, while there were boundaries within the profession, these were viewed by the leadership of the two bodies as being open to negotiation with the possibility of being redrawn. Second, it was a proportion of the Institute's members who rejected the merger proposals and, thereby, the revised organisational strategy that their leadership had proposed. In this way, in view of the mandated voting threshold of 75%, the members of the Institute who voted "No" defied the recommendations of their leaders and successfully protected the organisation's traditional boundaries.

As discussed previously, the boundaries of the Australian accounting profession were created around the different membership profiles of the Institute and the Society and the adoption of distinct organisational strategies in response to the "exclusiveness versus market control" dilemma (Macdonald & Ritzer, 1988, p. 257). However, the failed merger proposals highlight that this dilemma is best represented as a continuum rather than a dichotomy: that is, exclusiveness and market control are variables to be traded-off rather than being mutually exclusive concepts as may be presumed. Of necessity, the Society had traditionally prioritised a market control strategy, but it was far from being indifferent to matters of status. Conversely, while the Institute had fared better in the battle for exclusivity, it could not ignore the challenges it faced in terms of achieving market influence and economies of scale, particularly in a country such as Australia with a relatively small and widely spread population.

According to Gracia and Oats (2012, p. 308), "Boundaries are ubiquitous in modern social life" and the work of creating and maintaining boundaries is particularly evident within professions. The general council of the Institute apparently saw its own boundaries as being sufficiently "malleable and expandable" (Fournier, 2000, p. 83). In other words, while the Institute had traditionally favoured an exclusivity strategy constructed around the perceived superiority of public practice and its possession of a Royal Charter, the body's leadership at least was more receptive to a strategy of inclusiveness. While this would be the business model of the proposed new body, it would retain some vestiges of exclusivity by keeping the Royal Charter and the term Chartered Accountant in the title of the proposed merged body for all fully qualified members, including those who were formerly members of the Society. This certainly marked a "step up" for Society members, and the voting patterns reflect this view.

The failure to fully unify the Australian accounting profession, first attempted in 1969 and replicated in three subsequent merger proposals, has profoundly shaped the dynamics of the profession. In the case of the Society, a key issue it had to initially confront was its lack of a distinctive brand following its failure to gain access to the prestigious Chartered Accountant title. In the early 1980s, following the failure of the second merger proposal in 1981, it introduced a new professional designation of "CPA". However, this was not the "Certified Public Accountant" designation familiar in the US and several other countries. Rather, the Australian CPA was a "Certified Practising Accountant": a clever adaptation of the popular CPA designation to the circumstances of a professional body that had only a small portion of MIPP. The CPA designation, and the more rigorous educational program by which it was earned, raised the prospect of narrowing the differences between the Institute and the Society. This was tested with the merger proposals in each of 1991 and 1998, which emphasised that the Society, at last, had a professional designation that might be deemed at least almost equal to that of CA. However, in each case the Institute membership remained unconvinced and voted down the proposal, although by only a very small margin in the case of the third merger attempt.

New Zealand, located just to the south-east of Australia, was home to a single, broad-based professional accounting association: the New Zealand Society of Accountants. In 1996, this was renamed the New Zealand Institute of Charted Accountants (NZICA). This change in name did not involve the acquisition of a Royal Charter, but it did establish sufficient commonality to later enable a merger to proceed with the Australian Institute, leading to the creation of the Chartered Accountants Australia and New Zealand (CAANZ) in 2014. Paradoxically, while the Australian Institute was unable to achieve a merger with a broad-based Australian body, despite four proposals to do so, it was able to merge with a broad-based overseas body at the first attempt. Enabling this outcome was the common brand name of CA, even though the origins of this title were completely distinct for the two bodies, and the sweetener of lower membership fees in the event of merger success. This circumstance highlights the importance given to professional branding and membership self-interest, but perhaps also the extraordinary superficiality of intra-profession machinations: "Boundary work is… permeated by significant strands of arbitrariness and is vested in power relations" (Hazgui & Gendron, 2015, p. 1239).

A question also arises about future merger possibilities between CPA Australia and the newly formed CAANZ. However, recent conflict suggests that this seems unlikely. CPA Australia filed a defamation case against the NZICA for which judgement was handed down in August 2015 where Justice Dobson found that NZICA had been successful in its defence against allegations made by CPA Australia of defamation and in relation to an alleged breach of the New Zealand Fair-Trading Act. Accordingly, the relief sought by CPA Australia, a declaration of defamation and monetary damages, was denied. Until 2012, the NZICA held an effective monopoly in New Zealand when the Financial Markets Authority accredited CPA Australia for auditing work, putting it on a more equal footing with NZICA.

Whether the CAANZ and CPA Australia can foresee a merger is a question to be tested in the future only. However, in the course of the four failed merger attempts, the Society's brand positioning was strengthened and this included the adoption of the CPA brand in 1983. CPA Australia is still a large and dominant body in 2017 with 150,000 members in Australia and overseas, and both CAANZ and CPA Australia are still engaged in a complex interplay of competition and cooperation with each other, both in Australia and New Zealand.

The findings of the study will help leadership of these professional bodies in understanding the challenges posed by identity exclusiveness and will motivate them to overcome these challenges before they initiate any merger attempt in future. This may help the leadership in strengthening the accounting profession for common benefits of the members of both the professional accounting bodies.

The findings of this study of mergers will contribute to the ongoing growth of the accounting profession by redefining the roles of these professional accounting bodies, designing policies for attracting new members and through review of broader benefits or negative implications of these proposals in the wider public interest. It may also raise further questions in relation to the regulatory positioning of the accountants and the accounting profession. The failure of merger attempts in succession and the reported reasons for these failures contribute significantly to the future directions in re-shaping the accounting profession globally, more specifically in Australia. The research emphasises a strong need for members' awareness and education before any merger agenda is taken nationally or internationally. Also, there may be a need for strategic alliance of the leadership groups before planning the merger action plan including redefining the organisational boundaries, inter-organisational competition and their professional standing in the market.

References

Anderson, C. (2010). Presenting and evaluating qualitative research. *American Journal of Pharmaceutical Education, 74*(8), 141.

Annisette, M. (2017). Discourse of the professions: The making, normalizing and taming of Ontario's foreign-trained accountant. *Accounting, Organizations and Society, 60*, 37–61.

Anon. (1969h, September). Unity proposals submitted to members. *The Australian Accountant*, 394.

Anon. (1971, October). Status of accountants. *The Australian Accountant*, 420.

Anon. (1974, July). Joint message by G. W. Bottrill (President of Society) and E. H. Burgess (President of Institute). *The Australian Accountant*, 455.

Anon. (1976a). General council annual report 1975. *Annual Report, 1975*, p. 7.

Anon. (1976c, July 15). Accountants try again for merger. *The Australian*, p. 7.

Anon. (1981a, March). Integration forum. *The Australian Accountant*, pp. 90–93.

Anon. (1981e, June). Integration forum. *The Australian Accountant*, pp. 350–356.

Anon. (1981h, December 5). NSW key to poll. *Business Review*, p. 9.

Anon. (1981i, August). Integration forum. *The Australian Accountant*, pp. 480–484.

Anon. (1998a, May). New national president: David Boymal. *Australian CPA*, pp. 18–19.

Anon. (1998b, August). Merger: The key points. *Australian CPA*, p. 18.

Anon. (1998e, November). Members to vote on merger proposal. *Accountant*, p. 7.

Anon. (1998j, March 18). Accountants' olive branch. *The Daily Telegraph*, p. 8.

Anon. (1998l). A merger codenamed 'Newpro'. *Chartac Accountancy News, 22*(265), 1, p. 68.

Anon. (1999b, April). Research failed to predict merger result. *Charter,* 70(2), p. 12

Atkinson, R. (1999, February). It's time to get back to our roots. *Charter,* p. 4.

Australian Society of Accountants and the Institute of Chartered Accountants in Australia. (1969). *Report of Joint Meeting of Education Committees*. ASA Melbourne and ICAA Sydney, pp. 1–19.

Australian Society of Accountants and The Institute of Chartered Accountants in Australia. (1968a). Ninth Conference of representatives of The Institute of Chartered Accountants and the Australian Society of Accountants held in Melbourne on March 22–23, 1968 (1–18). ASA Melbourne and ICAA Sydney.

Australian Society of Accountants. (1967a). *Minutes of meeting of Executive Committee held on 17 February 1967* (1–20). Melbourne, Australia.

Australian Society of Accountants. (1970). *Annual report*. Melbourne, Australia.

Australian Society of Accountants. (1981). *Annual report*. Melbourne, Australia.

Australian Society of Accountants. (1984). *Annual report*. Melbourne, Australia.

Australian Society of Accountants. (1992). *Annual report*. Melbourne, Australia.

Australian Society of Accountants. (1998). *Annual report*. Melbourne, Australia.

Australian Society of Accountants. (1999). *Annual report*. Melbourne, Australia.

Bedeian, A. G. (1998). Exploring the past. *Journal of Management History, 4*(1), 4–15.

Boymal, D. (2016), Interview with David Boymal on February 8.

Brodkin, K. (1998). *How the Jews became white folk and what that says about race in America.* Rutgers University Press.

Carnegie, G. D. (1993). The Australian Institute of Incorporated Accountants (1892–1938). *ABFH, 3*(1), 61–80.

Carnegie, G. D. (2016). The accounting professional project and bank failures. *Journal of Management History, 22*(4), 389–412.

Carnegie, G. D., & Edwards, J. R. (2001). The construction of the professional accountant: The case of the Incorporated Institute of Accountants, Victoria (1886). *Accounting, Organisations and Society, 26*(4/5), 301–325.

Carnegie, G. D., & Napier, C. (2012). Accounting's past, present and future: The unifying power of history. *Accounting, Auditing & Accountability Journal, 25*(2), 328–369.

Carnegie, G. D., & O'Connell, B. T. (2012). Understanding the responses of professional accounting bodies to crises: The case of the Australian profession in the 1960s. *Accounting Auditing and Accountability Journal, 25*(5), 835–875.

Carnegie, G. D., & Parker, R. H. (1999). Accountants and empire: The case of co-membership of Australian and British accountancy bodies, 1885 to 1914. *Accounting, Business & Financial History, 9*(1), 77–102.

Carnegie, G. D., Edwards, J. R., & West, B. P. (2003). Understanding the dynamics of the Australian accounting profession: A prosopographical study of the founding members of the Incorporated Institute of Accountants, Victoria, 1886 to 1908. *Accounting, Auditing & Accountability Journal, 16*(5), 790–820.

Chua, W. F., & Poullaos, C. (1993). Rethinking the profession-state dynamic: The case of the Victorian Charter attempt, 1885–1906. *Accounting, Organisations and Society, 18*(7/8), 691–728.

Chua, W. F., & Poullaos, C. (1998). The dynamics of 'closure' amidst the construction of market, profession, empire and nationhood: An historical analysis of an Australian accounting association, 1886–1903. *Accounting, Organisations and Society, 23*(2), 155–187.

Dowling, J. (1998, March 18). Competing accountancy bodies in merger talks. *Courier Mail*, p. 11.

Eastwood, K. (1990d, October). From the president. *The Australian Accountant*, p. 5.

Farnham, C. (1998, March). ASCPA, ICAA merger mooted. Australian CPA,11.

Fleischman, R. K., Mills, P. A., & Tyson, T. N. (1996). A theoretical primer for evaluating and conducting historical research in accounting. *Accounting History, 1*(1), 55–75.

Fournier, V. (2000). Boundary work and the (un) making of the professions. Professionalism, boundaries and the workplace, 67.

Gavens, J. J. (1990). A historical perspective of integration of the Australian accounting profession. In R. H. Parker (Ed.), *Accounting in Australia: Historical essays* (pp. 381–407).

Gavens, J. J., & Gibson, R. W. (1992). An Australian attempt to internationalize accounting professional organisations. *The Accounting Historians Journal, 19*(2), 79–102.

Gettler, L. (1998b, December 12). Merger numbers fall well short. *The Age*, p. 13.

Gieryn, T. F. (1983). Boundary-work and the demarcation of science from non-science: Strains and interests in the professional ideologies of scientists. *American Sociological Review, 48*(6), 781–795.

Gieryn, T. F. (1995). Boundaries of science. In S. Jasanoff, G. E Markle, J. C Petersen, & T. Pinch (Eds.), *Handbook of science and technology studies* (393–443). SAGE.

Gieryn, T. F. (1999). *Cultural boundaries of science: Credibility on the line*. University of Chicago Press.

Gieryn, T. F., Bevins, G. M., & Zehi, S. C. (1985). Professionalization of American scientists: Public science in the creation/evolution trials. *American Sociological Review, 50*(3), 392–409.

Gracia, L., & Oats, L. (2012). Boundary work and tax regulation: A Bourdieusian view. *Accounting, Organizations and Society, 37*(5), 304–321.

Hazgui, M., & Gendron, Y. (2015). Blurred roles and elusive boundaries: On contemporary forms of oversight surrounding professional work. *Accounting, Auditing & Accountability Journal, 28*(8), 1234–1262.

Henderson, S. (1997). The expectations gap and the Australian accounting profession. *Accounting Forum, 21*(2), 175–188.

Ignatiev, N. (1995). *How the Irish became white*. Routledge.

Irving, H. R. (1966). Report on professional awards for accountants (designation of CPA) submitted on behalf of the Executive Committee by President, *The Australian Society of Accountants*. 7 October 1966, pp. 1–27.

Lamont, M., & Molnár, V. (2002). The study of boundaries in the social sciences. *Annual Review of Sociology, 28*(1), 167–195.

Lee, T. A. (2010). Consolidating the public accountancy profession: The case of the proposed Institute of Chartered Accountants of Great Britain, 1988–9. *Accounting History, 15*(1), 7–39.

Lewis, S. (1991a, January 29). Accountants try another path to merge professional bodies. *Financial Review*, p. 6.

Macdonald, K. M., & Ritzer, G. (1988). The sociology of the professions: Dead or alive? *Work and Occupations, 15*(3), 251–272.

McKeon, A. (1975a, April 4). Accountants in disarray. *Financial Review*, p. 2.

McMahon, S. (2007, 13 October 13). Two days that shook the world. *Herald Sun*. www.heraldsun.com.au/businessold/two-days-that-shook-the-world/story-e6frfh4f-1111114631654

Miller, J. (2015). Interview with John Miller on February 27.

Miller, P., Hopper, T., & Laughlin, R. (1991). The new accounting history: An introduction. *Accounting, Organisations and Society, 16*(5/6), 395–403.

Milner, D. (1996). Children and racism: Beyond the value of dolls. In P. W Robinson (Ed.), *Social groups and identities: Developing the legacy of Henri Tajfel* (pp. 249–68). Oxford, England: Butterworth Heinermann.

Munro, R. F. (1975c, March). Qualification requirements of the Australian Society of Accountants. p. 63.

Nancarrow, S. A., & Borthwick, A. M. (2005). Dynamic professional boundaries in the healthcare workforce. *Sociology of Health & Illness, 27*(7), 897–919.

Neilson, G. (2015). Interview with Geoff Neilson on February 20.

Orr, J. G. (2014). Interview with Geoff Orr on May 17.

Parker, L. D. (1999). Historiography for the new millennium: Adventures in accounting and management. *Accounting History, 4*(2), 11–42.

Parker, R. H. (1989). Importing and exporting accounting: The British experience. In A. G. Hopwood (Ed.), *International pressures for accounting change* (pp. 7–29). Prentice-Hall.

Persson, A. (2010). Soldiers and secretaries: Gendered boundary work in the Swedish Armed Forces. *Scandinavian Journal of Management, 26*, 166–175.

Poullaos, C. (1993). Making profession and state, 1907 to 1914: The ACPA's first charter attempt. *Abacus, 29*(2), 196–229.

Poullaos, C. (1994). *Making the Australian chartered accountant. New York.* Garland.

Richardson, A. J., & Jones, D. B. (2007). Professional 'brand', personal identity and resistance to change in the Canadian accounting profession: A comparative history of two accounting association merger negotiations. *Accounting History, 12*(2), 135–164.

Shackleton, K. & Walker, S. P. (2001). *A future for the accountancy profession: The quest for closure and integration, 1957–1970.* Edinburgh, Scotland: Institute of Chartered Accountants of Scotland.

Shackleton, K., & Walker. S. P. (1998). *Professional reconstruction: The coordination of the accountancy bodies, 1930–1957.* Edinburgh, Scotland: Institute of Chartered Accountants of Scotland.

Sharpe, M. (1983). President's overview. *Annual report*, , The Australian Society of Accountants, pp. 2–3.

Taylor, N. B. (1991c, October). Message of President. *Charter*, p. 66.

Taylor, N. B. (2016). Interview with Nick Burton Taylor on March 18.

The Institute of Chartered Accountants in Australia. (1965). *Annual report.* Australia.

The Institute of Chartered Accountants in Australia. (1968). *Annual report.* Australia.

The Institute of Chartered Accountants in Australia. (1969). *Annual report.* Australia.

The Institute of Chartered Accountants in Australia. (1970). *Annual report.* Australia.

The Institute of Chartered Accountants in Australia. (1980). *Annual report.* Australia.

The Institute of Chartered Accountants in Australia. (1981). *Annual report.* Australia.

The Institute of Chartered Accountants in Australia. (1999). *Annual report.* Australia.

Thomas, T. (1998a), Merger vote doubt, Business Review Weekly, April 13, p. 84.

Walker, S. P., & Shackleton, K. (1995). Corporatism and structural change in the British accountancy profession, 1930–1957. *Accounting, Organisations and Society, 20*(6), 467–503.

Willmott, H. (1986). Organising the profession: A theoretical and historical examination of the development of the major accountancy bodies in the UK. *Accounting, Organisations and Society, 11*(6), 555–580.
Wright, J. (2008, May 29). Top 10 Financial moments that shaped SA – ABC South Australia – Australian Broadcasting Corporation (ABC). Retrieved 18 August 2015 from *Blogs.abc.net.au.*
Zeff, S. A. (1973, March). Forging accounting principles in Australia. *Society Bulletin*, p. 14.

Appendix A1–A4: Accounting Bodies, Formation, Mergers and Dissolutions

A1: Accounting Bodies Formed Before 1901

SN	*Name*	*Year formed*	*Focus*	*Outcome*
1	The Adelaide Society of Accountants (ADSA)	1885	Public and non-public	Institute
2	The Incorporated Institute of Accountants of Victoria (IIAV) (1886–1918)	1886	Public and non-public	Society
3	The Queensland Institute of Accountants (QIA)	1891	Public and non-public	Society
4	The Sydney Institute of Public Accountants (SIPA)	1894	Public	Institute
5	The Tasmanian Institute of Accountants (TIA)	1897		Institute
6	Federal Institute of Accountants (FIA) (Australia)	1894		Society
7	The Corporations of Accountants of Australia (CAA)	1899	Public and non-public	Institute
8	The Society of Accountants and Auditors of Victoria (SAAV)	1900		Society
9	The Institute of Accountants and Auditors of Western Australia (IAAWA)	1900		Society
10	The Australian Institute of Incorporated Accountants (AIIA)	1892	Narrow regional focus	Dissolved 1938

(continued)

J. Sidhu et al., *Understanding the Sociology of the Accounting Profession*,
https://doi.org/10.1007/978-981-99-1572-9

(continued)

SN	Name	Year formed	Focus	Outcome
11	The North Queensland Institute of Accountants (NQIA)	1896	Regional focus	Dissolved in 1908
12	The Chartered Towers Institute of Accountants (CTIA)	1898		Dissolved in 1945

Sources Carnegie and Parker (1999), Gavens (1990), Gynther (1967a), Maskell (1944), and Walton (1970)

A2: Parent Bodies of the Society

SN	Name	Year formed	Outcome
1	The Incorporated Institute of Accountants of Victoria (IIAV) (1886–1918) Incorporated Institute of Accountants, Commonwealth of Australia (IIACA) (1918–1921) Commonwealth Institute of Accountants (CIA) (1921–1952)	1886	First antecedent body of the Society in 1952
2	The Queensland Institute of Accountants (QIA)	1891	Merged with CIA in 1921
3	Federal Institute of Accountants (FIA) (Australia)	1894	Foundation body to form Society in 1952
4	The Society of Accountants and Auditors of Victoria (SAAV)	1900	Merged with FIA
5	The Institute of Accountants and Auditors of Western Australia (IAAWA)	1900	Merged with CIA in 1923
6	The South Australian Society of Accountants (SASA)	1902	Merged with CIA in 1922
7	The Broken Hill Institute of Accountants	1903	Merged with CIA in 1923 Regional focus (Walton 1970)
8	The Institute of Public Accountants of Australasia (IPAA)	1907	Merged with CIA in 1929 Regional and state-based bodies (Gavens 1990)
9	The Institute of Incorporated Accountants of New South Wales (IIANSW)	1908	Merged with CIA in 1930 Regional and state-based body (Gavens 1990)

(continued)

(continued)

SN	*Name*	*Year formed*	*Outcome*
10	The Association of Accountants in Australia (AAA)	1910	Foundation body to form Society in 1952
11	The Corporation of Consulting Accountants (CCA) (1922–1955)	1922	Merged with Society in 1955
12	The Australian Accountants Corporation (AAC)	1922	Merged with Association of Accountants in Australia (AAA) in 1928
13	The International Institute of Accountants (IIA) (1933–1955)	1933	Merged with Society in 1955
14	Victorian Society of Public Accountants (VSPA) (1934–1955)	1934	Merged with Society in 1955
15	Australian Society of Accountants	1952	Foundation bodies of CIA, FIA and AAA
16	The Australasian Institute of Cost Accountants (AICA)	1921	Merged with Society 1966 Last successful merger of two accounting bodies in Australia

Sources Carnegie and Parker (1999), Gavens (1990), Gynther (1967a), Maskell (1944), and Walton (1970)

A3: Parent Bodies of Institute

SN	*Name*	*Year formed*	*Outcome*
1	The Adelaide Society of Accountants (ADSA) (1885–1891) The Adelaide Society of Accountants Incorporated (ADSAI) (1891–1899) The Institute of Accountants in South Australia (1899–1925)	1885	Merged with ACPA 1925
2	The Sydney Institute of Public Accountants (SIPA)	1894	Foundation body to form ACPA 1908
3	The Tasmanian Institute of Accountants (TIA)	1897	Foundation body to form ACPA 1908
4	The Corporations of Accountants of Australia (CAA)	1899	Foundation body to form ACPA 1908
5	Australasian Corporation of Public Accountants (ACPA)	1908	Dissolved to form ICAA

(continued)

(continued)

SN	*Name*	*Year formed*	*Outcome*
6	Institute of Chartered Accountants in Australia (ICAA)	1928	Formed with Royal Charter

Sources Carnegie and Parker (1999), Gavens (1990), Gynther (1967a), Maskell (1944), and Walton (1970)

A4: All Accounting Bodies Formed in Australia

SN	*Name*	*Details*	*Remarks*
1	The Adelaide Society of Accountants (ADSA) Later known as the Institute of Accountants of South Australia Incorporated	Formed November 1885 Incorporated March 1886 Merged with ACPA 1925	Fifteen accountants met on 20 November 1885 to form this body. Initially only open to public accountants, but since 1890, open to non-public accountants who passed the required exam (Gavens, 1990) Parker (1961) provided a list of 19 founding members

(continued)

(continued)

SN	*Name*	*Details*	*Remarks*
2	The Incorporated Institute of Accountants of Victoria (IIAV) (1886–1918) Incorporated Institute of Accountants, Commonwealth of Australia (IIACA) (1918–1921) Commonwealth Institute of Accountants (CIA) (1921–1952)	Formed 1886 Incorporated 1887 From very beginning, it adopted the view that it would include clerks in government and commercial employment as well as MIPP (Gavens, 1990) Admission to women allowed in 1918 after being rejected three times in 1899, 1912 and 1916 (Gynther, 1967a)	On 3 December 1885, 22 leading Melbourne accountants met and discussed the proposal to form a Victorian branch of SAA (Gavens, 1990). According to Marshall (1982, p. 87), Australian accountants were not ready to work 'under the tutelage of a body which functioned 12,000 miles away'. In their meeting they also rejected 'burdensome restrictions' imposed by the ICAEW (Gavens, 1990; Graham, 1978; Marshall, 1982) Published journal: *Commonwealth Journal of Accountancy* (1921–1936) Name changed to *The Australian Accountant* (1936–1998) *Australian CPA* (1998–2004) *In the Black* (2004–present)
3	The Queensland Institute of Accountants (QIA)	Formed August 1891 (Gynther 1967a)	Initially 18 members formed the QIA in Brisbane on 27 August 1891. Objectives and Memorandum similar to IIAV (Gavens, 1990)
4	The Sydney Institute of Public Accountants (SIPA)	Formed and incorporated May 1894 Merged with ACPA 1908	Restricted to MIPP and their clerks (Gavens 1990). It became a founder body for the Institute (ICAA)
5	The Tasmanian Institute of Accountants (TIA)	Formed December 1897 Merged with ACPA 1908	Initially 12 original members met on 2 December 1897 to form this body. Little is known about its activities, including the extent of its focus on public practice (Graham, 1978)

(continued)

(continued)

SN	*Name*	*Details*	*Remarks*
6	Federal Institute of Accountants (FIA) (Australia)	Formed 1894 Incorporated July 1894 (Gavens, 1990) In 1902, an application by a woman to join was rejected with a further rejection in 1911. Finally allowed the entry of women in 1925 (Gynther, 1967a) Ran a Journal *Federal Accountant* (1916–1935 and 1938–1952)	Its objective was to open its branches in other British colonies. This was the first body that aimed to extend its scope to form a global profession, rather than on the basis of regionalism, which had so far been the key feature of the Australian accounting profession (Gavens, 1990)
7	The Corporations of Accountants of Australia (CAA)	Formed and incorporated 1899 in New South Wales	Allowed both types of accountants, public and non-public. 'The decision of Sydney Institute to confine its membership to public accountants made it inevitable that a rival Sydney body would be formed' (Graham, 1970, p. 3) CAA started Australia's first accountancy journal *The Public Accountant* in 1901
8	The Society of Accountants and Auditors of Victoria (SAAV)	Incorporated November 1900 Merged with 6* (Gynther 1967a)	According to Gavens (1990), these bodies may have been formed as a local branch of SAA (London) but were later incorporated as separate entities within Victoria and Western Australia
9	The Institute of Accountants and Auditors of Western Australia (IAAWA)	Incorporated December 1900 Merged with 2* in 1923 with 104 members (Gynther, 1967a)	
10	The Australian Institute of Incorporated Accountants (AIIA)	Incorporated December 1892	There is no record that this body amalgamated with another body (Gavens, 1990; Gynther, 1967a) Its narrow membership focus on county Victoria led to a sharp decline in its membership base and it was dissolved on 14 January 1938 (Carnegie, 1993)

(continued)

(continued)

SN	*Name*	*Details*	*Remarks*
11	The North Queensland Institute of Accountants (NQIA)	Registered September 1896	Originally, there were 15 members. In 1908, its former president J. N. Parkes requested that NQIA be removed from the Companies Register because it had not held any meetings during the past five years (Gynther, 1967a)
12	The Chartered Towers Institute of Accountants (CTIA)	Registered May 1898 Name changed to the North Queensland Institute of Accountants (NQIA) in October 1908 (Gynther, 1967a)	CTIA was removed from the Companies Register in 1945 after receipt of a letter stating that it had not functioned for five or six years (Gynther, 1967a)
13	The South Australian Society of Accountants (SASA)	Incorporated 1902 (Gavens, 1990)	Gavens (1990) claimed that no historical records were found about its existence or operations Merged with 2* in 1922 with 81 members (Gynther, 1967a)
14	The Broken Hill Institute of Accountants	Formed 1903 and merged with Commonwealth Institute of Accountants (Walton, 1970)	Regional focus (Walton, 1970)
15	The Institute of Accountants in Central Queensland (IACQ)		Regional focus (Walton, 1970)
16	The Institute of Public Accountants of Australasia (IPAA)	Incorporated in 1907 (Gavens, 1990) Merged with 2* with 138 members in 1929 (Gynther, 1967a)	Regional and state-based bodies (Gavens, 1990)
17	The Institute of Incorporated Accountants of New South Wales (IIANSW)	Incorporated in 1908 Merged with 2* in 1930 with nearly 500 members (Gynther, 1967a)	Regional and state-based body (Gavens, 1990)

(continued)

(continued)

SN	Name	Details	Remarks
18	The Australasian Corporation of Public Accountants (ACPA)	Formed 1908	Initial suggested name was the Institute of Public Accountants in Australasia. However, to avoid confusion with the IPAA, a different name was adopted. Its objective was to be a national body with its branches in each state of Australia (Graham, 1978)
19	The Association of Accountants in Australia (AAA)	Incorporated November 1910	This body was formed after the ACPA and it was formed to serve the interests of commercial accountants. According to Kenley (1964), founders of this body claimed that existing bodies catered more for accountants in public practice
20	The Australasian Institute of Cost Accountants (AICA)	Formed 1921	Was modelled on the basis of the Institute of Cost and Works Accountants Limited (England), which was formed in 1919 Merged with Society in 1966
21	The Corporation of Consulting Accountants (CCA) (1922–1955)	Incorporated 1922	
22	The Australian Accountants Corporation	Formed 1922 and merged with AAA	

(continued)

(continued)

SN	*Name*	*Details*	*Remarks*
23	The Institute of Factory and Cost Accountants (IFCA) (1923–1950) Institute of Taxation and Cost Accountants (1950–1957) National Institute of Accountants (1957–1967) Institute of Commercial Studies (1967–1970) Institute of Affiliate Accountants (1970–1988) National Institute of Accountants (1988–2011) Institute of Public Accountants (2011–present)	Formed 1923 Incorporated 1926	This was a specialist institute to promote the 'elevation of the profession of factory and cost accountants' (Walton, 1961)
24	International Accountants Corporation and Bookkeepers Institute of Australasia Incorporated (IACBIA)		Gavens (1990) cites article from *The Accountant* that this was a lower status body and it was possible to join this merely by filling a form
25	The International Institute of Accountants (IIA) (1933–1955)	Incorporated 1933	
26	Victorian Society of Public Accountants (VSPA) (1934–1955)	Formed August 1934	
27	The Incorporated Association of Cost Accountants	Incorporated September 1936	

(continued)

(continued)

SN	*Name*	*Details*	*Remarks*
28	Association of Practising Accountants	Incorporated November 1938	
29	Society of Commercial Accountants	A paper by Young (1949) makes reference to these two bodies. However, Gavens (1990) could not find any records to trace their origins	
30	Association of Practising and Commercial Accountants		
31	Institute of Chartered Accountants in Australia	Formed in 1928 with Royal Charter	Published a journal *The Chartered Accountant in Australia*: the official organ of the Institute of Chartered Accountants in Australia. (1933–1988) *The Chartered Accountant*: journal of the Institute of Chartered Accountants in Australia (1989–1989) Charter (1990–present)
32	Australian Society of Accountants	Formed 1952 with the merger of CIA, FIA and AAA	

Sources Carnegie and Parker (1999), Gavens (1990), Gynther (1967a), Maskell (1944), and Walton (1970)

Index

J. Sidhu et al., *Understanding the Sociology of the Accounting Profession*,
https://doi.org/10.1007/978-981-99-1572-9

Kolibri 360 GmbH
Ferdinand-Jühlke-Straße 7
99095 Erfurt, Deutschland
produktsicherheit@kolibri360.de